Bankruptcy and Diligence etc. (Scotland) Act 2007

AUSTRALIA
Law Book Co.
Sydney

CANADA and USA
Carswell
Toronto

HONG KONG
Sweet & Maxwell Asia

NEW ZEALAND
Brookers
Wellington

SINGAPORE and MALAYSIA
Sweet & Maxwell Asia
Singapore and Kuala Lumpur

Bankruptcy and Diligence etc. (Scotland) Act 2007

Annotations by

Nicholas Grier, M.A., LL.B., W.S.
Solicitor,
Senior Lecturer in Law, Napier University

THOMSON

™

W. GREEN

Published in 2008 by
W. Green & Son Ltd
21 Alva Street
Edinburgh EH2 4PS

www.wgreen.thomson.com

*Printed and bound in Great Britain by
Athenaeum Press Ltd, Gateshead*

No natural forests were destroyed to make this product;
only farmed timber was used and replanted

A CIP catalogue record for this book is available from
the British Library.

ISBN-13 978-0-414-01685-9

© W. Green & Son Ltd 2008

CONTENTS

BANKRUPTCY AND DILIGENCE ETC. (SCOTLAND) ACT 2007*

(2007 asp 3)

CONTENTS

PART 1
BANKRUPTCY

*Annotations by Nicholas Grier, Senior Lecturer, Napier University, Edinburgh.

PART 2
FLOATING CHARGES

PART 3
ENFORCEMENT

PART 4
LAND ATTACHMENT AND RESIDUAL ATTACHMENT

CHAPTER 1
ABOLITION OF ADJUDICATION FOR DEBT

CHAPTER 2
ATTACHMENT OF LAND

Land attachment

Consequences of land attachment

Preparations for sale of attached land

The sale

CHAPTER 3
RESIDUAL ATTACHMENT

PART 8
ATTACHMENT OF MONEY

Money attachment

Execution of money attachment

Release of money attached

Statement of money attachment

General and miscellaneous

PART 9
DILIGENCE AGAINST EARNINGS

PART 10
ARRESTMENT IN EXECUTION AND ACTION OF FURTHCOMING

An Act of the Scottish Parliament to amend the law of sequestration and personal insolvency; to amend the law about floating charges; to establish a Scottish Civil Enforcement Commission and replace officers of court with judicial officers; to amend the law of diligence; and for connected purposes.
The Bill for this Act of the Scottish Parliament was passed by the Parliament on 30th November 2006 and received Royal Assent on 15th January 2007.

PROGRESS OF THE ACT

Introduced to the Scottish Parliament by Allan Wilson, Deputy Minister for Enterprise and Lifelong Learning on November 21, 2005.

Stage 1 in Enterprise and Culture Committee: December 6, 2005, January 17 and 24, February 7 and 28, March 7, 14, 21 and 28, April 18 and 25 and May 2, 9 and 16, 2006; Stage 1 in Finance Committee: January 10 and 31 and February 7, 21 and 28, 2006; Subordinate Legislation Committee: February 28 and March 7, 21 and 28, 2006; Parliament Stage 1 debated and agreed: May 24, 2006; Stage 2 in Enterprise and Culture Committee: June 13 and 20, September 12, 19 and 26, October 3 and 24 and November 7, 2006; Subordinate Legislation Committee: November 21 and 28, 2006; Finance Committee: November 28, 2006; Stage 3: November: 30, 2006; Bill passed: November 30, 2006; Royal Assent: January 15, 2007.

INTRODUCTION AND GENERAL NOTE

The Accountant in Bankruptcy

The Accountant in Bankruptcy, who is referred to in many sections of the 2007 Act, has various supervisory and other functions delegated to her by the Scottish Ministers in terms of the 1985 Act ss.1, 1A-1C. Amongst the tasks that she carries out are the supervision of trustees in sequestration (other than herself) and the maintenance of the register of insolvencies, which contains details of estates which have been sequestrated, registered trust deeds, and the winding up, receivership and administration of companies. Under the 2007 Act s.2(2), she is also to keep a register of BROs, interim BROs and BRUs. Under the 2007 Act s.18(5), she also has to keep in that register a record of payment orders and payment arrangements out of debtors' incomes (new s.1A(1)(b)(iia) of the 1985 Act).

She also is the DAS administrator by means of the 2002 Act s.8. In that capacity she maintains the DAS register, endorses variations of DPPs, approves money advisers and payment distributors.

In practice she (through the officials in her office) carries out most of the sequestrations in Scotland, but she may in turn appoint certain insolvency practitioners to act in her name. She is always appointed where no other trustee is appointed or has elected to be appointed.

Where she suspects criminal activity by a trustee or a debtor, she may report the matter to the Lord Advocate.

The office of the Accountant in Bankruptcy is now in Kilwinning, though there is a small office in Edinburgh. There is an excellent and very user-friendly website (*http://www.aib.gov.uk/*) for the Accountant in Bankruptcy, which gives a great deal of practical advice for debtors, lawyers and insolvency practitioners alike. In addition, the website has a complete list of the relevant primary and secondary legislation applicable to sequestration, and maintains a continually updated version of the Bankruptcy (Scotland) Act 1985 as amended, so that it is possible to see what the current state of the Act is.

One of the most important new functions of the 2007 Act is to enable the Accountant in Bankruptcy to deal with debtor applications for sequestration, or applications by a debtor with the concurrence of their creditors. This, it is thought, should make it easier for debtors to apply for their own sequestration and may avoid the embarrassing publicity of applying for sequestration within their own sheriffdom. Debtor applications for their own sequestration from the Accountant in Bankruptcy have been available with effect from 1 April 2008 (Bankruptcy and Diligence etc (Scotland) Act 2007 (Commencement No.3, Savings and Transitionals) Order 2008, SSI 2008 No.115).

Debt Arrangement Scheme

This was a scheme set up under the 2002 Act to enable certain debtors to approach, usually through such organisations as the Citizens Advice Bureaux and Money Advice Scotland, registered money advisers who would help each debtor set up a debt payment programme. Under the DPP, the debtor makes a regular payment usually each week or month out of his income to a payments distributor who divides up the payments between the debtor's creditors. The creditors normally have to object to the DPP within 21 days and if they do not object within 21 days they are deemed to have agreed to the DPP. Once a DPP is in place, creditors may not effect diligence against the debtor. In order to benefit from the DPP, a debtor needs to be in receipt of regular income, either from self-employment or employment. This is one of the reasons that DPPs have not been conspicuously successful, since they are of limited use to anyone with irregular or very little income. Formerly a DPP had no provision for writing off interest (this also limited the usefulness of DPPs), but following the Debt Arrangement Scheme (Scotland) Regulations 2007 (SSI 2007/262) a DPP may now provide that a debtor is released from interest, fees, penalties and other charges, as well as providing a mechanism for enabling debtors to cope with their debts. In many respects the DPP is similar to registered trust deeds for creditors and to Individual Voluntary Arrangements in England and Wales.

Introduction and general overview of the 2007 Act

This Act is the longest Act ever prepared for the Scottish Parliament and, given the political nature of some of its content, and the complex areas that it had to cover, the Parliamentary draftsmen should be given credit for doing their best to make a very difficult area of law relatively approachable. One of the commitments of the Scottish Government is to the greater use of plain English to make legislation readable (see its Plain Language and Legislation booklet, available at: *http://www.scotland.gov.uk/Publications/2006/02/17093804/0*) and intelligible, and by and large, this has been successfully carried out in this Act. There does seem to be a move away from the drafting principles of yesteryear, where the way the text was set out involved large blocks of succinct but therefore indigestible text, and little concession to those who might wish to read the legislation but did not have the benefit of legal training. The Scottish Government has prepared its own notes on the Act, and these are available on the Office of Public Sector Information website. Sometimes these give the impression of having been written in haste, which is wholly understandable given the length of the task and almost certainly the unreasonable timescale that the author will have been given in which to write it. From time to time one might wish that the notes would explain why a certain matter has been inserted or indeed omitted, because, as ever with legislation, it is hard to know a matter has been omitted deliberately, on the grounds that it is unnecessary or covered elsewhere, or whether something has been overlooked by mischance or the pressure of Parliamentary business.

The 2007 Act implements the Scottish Executive's commitment to modernise the law of bankruptcy and diligence within Scotland. The 17th century Scots laws on sequestration and diligence, based on Roman law, were originally designed for established businesses and landed estates and rarely were used for those much lower down the social or economic scale, mainly because the cost of sequestration meant that it was not worthwhile wasting time and money sequestrating those with few assets, or living in rented accommodation. The law remained in many respects remarkably little altered from 1621 until the Bankruptcy (Scotland) Act 1913 which in its own right preserved much of the old law including its terminology, which featured such phrases as "notour bankruptcy". The current law of sequestration in Scotland, which still preserves elements of the previous law, is to be found in the 1985 Act. However, the 2007 Act introduces significant new changes, such as the period of sequestration being limited to one year (formerly three years) and the introduction of Bankruptcy Restrictions Orders ("BROs"), which prohibit a debtor from certain activities (such as borrowing large sums of money) for certain periods of time. The Accountant in Bankruptcy is given greater powers and is made an officer of court. She is given greater authority to supervise protected trust deeds and to oversee the practice of sequestration in Scotland.

Much of the law of diligence is to be found in a confusing mixture of statute, rules of court and common law. The 2007 Act abolishes a number of ancient and little used forms of diligence, clarifies and updates the law relating to extant forms of diligence, and introduces various new diligences, including land attachment, money attachment and residual attachment, the first to replace the old diligence of adjudication, the second to allow cash to be attached (hitherto not possible) and the last to be a form of diligence which can be used against assets which failed to fit into any other category of assets over which diligence could safely be used. The emphasis throughout the parts relating to diligence is on redressing the balance in favour of the debtor, it being thought that some of the previous law was too generous to the creditor and failed to take enough account of debtors' interests, in particular the risk of the debtor becoming homeless or not having enough funds to maintain his family. The words "unduly harsh" appear from time to time as grounds for recalling or restricting some form of diligence. "Unduly harsh" are words which, like their predecessors, nimious and oppressive, are understandable, but inherently subjective. Much will be left to the discretion of the sheriff, and the words are likely to provide case law for many years to come. When a sheriff decides that some form of diligence might be unduly harsh, it does not mean that the debt disappears: it merely delays the enforcement of the debt through the particular means that the creditor had selected, while continuing to incur interest on the outstanding debt (unless a DAS had been set up).

It must not be forgotten that while much of the legislation here is bending backwards to be fair and kind to the debtor, there will be creditors who are just as desperate to be paid what they are owed by their debtors as debtors are keen not to pay their creditors. Not all creditors are banks, HMRC and local authorities all of which can possibly afford, or factor in, a certain amount of non-payment. Many creditors are small businesses or small scale organisations like credit unions which cannot necessarily afford any delay in payment of their accounts or repayment of their loans. Debtors who refuse or delay to pay their accounts may result in undue harshness for those creditors too, causing their businesses to collapse and their staff to be laid off.

The 2007 Act sets up a new quango, the Scottish Civil Enforcement Commission for the regulation of the profession of judicial officers, this being the new designation for sheriff officers and messengers at arms. Despite the provision in the Act, it would appear at the time of writing that neither will the Commission be set up nor the name change to judicial officer take place.

In addition the 2007 Act creates a new Register of Floating Charges in Scotland and makes various amendments to the 2002 Act.

Bankruptcy

One of the original aims of the 2007 Act was to shorten the period of bankruptcy to one year in the belief that by doing so, not only would debtors' positions generally be improved, but Scotland would become a more entrepreneurial society, by allowing entrepreneurs to start again in business with less difficulty. There was a subsidiary aim that by making bankruptcy easier and quicker it would also remove the social stigma of bankruptcy. The Enterprise Act 2002 introduced similar provisions in England and Wales, for much the same reasons. While the Enterprise Act 2002 certainly made it easier for people to be made bankrupt, it is arguable whether or not it has removed the stigma of bankruptcy, at least in England and Wales. What it did do was coincide throughout the United Kingdom with greater ease than hitherto of obtaining credit, particularly from credit cards and store cards, and a simultaneous, and some would say consequential, rise in the number of people unable to repay their debts and opting for bankruptcy. Whether the Enterprise Act 2002 actually encouraged more people to become bankrupt, secure in the knowledge that at most they would be likely to be bankrupt for only a year, or whether they would have chosen bankruptcy anyway, whatever the duration of the period of bankruptcy, is impossible to say. What the reduction of the period of bankruptcy to one year under the Enterprise Act 2002 did not appear to do in England and Wales is to make much difference to entrepreneurs. It was by no means clear that the threat of bankruptcy in itself was much of a deterrent to entrepreneurs, but more to the point, sensible entrepreneurs incorporated their businesses anyway. It is therefore unlikely that the Bankruptcy and Diligence etc. (Scotland) Act 2007 will make much difference to Scottish entrepreneurs, most of whom also incorporate their businesses, and indeed as the Bill was discussed in the Enterprise and Culture Committee at the Scottish Parliament it became evident that the then Executive, now Government, was no longer promoting the Bill as a surefire method of stimulating enterprise — while pointing out, probably correctly, that it would do no harm either.

Perhaps the most pragmatic reason for the new one year period of sequestration is, though the Executive was sometimes a little reluctant to admit it, parity with England and Wales. Scotland would be at a commercial disadvantage if Scotland did not have a similar one year period of bankruptcy.

Bankruptcy restrictions orders and bankruptcy restrictions undertakings

Where a debtor's conduct, either before or after the date of sequestration is such that the debtor deserves to be subject to a BRO, the sheriff can make such an order. This will bar the debtor from certain public offices and from being a company director. A debtor may also voluntarily apply for a BRU, thereby saving the court time and inconvenience. BROs and BRUs have been used in England and Wales since 2004. Breach of a BRU or BRO is a criminal offence. All BROs and BRUs are kept on a register maintained by the Accountant in Bankruptcy. Debtors are required to disclose to their potential creditors the existence of any applicable BROs and BRUs. The Act does not reveal what is to be done with debtors who leave Scotland before the expiry of their period of restriction, nor how the Scottish register will marry up with the English one. This may restrict the usefulness of BROs and BRUs.

Floating charges

The law on floating charges for companies has never sat comfortably within Scots law. This is partly because Scots law has never been entirely happy with the idea of a charge without some form of *traditio* (physical or deemed delivery, in the case of security, to the lender) and because there is a general feeling that it is unfair on outside creditors if it is not clear from a company's publicly registered documentation to what extent a company's assets are secured in favour of secured creditors. Publicity of a charge for the benefit of other creditors, or indeed investors, is a very old principle in Scots law-indeed, back to 1617, when the Register of Sasines was set up. The process of registration of a security both gives the secured creditor a real right, and tells creditors what the true position is. By contrast, English law seems to have less compunction in saying that a floating charge is a private bargain between the secured creditor and the company, and that outside creditors (or indeed investors) need not be much informed about the nature of the charge or the grounds that would cause the charge to attach to the company's assets. This approach may occasionally be seen in Scotland, as in the Sale of Goods Act 1979 s.17 and the Floating Charges (Scotland) Act 1961. The Scottish Law Commission, recognising some of the difficulties, issued a thoughtful Discussion Paper on Registration of Rights in Security by Companies (SLC Paper 121, October 2002) and later a Report on Registration of Rights in Security by Companies (SLC Report 197, 2004). Between the issue of that paper and report and the present day, there have been other concerns relating to the registration of charges throughout the United Kingdom, because of, amongst other things: (a) the 21 day period of invisibility, during which it is not necessarily clear whether other creditors may have taken a charge over a company's assets and (b) the cost to the Registrar of Companies of having an army of clerks checking charges and issuing certificates of registration of charge. From the Government's point of view there is no benefit in issuing certificates of registration of charge for the convenience of the charger and the chargee, although there is a counter-argument that the reassurance given by the Government by way of these certificates is actually a boon to banking and thereby to commerce generally, not to mention employment and tax revenue. While these potential changes were being debated, and in the light of the SCL paper and report, it was decided to take the opportunity to give Scotland in this Act its own register of floating charges. The overwhelming benefit of the new register of floating charges will be that a charge is created on registration: there is no 21-day period of invisibility, and no danger of an intervening charge unexpectedly taking priority. The regulations spelling out the fine detail of the operation of the new register are yet to be drafted, and were the subject of a consultation document issued by the then DTI (now the DBERR) in May 2007. In addition, though not strictly relevant to the registration of floating charges, there is much discussion about the attachment of floating charges in the Scottish Law Commission's Report on *Sharp v Thomson* (SLC Report 208, December 2007).

Scottish Civil Enforcement Commission

Messengers at Arms and Sheriff Officers, despite their long and distinguished history as servants of the Crown, enforcers of court decrees and officers of Lord Lyon King of Arms, were perceived as a collective body to be in need of greater public accountability: self-regulation was no longer acceptable. Accordingly a new body, a quango to be known as the Scottish Civil Enforcement Commission, to be staffed by senior representatives of the judiciary, lay members and others, would oversee the practice of these officials, who would henceforth be known as Judicial Officers. As the Scottish Government is very reluctant to fund any new quangos, and indeed regularly speaks of "bonfires" of quangos, it may well be that this quango is not set up as envisaged in the 2007 Act, if indeed it is set up at all. At the time of writing, it would appear the Commission will not be set up for these very reasons. This is not to say that the idea may not be revived at a later date.

Diligence

The new Act introduces a new form of diligence, land attachment, to replace adjudication for debt. Adjudication for debt was a long drawn out and rarely used process which enabled a creditor to seize a debtor's heritage after 10 years. Although it might once have been useful in a predominantly agricultural society, it has been of little use recently, and Scotland has been unusual amongst developed economies in not having a quick and effective method whereby a creditor can force the sale of a recalcitrant debtor's land. This is particularly useful when a wealthy debtor is perfectly able to pay his debts but refuses to do so, such a debtor being known as a "won't pay" debtor. A creditor could choose to sequestrate such a debtor, or were the debtor a company, put it into liquidation, but this may be more than the situation requires. It would not therefore be particularly harsh to make such a debtor lose his rights in any land he owns and to let the creditor have the benefit of the land instead. The new diligence that deals with this is land attachment.

At the same time, it would be oppressive if land attachment were used on debtors whose only asset is their home and who are in no position to pay, these people being known as "can't pays" and who may be further affected in that, if their house is sold, they become homeless. Land attachment also effectively makes an unsecured debt into a secured debt without a reduction in interest rate, which is seen as unfair. Despite the outbursts in the Scottish Parliament (see *Hansard* on November 30, 2006) concerning this diligence, which some MSPs feared would be used harshly and on every occasion, in a manner similar to the increasing use of charging orders in England, the new legislation tries to find a balance between the justified concern that land attachment could be used oppressively against the indigent, and the equally justified unfairness were a creditor unable to satisfy his claim against a debtor who either had spare houses or land he could sell, or who had ample equity in his home. At the time of writing one of the reasons that the Act has not been brought into force is that the precise figure for which land attachment may take place has yet to be established. The Act says £3,000: the SNP, in power at the time of writing, violently objected to this at the time the Act was passed, as being far too low, or wrong in principle, and therefore have not at the time of writing brought the part of the Act relating to land attachment into force.

Residual attachment is a new form of attachment that catches assets that hitherto may not have been entirely amenable to attachment, such as intellectual property rights.

The process of inhibition is being rationalised and made more "user-friendly".

The law on diligence on the dependence is being put on a statutory basis and dispenses with some of the old Latin terminology.

Attachment of money allows a creditor to seize cash in a debtor's premises, something hitherto not possible. There are safeguards to protect third parties where necessary.

The rules relating to diligence against earnings are being clarified, particularly in respect of holiday pay, although in practice holiday pay is very rare following recent changes in employment law.

The process of arrestment and furthcoming is regularised, two of the principal changes being that there will be no need to have a separate action of furthcoming and that a bank account may not be evacuated by a creditor: the creditor must leave some funds in the account for the benefit of the debtor and his family.

There are changes to the practice and procedure of admiralty arrestments and to actions for removing people from heritable property.

Although not all of the 2007 Act is in force, where it is in force the consequential amendments to the Rules of the Court of Session and the Sheriff Court Rules have been made and, for some of the details of the practicalities of carrying out diligence, it will be necessary to follow the procedures therein.

Much of the thinking behind the 2007 Act's changes to diligence may be found in the Scottish Law Commission's Report on Diligence (SLC Report 207, May 2001). By way of contrast, it is enlightening to see a sceptical debtor's view of the whole process of diligence: the website *http://www.edinburghclaimants.org/debtworriesleaflet.html* provides earthy practical advice on how to outwit sheriff officers and deal with debt-enforcers' threats.

What does the 2007 Act not do?

What the 2007 Act does not do is tidy up all the difficulties in the process of sequestration. Much is left to regulations yet to be drafted, and it is likely that insolvency practitioners and debt advisers will have to consult the 2007 Act, the 1985 Act and various yet to be drafted regulations if they wish to be sure what the new rules are. This is undoubtedly a recipe for confusion and error, not least because, with the best will in the world, it is difficult for practitioners to keep abreast of statutory instruments, to know when they come into force and what existing arrangements are changed by the new regulations. It is therefore most commendable that the Accountant in Bankruptcy maintains continually updated versions of the 1985 Act, the 1987 Act and the 2002 Act.

The Act does not resolve all the difficulties of the Debt Arrangement Programmes, which, while working well enough for those who use them, have not been found particularly useful for those not in employment or only in intermittent employment. The Act also does not entirely resolve the intractable problem, not unique to Scotland, of dealing with "no income no assets" debtors, sometimes known as "NINAs" though it does take some steps to deal with "low income low assets" debtors (see The Bankruptcy (Scotland) Act 1985 (Low Income, Low Asset Debtors etc.) Regulations 2008 (SSI 2008/81), in force on April 1, 2008). In 2005 New Zealand introduced an Insolvency Law Reform Bill allowing such debtors the opportunity to write off all their debts, and a similar scheme is being considered in England (see the Department of Constitutional Affairs' consultation document *A Choice of Paths* 23/04 and the Debt Relief Orders envisaged under the Courts and Tribunals Bill introduced in 2006). While this would possibly concentrate lenders' minds on the wisdom of lending to the very poor, it might also deprive people in neighbourhoods with a high incidence of NINA debtors of any opportunity of obtaining credit (sometimes known as post-code deprivation), thus driving debtors into the hands of loan sharks, unless there happen to be particularly active and well run credit unions nearby. In any event, the general credit squeeze arising out of the sub-prime lending scandal is already making it harder for poor people to borrow money. There is also the wider issue of whether it is a good message to send to the population generally that if a debtor's financial problems are severe enough, his debts may all be written off: such an attitude, it is said, does not encourage thrift or prudence, virtues traditionally associated with Scotland. The same criticism, indeed, is made of the fact that the period of bankruptcy is now only to be one year.

The Act does not make the concept of "apparent insolvency" any easier to understand. Apparent insolvency is defined in a number of ways at s.7 of the 1985 Act and for a debtor to present his own application for sequestration, or for a creditor to sequestrate a debtor, the debtor must have been apparently insolvent. The concept of "apparent insolvency" is not an easy one to grasp for anyone, let alone anxious debtors, and if the aim of the 2007 Act is to make life better for debtors, a good start would be to rewrite the ss.5 and 7 of the 1985 Act in a more approachable manner so that debtors, not to mention lawyers and insolvency practitioners, could easily understand what the law expects. It is nevertheless worth stating that, with effect from April 1, 2008 the sum for which a creditor may sequestrate a debtor within 21 days in the absence of payment or security is raised to £1,500 (1985 Act s.7(1)(d), as amended by the Bankruptcy (Scotland) Regulations 2008 (SSI 2008/82, para.13)).

For a general critique of the effectiveness of the bankruptcy regimes in Scotland and in England, see Mackenzie Skene and Walters *Consumer Bankruptcy Law Reform in England, Wales and Scotland* May 2006 available at: *http://www.insolvency.gov.uk/insolvencyprofessionandlegislation/research/personaldocs/McKenzieSkeneWalters-Jul06fv.doc.*

COMMENCEMENT

Section 22 of the Act came into force on the day after Royal Assent. The remaining provisions of this Act, except ss.227, 224 and 225, come into force on such day as the Scottish Ministers may, by order, appoint. Part 1 of the Act came into force on 1st April 2008, with the exception of ss.18(5), 21, 25 and some parts of s.36 (see (Bankruptcy and Diligence etc (Scotland) Act 2007 (Commencement No.3, Savings and Transitionals) Order 2008, SSI 2008 No.115). Parts 7, 9 and 12 came into force on the same date, as did most of Sch.1.

ABBREVIATIONS

"the 1985 Act":	the Bankruptcy (Scotland) Act 1985
"the 1987 Act":	the Debtors (Scotland) Act 1987
"the 2002 Act":	the Debt Arrangement and Attachment (Scotland) Act 2002
"the 2007 Act":	the Bankruptcy and Diligence etc. (Scotland) Act 2007
"BRO":	Bankruptcy Restrictions Order
"BRU":	Bankruptcy Restrictions Undertaking
"DAS":	Debt Arrangement Scheme
"DPP":	Debt Payment Programme

PART 1

BANKRUPTCY

Duration of bankruptcy

1. Discharge of debtor

(1) Section 54 of the Bankruptcy (Scotland) Act 1985 (c.66) (in this Act, the "1985 Act") (automatic discharge of debtor) is amended as follows.

(2) In subsection (1), for the words "3 years" substitute "1 year".

(3) In subsection (3), the words "2 years and" are repealed.

(4) The heading to that section becomes "Automatic discharge of debtor".

GENERAL NOTE

This section reduces the period of sequestration for a debtor from three years from the date of sequestration to one year. The date of sequestration, as stated in the 1985 Act s.12(4), is as follows: where the debtor presents his own petition for sequestration, the date of sequestration is the date sequestration is granted; where the petition is presented by a creditor or a trustee under a trust deed, the date of sequestration is the date the court grants warrant to cite the debtor to appear before the court hearing to decide on the debtor's sequestration (see the 1985 Act s.12(2)).

However, under this new section, the trustee in sequestration, or any creditor, may, not later than nine months after the date of sequestration, apply to the sheriff to have the discharge of the sequestration deferred (1985 Act s.54(3)). The sheriff will order the application for deferral to be served on the debtor, and the debtor is then entitled to lodge in court a declaration indicating that he has fully and fairly surrendered his estate to the trustee in sequestration and handed over to the trustee all the documentation relating to his estate. If the debtor fails to make that declaration, the sheriff must, without a hearing, defer the discharge for a further two years (1985 Act s.54(4)). If the debtor does lodge the declaration, the sheriff will fix a hearing not earlier than 28 days from the date of lodging of the declaration, and order the applicant to notify the debtor and, where necessary, the trustee of the date of the hearing. The trustee must then lodge in court a report on the debtor's assets and liabilities, his financial and business affairs and his conduct both in relation to those affairs and to his conduct in the court of the sequestration (1985 Act s.54(5)). The sheriff may then defer the discharge for a period of up to a further two years (1985 Act s.54(6)).

Bankruptcy restrictions orders and undertakings

2. Bankruptcy restrictions orders and undertakings

(1) After section 56 of the 1985 Act, insert-

"Bankruptcy restrictions orders and undertakings

56A Bankruptcy restrictions order

(1) Where sequestration of a living debtor's estate is awarded, an order (known as a "bankruptcy restrictions order") in respect of the debtor may be made by the sheriff.

(2) An order may be made only on the application of the Accountant in Bankruptcy.

56B   Grounds for making order

(1) The sheriff shall grant an application for a bankruptcy restrictions order if he thinks it appropriate having regard to the conduct of the debtor (whether before or after the date of sequestration).

(2) The sheriff shall, in particular, take into account any of the following kinds of behaviour on the part of the debtor-

(a) failing to keep records which account for a loss of property by the debtor, or by a business carried on by him, where the loss occurred in the period beginning 2 years before the date of presentation of the petition for sequestration or, as the case may be, the date the debtor application was made and ending with the date of the application for a bankruptcy restrictions order;

(b) failing to produce records of that kind on demand by-
(i) the Accountant in Bankruptcy;
(ii) the interim trustee; or
(iii) the trustee;

(c) making a gratuitous alienation or any other alienation for no consideration or for no adequate consideration which a creditor has, under any rule of law, right to challenge;

(d) creating an unfair preference or any other preference which a creditor has, under any rule of law, right to challenge;

(e) making an excessive pension contribution;

(f) failing to supply goods or services which were wholly or partly paid for which gave rise to a claim submitted by a creditor under section 22 or 48 of this Act;

(g) trading at a time before the date of sequestration when the debtor knew or ought to have known that he was to be unable to meet his debts;

(h) incurring, before the date of sequestration, a debt which the debtor had no reasonable expectation of being able to pay;

(j) failing to account satisfactorily to-
(i) the sheriff;
(ii) the Accountant in Bankruptcy;
(iii) the interim trustee; or
(iv) the trustee,

for a loss of property or for an insufficiency of property to meet his debts;

(k) carrying on any gambling, speculation or extravagance which may have materially contributed to or increased the extent of his debts or which took place between the date of presentation of the petition for sequestration or, as the case may be, the date the debtor application was made and the date on which sequestration is awarded;

(l) neglect of business affairs of a kind which may have materially contributed to or increased the extent of his debts;

(m) fraud or breach of trust;

(n) failing to co-operate with-
(i) the Accountant in Bankruptcy;
(ii) the interim trustee; or
(iii) the trustee.

(3) The sheriff shall also, in particular, consider whether the debtor-

    (a) has previously been sequestrated; and

    (b) remained undischarged from that sequestration at any time during the period of 5 years ending with the date of the sequestration to which the application relates.

(4) For the purposes of subsection (2) above-

"excessive pension contribution" shall be construed in accordance with section 36A of this Act; and

"gratuitous alienation" means an alienation challengeable under section 34(1) of this Act.

56C   Application of section 67(9)

(1) Where the sheriff thinks it appropriate, the sheriff may specify in the bankruptcy restrictions order that subsection (9) of section 67 of this Act shall apply to the debtor during the period he is subject to the order as if he were a debtor within the meaning of subsection (10)(a) of that section.

(2) For the purposes of subsection (1) above, section 67(10) of this Act shall have effect as if, for paragraph (c) of that subsection, there were substituted-

    "(c) the relevant information about the status of the debtor is the information that-

        (i) he is subject to a bankruptcy restrictions order; or

        (ii) where his estate has been sequestrated and he has not been discharged, that fact.".

56D   Timing of application for order

(1) An application for a bankruptcy restrictions order must be made, subject to subsection (2) below, within the period beginning with the date of sequestration and ending with the date on which the debtor's discharge becomes effective.

(2) An application may be made after the end of the period referred to in subsection (1) above only with the permission of the sheriff.

56E   Duration of order and application for annulment

(1) A bankruptcy restrictions order-

    (a) shall come into force when it is made; and

    (b) shall cease to have effect at the end of the date specified in the order.

(2) The date specified in a bankruptcy restrictions order under subsection (1)(b) above must not be-

    (a) before the end of the period of 2 years beginning with the date on which the order is made; or

    (b) after the end of the period of 15 years beginning with that date.

(3) On an application by the debtor the sheriff may-

    (a) annul a bankruptcy restrictions order; or

    (b) vary such an order, including providing for such an order to cease to have effect at the end of a date earlier than the date specified in the order under subsection (1)(b) above.

56F Interim bankruptcy restrictions order

(1) This section applies at any time between-
    (a) the making of an application for a bankruptcy restrictions order; and
    (b) the determination of the application.
(2) The sheriff may make an interim bankruptcy restrictions order if he thinks that-
    (a) there are prima facie grounds to suggest that the application for the bankruptcy restrictions order will be successful; and
    (b) it is in the public interest to make an interim order.
(3) An interim order may be made only on the application of the Accountant in Bankruptcy.
(4) An interim order-
    (a) shall have the same effect as a bankruptcy restrictions order; and
    (b) shall come into force when it is made.
(5) An interim order shall cease to have effect-
    (a) on the determination of the application for the bankruptcy restrictions order;
    (b) on the acceptance of a bankruptcy restrictions undertaking made by the debtor; or
    (c) if the sheriff discharges the interim order on the application of the Accountant in Bankruptcy or of the debtor.
(6) Where a bankruptcy restrictions order is made in respect of a debtor who is subject to an interim order, section 56E(2) of this Act shall have effect in relation to the bankruptcy restrictions order as if the reference to the date on which the order is made were a reference to the date on which the interim order was made.

56G Bankruptcy restrictions undertaking

(1) A living debtor who is not subject to a bankruptcy restrictions order may offer an undertaking (known as a "bankruptcy restrictions undertaking") to the Accountant in Bankruptcy.
(2) In determining whether to accept a bankruptcy restrictions undertaking, the Accountant in Bankruptcy shall have regard to the matters specified in section 56B(2) and (3) of this Act.
(3) A bankruptcy restrictions undertaking-
    (a) shall take effect on being accepted by the Accountant in Bankruptcy; and
    (b) shall cease to have effect at the end of the date specified in the undertaking.
(4) The date specified under subsection (3)(b) above must not be-
    (a) before the end of the period of 2 years beginning with the date on which the undertaking is accepted; or
    (b) after the end of the period of 15 years beginning with that date.
(5) On an application by the debtor the sheriff may-
    (a) annul a bankruptcy restrictions undertaking; or
    (b) vary such an undertaking, including providing for a bankruptcy restrictions undertaking to cease to have effect at the end of a date earlier than the date specified in the undertaking under subsection (3)(b) above.

56H Bankruptcy restrictions undertakings: application of section 67(9)

(1) A debtor may, with the agreement of the Accountant in Bankruptcy, specify in a bankruptcy restrictions undertaking that subsection (9) of section 67 of this Act shall apply to the debtor during the period the undertaking has effect as if he were a debtor within the meaning of subsection (10)(a) of that section.

(2) For the purposes of subsection (1) above, section 67(10) of this Act shall have effect as if, for paragraph (c) of that subsection, there were substituted-

"(c) the relevant information about the status of the debtor is the information that-

(i) he is subject to a bankruptcy restrictions undertaking; or

(ii) where his estate has been sequestrated and he has not been discharged, that fact.".

56J Effect of recall of sequestration

(1) Where an award of sequestration of a debtor's estate is recalled under section 17(1) of this Act-

(a) the sheriff may annul any bankruptcy restrictions order, interim bankruptcy restrictions order or bankruptcy restrictions undertaking which is in force in respect of the debtor;

(b) no new bankruptcy restrictions order or interim order may be made in respect of the debtor; and

(c) no new bankruptcy restrictions undertaking by the debtor may be accepted.

(2) Where the sheriff refuses to annul a bankruptcy restrictions order, interim bankruptcy restrictions order or bankruptcy restrictions undertaking under subsection (1)(a) above the debtor may, no later than 28 days after the date on which the award of sequestration is recalled, appeal to the sheriff principal against such a refusal.

(3) The decision of the sheriff principal on an appeal under subsection (2) above is final.

56K Effect of discharge on approval of offer of composition

(1) This section applies where a certificate of discharge is granted under paragraph 11(1) of Schedule 4 to this Act discharging a debtor.

(2) Subject to sections 56E(3)(a), 56F(5)(c) and 56G(5)(a) of this Act, the debtor shall remain subject to any bankruptcy restrictions order, interim bankruptcy restrictions order or bankruptcy restrictions undertaking which is in force in respect of him.

(3) The sheriff may make a bankruptcy restrictions order in relation to the debtor on an application made before the discharge.

(4) The Accountant in Bankruptcy may accept a bankruptcy restrictions undertaking offered before the discharge.

(5) No application for a bankruptcy restrictions order or interim order may be made in respect of the debtor.

(2) In section 1A(1)(b) of that Act (duty of the Accountant in Bankruptcy to maintain register of insolvencies), after sub-paragraph (ii) insert-

> "(iia) bankruptcy restrictions orders, interim bankruptcy restrictions orders and bankruptcy restrictions undertakings;".

GENERAL NOTE

This is a new provision of the Act and echoes similar legislation in the Enterprise Act 2002, applicable to England and Wales. It inserts new s.56A-K into the 1985 Act. The Accountant in Bankruptcy is expected to set up a new Scottish Register for BROs and BRUs although at the time of writing the practical details of this are not available. It is to be hoped that there will be some method whereby the Scottish Register will interact with the one maintained by the Official Receiver in England and Wales, otherwise there will be nothing to prevent a Scottish debtor subject to a BRO or BRU moving south and ignoring the Scottish BRO or BRU as the case may be. Indeed, at present, there is little to prevent a person subject to an English BRO or BRU moving to Scotland or Ireland and ignoring his restrictions. When BROs and BRUs were being discussed by the Culture and Enterprise Committee, there were concerns as to the effectiveness of the Scottish Register, since an unscrupulous debtor would change his name and address and fail to pass on these changes to the Register. Debtors, when applying for loans from banks, would be likely to have checks run against them in the new Scottish Register which should disclose, at least some of the time, the BROs and BRUs; but lenders other than banks would be less likely to make use of the Scottish Register. This may reduce the effectiveness of BROs and BRUs.

Subsection 1 inserts the following provisions into the 1985 Act.

Section 56 A

DEFINITION

"Accountant in bankruptcy": 1985 Act ss.1, 1A-C

Only the sheriff may make a BRO, and it may only be imposed on living debtors. Only the Accountant in Bankruptcy may apply for the BRO. Trustees in sequestration other than the Accountant in Bankruptcy do not have the authority to make such an application and will have to request the Accountant in Bankruptcy to do this for them.

Section 56 B

DEFINITIONS

"Date of presentation of petition for sequestration": 1985 Act s.5
"Debtor application": 2007 Act s.14
"Accountant in bankruptcy": 1985 Act ss.1, 1A-C
"Interim trustee": 1985 Act s.2
"Gratuitous alienation": 1985 Act s.34
"Unfair preference": 1985 Act s.36
"Excessive pension contribution": 1985 Act s.36A-F
"Trustee": 2007 Act s.6

This section explains that if a debtor has failed to conduct himself with the propriety with which he should have conducted himself, the sheriff, having taken account of all the circumstances and the factors indicated in this section, should grant a BRO. The significance for a debtor of having received a BRO is that it prohibits the debtor from certain activities, such as being appointed a receiver in terms of the Insolvency Act 1985 s.51 (s.3), holding public office within a local authority (s.4), but perhaps most importantly on a practical basis, where the sheriff thinks fit, not being able to obtain credit for more than £500 (or any sum if the debtor already has debts amounting to over £1,000) without indicating to the lender that he is subject to a BRO (but not a BRU) or that he has been sequestrated or bankrupt elsewhere in the United Kingdom and that he has not been discharged (1985 Act s.56C, as inserted by 2007 Act s.2). If the debtor fails to disclose his BRO he may be prosecuted, and if found guilty, may be sentenced in accordance with the provisions of the 1985 Act s.67(12). Section 67 is amended by the 2007 Act s.24.

The grounds under which the sheriff may make an order are wide. They include not only the obviously fraudulent or unhelpful activities carried out by the debtor both before and after the date of sequestration, but such activities as "gambling, speculation or extravagance" which may have materially contributed to or increased the extent of his debts. Subsection (f) refers to the failure by the debtor to supply goods or services, partly or wholly paid for, giving rise to a claim submitted by a creditor under ss.22 or 48 of the 1985 Act. These are claims submitted by creditors to the initial statutory meeting of creditors and to the creditors' meeting for the adjudication of claims.

Section 56B(2)(c) refers to a gratuitous alienation or any other alienation for no consideration, or for no adequate consideration, which a creditor has, under any rule of law, right to challenge, this is qualified by s.56B(4) which states that a "gratuitous alienation" means an alienation challengeable under the 1985 Act s.34(1). "Any other alienation" presumably therefore refers to the admittedly rarely used common law gratuitous alienation. On a connected note, s.56B refers to an unfair preference or any other preference which a creditor has under any rule of law a right to challenge, but this is not defined within the terms of the 1985 Act s.36 as one might have expected.

The sheriff must also take into account any excessive pension contributions, as defined in the 1985 Act s.36A and introduced by the Welfare Reform and Pensions Act 1999. Despite the extensive and very complex legislation on the definition and recovery of excessive pension contributions made by a debtor to a pension scheme, there appear at the time of writing to have been no Scottish cases where the legislation has been invoked and which might therefore have been of guidance.

The wording of this section is very similar to the Insolvency Act 1986 Sch.4A para.2, as inserted by the Enterprise Act 2002. This introduced BROs and BRUs to England and Wales.

Section 56C

This provides that the sheriff may order that where the debtor obtains credit in excess of £500 (or any sum if the debtor already has debts of over £1,000) from any creditor without disclosing the fact that he is sequestrated or bankrupt elsewhere in the United Kingdom, or subject to a BRO, he may be prosecuted in terms of the 1985 Act s.67(12). Section 67 of the 1985 is amended by virtue of s.24 of the 2007 Act.

Section 56D

DEFINITIONS

"Date of sequestration": 1985 Act s.12(4)
"Date of discharge": 1985 Act s.54

This provides that an application for a BRO is only permissible between the date of sequestration and the effective date of discharge of the sequestration (normally one year after the date of sequestration), unless the sheriff permits otherwise.

Section 56E

This provides that the minimum period of a BRO is two years and the maximum is 15 years. According to the Insolvency Service statistics for the years 2004 to 2006 the average BRO in England and Wales was imposed for a period of four years.

Section 56F

DEFINITIONS

"Bankruptcy Restrictions Undertaking": 1985 Act s.56G (as inserted by the 2007 Act s.2)

Only the Accountant in Bankruptcy may apply for an interim BRO. An interim BRO ceases to have effect once the original application for a BRO has been granted or refused, where the court accepts a BRU or where the sheriff discharges the interim BRO. If an interim BRO is granted, and a subsequent BRO is granted thereafter, the period during which the debt is subject to the BRO is backdated to the date when the interim BRO was granted.

Section 56G

A debtor may, if he wishes, offer a BRU to the Accountant in Bankruptcy (not the sheriff). Before she accepts it, she should consider the same grounds as the sheriff does in granting a BRO under s.56B(2) and(3). If she accepts it, the BRU takes effect on acceptance but it must endure for at least two years and terminate no more than 15 years after the date of acceptance. It is for the debtor to suggest an appropriate period for his BRU: no doubt this might require some negotiation with the Accountant in Bankruptcy.

Under subs.(5), if the debtor at a later date wishes to annul or vary (including shortening) the BRU, he must apply to the sheriff for this.

Section 56H

This section, which replicates s.56C, permits the debtor to specify in his BRU that the same criminal sanctions as in s.56C would apply to him if he tried to obtain credit in excess of £500 (or any sum if the debtor already has debts of over £1,000) with disclosing the fact that he was subject to a BRU or was sequestrated and as yet undischarged. Although this section says "with the agreement of the Accountant in Bankruptcy" it is likely that she would insist on s.67(9) of the 1985 Act applying. s.67(9) of the 1985 Act is amended by s.24 of the 2007 Act to the effect that the former figure of £100 is replaced by £500 (or £1,000 if the debtor already has debts of over £1,000).

Section 56J

Recall of sequestration is the process of restoring the debtor to the position he was in before the award of sequestration was granted, so far as practicable, in terms of s.17 of the 1985 Act. It will be noted that the sheriff is now able to recall the award (2007 Act s.16(4)): hitherto only the Court of Session could do so. Where an award is set aside, the sheriff may annul any BRO, interim BRO or BRU in force, and no new BROs, interim BROs or BRUs may be made or accepted. If the sheriff refuses to annul any BRO, interim BRO or BRU, an appeal may be made to the sheriff principal. Recall is only available if the sheriff is satisfied that the debtor has paid his debts in full or given sufficient security for their payment, that a majority of the debtor's creditors reside in a country outside Scotland and it is more appropriate for the debtor's estate to be dealt with in that country, or one or more awards of sequestration (or bankruptcy in England, Wales and Northern Ireland) has been granted already (1985 Act s.17(1)).

Section 56K

DEFINITION

"Composition": 1985 Act s.56 and Sch.4 (as amended by the 2007 Act s.21)

An offer of composition is usually where the debtors' family or representatives approach the trustee, offering to make a settlement with the debtor's creditors.

To be acceptable, the composition must offer to pay the ordinary creditors a dividend of at least 25p in the pound after satisfaction of the preferred creditors, and within a reasonable time-span. The creditors are invited to accept it, and if a majority in number and not less than one third in value have not rejected it, the trustee presents the offer to the sheriff for his approval.

This section provides that even where a certificate of discharge of composition has been granted, any BRO, interim BRO or BRU remains in place unless expressly annulled or discharged by the sheriff. The sheriff may make a BRO and the Accountant in Bankruptcy may accept a BRU before the discharge, but under (e) once the certificate of discharge following a successful composition has been granted, no new BRO or interim BRO may be made.

Subsection (2) directs the Accountant in Bankruptcy to set up a new register of BROs, interim BROs and BRUs.

Effect of bankruptcy restrictions orders and undertakings

3. Disqualification from being appointed as receiver

(1) Section 51 of the Insolvency Act 1986 (c.45) (appointment of receiver) is amended as follows.
(2) In subsection (3), after paragraph (b), insert-
    "(ba) a person subject to a bankruptcy restrictions order;".
(3) In subsection (5), after "bankrupt" insert "or a person subject to a bankruptcy restrictions order".

(4) In subsection (6), after "receivers" insert; and
"bankruptcy restrictions order" means-

      (a) a bankruptcy restrictions order made under section 56A of the Bankruptcy (Scotland) Act 1985 (c.66);

      (b) a bankruptcy restrictions undertaking entered into under section 56G of that Act;

      (c) a bankruptcy restrictions order made under paragraph 1 of Schedule 4A to this Act; or

      (d) a bankruptcy restrictions undertaking entered into under paragraph 7 of that Schedule.".

DEFINITIONS

"Receiver": Insolvency Act 1986 s.51

GENERAL NOTE

This section amends the Insolvency Act 1986 to prevent persons subject to BROs and BRUs from acting as receivers appointed by floating charge holders. This section is unlikely to be of much practical use since receivers nowadays have to be insolvency practitioners, and secondly, since the Enterprise Act 2002, nearly all new floating charges, with a few limited exceptions, are qualifying floating charges, which prohibit the appointment of a receiver and require the appointment of an administrator instead. However, there will be still many companies with floating charges granted before September 15, 2003 (the date of implementation of the Enterprise Act) whose floating charge holders are still permitted to appoint receivers.

Subsection (4)(c) refers to the Insolvency Act 1986 Sch.4A inserted by the Enterprise Act 2002, and which introduced BROs and BRUs in England and Wales.

4. Disqualification for nomination, election and holding office as member of local authority

In section 31 of the Local Government (Scotland) Act 1973 (c.65) (disqualifications for nomination, election and holding office as member of local authority)-

      (a) after subsection (1)(b), insert-

          "(ba) he is subject to a bankruptcy restrictions order;"; and

      (b) after subsection (3A), insert-

          "(3B) In subsection (1)(ba) above, "bankruptcy restrictions order" means-

          (a) a bankruptcy restrictions order made under section 56A of the Bankruptcy (Scotland) Act 1985;

          (b) a bankruptcy restrictions undertaking entered into under section 56G of that Act;

          (c) a bankruptcy restrictions order made under paragraph 1 of Schedule 4A to the Insolvency Act 1986 (c.45); or

          (d) a bankruptcy restrictions undertaking entered into under paragraph 7 of that Schedule.".

GENERAL NOTE

This section prevents someone subject to a BRO or BRU in either Scotland or England and Wales from being nominated, elected or holding office as a member of a local authority.

5. Orders relating to disqualification

After section 71A of the 1985 Act, insert-

"71B Disqualification provisions: power to make orders

(1) The Scottish Ministers may make an order under this section in relation to a disqualification provision.

(2) A "disqualification provision" is a provision made by or under any enactment which disqualifies (whether permanently or temporarily and whether absolutely or conditionally) a relevant debtor or a class of relevant debtors from-

    (a) being elected or appointed to an office or position;

    (b) holding an office or position; or

    (c) becoming or remaining a member of a body or group.

(3) In subsection (2) above, the reference to a provision which disqualifies a person conditionally includes a reference to a provision which enables him to be dismissed.

(4) An order under subsection (1) above may repeal or revoke the disqualification provision.

(5) An order under subsection (1) above may amend, or modify the effect of, the disqualification provision-

    (a) so as to reduce the class of relevant debtors to whom the disqualification provision applies;

    (b) so as to extend the disqualification provision to some or all individuals who are subject to a bankruptcy restrictions order;

    (c) so that the disqualification provision applies only to some or all individuals who are subject to a bankruptcy restrictions order;

    (d) so as to make the application of the disqualification provision wholly or partly subject to the discretion of a specified person, body or group.

(6) An order by virtue of subsection (5)(d) above may provide for a discretion to be subject to-

    (a) the approval of a specified person or body;

    (b) appeal to a specified person, body, court or tribunal.

(7) The Scottish Ministers may be specified for the purposes of subsection (5)(d) or (6)(a) or (b) above.

(8) In this section-

    "bankruptcy restrictions order" includes-

        (a) a bankruptcy restrictions undertaking;

        (b) a bankruptcy restrictions order made under paragraph 1 of Schedule 4A to the Insolvency Act 1986 (c.45); and

        (c) a bankruptcy restrictions undertaking entered into under paragraph 7 of that Schedule;

    "relevant debtor" means a debtor-

        (a) whose estate has been sequestrated;

        (b) who has granted (or on whose behalf there has been granted) a trust deed;

        (c) who has been adjudged bankrupt by a court in England and Wales or in Northern Ireland; or

        (d) who, in England and Wales or in Northern Ireland, has made an agreement with his creditors for a composition

in satisfaction of his debts or a scheme of arrangement of his affairs or for some other kind of settlement or arrangement.

(9) An order under this section-

    (a) may make provision generally or for a specified purpose only;

    (b) may make different provision for different purposes; and

    (c) may make transitional, consequential or incidental provision.

(10) An order under this section-

    (a) shall be made by statutory instrument; and

    (b) shall not be made unless a draft has been laid before and approved by a resolution of the Scottish Parliament.".

DEFINITIONS

"Bankruptcy restrictions order": 1985 Act s.56B (as inserted by the 2007 Act s.2)

"Bankrupcty restrictions undertaking": 1985 Act s.56G (as inserted by the 2007 Act s.2)

"Trust deed": 1985 Act s.59 and Sch.5

GENERAL NOTE

This section allows the Scottish Ministers to make an order or orders in relation to a disqualification provision. This is to enable them to bring in an order to permit them to repeal, revoke or change any provision in any legislation which prevents a debtor being elected to an office, holding an office or remaining a member of a "body or a group", this vague term presumably being some sort of organisation with responsibilities and duties which would be inappropriate for a debtor to be part of. The power that is being granted to the Ministers is wide: it enables them to extend the scope or reduce the scope of any enactment, and to provide that the application of the disqualification provision may be at the discretion of some specified group, which in turn may be subject to some other person or body and on appeal to the court. Although this is a very wide power, any such order may only be made by statutory instrument and a draft of it must have been approved by the Scottish Parliament.

The reasoning behind this section is that as part of the consultation exercise that lay behind this Act, consultees were asked whether or not bankrupts should be allowed to hold public office: opinion was divided on the matter. In principle, bankrupts are prohibited from holding public office because of the risk of their integrity being compromised. This section allows Ministers the option to extend or indeed reduce that prohibition to persons who are subject to BROs and BRUs. Bankrupts are prohibited from being company directors by virtue of the Company Directors Disqualification Act 1986 s.11.

The trustee in the sequestration

6. Amalgamation of offices of interim trustee and permanent trustee

(1) In section 2 of the 1985 Act (appointment and functions of interim trustee)-

    (a) after subsection (2), insert-

        "(2A) Where the sheriff awards sequestration of the debtor's estate and an interim trustee has been appointed in pursuance of subsection (5) below, the sheriff may appoint-

        (a) the interim trustee; or

        (b) subject to subsection (2B) below, such other person as may be nominated by the petitioner,

    to be the trustee in the sequestration.

(2B) A person nominated under subsection (2A)(b) above may be appointed to be the trustee in the sequestration only if-

(a) it appears to the sheriff that the person satisfies the conditions mentioned in subsection (3) below; and

(b) a copy of the undertaking mentioned in subsection (3)(c) below has been lodged with the sheriff.

(2C) Where the sheriff does not appoint a person to be trustee in pursuance of subsection (2A) above, the sheriff shall appoint the Accountant in Bankruptcy to be the trustee in the sequestration.";

(b) after subsection (6), insert-

"(6A) The interim trustee's general function shall be to safeguard the debtor's estate pending the determination of the petition for sequestration.

(6B) Whether or not the interim trustee is still acting in the sequestration, the interim trustee shall supply the Accountant in Bankruptcy with such information as the Accountant in Bankruptcy considers necessary to enable him to discharge his functions under this Act."; and

(c) the heading to that section becomes "Appointment and functions of the trustee in the sequestration".

(2) The heading to section 3 of that Act becomes "Functions of the trustee".

(3) Unless the context otherwise requires, any reference in any enactment to-

(a) an "interim trustee"; or

(b) a "permanent trustee",

is to be construed as a reference to a trustee in the sequestration.

GENERAL NOTE

This section causes the offices of interim and permanent trustee to be united. Historically an interim trustee was appointed on sequestration and at the first meeting of the creditors he would either be appointed permanent trustee or some other insolvency practitioner would be appointed in his place. Since most of the time the Accountant in Bankruptcy was the trustee anyway, or the interim trustee was in any case elected permanent trustee, the law has been changed to reflect what generally happens in practice.

There is a secondary meaning of "interim trustee" which applies under the 1985 Act s.2(5): this is a trustee appointed to safeguard the debtor's assets until the determination of the petition for sequestration.

This particular meaning of "interim trustee" still applies and would apply where a petition for sequestration is presented by a creditor or a trustee under a trust deed if the debtor consented to the petition, or if the trustee under the trust deed or any creditor showed cause why an interim trustee should be appointed. An interim trustee must give an undertaking that he will both act as interim trustee and as the trustee if no other trustee is later appointed (1985 Act s.3).

7. Repeal of trustee's residence requirement

(1) In section 2(3) of the 1985 Act (conditions to be met by interim trustee), paragraph (a) is repealed.

(2) In section 24(2) of that Act (eligibility for election as permanent trustee), paragraph (d) is repealed.

GENERAL NOTE

This section removes the previous requirement that the trustee had to reside within the jurisdiction of the Court of Session.

This section caused much disquiet amongst insolvency practitioners on the grounds that insolvency practitioners working from England and Wales would not serve their clients well because of their ignorance of the Scots law of bankruptcy. This objection was seen as accountants defending their own patch and was not accepted.

8. Duties of trustee

(1) In section 3 of the 1985 Act (functions of permanent trustee)-
   (a) after subsection (3), insert-
     "(3A) If the trustee has reasonable grounds to believe that any behaviour on the part of the debtor is of a kind that would result in a sheriff granting, under section 56B(1) of this Act, an application for a bankruptcy restrictions order, he shall report the matter to the Accountant in Bankruptcy.";
   (b) in subsection (4), after "(3)" insert "or (3A)";
   (c) in subsection (5), for "subsection (3)" substitute "subsections (3) and (3A)"; and
   (d) after subsection (7), insert-
     "(8) The trustee shall comply with the requirements of subsections (1)(a) to (d) and (2) above only in so far as, in his view, it would be of financial benefit to the estate of the debtor and in the interests of the creditors to do so.".

(2) In section 39 of that Act (management and realisation of estate), after subsection (8), insert-
   "(9) The trustee-
     (a) shall comply with the requirements of subsection (4) of this section; and
     (b) may do anything permitted by this section,
     only in so far as, in his view, it would be of financial benefit to the estate of the debtor and in the interests of the creditors to do so.".

(3) In section 49 of that Act (adjudication of claims), after subsection (2), insert-
   "(2A) On accepting or rejecting, under subsection (2) above, every claim submitted or deemed to have been re-submitted, the trustee shall, as soon as is reasonably practicable, send a list of every claim so accepted or rejected (including the amount of each claim and whether he has accepted or rejected it) to-
     (a) the debtor; and
     (b) every creditor known to the trustee.".

DEFINITIONS

"Bankruptcy restrictions order": 1985 Act s.56B (as inserted by the 2007 Act s.2)

GENERAL NOTE

Section 8(1) makes certain alterations to the duty of the trustee. If a trustee suspects that the debtor's behaviour might warrant a BRO, he should inform the Accountant in Bankruptcy of the matter.

The new subs.8 of s.3 of the 1985 Act inserted hereby is a provision designed to ensure that where it is uneconomic from the estate's and the creditors' point of view to: (a) recover, manage and realise the debtor's estate; (b) distribute the estate amongst the creditors; (c) find out the reasons for the debtor's insolvency and (d) ascertain the extent of the debtor's assets and liabilities, the trustee is no longer obliged to carry out these tasks.

Under s.8(2) the same principle applies to the realisation of the estate under the 1985 Act s.39.

Section 8(3) has the effect of making the trustee's decisions when adjudicating which of the creditors' claims he has accepted or rejected more transparent, by sending a list of every claim accepted or rejected to the debtor and to all the creditors. This may possibly make it slightly more difficult to carry out the "false creditor" fraud where friends of the debtor submit bogus claims, thus reducing the distributions to genuine creditors.

9. Grounds for resignation or removal of trustee

(1) In section 13 of the 1985 Act (resignation, removal etc. of interim trustee)-
   (a) in subsection (2)(a)-
      (i) for "(whether)" substitute "for any reason mentioned in subsection (2A) below or";
      (ii) for "a" substitute "any other"; and
      (iii) the words "or from any other cause whatsoever)" are repealed; and
   (b) after subsection (2), insert-
      "(2A) The reasons referred to in subsection (2)(a) above are that the interim trustee-
         (a) is incapable within the meaning of section 1(6) of the Adults with Incapacity (Scotland) Act 2000 (asp 4); or
         (b) has some other incapacity by virtue of which he is unable to act as interim trustee.".

(2) In section 28 of that Act (resignation and death of permanent trustee), in subsection (1), for the words from "either" to "he" substitute
   the trustee-
      (a) is unable to act (whether by, under or by virtue of a provision of this Act or from any other cause whatsoever); or
      (b) has so conducted himself that he should no longer continue to act,
   the Accountant in Bankruptcy".

DEFINITIONS
   "Interim trustee": 1985 Act s.2(5)

GENERAL NOTE
   Section 9(1) restricts the reasons indicated in the 1985 Act s.13(2) for the removal of the interim trustee from the rather wide terms hitherto employed, so that an interim trustee may only be removed where the trustee is *incapax* or has some other incapacity (such as, say, a conflict of interest) preventing him from acting as interim trustee.
   Section 9(2) alters s.28 of the 1985 Act by deleting the former reference to s.13(2)(a) and (b), but using their former wording in respect of the resignation but not removal of the trustee. Although s.28(1), (1A) and (2) refer to the sheriff throughout, the sheriff's role is now replaced by the Accountant in Bankruptcy (2007 Act Sch.1 para.28(2)).

10. Termination of interim trustee's functions

After section 13 of the 1985 Act, insert-

"13A Termination of interim trustee's functions where not appointed as trustee

(1) This section applies where an interim trustee (not being the Accountant in Bankruptcy) is appointed under section 2(5) of this Act and the sheriff-

    (a) awards sequestration and appoints another person as trustee under subsection (2A) or (2C) of section 2 of this Act; or

    (b) refuses to award sequestration.

(2) Where the sheriff awards sequestration and appoints another person as trustee, the interim trustee shall hand over to the trustee everything in his possession which relates to the sequestration and shall thereupon cease to act in the sequestration.

(3) The sheriff may make such order in relation to liability for the outlays and remuneration of the interim trustee as may be appropriate.

(4) Within 3 months of the sheriff awarding or, as the case may be, refusing to award sequestration, the interim trustee shall-

    (a) submit to the Accountant in Bankruptcy-

        (i) his accounts of his intromissions (if any) with the debtor's estate; and

        (ii) a claim for outlays reasonably incurred, and for remuneration for work reasonably undertaken, by him; and

    (b) send a copy of his accounts and the claim to-

        (i) the debtor;

        (ii) the petitioner; and

        (iii) in a case where sequestration is awarded, the trustee and all creditors known to the interim trustee.

(5) On a submission being made to him under subsection (4)(a) above, the Accountant in Bankruptcy shall-

    (a) audit the accounts;

    (b) issue a determination fixing the amount of the outlays and remuneration payable to the interim trustee;

    (c) send a copy of the determination to-

        (i) the interim trustee; and

        (ii) the persons mentioned in subsection (4)(b) above; and

    (d) where a trustee (not being the Accountant in Bankruptcy) has been appointed in the sequestration, send a copy of the audited accounts and of the determination to the trustee, who shall insert them in the sederunt book.

(6) Where the Accountant in Bankruptcy has been appointed as the trustee in the sequestration, the

Accountant in Bankruptcy shall insert a copy of the audited accounts and the determination in the sederunt book.

(7) The interim trustee or any person mentioned in subsection (4)(b) above may, within 14 days after the issuing of the determination under subsection (5)(b) above, appeal to the sheriff against the determination.

(8) On receiving a copy of the Accountant in Bankruptcy's determination sent under subsection (5)(c)(i) above the interim trustee may apply to him for a certificate of discharge.

(9) The interim trustee shall send notice of an application under subsection (8) above to the persons mentioned in subsection (4)(b) above and shall inform them-

(a) that they may make written representations relating to the application to the Accountant in Bankruptcy within the period of 14 days after such notification; and

(b) of the effect mentioned in subsection (16) below.

(10) On the expiry of the period mentioned in subsection (9)(a) above the Accountant in Bankruptcy, after considering any representations duly made to him, shall-

(a) grant or refuse to grant the certificate of discharge; and

(b) notify the persons mentioned in subsection (4)(b) above accordingly.

(11) The interim trustee or any person mentioned in subsection (4)(b) above may, within 14 days after the issuing of the determination under subsection (10) above, appeal therefrom to the sheriff.

(12) If, following an appeal under subsection (11) above, the sheriff determines that a certificate of discharge which has been refused should be granted he shall order the Accountant in Bankruptcy to grant it.

(13) If, following an appeal under subsection (11) above, the sheriff determines that a certificate of discharge which has been granted should have been refused he shall revoke the certificate.

(14) The sheriff clerk shall send a copy of the decree of the sheriff following an appeal under subsection (11) above to the Accountant in Bankruptcy.

(15) The decision of the sheriff in an appeal under subsection (7) or (11) above shall be final.

(16) The grant of a certificate of discharge under this section by the Accountant in Bankruptcy shall have the effect of discharging the interim trustee from all liability (other than any liability arising from fraud) to the debtor, to the petitioner or to the creditors in respect of any act or omission of the interim trustee in exercising the functions conferred on him by this Act.

13B Termination of Accountant in Bankruptcy's functions as interim trustee where not appointed as trustee

(1) This section applies where the Accountant in Bankruptcy is appointed as interim trustee under section 2(5) of this Act and the sheriff-

    (a) awards sequestration and appoints another person as trustee under section 2(2A) of this Act; or

    (b) refuses to award sequestration.

(2) Where the sheriff awards sequestration and appoints another person as trustee, the Accountant in Bankruptcy shall hand over to the trustee everything in his possession which relates to the sequestration and shall thereupon cease to act in the sequestration.

(3) The sheriff may make such order in relation to liability for the outlays and remuneration of the Accountant in Bankruptcy as may be appropriate.

(4) Within 3 months of the sheriff awarding or, as the case may be, refusing to award sequestration, the Accountant in Bankruptcy shall-

    (a) send to the debtor and the petitioner-

        (i) his accounts of his intromissions (if any) with the debtor's estate;

        (ii) a determination of his fees and outlays calculated in accordance with regulations made under section 69A of this Act; and

        (iii) the notice mentioned in subsection (5) below; and

    (b) in a case where sequestration is awarded, send a copy of his accounts, the claim and the notice to all creditors known to him.

(5) The notice referred to in subsection (4)(a)(iii) above is a notice in writing stating-

    (a) that the Accountant in Bankruptcy has commenced procedure under this Act leading to discharge in respect of his actings as interim trustee;

    (b) that an appeal may be made to the sheriff under subsection (7) below; and

    (c) the effect mentioned in subsection (9) below.

(6) The Accountant in Bankruptcy shall, unless the sheriff refuses to award sequestration, insert a copy of the accounts and the determination in the sederunt book.

(7) The debtor, the petitioner and any creditor may, within 14 days after the sending of the notice under subsection (4)(a)(iii) or, as the case may be, subsection (4)(b) above, appeal to the sheriff against-

    (a) the determination of the Accountant in Bankruptcy mentioned in subsection (4)(a)(ii) above;

    (b) the discharge of the Accountant in Bankruptcy in respect of his actings as interim trustee;

(c) both such determination and discharge,

and the sheriff clerk shall send a copy of the decree of the sheriff to the Accountant in Bankruptcy.

(8) The decision of the sheriff in an appeal under subsection (7) above shall be final.

(9) Where-

(a) the requirements of this section have been complied with; and

(b) no appeal is made to the sheriff under subsection (7) above or such an appeal is made but is refused as regards the discharge of the Accountant in Bankruptcy,

the Accountant in Bankruptcy shall be discharged from all liability (other than any liability arising from fraud) to the debtor, to the petitioner or to the creditors in respect of any act or omission of the Accountant in Bankruptcy in exercising the functions of interim trustee conferred on him by this Act.".

DEFINITIONS

"Interim trustee": 1985 Act s.2(5)

GENERAL NOTE

This section inserts the following sections in the 1985 Act.

Section 13A

The purpose of this new section is to deal with the situation where the interim trustee is not appointed as the trustee under subss.2A and 2C of the 1985 Act s.2 (for which see s.6(1) of the 2007 Act). The interim trustee must make over to the appointed trustee everything in his possession which relates to the sequestration. The rest of the section deals with the audit and determination of the payment of the interim trustee's fees by the Accountant in Bankruptcy and the interim trustee's intromissions with the estate, the discharge of the interim trustee, and an appeal to the sheriff against any determination by the Accountant in Bankruptcy.

Section 13B

This section deals with the situation where the Accountant in Bankruptcy is appointed interim trustee but is not appointed trustee under subs.2A of the 1985 Act s.2 (for which see s.6(1) of the 2007 Act). The Accountant in Bankruptcy must make over to the appointed trustee everything in his possession which relates to the sequestration. The rest of the section deals with the determination of the Accountant in Bankruptcy's fees and his intromissions with the estate, and sets out the time-limits with which an appeal against the determination and/or the discharge of the Accountant in Bankruptcy may be made to the sheriff by the debtor, the petitioner and any creditor. Where there is no appeal, or an unsuccessful appeal, the Accountant in Bankruptcy is discharged from all liability (other than any liability arising from fraud) arising out of his acts and omissions in his capacity as interim trustee of the estate.

11. Statutory meeting and election of trustee

(1) Section 21 of the 1985 Act (requirement to call statutory meeting) is repealed.

(2) In section 21A of that Act (calling of statutory meeting where interim trustee is Accountant in Bankruptcy)-

(a) in subsection (1), the words from "where" to "Bankruptcy", are repealed; and

(b) the heading to that section becomes "Calling of statutory meeting".

(3) The heading to section 23 of that Act becomes "Proceedings at statutory meeting before trustee vote".

(4) In section 24 of that Act (election of permanent trustee)-

(a) in subsection (1), for the words "the election of the permanent trustee" substitute

a vote at which they shall-

(a) confirm the appointment of the trustee appointed under section 2 of this Act (referred to in this section and in sections 25 to 27 of this Act as the "original trustee"); or

(b) elect another person as the trustee in the sequestration (referred to in this section and in sections 13 and 25 to 29 of this Act as the "replacement trustee"),

such a vote being referred to in this Act as a "trustee vote"." ; and

(b) the heading to that section becomes "Trustee vote".

(5) In section 25 of that Act (confirmation of permanent trustee)-

(a) before subsection (1) insert-

(A1) This section applies where a replacement trustee is elected by virtue of a trustee vote.";

and

(b) the heading to that section becomes "Appointment of replacement trustee".

(6) Schedule 2 to that Act (adaptation of procedure etc. where permanent trustee not elected) is repealed.

GENERAL NOTE

Section 11(1) repeals the requirement under s.21 of the 1985 Act for the interim trustee to have a statutory meeting. This used to take place usually within 60 days of the date of sequestration. At the meeting the permanent trustee would be appointed by the body of creditors. As the role of the interim trustee is now changed, so that he only holds office until the date of sequestration, there is no need for s.21 any longer.

Section 11(2), altering s.21A of the 1985 Act, narrates that where there is an interim trustee, and that interim trustee is the Accountant of Bankruptcy, appointed to maintain the estate until the award of sequestration is granted, he may hold the statutory meeting at such time and place as she sees fit. As for the date of the meeting, this must take place within 60 days of the date of sequestration and all the creditors must be given notice of the meeting (1985 Act s.21A(2)). On request by a quarter in value of the debtor's creditors, the meeting may be held within 28 days of the date of sequestration (1985 Act s.21A (5), (6)).

Section 11(4) deals with the point that there is no longer a permanent trustee, his role being filled by the trustee appointed on the date of sequestration. For the purposes of ss.25 and 27 of the 1985 Act he is known as the "original trustee" where that trustee was originally the interim trustee, and for the purposes of ss.13 and 25-29 of the 1985 Act as the "replacement trustee" to indicate that the replacement trustee was not the same person as the interim trustee. Replacement trustees must indicate their appointment using Form 5 (Notice by Replacement Trustee in the Edinburgh Gazette of Confirmation of Office) in the Schedule to the Bankruptcy (Scotland) Regulations 2008 (SSI 2008/82) in force with effect from April 1, 2008.

Section 11(6) dispenses with Sch.2 of the 1985 Act. This dealt with the position where no permanent trustee was elected. Unless the Accountant in Bankruptcy was the interim trustee, in which case he stayed in office, the interim trustee would become the permanent trustee. As this procedure no longer applies, there is no need for Sch.2.

12. Replacement of trustee acting in more than one sequestration

After section 28 of the 1985 Act, insert-

"28A Replacement of trustee acting in more than one sequestration

(1) This section applies where a trustee acting as such in two or more sequestrations-
  (a) dies; or
  (b) ceases to be qualified to continue to act as trustee by virtue of section 24(2) of this Act.
(2) The Accountant in Bankruptcy may, by a single petition to the Court of Session, apply-
  (a) in a case where subsection (1)(b) above applies, for the removal of the trustee from office in each sequestration in which he has so ceased to be qualified; and
  (b) for the appointment of-
    (i) the Accountant in Bankruptcy; or
    (ii) such person as may be nominated by the Accountant in Bankruptcy (being a person who is not ineligible for election as replacement trustee under section 24(2) of this Act) if that person consents to the nomination,
  as the trustee in each sequestration in which the trustee was acting.
(3) The procedure in a petition under subsection (2) above shall be as the Court of Session may, by act of sederunt, prescribe.
(4) An act of sederunt made under subsection (3) above may, in particular, make provision as to the intimation to each sheriff who awarded sequestration or to whom sequestration was transferred under section 15(2) of this Act of the appointment by the Court of Session of a trustee in that sequestration.".

GENERAL NOTE

This section deals with the practicalities of replacing a replacement trustee (see s.11 above) who was acting in more than one sequestration and who had either died or who was no longer qualified to act as a replacement trustee because of s.24(2) of the 1985 Act. The Accountant in Bankruptcy may apply by the one petition to the Court of Session for a replacement rather than having to apply to each sheriffdom. As the wording says the Accountant in Bankruptcy "may" apply to the Court of Session, it is presumably not necessary to do so if the former trustee's sequestrations were in the same sheriffdom.

13. Requirement to hold money in interest bearing account

In section 43 of the 1985 Act (money received by permanent trustee)-
  (a) in subsection (1)-
    (i) for "subsection (2)" substitute "subsections (1A) and (2)"; and
    (ii) after "an" insert "interest-bearing account in an"; and
  (b) after subsection (1), insert-

"(1A) In any case where the Accountant in Bankruptcy is the trustee, subject to subsection (2) below, all money received by the Accountant in Bankruptcy in the exercise of his functions as trustee shall be deposited by him in an interest bearing account in the name of the debtor's estate or in the name of the Scottish Ministers in an appropriate bank or institution.".

GENERAL NOTE

The existing legislation at s.43 of the 1985 Act did not specifically provide that money received by the trustee should be held in an interest-bearing account. Now where the trustee is the Accountant in Bankruptcy or any other trustee, any monies received must be placed in an interest-bearing account.

Debtor applications

14. Debtor applications

(1) In section 1A of the 1985 Act (supervisory functions of the Accountant in Bankruptcy), in subsection (1), after paragraph (a), insert-

"(aa) the determination of debtor applications;".

(2) In section 2 of that Act (appointment and functions of interim trustee), after subsection (1), insert-

"(1A) Subject to subsection (1C) below, where the Accountant in Bankruptcy awards sequestration of the debtor's estate and the debtor application-

(a) nominates a person to be the trustee;

(b) states that the person satisfies the conditions mentioned in subsection (3) below; and

(c) has annexed to it a copy of the undertaking mentioned in subsection (3)(c) below,

the Accountant in Bankruptcy may, if it appears to him that the person satisfies those conditions, appoint that person to be the trustee in the sequestration.

(1B) Where the Accountant in Bankruptcy awards sequestration of the debtor's estate and does not appoint a person to be the trustee in pursuance of subsection (1A) above, the Accountant in Bankruptcy shall be deemed to be appointed to be the trustee in the sequestration.

(1C) Where-

(a) the debtor application is made by a debtor to whom section 5(2B)(c)(ia) applies; and

(b) the Accountant in Bankruptcy awards sequestration of the debtor's estate,

the Accountant in Bankruptcy shall be deemed to be appointed as trustee in the sequestration.".

(3) In section 5 of that Act (sequestration of the estate of living or deceased debtor)-

(a) for subsection (2) substitute-

"(2) The sequestration of the estate of a living debtor shall be-

    (a) by debtor application made by the debtor, if either subsection (2A) or (2B) below applies to the debtor; or

    (b) on the petition of-

        (i) subject to subsection (2D) below, a qualified creditor or qualified creditors, if the debtor is apparently insolvent;

        (ii) a temporary administrator;

        (iii) a member State liquidator appointed in main proceedings; or

        (iv) the trustee acting under a trust deed if, and only if, one or more of the conditions in subsection (2C) below is satisfied."; and

(b) after subsection (4A), insert-

"(4B) A debtor application shall-

    (a) be made to the Accountant in Bankruptcy; and

    (b) be in such form as may be prescribed.

(4C) The Scottish Ministers may, by regulations, make provision-

    (a) in relation to the procedure to be followed in a debtor application (in so far as not provided for in this Act);

    (b) prescribing the form of any document that may be required for the purposes of making a debtor application; and

    (c) prescribing the fees and charges which may be levied by the Accountant in Bankruptcy in relation to debtor applications.".

(4) In section 6 of that Act (sequestration of other estates)-

(a) in subsection (3), for the words from "on" to the end of that subsection substitute-

"(a) by debtor application made by a majority of trustees, with the concurrence of a qualified creditor or qualified creditors; or

    (b) on the petition of-

        (i) a temporary administrator;

        (ii) a member State liquidator appointed in main proceedings; or

        (iii) a qualified creditor or qualified creditors, if the trustees as such are apparently insolvent.";

(b) in subsection (4), for the words from "on" to the end of that subsection substitute-

"(a) by debtor application made by the partnership with the concurrence of a qualified creditor or qualified creditors; or

    (b) on the petition of-

        (i) a temporary administrator;

        (ii) a member State liquidator appointed in main proceedings;

(iii) a trustee acting under a trust deed; or

(iv) a qualified creditor or qualified creditors, if the partnership is apparently insolvent.";

(c) in subsection (6), for the words from "on" to the end of that subsection substitute-

"(a) by debtor application made by a person authorised to act on behalf of the body, with the concurrence of a qualified creditor or qualified creditors; or

(b) on the petition of-

(i) a temporary administrator;

(ii) a member State liquidator appointed in main proceedings; or

(iii) a qualified creditor or qualified creditors, if the body is apparently insolvent." ; and

(d) in subsection (8), for "and (8)" substitute ", (6A), (8) and (8A)".

(5) After section 6A of that Act, insert-

"6B Debtor application: provision of information

(1) Where a debtor application is made, the debtor shall state in the application-

(a) whether or not the debtor's centre of main interests is situated-

(i) in the United Kingdom; or

(ii) in another member State; and

(b) whether not the debtor possesses an establishment-

(i) in the United Kingdom; or

(ii) in any other member State.

(2) If, to the debtor's knowledge, there is a member State liquidator appointed in main proceedings in relation to the debtor, the debtor shall, as soon as reasonably practicable, send a copy of the debtor application to that member State liquidator.".

(6) After section 8 of that Act, insert-

"8A Further provisions relating to debtor applications

(1) Subject to subsection (2) below, a debtor application may be made at any time.

(2) A debtor application made in relation to the estate of a limited partnership may be made within such time as may be prescribed.

(3) The making of, or the concurring in, a debtor application shall bar the effect of any enactment or rule of law relating to the limitation of actions.

(4) Where, before sequestration is awarded, it becomes apparent that a creditor concurring in a debtor application was ineligible to so concur the Accountant in Bankruptcy shall withdraw him from the application but another creditor may concur in the place of the

ineligible creditor and that other creditor shall notify the Accountant in Bankruptcy of that fact.".

(7) In section 9 of that Act (jurisdiction)-

(a) in subsection (1), at the beginning insert "Where a petition is presented for the sequestration of an estate,";

(b) after subsection (1), insert-

"(1A) The Accountant in Bankruptcy may determine a debtor application for the sequestration of the estate of a living debtor if the debtor had an established place of business in Scotland, or was habitually resident there, at the relevant time.";

(c) in subsection (2), at the beginning insert "Where a petition is presented for the sequestration of an estate,";

(d) after subsection (2), insert-

"(2A) The Accountant in Bankruptcy may determine a debtor application for the sequestration of the estate of any entity which may be sequestrated by virtue of section 6 of this Act, if the entity-

(a) had an established place of business in Scotland at the relevant time; or

(b) was constituted or formed under Scots law, and at any time carried on business in Scotland."; and

(e) after subsection (3), insert-

"(3A) Any proceedings under this Act which-

(a) relate to-

(i) a debtor application; or

(ii) the sequestration of a debtor's estate awarded following such an application; and

(b) may be brought before a sheriff,

shall be brought before the sheriff who would, under subsection (1) or (2) above, have had jurisdiction in respect of a petition for sequestration of the debtor's estate.".

(8) In section 12 of that Act (when sequestration is awarded), in subsection (1), for the words from "petition", where it first occurs, to the end of paragraph (a), substitute

debtor application is made, the Accountant in Bankruptcy shall award sequestration forthwith if he is satisfied-

(a) that the application has been made in accordance with the provisions of this Act and any provisions made under this Act;".

DEFINITIONS

"Member State liquidator": Cross Border Insolvency Regulations 2006 Sch.3 Pt 1
"Main proceedings": Cross Border Insolvency Regulations 2006 Sch.3 Pt 1
"Limited partnership": Limited Partnership Act 1907
"Administrator": Proceeds of Crime Act 2002 s.125

GENERAL NOTE

The purpose of this section is to enable debtors to apply for their sequestration from the Accountant in Bankruptcy rather than from their local sheriff court as has hitherto been the case. This should attract less publicity and may be more convenient for some debtors. The Accountant in Bankruptcy is given express power in subs.(1) to determine debtor applications.

Subsection (2) provides that where a debtor has specifically nominated a trustee, and the Accountant in Bankruptcy is satisfied that the trustee is suitably qualified as an insolvency practitioner and has provided the required undertaking under s.2(3)(c) of the 1985 Act (i.e. that he will act as trustee), the Accountant in Bankruptcy may appoint that person to be the trustee. Where the Accountant in Bankruptcy is not so satisfied, she will be deemed to be the trustee, and where the debtor is one to whom s.5(2B)(c)(ia) applies (i.e. the debtor is a "low income, low asset" debtor (see s.15 of the 2007 Act)) the Accountant in Bankruptcy is again deemed to be appointed. For more details about "low income, low asset" debtors, see the Bankruptcy (Scotland) Act 1985 (Low Income, Low Asset Debtors etc) Regulations 2008 (SSI 2008/81), and see also para.15 of the Bankruptcy (Scotland) Regulations 2008 (SSI 2008/82).

Subsection (3) substitutes a new subs.(2) for s.5 of the 1985 Act to take account of the fact that debtor applications may now be made by the debtor. Power is given to the Scottish Ministers to issue regulations for the procedure and documentation required for a debtor's application. See the Bankruptcy (Scotland) Regulations 2008 (SSI 2008/82) and in particular, para.14. These explain which forms should be used, how to apply to the Accountant in Bankruptcy, and what steps she should take having granted the award of sequestration.

Subsection (4) substitutes new wording in s.6(3), (4) and (6) of the 1985 Act to take account of debtor applications for respectively trust estates, partnerships, bodies corporate and unincorporated bodies (i.e. clubs, associations, colleges, etc.).

Subsection (5) inserts a new s.6B into the 1985 Act. This makes it a requirement that the debtor in his application indicates whether his centre of main interests is located in the United Kingdom or in another Member State within the European Union, and whether or not the debtor possesses an establishment in the United Kingdom or in a Member State. "Centre of main interests" is not a defined term in terms of the Cross Border Insolvency Regulations 2006 but covers the debtor's habitual residence, and an "establishment" means a place of operations where the debtor carries out a non-transitory economic activity with human means or assets or services (Cross Border Insolvency Regulations 2006 Sch.1, UNCITRAL Model Law on Cross Border Insolvency Art.2(e)). Furthermore, if there is a Member State liquidator appointed in main proceedings in relation to the debtor, the debtor must send a copy of the application to that liquidator. This section enables cross-border bankruptcies to proceed more smoothly in line with the Cross Border Insolvency Regulations 2006 which no longer require a foreign insolvency practitioner to seek special licences or other formal approval, though the Member State liquidator appointed in main proceedings will nevertheless need to produce evidence of the Member State proceedings and the appointment of its liquidator.

The effect of Member State proceedings are that other actions against the debtor are stayed, execution of diligence is stayed and the right to transfer any of the debtor's assets is stayed as well.

Subsection (6) inserts a new s.8A to the 1985 Act and ties in with the new debtor applications. It provides that a debtor application may be made at any time and that, where a debtor application is made, or where a creditor concurs in a debtor application (in terms of s.2A of the 1985 Act), the application serves to prevent the operation of any rule on the limitation of actions, especially the Prescription and Limitations (Scotland) Act 1973. If the concurring creditor turns out to be ineligible to concur in a debtor application, another creditor may take his place, though that later creditor must inform the Accountant in Bankruptcy of this fact. As regards debtor applications for limited partnerships, see para.9 of the Bankruptcy (Scotland) Regulations 2008/SSI 2008/82).

Subsection (7)(a) inserts new wording into s.9(1) of the 1985 Act, so that where there is a petition for sequestration, the sheriff has jurisdiction if the debtor had an established place of business or was resident in the sheriffdom at the relevant time (i.e. within a year immediately preceding the date of presentation of a petition for sequestration or the date of death of the debtor, as the case may be (1985 Act s.9(5)).

The words "sheriff" and "sheriff court" are substituted for the words "Court of Session" and "Scotland" (see the 2007 Act s.16(1)).

Subsection (7)(b) inserts a subs.1A into s.9 of the 1985 Act, permitting the Accountant in Bankruptcy to determine a debtor application provided the debtor had an established place of business or was resident in Scotland at the relevant time.

Subsection (7)(c) inserts new wording into s.9(2) of the 1985 Act and is similar to subs.(7)(a) above, save that it permits the sheriff to deal with the sequestration of the estate of any entity (an entity being a trust, partnership, a body corporate or an unincorporated body or a limited partnership) which had an established business in Scotland at the relevant time or was constituted or formed under Scots law and at any time carried on business in Scotland.

Subsection (7)(d) is similar to subs.(7)(b) in that it permits the Accountant in Bankruptcy to determine a debtor application for such an estate as is mentioned in subs.(7)(c).

Subsection (7)(e) inserts a new subs.3A into s.9 of the 1985 Act to the effect that any proceedings relating to debtor applications and which may be brought before a sheriff should be brought before the sheriff if the debtor had an established place of business or was resident in the sheriffdom at the relevant time (under subs.(1), as amended by subs.(7)(c) above), or, in the case of the sequestration of an entity's estate, and which may be brought before a sheriff, should be brought before the sheriff who would have jurisdiction as the estate had an established business in Scotland at the relevant time or was constituted or formed under Scots law and at any time carried on business in Scotland (under subs.2, as amended by subs.(7)(c) above). Subsection (8) deletes words from s.12(1) of the 1985 Act and in so doing provides that the Accountant in Bankruptcy may award sequestration provided the debtor's application has been made in accordance with the requirements of the 1985 Act.

15. Debtor applications by low income, low asset debtors

(1) In section 5 of the 1985 Act, in subsection (2B)(c)-
    (a) the word "either" is repealed; and
    (b) after sub-paragraph (i) insert-
           "(ia) is unable to pay his debts and each of the conditions in section 5A of this Act is met;".

(2) After section 5 of that Act insert-

"5A Debtor applications by low income, low asset debtors

(1) The conditions referred to in section 5(2B)(c)(ia) of this Act are as follows.

(2) The debtor's weekly income (if any) on the date the debtor application is made does not exceed £100 or such other amount as may be prescribed.

(3) The debtor does not own any land.

(4) The total value of the debtor's assets (leaving out of account any liabilities) on the date the debtor application is made does not exceed £1000 or such other amount as may be prescribed.

(5) The Scottish Ministers may by regulations-
    (a) make provision as to how the debtor's weekly income is to be determined;
    (b) provide that particular descriptions of income are to be excluded for the purposes of subsection (2) above;
    (c) make provision as to how the value of the debtor's assets is to be determined;
    (d) provide that particular descriptions of asset are to be excluded for the purposes of subsection (4) above;

(e) make different provision for different classes or description of debtor;
(f) add further conditions which must be met before a debtor application may be made by virtue of section 5(2B)(c)(ia) of this Act; and
(g) where such further conditions are added-
    (i) remove; or
    (ii) otherwise vary,
those conditions.".

DEFINITIONS
"Debtor application": 2007 Act s.14

GENERAL NOTE
Low income, low assets debtors were a particular concern for the framers of the Bill, since it had become apparent that some debtors very much wished to be sequestrated in order to stop harassment from and diligence by their creditors. However, it was often not worth while for creditors to sequestrate such debtors, for there was always the chance that diligence might bring them some repayment, while sequestration would take a long time and would be unlikely to bring much return. Equally, the debtors themselves often did not qualify for sequestration, because their debts did not amount to the required apparent insolvency figure of £1,500. This section tries to amend this difficulty as far as these debtors are concerned, though it does not make "apparent insolvency" any less less opaque as a concept.

Section 15(1) amends s.5(2B)(c) of the 1985 Act to provide a further ground for a debtor to apply to the Accountant in Bankruptcy, namely that the debtor is unable to pay his debts and the conditions of s.5A of the 1985 Act apply to that debtor.

Section 5A of the 1985 Act (as provided for by s.15(2) of the 2007 Act) states the conditions are that the debtor's weekly income is no more than £100 per week, that the debtor does not own any land, and that the debtor's total assets (not net assets) at the time of the debtor application are no more than £1,000. The other subsections of s.5A permit the Scottish Ministers by regulations to vary the above figures, to determine how the debtor's income is to be calculated (possibly by excluding certain categories of income), how the debtor's assets are to be calculated (again possibly by excluding certain categories of asset) and make such other conditions as they choose to impose.

Since the Act was printed, regulations have come into force amending the above figures. They are to be found at The Bankruptcy (Scotland) Act 1985 (Low Income, Low Asset Debtors etc.) Regulations 2008 (SSI 2008/81) and came into force on April 1, 2008. The income figure changes to £220.20 per week and the total asset figure to £10,000 with no one asset being worth more than £1,000. There are further provisions to take account of the source of the debtor's income.

Jurisdiction

16. Sequestration proceedings to be competent only before sheriff

(1) In section 9 of the 1985 Act (jurisdiction)-
    (a) in subsection (1)-
        (i) for "Court of Session" substitute "sheriff"; and
        (ii) for "Scotland" substitute "the sheriffdom";
    (b) in subsection (2)-
        (i) for "Court of Session" substitute "sheriff"; and
        (ii) for "Scotland", in both places where it occurs, substitute "the sheriffdom";
    (c) in subsection (3), for "Court of Session" substitute "sheriff"; and
    (d) subsection (4) is repealed.

(2) In section 15 of that Act (further provisions relating to award of sequestration)-

(a) subsection (1) is repealed;

(b) in subsection (2)-

(i) for "Court of Session" substitute "sheriff";

(ii) for "it", where it first occurs, substitute "him and subject to subsection (2A) below"; and

(iii) the words from "from" to "remitted" are repealed;

(c) after subsection (2), insert-

(2A) The debtor may, with leave of the sheriff, appeal to the sheriff principal against a transfer under subsection (2) above.";

(d) in subsection (3), for "court" substitute "sheriff"; and

(e) in subsection (5), for "clerk of the court" substitute "sheriff clerk".

(3) In section 16 of that Act (petitions for recall), in subsection (1), for "Court of Session" substitute "sheriff".

(4) In section 17 of that Act (recall)-

(a) in subsection (1)-

(i) for "Court of Session" substitute "sheriff"; and

(ii) for "it", in the first and third places where it occurs, substitute "he";

(b) in subsection (2)-

(i) for "Court" substitute "sheriff"; and

(ii) for "it" substitute "he";

(c) in subsection (3)-

(i) for "Court" substitute "sheriff"; and

(ii) in paragraph (c), for "it" substitute "he";

(d) in subsection (6)-

(i) for "Court" substitute "sheriff"; and

(ii) for "it", in the second and third places where it occurs, substitute "he";

(e) in subsection (7)-

(i) for "Court" substitute "sheriff"; and

(ii) for "it" substitute "he"; and

(f) in subsection (8), for "clerk of the court" substitute "sheriff clerk".

GENERAL NOTE

This section provides that in certain places throughout the 1985 Act where the word "Court of Session" is used, "sheriff" should be used instead, and likewise, "sheriffdom" substituted for "Scotland". This reflects the fact that henceforth sequestration will no longer take place before the Court of Session.

Vesting of estate and dealings of debtor

17. Vesting of estate and dealings of debtor

(1) In section 31 of the 1985 Act (vesting of estate in trustee at date of sequestration)-

(a) after subsection (1) insert-

"(1A) It shall not be competent for-

(a) the trustee; or

(b) any person deriving title from the trustee,

to complete title to any heritable estate in Scotland vested in the trustee by virtue of his appointment before the expiry of the period mentioned in subsection (1B) below.

(1B) That period is the period of 28 days (or such other period as may be prescribed) beginning with the day on which-

(a) the certified copy of the order of the sheriff granting warrant is recorded under subsection (1)(a) of section 14 of this Act; or

(b) the certified copy of the determination of the Accountant in Bankruptcy awarding sequestration is recorded under subsection (1A) of that section,

in the register of inhibitions."; and

(b) in subsection (8), after paragraph (a) insert-

"(aa) any property of the debtor, title to which has not been completed by another person deriving right from the debtor;".

(2) In section 32 (vesting of estate, and dealings of debtor, after sequestration)-

(a) in subsection (8) (dealings with debtor after sequestration to be of no effect), after "under" insert "this section or";

(b) in subsection (9) (circumstances where post-sequestration dealings with debtor remain valid), after paragraph (b)(iii) insert; or

(iv) one which satisfies the conditions mentioned in subsection (9ZA) below,"; and

(c) after that subsection insert-

"(9ZA) The conditions are that-

(a) the dealing constitutes-

(i) the transfer of incorporeal moveable property; or

(ii) the creation, transfer, variation or extinguishing of a real right in heritable property,

for which the person dealing with the debtor has given adequate consideration to the debtor, or is willing to give adequate consideration to the trustee;

(b) the dealing requires the delivery of a deed; and

(c) the delivery occurs during the period beginning with the date of sequestration and ending on the day which falls 7 days after the day on which-

(i) the certified copy of the order of the sheriff granting warrant is recorded under subsection (1)(a) of section 14 of this Act; or

(ii) the certified copy of the determination of the Accountant in Bankruptcy awarding sequestration is recorded under subsection (1A) of that section, in the register of inhibitions.".

DEFINITIONS
"The date of sequestration": 1985 Act s.12(4)

GENERAL NOTE
This section inserts new provisions into s.31 of the 1985 Act in connection with the vesting of the estate in the trustee. In essence, it gives some degree of protection to those who deal in good faith and for value with a sequestrated debtor without being aware that the debtor should not be divesting himself of any part of his estate. It stems from the difficulties arising out of the two cases, *Sharp v Thompson*, 1997 SC (HL) 66 and *Burnett's Tr. v Grainger*, 2004 SC (HL) 19 and a desire to ensure that a purchaser in good faith for value should not lose his chance to own the property he thought he was buying. It also takes account of the recommendations of the Scottish Law Commission in its discussion paper 2001/114.

Subsection (1)(a), by inserting new subss.(1A) and (1B) into s.31 of the 1985 Act, states that, in essence, neither the trustee, nor anyone deriving title from the trustee, may complete title to any heritage vested in the trustee following his appointment until at least 28 days from the day of recording of the certified copy of the sheriff's grant of the warrant to cite the debtor (in terms of s.14(1)(a) of the 1985 Act) or day of recording of the certified copy of the determination of a debtor application by the Accountant in Bankruptcy, in either case in the register of inhibitions (formerly known as the register of inhibitions and adjudications).

The 28 day period ties in with s.11(2) of the 2007 Act (i.e. s.21A as amended by the 1985 Act).

This gives a purchaser of heritage from the debtor 28 days from the date of sequestration in which to register his deed (see new s.31(1A) and (1B) of the 1985 Act inserted by subs.(1)(a)). After the expiry of the 28 day deadline the trustee may complete his own title instead and the purchaser has lost his opportunity.

Subsection (1)(b) adds a new para.(aa) to subs.(8) of s.31 of the 1985 Act to the effect that the whole estate of the debtor comprises, in addition to the assets already indicated there, "any property of the debtor, title to which has not been completed by any person deriving right from the debtor". This means that if the purchaser has not recorded his title within the 28 day period as indicated in the previous paragraph, the debtor's estate will include the heritable property that the debtor was trying to sell but to which the purchaser failed to record title. It is worth noting that this, at least for the 28 day period, protects a purchaser who may have received the signed deed from the debtor *before* the debtor's sequestration but has not got round to registering it. If the purchaser receives the deed *after* the debtor's sequestration, the matter is covered by new subs.9ZA in s.32 of the 1985 Act as indicated below.

Subsection (2)(a), amending s.32(8) of the 1985 Act, refers to dealings, after the date of sequestration, of or with the debtor relating to the estate vested in the trustee, and extends the invalidity of those dealings in a dispute with the trustee to cover the matters referred to in s.31 (vesting of the estate in the trustee as at the date of sequestration) and the matters referred to in s.32 (vesting of the estate in the trustee, and the dealings of the debtor, after sequestration) as well.

What this means is that if a purchaser tries to acquire some asset within the debtor's estate at the time of sequestration or after the debtor has been sequestrated, the trustee normally can reduce the acquisition, since the debtor has no title to the estate. The only person who could give title to any asset within the debtor's estate would be the trustee.

However, it is recognised that some post-sequestration dealings of or with the debtor do take place, and so subs.9 of s.32 of the 1985 Act indicates a number of permitted exceptions to the right of the trustee to reduce these dealings.

Accordingly, subss.(2)(b) and (2)(c) insert a further permitted exception to the provisions of s.32(8) of the 1985 Act, thus giving a set of conditions when post-sequestration dealings of or with the debtor remain valid. These conditions, indicated in new subs.9ZA of the 1985 Act, are: (i) that the debtor's dealings are in respect of the transfer of incorporeal moveable property (such as debts, shares, intellectual property rights, claims etc.) or the creation of real rights for which the person contracting dealing with the debtor has either paid the debtor or is willing to pay the trustee;(ii) that the dealing requires the delivery of a deed and (iii) the delivery of the deed takes place within a period starting with the date of sequestration and ending either seven days after the date of recording of the warrant to cite the debtor under s.14(1)(a) of the 1985 Act, which in turn refers to s.12(2) of the 1985 Act, or with the recording of certified copy of the determination of the Accountant in Bankruptcy under s.14(1A), in each case the recording being in the register of inhibitions.

These conditions are designed to protect the position of people dealing with the debtor, who have in good faith given value to the debtor (or at least are willing to pay the trustee in the absence of the debtor), who need a deed (this would be in any case be necessary for the creation, transfer, variation or extinguishing of a real right and property, and for the transfer of certain incorporeal moveable assets, such as shares or assignments of life assurance policies), have that deed delivered to them within the required time limit of seven days, and who had no knowledge of the debtor's sequestration. It also means that they have only a limited period of time to take advantage of this provision, which in turn means that if the deed is not delivered in time, they cease to have the protection of new subs.9ZA. What it does do is to take account of the fact that someone dealing with a debtor (who is in the process of sequestration) might well not know that the debtor is being sequestrated (since a debtor might well not tell the purchaser) and the information about the sequestration would not have had time to be registered in the Register of Inhibitions or be notified in the Edinburgh Gazette.

Equally it protects the sequestrated estate since anyone claiming under the new subsection has to be quick off the mark.

A purchaser would not be protected by this section if no deed were delivered within the seven day period, or if the incorporeal moveable assets were transferred without a deed. There should be few incorporeal moveable assets which would not require some form of deed of transfer, apart perhaps bearer instruments, and where they do not require a deed for transfer, they would not receive the protection of this section and the purchaser would need to relinquish them to the trustee.

Note that this section does not apply to corporate insolvencies and only applies where the debtor is being sequestrated in Scotland. It does not apply where the debtor is being made bankrupt elsewhere and has assets in Scotland.

Income received by debtor after sequestration

18.   Income received by debtor after sequestration

(1) Section 32 of the 1985 Act (vesting of estate and dealings of debtor after sequestration) is amended as follows.

(2) In subsection (1), for "subsection (2)" substitute "subsections (2) and (4B)".

(3) After subsection (2), insert-

"(2WA) Subject to subsection (4L) below, no application may be made under subsection (2) above after the date on which the debtor's discharge becomes effective.

(2XA) An order made by the sheriff under subsection (2) above shall specify the period during which it has effect and that period-

(a) may end after the date on which the debtor's discharge becomes effective; and

(b) shall end no later than 3 years after the date on which the order is made.

(2YA) An order made by the sheriff under subsection (2) above may provide that a third person is to pay to the trustee a specified proportion of money due to the debtor by way of income.

(2ZA) If the debtor fails to comply with an order made under subsection (2) above, he shall be guilty of an offence and liable on summary conviction to a fine not exceeding level 5 on the standard scale or to imprisonment for a term not exceeding 3 months or to both.".

(4) After subsection (4), insert-

"(4A) The sheriff clerk shall send a copy of any order made under subsection (2) above (and a copy of any variation or recall of such an order) to the Accountant in Bankruptcy.

(4B) Where no order has been made under subsection (2) above, a debtor may enter into an agreement in writing with the trustee which provides-

(a) that the debtor is to pay to the trustee an amount equal to a specified part or proportion of his income; or

(b) that a third person is to pay to the trustee a specified proportion of money due to the debtor by way of income.

(4C) No agreement under subsection (4B) above may be entered into after the date on which the debtor's discharge becomes effective.

(4D) Subsection (2XA) above applies to agreements entered into under subsection (4B) above as it applies to orders made under subsection (2) above.

(4E) An agreement entered into under subsection (4B) above may, if subsection (4K) below has been complied with, be enforced, subject to subsection (4F) below, as if it were an order made under subsection (2) above.

(4F) Subsection (2ZA) above does not apply to an agreement entered into under subsection (4B) above.

(4G) An agreement entered into under subsection (4B) above may be varied-

(a) by written agreement between the parties; or

(b) by the sheriff, on an application made by the trustee, the debtor or any other interested person.

(4H) The sheriff-

(a) may not vary an agreement entered into under subsection (4B) above so as to include provision of a kind which could not be included in an order made under subsection (2) above; and

(b) shall grant an application to vary such an agreement if and to the extent that the sheriff thinks variation is necessary to determine a suitable amount to allow for the purposes specified in paragraphs (a) and (b) of subsection (2) above, being an amount which shall not be included in the amount to be paid to the trustee.

(4J) Where a third person pays a sum of money to the trustee under subsection (2YA) or (4B)(b) above, that person shall be discharged of any liability to the debtor to the extent of the sum of money so paid.

(4K) The trustee shall (unless he is the Accountant in Bankruptcy) send a copy of any agreement entered into under subsection (4B) above (and a copy of any variation of such an agreement) to the Accountant in Bankruptcy.

(4L) If the debtor fails to comply with an agreement entered into under subsection (4B) above, the sheriff, on the application of the trustee, may make an order under subsection (2) above-

    (a) ending on the date on which the agreement would, had the debtor continued to comply with it, have ended; and

    (b) on the same terms as the agreement,".

(5) In section 1A of that Act (supervisory functions of the Accountant in Bankruptcy), after subsection (1)(b)(iia) (as inserted by section 2(2) of this Act), insert-

"(iib) orders made under subsection (2) of section 32 of this Act and agreements made under subsection (4B) of that section;".

GENERAL NOTE

This section inserts new provisions into s.32 of the 1985 Act in respect of income received by the debtor after sequestration. The general rule is that the debtor is allowed to keep some of his income but if he is earning enough that he could make a payment to his creditors, he should do so. What this section (in subss.(1), (2) and (3)) initially provides is that the trustee may apply to the sheriff for an order, known as an income payment order, directing the debtor to make such a payment but such application may only be made before the discharge of the debtor (new subs.2WA). Where an application is made, and an order granted, that order may specify the period during which the order will remain in force, even though it may continue after the discharge of the debtor; nevertheless, the maximum duration of such an order is only three years (new subs.2XA). Alternatively, under the order, some third person, perhaps a family trust or a family member, or even a debtor of the debtor, may provide that that person should pay to the trustee a specified proportion of money due to the debtor by way of income (new subs.2YA).

If the debtor fails to make his own payments (i.e. not the payments required to be made by the third person), he commits a criminal offence (new subs.2ZA).

Section 18(4), after requiring that a copy of any order made under subs.2 of s.32 of the 1985 Act must be sent by the sheriff clerk to the Accountant in Bankruptcy (new subs.4A), introduces the option of the debtor making an arrangement with the trustee to pay a certain proportion of his income to the trustee, or a third person making the payments to the trustee as above (new subs.4B), within the same time limits as the sheriff's order above, but without the necessity or expense of applying to the sheriff and without the criminal sanctions of subs.2 (new subs.4F). Such an arrangement, known as an income payment agreement, may be varied if necessary, either by written agreement by the trustee, the debtor and the third person where appropriate (new subs.4G), though if the sheriff varies the arrangement, he may not do so in such a manner as to include provisions which he could not have included in an order under subs.2 (subs.4H).

When the third person makes his payment to the trustee, he is discharged of any liability to the debtor to the extent of his payment (new subs.4J).

If the debtor fails to adhere to the arrangement, the sheriff may make an order in terms of subs.2.

Subsection 5 refers to the record of income payment orders and agreements in the register of insolvencies. This subsection is not yet in force (Bankruptcy and Diligence, etc (Scotland) Act 2007 (Commencement No. 3, Savings and Transitions Order 2008 (SSI 2008/115), para.3(a)(i)),

Debtor's home and other heritable property

19.   Debtor's home and other heritable property

(1) After section 32(9) of the 1985 Act (circumstances where dealings with debtor not challengeable by permanent trustee), insert-

"(9A) Where the trustee has abandoned to the debtor any heritable property, notice in such form as may be prescribed given to the debtor by the trustee shall be sufficient evidence that the property is vested in the debtor.

(9B) Where the trustee gives notice under subsection (9A) above, he shall, as soon as reasonably practicable after giving the notice, record a certified copy of it in the register of inhibitions.".

(2) After section 39 of that Act, insert-

"39A   Debtor's home ceasing to form part of sequestrated estate

(1) This section applies where a debtor's sequestrated estate includes any right or interest in the debtor's family home.

(2) At the end of the period of 3 years beginning with the date of sequestration the right or interest mentioned in subsection (1) above shall-

(a) cease to form part of the debtor's sequestrated estate; and

(b) be reinvested in the debtor (without disposition, conveyance, assignation or other transfer).

(3) Subsection (2) above shall not apply if, during the period mentioned in that subsection-

(a) the trustee disposes of or otherwise realises the right or interest mentioned in subsection (1) above;

(b) the trustee concludes missives for sale of the right or interest;

(c) the trustee sends a memorandum to the keeper of the register of inhibitions under section 14(4) of this Act;

(d) the trustee registers in the Land Register of Scotland or, as the case may be, records in the Register of Sasines a notice of title in relation to the right or interest mentioned in subsection (1) above;

(e) the trustee commences proceedings-

(i) to obtain the authority of the sheriff under section 40(1)(b) of this Act to sell or dispose of the right or interest;

(ii) in an action for division and sale of the family home; or

(iii) in an action for the purpose of obtaining vacant possession of the family home;

(f) the trustee and the debtor enter into an agreement such as is mentioned in subsection (5) below.

(4) The Scottish Ministers may, by regulations, modify paragraphs (a) to (f) of subsection (3) above so as to-

(a) add or remove a matter; or

(b) vary any such matter,

referred to in that subsection.

(5) The agreement referred to in subsection (3)(f) above is an agreement that the debtor shall incur a specified

48

liability to his estate (with or without interest from the date of the agreement) in consideration of which the right or interest mentioned in subsection (1) above shall-

    (a) cease to form part of the debtor's sequestrated estate; and

    (b) be reinvested in the debtor (without disposition, conveyance, assignation or other transfer).

(6) If the debtor does not inform the trustee or the Accountant in Bankruptcy of his right or interest in the family home before the end of the period of 3 months beginning with the date of sequestration, the period of 3 years mentioned in subsection (2) above-

    (a) shall not begin with the date of sequestration; but

    (b) shall begin with the date on which the trustee or the Accountant in Bankruptcy becomes aware of the debtor's right or interest.

(7) The sheriff may, on the application of the trustee, substitute for the period of 3 years mentioned in subsection (2) above a longer period-

    (a) in prescribed circumstances; and

    (b) in such other circumstances as the sheriff thinks appropriate.

(8) The Scottish Ministers may, by regulations-

    (a) make provision for this section to have effect with the substitution, in such circumstances as the regulations may prescribe, of a shorter period for the period of 3 years mentioned in subsection (2) above;

    (b) prescribe circumstances in which this section does not apply;

    (c) prescribe circumstances in which a sheriff may disapply this section;

    (d) make provision requiring the trustee to give notice that this section applies or does not apply;

    (e) make provision about compensation;

    (f) make such provision as they consider necessary or expedient in consequence of regulations made under paragraphs (a) to (e) above.

(9) In this section, "family home" has the same meaning as in section 40 of this Act.".

DEFINITIONS

"Family home": 2007 Act s.40(4)(a)

"Date of sequestration": 1985 Act s.12(4)

GENERAL NOTE

The Scottish Ministers were concerned by stories that trustees in sequestration sometimes delayed in selling heritage owned, or part-owned by the debtor, leaving the debtor and his family in an uncertain position, particularly if the heritage in question was the debtor's family's home. This section therefore requires the trustee to deal with the debtor's home expeditiously, and if the trustee fails to deal with the debtor's interest in the debtor's home within a period of three years, the home ceases to be part of the debtor's sequestrated estate and is automatically reinvested in the debtor.

Section 19(1) inserts new provisions into s.32(9) of the 1985 Act which refers to the abandonment of any heritable property by the trustee to the debtor. New subss.9A and 9B of s.32 provide that the trustee's notice of abandonment will be sufficient evidence of the vesting of the property in the debtor. A copy of the notice is then to be registered in the register of inhibitions. The notice is available as Form 21 in the Schedule to the Bankruptcy (Scotland) Regulations 2008 (SSI 2008/82). See also para.19 of the same Regulations.

Section 19(2) introduces a new s.39A into the 1985 Act. It applies where the debtor's sequestrated estate includes any right or interest in the debtor's family home. Family home is defined in s.40(4)(a) of the 1985 Act and is any property in which the debtor had a right or interest, either alone or in common with another person, and occupied as a residence by the debtor and his spouse or civil partner, or his spouse or civil partner, or former spouse or former civil partner, or by the debtor with a child of the family.

Section 39A

Where the sequestrated estate includes any right or interest in the debtor's family home, if the trustee does not, within three years beginning with the date of sequestration, do any of the acts in subs.3, these being:

(a)   disposing or realisation of the debtor's right or interest;

(b)   concluding missives for the sale of the right or interest;

(c)   sending a memorandum to the register of inhibition extending any existing three year inhibition of the debtor for a further period of three years in terms of s.14(4) of the 1985 Act;

(d)   the registration in the Land Register or the Register of Sasines (as appropriate) of a notice of title in relation to the debtor's right of interest;

(e)   the commencement of proceedings to obtain permission from the sheriff to sell or dispose of the right or interest, for an action of division and sale or an action for obtaining vacant possession of the family home; and

(f)   the trustee and the debtor enter into an arrangement under subs.(5),

the right or interest will cease to be part of the sequestrated estate and is reinvested in the debtor without the need for any formal conveyancing deed or any other transfer requirements (subs.2).

The Scottish Ministers have the right to vary, add to or remove any of the above requirements (a)-(f). This they have done by The Bankruptcy (Scotland) Act 1985 (Low Income, Low Asset Debtors etc.) Regulations 2008 (SSI 2008/81), para.4, which introduces a further para.(g). It reads as follows:

> the trustee has commenced an action under section 34 of this Act in respect of any right or interest mentioned in sub-section (1) above or the trustee has not known about the facts giving rise to a right of action under section 34 of this Act, provided the trustee commences such an action reasonably soon after the trustee becomes aware of such right.

What this does is to add one more circumstance which will preclude the right of the debtor to be reinvested in his family home after the three year period. These regulations came into force on April 1, 2008, thereby adding this paragraph to s.39A.

The arrangement in subs.5 is an agreement that the debtor will effectively pay or owe his sequestrated estate money (and possibly interest) in return for which the sequestrated estate will no longer hold that right or interest in the debtor's home. The debtor will then have it reinvested in him without any formal conveyancing deed or any other transfer requirements (subs.5).

It is thought that these requirements should make trustees proceed more swiftly than has perhaps always been the case in the past.

Should the debtor not disclose his right or interest in the family home to the trustee or Accountant in Bankruptcy before the end of the period of three months beginning with the date of sequestration, the three year period is deemed to begin on the date on which the trustee or the Accountant in Bankruptcy becomes aware of the debtor's right or interest (subs.6). The remaining rules give discretion to the sheriff to prescribe a longer period than that of three years where necessary (subs.7) and permit the Scottish Ministers to make regulations concerning the provisions of this section.

20. Modification of provisions relating to protected trust deeds

(1) For paragraphs 5 to 13 of Schedule 5 to the 1985 Act (protected trust deeds) substitute-

"**5.**

(1) The Scottish Ministers may by regulations make provision as to-

(a) the conditions which require to be fulfilled in order for a trust deed to be granted the status of a protected trust deed;

(b) the consequences of a trust deed being granted that status;

(c) the rights of any creditor who does not accede to a trust deed which is granted protected status;

(d) the extent to which a debtor may be discharged, by virtue of a protected trust deed, from his liabilities or from such liabilities or class of liabilities as may be prescribed in the regulations;

(e) the circumstances in which a debtor may bring to an end the operation of a trust deed in respect of which the conditions provided for under subparagraph (a) above are not fulfilled;

(f) the administration of the trust under a protected trust deed (including provision about the remuneration payable to the trustee).

(2) Regulations under this paragraph may-

(a) make provision enabling applications to be made to the court;

(b) contain such amendments of this Act as appear to the Scottish Ministers to be necessary in consequence of any other provision of the regulations.".

(2) In section 73(1) of that Act (interpretation), for the definition of "protected trust deed" substitute-

"protected trust deed" means a trust deed which has been granted protected status in accordance with regulations made under paragraph 5 of Schedule 5 to this Act;".

DEFINITIONS
"Protected trust deeds": 1985 Act Sch.5 paras 5-13

GENERAL NOTE
A protected trust deed is a trust deed for creditors that involves the transfer of some or all of the debtor's assets to a trust, to be managed by an insolvency practitioner, who will pay out the income therefrom (and sometimes the capital) to the creditors. The trustee will prepare the trust deed and send a copy to each of the debtor's creditors.

There have been concerns that some insolvency practitioners were either charging too much for their services or were generating a poor return for creditors. It was felt that there needed to be more oversight of the operation of protected trust deeds by the Accountant in Bankruptcy and debtors needed to be made more aware of the significance of granting such deeds and the relative merits of sequestration and protected trust deeds.

All these matters were considered in a Scottish Executive consultation document, *Consultation on Protected Trust Deed Reform*, January 2006 and an accompanying document, *Partial regulatory impact assessment to accompany the SE consultation document on protected trust deed reform*, February 2006.

Section 20 provides that the Scottish Ministers may make regulations concerning protected trust deeds. The Regulations were to be seen in the Protected Trust Deeds (Scotland) Regulations 2008 (SSI 2008/243), in force with effect from April 1, 2008.

This section came into force on February 19, 2008 (see the Bankruptcy and Diligence etc (Scotland) Act 2007 (Commencement No.2 and Saving) Order 2008 (SSI 2008/45).

Modification of composition procedure

21. Modification of composition procedure

(1) Schedule 4 to the 1985 Act (discharge on composition) is amended as follows.

(2) In paragraph 1(1), for "clerk issues the act and warrant to the permanent" substitute " or, as the case may be, the Accountant in Bankruptcy appoints the".

(3) In paragraph 4, for sub-paragraphs (c) and (d) substitute-

    (c) not later than 1 week after the date of publication of such notice, send to every creditor known to him-

        (i) a copy of the terms of offer; and

        (ii) such other information as may be prescribed.".

(4) For paragraphs 5 to 8, substitute-

    "**5.** The notice mentioned in paragraph 4(b) of this Schedule shall be in the prescribed form and shall contain such information as may be prescribed.

    6. Where, within the period of 5 weeks beginning with the date of publication of the notice under paragraph 4(b) of this Schedule, the trustee has not received notification in writing from a majority in number or not less than one third in value of the creditors that they reject the offer of composition, the offer of composition shall be approved by the trustee.

    7. Where the trustee has received notification within the period and to the extent mentioned in paragraph 6 of this Schedule, the offer of composition shall be rejected by the trustee.

    8. Any creditor who has been sent a copy of the terms of the offer as referred to in paragraph 4(c)(i) of this Schedule and who has not notified the trustee as mentioned in paragraph 6 of this Schedule that he objects to the offer shall be treated for all purposes as if he had accepted the offer.

8A

(1) The Scottish Ministers may by regulations amend paragraphs 4 to 8 of this Schedule by replacing them, varying them or adding to or deleting anything from them.

(2) Regulations made under sub-paragraph (1) above may contain such amendments of this Act as appear to the Scottish Ministers to be necessary in consequence of any amendment made by the regulations to the said paragraphs 4 to 8.

8B

(1) Where an offer of composition is approved, a creditor who has not been sent a copy of the terms of the offer as mentioned in paragraph 4(c)(i) of this Schedule or who has notified the trustee of his rejection of the offer as mentioned in paragraph 6 of this Schedule may, not more than 28 days after the expiry of the period mentioned in said paragraph 6, appeal to the Accountant in Bankruptcy against such approval.

(2) In determining an appeal under sub-paragraph (1) above, the Accountant in Bankruptcy may-

    (a) approve or reject the offer of composition; and

    (b) make such other determination in consequence of that approval or rejection as he thinks fit.".

(5) In paragraph 9(3), for "paragraph 9(2) and (3) of Schedule 2 to" substitute "section 53A of".

(6) In paragraph 10-

    (a) for "lodged with the sheriff clerk" substitute "sent to the Accountant in Bankruptcy"; and

    (b) in sub-paragraph (a), for "permanent trustee" substitute "trustee (where he is not the Accountant in Bankruptcy)".

(7) For paragraph 11, substitute-

"11.

(1) Where the documents have been sent to the Accountant in Bankruptcy under paragraph 10 of this Schedule and either-

    (a) the period mentioned in paragraph 8B(1) of this Schedule has expired; or

    (b) the Accountant in Bankruptcy, in determining an appeal under said paragraph 8B(1), has approved the offer of composition,

the Accountant in Bankruptcy shall grant the certificates of discharge referred to in sub-paragraph (2) below.

(2) Those certificates are-

    (a) a certificate discharging the debtor; and

    (b) a certificate discharging the trustee.

(3) A certificate granted under sub-paragraph (1) above shall be in the prescribed form.

(4) The Accountant in Bankruptcy shall

(a) send a certified copy of the certificate discharging the debtor to the keeper of the register of inhibitions for recording in that register; and

(b) send a copy of that certificate to the trustee who shall insert it in the sederunt book or, where the Accountant in Bankruptcy is the trustee, insert a copy of that certificate in the sederunt book.".

(8) In paragraph 12, for "An order under paragraph 11" substitute "A certificate granted under paragraph 11(1)".

(9) In paragraph 14-

(a) the words "the sheriff makes an order approving" are repealed; and

(b) after "composition", where it first occurs, insert "is approved".

(10) In paragraph 16-

(a) in sub-paragraph (1), for the words from "an" to "effective" substitute "the granting of a certificate under paragraph 11(1) of this Schedule discharging the debtor"; and

(b) in sub-paragraph (2), for "an order under paragraph 11 above" substitute "the granting of a certificate under paragraph 11(1) of this Schedule".

(11) In paragraph 17(1)-

(a) the words from "Without" to "decrees," are repealed; and

(b) for the words from "order" to "and", where it first occurs, substitute "approval of the offer of composition and the granting of certificates".

(12) In paragraph 18(1)-

(a) the words from "Without" to "decrees," are repealed; and

(b) for "an order under paragraph 11" substitute "a certificate granted under paragraph 11(1)".

(13) In paragraph 4 of Schedule 1 to that Act (determination of amount of creditor's claim), the words "by the sheriff" are repealed.

GENERAL NOTE

A composition under the 1985 Act Sch.4 is where, after the trustee has been appointed, an offer of composition is made by the debtor, or on behalf of the debtor, to the trustee. A composition is effectively a voluntary undertaking by the debtor, or his friends and family, to pay, if not all, at least a proportion of his debts, to the trustee swiftly, rather than letting the matter drag on. Once offered, it should be submitted to the debtor's commissioners (if there are any) whom failing the trustee or the Accountant in Bankruptcy (assuming the trustee is not already the Accountant in Bankruptcy). If they, or she, considers that the composition could be implemented timeously and that it would generate a dividend of at least 25p in the pound, and provided the offer of composition is accepted by a majority in number and two thirds in value, the composition is presented to the sheriff for his approval. If approved and assuming everything required under the composition takes place, the debtor is discharged. It will be noticed that the creditors have to opt in to the offer of composition. If they do not, the offer will fail.

The new arrangements under the 2007 Act and this section in particular alter Sch.4. paras 4-8. They do not substantially alter the practicalities except that the new arrangements set out time limits within which the creditors must be informed of the offer (one week from the publication in the Edinburgh Gazette of the notice of the offer) and have only five weeks from the same date of publication in which to reject the offer. Furthermore, the trustee must receive notification of rejection in writing from a majority in number or not less than one third in value of the creditors; and without such notification of rejection the composition is deemed to be accepted. In other words, the creditors have specifically to opt out of the offer. Inertia will count as assent.

The section further provides that the Scottish Ministers may by regulation vary the terms of paras 4–8.

The remaining paragraphs deal with the fact that the Accountant in Bankruptcy takes over the role of the sheriff (or as the case may be, sheriff clerk) and therefore receives copies of the accounts and issues certificates of discharge. In particular she takes over as the person to whom creditors may appeal if they have not been informed of the offer, or have rejected it, provided the appeal is within the 28 day time limit for the appeal (new Sch 4 para.8B(1)). The wording does not make it clear on what grounds creditors may appeal other than that they may do so, and on determining the appeal, the Accountant in Bankruptcy may approve or reject the offer or make such other determination as it sees fit.

Status and powers of Accountant in Bankruptcy

22.   Status of Accountant in Bankruptcy as officer of the court

In section 1 of the 1985 Act (Accountant in Bankruptcy), after subsection (1), insert-
> "(1A) The Accountant in Bankruptcy shall be an officer of the court.".

GENERAL NOTE

This section makes the Accountant in Bankruptcy an officer of the court, and thus in the same position as lawyers and others who have a duty to uphold the law. This gives the Accountant in Bankruptcy a legal function as well as an executive function, which is appropriate given that she will be carrying out a role formerly carried out by a sheriff.

23.   Accountant in Bankruptcy's power to investigate trustees under protected trust deeds

(1) In Schedule 5 to the 1985 Act (voluntary trust deeds for creditors), after paragraph 1, insert-

"Accountant in Bankruptcy's power to carry out audit

1A The Accountant in Bankruptcy may, at any time, audit the trustee's accounts and fix his remuneration.".

(2) In section 1A(1)(a) of that Act (supervision of persons by the Accountant in Bankruptcy), after sub-paragraph (ii), insert-
"(iia) trustees under protected trust deeds;".

GENERAL NOTE

This gives the Accountant in Bankruptcy the power to audit trustees' accounts for protected trust deeds for creditors, and to fix their remuneration.

Offences

24.   Modification of offences under section 67 of the 1985 Act

(1) Section 67 of the 1985 Act (general offences by debtor) is amended as follows.
(2) In subsection (2), after "conceals" insert ", disposes of".
(3) Subsection (8) is repealed.
(4) In subsection (9), for "to the extent of £100 (or such other sum as may be prescribed) or more" substitute-

"(a) to the extent of £500 (or such other sum as may be prescribed) or more; or

(b) of any amount, where, at the time of obtaining credit, the debtor has debts amounting to £1,000 (or such other sum as may be prescribed) or more,".

(5) After subsection (9), insert-

"(9A) For the purposes of calculating an amount of-

(a) credit mentioned in subsection (9) above; or

(b) debts mentioned in paragraph (b) of that subsection,

no account shall be taken of any credit obtained or, as the case may be, any liability for charges in respect of-

(i) any of the supplies mentioned in section 70(4) of this Act; and

(ii) any council tax within the meaning of section 99(1) of the Local Government Finance Act 1992 (c.14).".

(6) In subsection (10)(a)-

(a) the word "or" after sub-paragraph (i) is repealed;

(b) after sub-paragraph (ii) insert

"; or

(iii) a person subject to a bankruptcy restrictions order, or a bankruptcy restrictions undertaking, made in England or Wales," ; and

(c) for "either case" substitute "the case mentioned in sub-paragraph (i) or (ii) above".

(7) For subsection (10)(c) substitute-

"(c) the relevant information about the status of the debtor is the information that-

(i) his estate has been sequestrated and that he has not been discharged;

(ii) he is an undischarged bankrupt in England and Wales or Northern Ireland; or

(iii) he is subject to a bankruptcy restrictions order, or a bankruptcy restrictions undertaking, made in England or Wales,

as the case may be.".

(8) After subsection (11) insert-

"(11A) A person shall be guilty of an offence under subsection (1), (2), (4), (5), (6) or (7) above if that person does or, as the case may be, fails to do, in any place in England and Wales or Northern Ireland, anything which would, if done or, as the case may be, not done in Scotland, be an offence under the subsection in question.".

GENERAL NOTE

This makes various changes to s.67 of the 1985 Act, which deals with criminal penalties for the debtor. Subsection 8, which is repealed, referred to a debtor who was in business and had failed to keep proper business records for the previous two years, unless he could prove that his failure was neither reckless nor dishonest. Since this was quite a high hurdle over which the debtor was expected to leap, it was removed in the interests of fairness to the debtor. Subsection 9 of s.67 now states that the minimum figure at which the requirement for the debtor to disclose his sequestration or any BRO or BRU to a potential creditor is now £500, unless the debtor already has debts amounting to £1,000 in which any further request for credit is criminal. These figures do not need to take account of any sums due in respect of services for gas, water, electricity or electronic communications (under s.70(4) of the 1985 Act) or any council tax. The rest of the section outlines the meaning of "debtor" for the purposes of the criminal sanctions.

Miscellaneous and general

25. Debt limits in sequestrations

In section 5 of the 1985 Act (sequestration of the estate of living or deceased debtor)-

    (a) in subsection (2B)(a), for "£1,500" substitute "£3,000 or such sum as may be prescribed"; and

    (b) in subsection (4), for "£1,500", in both places where it occurs, substitute "£3,000".

GENERAL NOTE

This section increases the minimum amount for which a debtor application may be made to £3,000 (s.5(2B)(a) of the 1985 Act). The same amount is to be used in s.5(4) as the minimum amount to enable a creditor to be qualified to petition for a debtor's sequestration. The figure was formerly £1,500 and was merely doubled to take account of inflation. Notwithstanding what has just been stated, subsection (a) has not yet been brought into force, being specifically excluded from the provisions of Part 1 that were brought into force on April 1, 2008 by means of the Bankruptcy and Diligence etc (Scotland) Act 2007 (Commencement No.3, Savings and Transitionals) Order 2008 (SSI 2008/115). This means that at the time of writing the existing figures of the 1985 Act remain in place, and so a debtor may apply for his own sequestration where the total amount of his debts is not less than £1,500.

Subsection (b) is, however, in force, except where a debtor application is involved, in which case the qualified creditor must be owed at least £1,500 (not £3,000). The purpose of this part-implementation of this section is to enable creditors to apply for their own sequestration with relative ease.

26. Creditor to provide debt advice and information package

In section 5 of the 1985 Act, after subsection (2C), insert-

    "(2D) No petition may be presented under subsection (2)(b)(i) above unless the qualified creditor has provided, by such time prior to the presentation of the petition as may be prescribed, the debtor with a debt advice and information package.

    (2E) In subsection (2D) above, "debt advice and information package" means the debt advice and information package referred to in section 10(5) of the Debt Arrangement and Attachment (Scotland) Act 2002 (asp 17).".

GENERAL NOTE

This requires a creditor petitioning for a debtor's sequestration to provide the debtor with a debt advice and information package. As indicated in the text, this is the package referred to in the Debt Arrangement and Attachment (Scotland) Act 2002 s.10(5). It is available from the Scottish Executive website and in hard copy form. The package in use is known as "Dealing with debt: finding your feet" and contains much useful information for debtors on how to find help and advice on how to deal with their debts. It may be seen at: *http://www.scotland.gov.uk/Publications/2005/09/15105247/52488.*

With effect from April 1, 2008 the package must be provided no less than 14 days before the presentation of the petition and not more than 12 weeks before the presentation of the petition. The requirement to provide the debtor with a debt advice and information package does not apply where the creditor states that the address of the debtor is not known (see the Bankruptcy (Scotland) Regulations 2008 (SSI 2008/82), para.12).

27. Continuation of sequestration proceedings

(1) Section 12 of the 1985 Act is amended as follows.

(2) In subsection (3), for "subsection (3A)" substitute "subsections (3A) to (3C)".

(3) After subsection (3A) insert-

"(3B) Where the sheriff is satisfied that the debtor shall, before the expiry of the period of 42 days beginning with the day on which the debtor appears before the sheriff, pay or satisfy-

(a) the debt in respect of which the debtor became apparently insolvent; and

(b) any other debt due by the debtor to the petitioner and any creditor concurring in the petition,

the sheriff may continue the petition for a period of no more than 42 days.

(3C) Where the sheriff is satisfied-

(a) that a debt payment programme (within the meaning of Part 1 of the Debt Arrangement and Attachment (Scotland) Act 2002 (asp 17)) relating to-

(i) the debt in respect of which the debtor became apparently insolvent; and

(ii) any other debt due by the debtor to the petitioner and any creditor concurring in the petition,

has been applied for and has not yet been approved or rejected; or

(b) that such a debt payment programme will be applied for,

the sheriff may continue the petition for such period as he thinks fit.".

DEFINITIONS

"Apparent insolvency": 1985 Act s.7

"Debt payment programme": 2002 Act Pt 1

GENERAL NOTE

This section is one where the legislation has been made more merciful to debtors (or alternatively, unhelpful to creditors) in order to give debtors one more chance to pay their debts. Under the 1985 Act sheriffs had very little discretion to refuse the award of sequestration, but this section allows the sheriff deciding on a petition from a creditor or a trustee under a trust deed to continue the petition for a period of no more than 42 days if he believes that the debtor will pay the debt for which the debtor became apparently insolvent and any other debt due by the debtor to the petitioner and any other concurring creditor.

Similarly, the sheriff may continue the case for a further period of 42 days to enable the debtor to apply for a debt payment programme. If a debtor can satisfy the court that a DPP application has been applied for and not yet approved or rejected or will be applied for, the sheriff has the power under subs.(3C) to delay awarding sequestration for as long as the sheriff thinks fit. Under s.4(3) of the 2002 Act, a creditor may not petition for sequestration for a debt which is covered by a DPP. If the DPP is approved during the period of continuation granted by the sheriff under new subs.(3C), no sequestration of the debtor on that petition could take place.

28. Abolition of summary administration

(1) The following provisions of the 1985 Act are repealed.

(2) In section 21A of that Act (calling of statutory meeting where interim trustee is Accountant in Bankruptcy), in subsection (3)(b)-
  (a) sub-paragraph (ii); and
  (b) the word "and" immediately preceding that sub-paragraph.

(3) Section 23A of that Act (summary administration) and Schedule 2A to that Act.

(4) In section 24 of that Act (election of permanent trustee), subsections (3B), (4A) and (5).

(5) In section 25 of that Act (confirmation of permanent trustee), subsection (2A).

GENERAL NOTE

Summary administration had become virtually extinct. It used to be used for very small debt cases and was not generally economic for debtor, trustee and creditors alike. It is now abolished.

29. Non-vested contingent interest reinvested in debtor

In section 31 of the 1985 Act (vesting of estate at date of sequestration), after subsection (5), insert-

"(5A) Any non-vested contingent interest vested in the trustee by virtue of subsection (5) above shall, where it remains so vested in the trustee on the date on which the debtor's discharge becomes effective, be reinvested in the debtor as if an assignation of that interest had been executed by the trustee and intimation thereof made at that date.".

GENERAL NOTE

This clarifies the position where a non-vested contingent interest (such as a right to inherit money) is still vested in the trustee at the date of discharge of the debtor. Just as such an interest automatically vests in the trustee at the date of sequestration (s.31(5) of the 1985 Act) so is it automatically reinvested in the debtor on the date of the debtor's discharge under this provision, inserting a new s.31(5A).

30. Debtor's requirement to give account of state of affairs

After section 43 of the 1985 Act, insert-

"43A Debtor's requirement to give account of state of affairs

(1) This section applies to a debtor who-
  (a) has not been discharged under this Act; or
  (b) is subject to
    (i) an order made by the sheriff under subsection (2) of section 32 of this Act; or
    (ii) an agreement entered into under subsection (4B) of that section.

(2) The trustee shall, at the end of-
  (a) the period of 6 months beginning with the date of sequestration; and
  (b) each subsequent period of 6 months,
  require the debtor to give an account in writing, in such form as may be prescribed, of his current state of affairs.".

GENERAL NOTE

Where a sheriff makes an order that the debtor should pay a sum out of his income (income payment order) to the trustee for the benefit of the debtor's creditors, in terms of s.32(2) of the 1985 Act, or where the debtor makes an arrangement (income payment agreement) with the trustee for the same purposes in terms of s.32(4B), this section, inserting a new s.43A to the 1985 Act, enables the trustee to require from the debtor every six months a statement in writing of his current state of affairs, presumably to enable him to establish whether or not the debtor is managing his affairs properly. Form 23 is the required form for such a statement. See para.20 of the Bankruptcy (Scotland) Regulations 2008 (SSI 2008/82).

31. Restriction of debtor's right to appeal under sections 49(6) and 53(6) of the 1985 Act

(1) In section 49 of the 1985 Act (adjudication of claims)-
   (a) in subsection (6), after "debtor" insert "(subject to subsection (6A) below)"; and
   (b) after subsection (6), insert-
      "(6A) A debtor may appeal under subsection (6) above if, and only if, he satisfies the sheriff that he has, or is likely to have, a pecuniary interest in the outcome of the appeal.".
(2) In section 53 of that Act (procedure after end of accounting period)-
   (a) in subsection (6), after "debtor" insert "(subject to subsection (6A) below)"; and
   (b) after subsection (6), insert-
      "(6A) A debtor may appeal under subsection (6) above if, and only if, he satisfies the Accountant in Bankruptcy or, as the case may be, the sheriff that he has, or is likely to have, a pecuniary interest in the outcome of the appeal.".

GENERAL NOTE

The trustee, when adjudicating on the creditors' claims, is required to send a list of every accepted or rejected claim to the debtor and to the creditors. Under s.49(6) of the 1985 Act, the debtor is entitled to appeal to the sheriff against any rejection or acceptance of any claim of any of the creditors. However, this section introduces a new subs.6A which limits the debtor's claim to those occasions where the debtor himself has a pecuniary interest in the matter, as, for example, where the debtor considers that a creditor's claim is so large that it precludes any chance of repayment to the debtor himself.

The same principle applies to the remuneration of the trustee. The debtor may only appeal against the determination of the remuneration of the trustee if he has a pecuniary interest in the matter himself (new s.53(6A) in the 1985 Act).

32. Status of order on petition to convert protected trust deed into sequestration

After section 59C(2) of the 1985 Act (content of court order converting protected trust deed into sequestration), insert-
   "(2A) The provisions of this Act shall apply to an order made by the sheriff under subsection (1) above as if it was a determination by the Accountant in Bankruptcy of a debtor application under section 12(1) of this Act and in relation to which the member State liquidator was a concurring creditor.".

GENERAL NOTE

This refers to the situation where a Member State liquidator applies to the court for the conversion of a protected trust deed into sequestration, in terms of ss.59A and 59B of the 1985 Act, on the grounds that it is in the interests of the creditors to do this.

The sheriff, in deciding whether or not to approve the application by the Member State liquidator, should grant the petition (provided the requirements of s.12(1) are satisfied) as if it were a debtor application, with the substitution of the sheriff for the Accountant in Bankruptcy and with the Member State liquidator concurring in the application.

33. Power to provide for lay representation in sequestration proceedings

In section 32(1) of the Sheriff Courts (Scotland) Act 1971 (c.58) (power of Court of Session to regulate civil procedure in sheriff court), after paragraph (l) insert-

"(m) permitting a debtor appearing before a sheriff under section 12 of the Bankruptcy (Scotland) Act 1985 (c.66) (award of sequestration) to be represented, in such circumstances as may be specified in the act of sederunt, by a person who is neither an advocate nor a solicitor.".

GENERAL NOTE

Organisations such as the Citizens Advice Bureaux Scotland and Money Advice Scotland were very keen that debtors could be represented in the sheriff court in connection with bankruptcy matters (specifically in terms of the 1985 Act s.12) by people who were not qualified as lawyers. It was felt that lawyers might not always be the most appropriate people for debtors to turn to for help and that other professionals working to help the needy might be better placed to plead debtors' cases. This section provides that an Act of Sederunt may be drawn up to allow for such lay representation before the court.

34. Treatment of student loans on sequestration

(1) In section 73B(12) of the Education (Scotland) Act 1980 (c.44) (power to make provision in relation to treatment of student loans upon discharge under the 1985 Act), after "receive," insert "before, on or".

(2) In paragraph 6 of Schedule 2 to the Education (Student Loans) Act 1990 (c.6) (treatment of student loans on sequestration), which, notwithstanding its repeal by section 44 of and Schedule 4 to the Teaching and Higher Education Act 1998 (c.30), is saved by virtue of article 3 of the Teaching and Higher Education Act 1998 (Commencement No. 2 and Transitional Provisions) Order 1998 (S.I. 1998 No. 2004)-

(a) after "Where," insert "before, on or"; and

(b) after "before" insert ", on".

GENERAL NOTE

This refers to student loans. Although most commercial debts are written off on discharge from sequestration, henceforth student loans will not be written off and will continue in force notwithstanding discharge. This is because student loans are subsidised by the Government, are only exigible once the former student/debtor starts to earn over £10,000 a year, and are repayable at a fixed rate on the marginal income about that income earned by the former student/debtor. This section provides for the remaining in force of the student debt after discharge.

35. Certain regulations under the 1985 Act: procedure

In section 72 of the 1985 Act (regulations)-
(a) the existing words become subsection (1);
(b) at the beginning insert "Subject to subsection (2) below,"; and
(c) at the end insert-

> "(2) No regulations such as are mentioned in subsection (3) below may be made unless a draft of the statutory instrument containing the regulations has been laid before, and approved by a resolution of, the Scottish Parliament.
>
> (3) The regulations are-
> (a) regulations made under-
> (i) subsection (2B)(a) and (4) of section 5;
> (ii) section 5A; and
> (iii) section 39A(4),
> of this Act; and
> (b) the first regulations under paragraph 5 of Schedule 5 to this Act made after the commencement of section 20 of the Bankruptcy and Diligence etc. (Scotland) Act 2007 (asp 3).".

GENERAL NOTE

This provides that the regulations to be made in respect of the various subsections indicated below may be made unless the draft of the relevant statutory instrument is laid before and approved by a resolution of the Scottish Parliament.

Subsection (2B)(a) and (4) of s.5 of the 1985 Act refers to the current figure of £3,000 (see the 2007 Act s.25 above) which may be varied by regulation later. See the note to s.25 of the 2007 Act.

Section 5A of the 1985 Act refers to suitable regulations to be drafted for low income low assets debtors (now provided-see the notes to s.15 of the 2007 Act).

Section 39A4 deals with regulations to be drafted for dealing with the situation when the trustee wishes to sell the family home. The first regulations under para.5, Sch.5 of the 1985 Act deal with protected trust deeds.

This section came into force on February 19, 2008 (see the Bankruptcy and Diligence etc. (Scotland) Act 2007 (Commencement No.2 and Saving) Order 2008 (SSI 2008/45).

36. Minor and consequential amendments of the 1985 Act

Schedule 1 to this Act, which contains minor amendments of the 1985 Act and amendments of that Act consequential on the provisions of this Part, has effect.

GENERAL NOTE

This provides for various minor changes throughout the 1985 Act reflecting consequential and grammatical changes. This section came into force on March 31, 2007.

PART 2

FLOATING CHARGES

GENERAL NOTE

Floating charges were originally an invention of English Chancery lawyers in the late 19th century, and in many ways are a remarkably sensible and effective form of security. Although they are in England and Wales a creature of the common law, in Scotland they were introduced on a statutory basis in the Floating Charges (Scotland) Act 1961. The appointment of a receiver for

Scottish floating charges was put on a statutory basis in the Insolvency Act 1986. The principle on which floating charges work is very simple. Under the pre-Enterprise Act 2002 requirements, the company granted a floating charge which, as it were, hovered over the assets of the company, howsoever constituted, thus allowing the company continually to change its assets, or increase or diminish them, as it saw fit. Provided the floating charge holder (generally a bank) was confident of the total value of the assets, he would generally continue to deal with the company, but in the event of his losing confidence in the company, perhaps by its failure to adhere to certain terms of the floating charge documentation, or the breach of s.52 of the Insolvency Act 1986 (circumstances justifying appointment of a receiver, such as the liquidation of the company) he would cause the floating charge to attach (also known as crystallise) on the assets on the company, and thereafter, at least until the Enterprise Act 2002, appoint a receiver. The receiver, where one was appointed, took charge of the assets of the company as at the time of attachment, and then either took over the management of the company in order to repay the floating charge holder his loan and other sums owing to the floating charge holder, or might sell all or some of the business in an attempt to recoup something for the floating charge holder. This procedure remains in place for floating charges granted before the implementation of the Enterprise Act 2002 and for a few specialised types of company exempted from the requirements of that Act. Following the Enterprise Act 2002, and the introduction of qualifying floating charges, the same general practice applies but a floating charge holder with the benefit of a qualifying floating charge will appoint an administrator instead. The administrator, depending on the circumstances, will try either to rescue the company as a going concern, try to obtain as good a return as possible for all the creditors, or should neither of those be possible, at least try to return something for the secured creditors.

Under the existing legislation, there are certain difficulties with floating charges.

The first is that the floating charge (and this includes qualifying floating charges) must be registered within 21 days of creation. If it is not registered within that period, the charge is void against any creditor, liquidator or administrator. Very occasionally it happens that a charge is not registered within the required 21 day period and a creditor pounces. This means that the sums advanced by the floating charge holder, in the belief that he would have a secured charge, are not secured, and he becomes an unsecured creditor. It is possible, but awkward, to register a charge late on application to the sheriff under the Companies Act 1985 s.420 (or its equivalent under the Companies Act 2006 s.888). The difficulty of the 21 day period is that within that period another charge may have been registered ahead of the floating charge holder's floating charge. For a company to have secretly granted a charge ranking ahead of the floating charge holder's floating charge may well be a breach of the covenants between the company and the floating charge holder, but does not in itself invalidate the secret charge. The 21 day period is sometimes known as the invisibility period.

The second difficulty is that a floating charge may encompass all the assets of the company. This means that it could encompass heritage owned by the company, even though a search in the Register of Sasines or the Land Register against each property owned by the company would not reveal the existence of that floating charge.

Although this offends the general principle of Scots law that any charge must be publicised, it is specifically provided for in the Companies Act 1985 s.462(5). In practice this difficulty can be cured by a search in the Registrar of Companies and the production of a letter of non-crystallisation or some other undertaking by the floating charge holder.

The reason for this procedure is purely practical: when floating charges were introduced in 1961 there was no means whereby a floating charge could be noted against each property that a company owned or might own. Once all the property registers are put on an electronic database, it might, in an ideal world, be possible to do this, but this is not yet available. In the meantime, a floating charge is an "overriding interest" in terms of s.28 of the Land Registration (Scotland) Act 1979 and will continue not to be entered into the Register of Sasines or the Land Register.

The third difficulty was the creation of the "beneficial ownership" arising out of the case of *Sharp v Thomson* (1997) S.C. (H.L.) 77, which gave to an uninfeft proprietor a right of ownership in preference to that of a receiver. This problem has since been dealt with by changes in conveyancing practice, and so should not arise again, though technically it is still extant. In any case the concept of beneficial ownership is only restricted to receivership (as opposed to sequestration) (see *Burnett's Trustee v Grainger* (2004 SC (HL) 19) and as there are over time going to be fewer and fewer old style floating charges extant (as opposed to the new qualifying floating charges) it may not be a particular difficulty.

The fourth difficulty is that the Government has long been unhappy about being the effective guarantor of any company charge, where that charge can be evidenced by the issue by Companies House of a certificate of registration which is conclusive evidence of the registration of the charge. The Government would be keen to shelve that responsibility, while aware that the security of registration in a Government-run register, as evidenced by a Government-backed certificate, does make the United Kingdom a better place in which to do business.

The fifth difficulty is the problem of the floating charge granted by a foreign company over Scottish property. Given the need for publicity, how is a creditor to know whether that foreign company has granted a floating charge over the Scottish assets?

A sixth difficulty is that the creation of a floating charge takes place on the date that it is executed, which is not necessarily the date of registration. The charge must be registered within 21 days in order not to be void against creditors, a liquidator or an administrator, but the date of execution is not the date of registration. This can lead to confusion as to whose floating charge has priority.

It is believed that the creation of a Scottish register of floating charges (to be known as the Register of Floating Charges) will remedy some of these difficulties.

At the time of writing, as indicated above, the process of creating the Register of Floating Charges, how it is to be set up, financed and organised is still a matter of discussion. It is understood that the earliest likely date for the Register to be operational is October 2010. Important features of the Register are that the whole of any charging document will be visible on the Register and that ultimately it will possible to register any document electronically (s.37(9)), although there may perhaps in the short term need to be a method whereby paper copies may still be delivered and scanned into the register. A feature of the Scottish floating charge registration system will be that under s.39 it will be possible to register advance notice of a floating charge in the Register and provided that this is followed up by the actual document granting the floating charge, the charge will be back-dated to the date when the notice was created. It is expected that most floating charge holders will wish to use this provision.

Finally, it must be appreciated that the Register must be used whenever a floating charge, created by any company, is granted over assets situated in Scotland, and without registration, the floating charge will not be valid.

At present, when any Scottish company grants a floating charge, it is registered at the (Scottish) Register of Companies using a form 410. This covers assets throughout the United Kingdom. The registration of the charge is visible on the company's published particulars at the Register of Companies. When an English company grants a floating charge over assets anywhere in the United Kingdom, the form 395 is used, and some published particulars are visible. There are cross-border provisions to enable recognition of a receiver appointed in one country over assets in another, subject to the *lex situs* in each case (Insolvency Act 1986 s.72). While no one would pretend that this is perfect, and does not wholly satisfy the Scottish requirement for publicity, it seems to operate reasonably well in practice.

It is envisaged, at least at the time of writing, with the new Register of Floating Charges ("the Register"), that whenever a floating charge is granted over assets in Scotland, it will need to be registered in the Register and would not be registered with the Register of Companies (as it is at present). So if a Scottish company grants a floating charge over assets in Scotland, it registers its floating charge in the Register.

If the Scottish company also has assets in England, it is envisaged that the registration of the floating charge in the Register would also cover the English assets, since there is no English Register of Floating Charges.

If an English company, having no assets in England, wishes to grant a floating charge over Scottish assets, it will need to register its floating charge in the Register. If an English company grants a floating charge over assets solely in England, it will continue to register its charge with the English Register of Companies. Since one of the requirements of the Hampton Report 2005 *Reducing administrative burdens; effective inspection and enforcement* (available at: *http://www.hmtreasury.-gov.uk/media/A63/EF/bud05hamptonv1.pdf*) is that business should not have to suffer unnecessary burdens such as having to give information twice, it is clearly desirable that one registration of any document should be sufficient. One possibility is that an English company having assets in both countries would register its charge with the English Register of Companies, but there would be an electronic link to the Register of Floating Charges to ensure that the floating charge would be validly registered in Scotland in order to be effective over Scottish property.

But if there were an English company with only English assets, having granted a floating charge over its English assets, duly registered in the English Register of Companies, and should it subsequently acquire Scottish assets, would it be required to register the same charge again in Scotland in order to ensure the validity of its pre-existing floating charge, or would it be required to register a new charge in Scotland?

Either way, would that not place an unnecessary burden on the English company by requiring dual registration? And what would the date of the creation of the floating charge be for Scottish purposes? Would the one charge have two dates of registration, one in England and one in Scotland? Would the existing English charge have to be varied so that it could be registered in Scotland in the Register? Would it matter if the date of an English charge and the date of the later Scottish charge were different?

If two registrations were required, there might be an outcry, since it would be more burdensome than the current position, as well as irritation at the fact that there might be expense involved, not to mention a suspicion that the purpose of the exercise was to benefit Scottish lawyers. It would be seen as one-sided (since Scottish companies would not have to do the same in England) and as a bureaucratic, legalistic nicety which may well satisfy Scots law but is arguably not very commercial.

Or would banks, being the main floating charge holders, insist that all English companies register simultaneously all their floating charges in the Register just to be on the safe side? But if so, would it be conceptually possible to register a floating charge in the Register even if there were no assets in Scotland over which the company could grant the floating charge? Alternatively, could a floating charge granted by an English company over Scottish property and registered in the Register automatically act as a registered charge over English assets too? If that is the case, there might be an enormous volume of floating charge registration taking place in Edinburgh and the more nationalistic English companies might wonder what the point was of making English companies register their charges in Edinburgh. One can imagine English lawyers trying, not always successfully, to explain the reasoning for the Edinburgh registration to baffled clients, who would see little commercial logic in this.

Once the Register is in place it will be registering both qualifying floating charges and any old-style floating charges that are exempt from the Enterprise Act 2002 requirements. It is suggested that, to avoid confusion, all floating charges registered in the register should be known as Scottish Floating Charges, to make their status and import clear to creditors and investors alike.

At the time of writing, the solution to these problems is not known, but it seems to be agreed that if new arrangements for a new Register are to be put in place, those arrangements must be easier, better and no more expensive than the current arrangements. They must both satisfy Scots law's requirement for publicity and satisfy the Hampton Report's requirement for minimal inconvenience. How this is done remains to be seen.

Notwithstanding all these difficulties, which may be less burdensome in practice than they may appear in theory, one should not lose sight of the overwhelming advantage of the proposed new Scottish floating charge: that the creation of the floating charge is on registration not on execution; there is no 21 day period of invisibility allowing other unforeseen secured creditors to steal a march on the supposedly secured creditor who thought his charge had prior ranking; there will be no need for negative pledge clauses; and unsecured creditors can have a better idea of the extent to which a company's assets are secured, on the basis of which they can make an informed decision on whether or not to deal with the company. The new system should be transparent and clear, and it is not entirely fanciful to say that its advantages should soon become apparent to rival jurisdictions whose methods of registration of floating charges lead to opacity and uncertainty.

Registration and creation etc

37. Register of Floating Charges

(1) The Keeper of the Registers of Scotland (in this Part, the "Keeper") must establish and maintain a register to be known as the Register of Floating Charges.

(2) The Keeper must accept an application for registration of-

(a) any document delivered to the Keeper in pursuance of section 38, 41, 42, 43 or 44 of this Act; and

(b) any notice delivered to the Keeper in pursuance of section 39 or 45(2) of this Act,

provided that the application is accompanied by such information as the Keeper may require for the purposes of the registration.

(3) On receipt of such an application, the Keeper must note the date of receipt of the application; and, where the application is accepted by the Keeper, that date is to be treated for the purposes of this Part as the date of registration of the document or notice to which the application relates.

(4) The Keeper must, after accepting such an application, complete registration by registering in the Register of Floating Charges the document or notice to which the application relates.

(5) The Keeper must-

(a) make the Register of Floating Charges available for public inspection at all reasonable times;

(b) provide facilities for members of the public to obtain copies of the documents in the Register; and

(c) supply an extract of a document in the Register, certified as a true copy of the original, to any person requesting it.

(6) An extract certified as mentioned in subsection (5)(c) above is sufficient evidence of the original.

(7) The Keeper may charge such fees-

(a) for registering a document or notice in the Register of Floating Charges; or

(b) in relation to anything done under subsection (5) above,

as the Scottish Ministers may by regulations prescribe.

(8) The Scottish Ministers may by regulations make provision as to-

(a) the form and manner in which the Register of Floating Charges is to be maintained;

(b) the form of documents (including notices as mentioned in sections 39(1) and 45(2) of this Act) for registration in that Register, the particulars they are to contain and the manner in which they are to be delivered to the Keeper.

(9) Provision under subsection (8) above may, in particular, facilitate the use-

(a) of electronic communication;

(b) of documents in electronic form (and of certified electronic signatures in documents).

GENERAL NOTE

Section 37(1) provides for the creation of a dedicated Register of Floating Charges, to be set up and maintained by the Keeper of the Registers of Scotland ("the Keeper").

We await the relevant regulations applicable to the Register. Subsection (2) provides for the registration of the entire document (not just the particulars) in respect of any floating charge (s.38), ranking agreement (s.41), assignation of a floating charge (s.42), document of alteration (s.43) or discharge of floating charge (s.44). It will also be possible to register an advance notice of floating charge (s.39). The date of registration will be the date of receipt of the application of the document or notice (subs.(3)). Registration of the floating charge will not be possible unless there is a document to register (subs.(4)). The Keeper must make the Register available for public inspection and allows extract copies to be made as necessary (subs.(5)). A certified extract will be equivalent to the original (subs.(6)).

38. Creation of floating charges

(1) It continues to be competent, for the purpose of securing any obligation to which this subsection applies, for a company to grant in favour of the creditor in the obligation a charge (known as a "floating charge") over all or any part of the property which may from time to time be comprised in the company's property and undertaking.

(2) Subsection (1) above applies to any debt or other obligation incurred or to be incurred by, or binding upon, the company or any other person.

(3) From the coming into force of this section, a floating charge is (subject to section 39 of this Act) created only when a document—

    (a) granting a floating charge; and

    (b) subscribed by the company granting the charge,

is registered in the Register of Floating Charges.

(4) References in this Part to a document which grants a floating charge are to a document by means of which a floating charge is granted.

DEFINITIONS
  "Company": 2007 Act s.47

GENERAL NOTE

The wording of subss.(1) and (2) is taken originally from the Companies Act 1985 s.462(1) and gives continuing statutory authority to the existence of floating charges in Scotland. Subsection (3) states that the floating charge is created when a document granting a floating charge, and subscribed by the company granting the floating charge, is registered in the Register. The date of creation is, therefore, not the date of execution (as it has been formerly) but the date of registration. It would appear that only companies may grant floating charges registrable in the new Register. A floating charge not granted by a company will not be registrable under this legislation, and indeed, therefore, would not be deemed to be created under this legislation. The word "company" is defined in s.47 as an incorporated company (whether or not a company within the meaning of the Companies Act 1985). It would appear that the word "company" therefore covers UK registered companies, and unregistered but incorporated companies, but not limited liability partnerships, despite the fact that they too under their own legislation can grant floating charges. The Scottish Justice Department is consulting with the Department of Business Enterprise and Regulatory Reform to ensure that changes are made to the Limited Liability Partnership Regulations 2001 (SI 2001/1090) and The European Economic Interest Grouping Regulations 1989 (SI 1989/638) to enable those two entities also to be able to register their floating charges in the Scottish Floating Charge Register. Consideration is also being given to the position of overseas companies that currently register with Companies House under s.1046 of the Companies Act 2006.

39. Advance notice of floating charges

(1) Where a company proposes to grant a floating charge, the company and the person in whose favour the charge is to be granted may apply to have joint notice of the proposed charge registered in the Register of Floating Charges.

(2) Subsection (3) below applies where—

    (a) a notice under subsection (1) above is registered in the Register of Floating Charges; and

    (b) within 21 days of the notice being so registered, a document—

        (i) granting a floating charge conforming with the particulars contained in the notice; and

        (ii) subscribed by the company granting the charge,

is registered in the Register of Floating Charges.

(3) Where this subsection applies, the floating charge so created is to be treated as having been created when the notice under subsection (1) above was so registered.

GENERAL NOTE

This allows a company and the floating charge holder to apply jointly (but not unilaterally) to have notice of a floating charge registered in the Register. Within 21 days, the notice must be followed up by the registration of a floating charge consistent with the information in the notice and subscribed by the company in question. If this is done, the date of creation of the floating charge is backdated to the date of the notice. The purpose of this section is to enable priority of ranking to be established and to prevent the current difficulty of not knowing if some secret charge has obtained priority instead. It is anticipated that the regulations yet to be issued will allow for the notice to be signed either by the company and floating charge holder or by their solicitors.

40. Ranking of floating charges

(1) Subject to subsections (4) and (5) below, a floating charge-
  (a) created on or after the coming into force of this section; and
  (b) which has attached to all or any part of the property of a company,
  ranks as described in subsection (2) below.

(2) The floating charge referred to in subsection (1) above-
  (a) ranks with-
    (i) any other floating charge which has attached to that property or any part of it; or
    (ii) any fixed security over that property or any part of it,
  according to date of creation; and
  (b) ranks equally with any floating charge or fixed security referred to in paragraph (a) above which was created on the same date as the floating charge referred to in subsection (1) above.

(3) For the purposes of subsection (2) above-
  (a) the date of creation of a fixed security is the date on which the right to the security was constituted as a real right; and
  (b) the date of creation of a floating charge subsisting before the coming into force of this section is the date on which the instrument creating the charge was executed by the company granting the charge.

(4) Where all or any part of the property of a company is subject to both-
  (a) a floating charge; and
  (b) a fixed security arising by operation of law,
  the fixed security has priority over the floating charge.

(5) Where the holder of a floating charge over all or any part of the property of a company has received intimation in writing of the subsequent creation of-
  (a) another floating charge over the same property or any part of it; or
  (b) a fixed security over the same property or any part of it,
  the priority of ranking of the first-mentioned charge is restricted to security for the matters referred to in subsection (6) below.

(6) Those matters are-
  (a) the present debt incurred (whenever payable);
  (b) any future debt which, under the contract to which the charge relates, the holder is required to allow the debtor to incur;
  (c) any interest due or to become due on the debts referred to in paragraphs (a) and (b) above;

(d) any expenses or outlays which may be reasonably incurred by the holder; and

(e) in the case of a floating charge to secure a contingent liability (other than a liability arising under any further debts incurred from time to time), the maximum sum to which the contingent liability is capable of amounting, whether or not it is contractually limited.

(7) Subsections (1) to (6) above, and any provision made under section 41(1) of this Act, are subject to sections 175 and 176A (provision for preferential debts and share of assets) of the Insolvency Act 1986 (c.45).

DEFINITIONS

"Floating charge": 2007 Act s.38
"Fixed security": 2007 Act s.47
"Preferential debts": IA 1986 s.175
"Register of Floating Charges": 2007 Act s.37
"Share of assets": IA 1986 s.176A

GENERAL NOTE

This states the priority of floating charges. The normal rule is that of priority following the date of creation, so an earlier created charge has priority over a later created one (s.40 (1), (2)(a)). Fixed securities arising by operation of law (e.g. liens) on the same assets will automatically rank ahead of floating charges (s.40(4)) but where any fixed security, whether arising by operation of law or otherwise, and a floating charge are created on the same day, they are treated as ranking equally (s.40(2)(b)). Likewise, two floating charges created on the same date are treated as ranking equally (s.40(2)(b)). A floating charge is deemed to be created on registration (see s.38) but a fixed security is created when the right to the security is constituted as a real right (s.40(3)(a)). The creation of a real right in the case of heritable security takes place on the registration of that heritable security in the Register of Sasines or the Land Register as the case may be, and as regards any other type of fixed security, will be, for example, on delivery or pledge of the asset to the security-holder. For the avoidance of doubt, the date of creation of a floating charge created before the coming into force of this section of the 2007 Act is the date when the company executed (not registered) that floating charge.

Where an existing floating charge holder is told of the creation of another floating charge, or of a fixed charge, in each case over the same property or any part of it, the existing floating charge has its priority restricted to the items in subs.(6).

This is to prevent the existing floating charge holder effectively having the chance to increase the extent of its security and thus take for its own account, in the event of insolvency, the sums advanced by the postponed floating charge holder. The terms of many companies' floating charges prohibit the granting of any further charge over the already charged assets and were a company to do so without permission from the existing floating charge holder, the existing charge holder would have grounds for exercising its rights to appoint a receiver or administrator as the case may be.

Any sums secured under this section are always subject to the provisions of IA 1986 ss.175 and 176A. The former of these, under s.175, are the preferential debts, stated in the Insolvency Act 1986 s.386 and Sch.6 of the Insolvency Act 1986. Until the Enterprise Act 2002, these used to be mainly government taxes, but are now contributions to occupational pension schemes, remuneration of employees (up to £800 per employee) plus sums advanced for such remuneration, and levies on coal and steel production. The latter of these, under s.176A, comprise the "prescribed part" for unsecured creditors. Depending on the size of the company this amounts to a proportion of the company's assets which are to be directed by the administrator, receiver, or liquidator to the unsecured creditors, effectively out of the sums otherwise due to the floating charge holder. The rules for this may be found in the Insolvency Act 1986 (Prescribed Part) Order 2003 (SI 2003/2097) and are as follows:

(a) where the company's net property is less than £10,000, 50 per cent of that property;
(b) where the company's net property is more than £10,000, 50 per cent of the first £10,000 worth of that company's property; plus
(c) 20 per cent of the remainder in excess of that first £10,000 worth of property; and
(d) all subject to a maximum overall prescribed part of £600,000.

The Government is of the view that the prescribed part will go some way towards helping the position of unsecured creditors in a company's insolvency, and may thus keep in business some unsecured creditors who would otherwise have collapsed following the company's demise. In practice, a good deal of the prescribed part goes towards paying the unpaid wages of employees. The administrator, liquidator or receiver is not obliged to make these payments if the cost of doing so exceeds the benefit (IA 1986 s.176A(3)).

41. Ranking clauses

(1) The document granting a floating charge over all or any part of the property of a company may make provision regulating the order in which the charge ranks with any other floating charge or any fixed security (including a future floating charge or fixed security) over that property or any part of it.

(2) Provision under subsection (1) above-

  (a) may displace in whole or part-

    (i) subsections (1) and (2) of section 40 of this Act;

    (ii) subsections (5) and (6) of that section;

  (b) may not affect the operation of subsection (4) of that section (whether as against subsections (1) and (2) of that section or other provision under subsection (1) above).

(3) Accordingly, subsections (1), (2), (5) and (6) of that section have effect subject to any provision made under subsection (1) above.

(4) Provision under subsection (1) above is not valid unless it is made with the consent of the holder of any subsisting floating charge, or any subsisting fixed security, which would be adversely affected by the provision.

(5) A document of consent for the purpose of subsection (4) above may be registered in the Register of Floating Charges.

DEFINITIONS

"Fixed security": 2007 Act s.47
"Floating charge": 2007 Act s.38
"Register of Floating Charges": 2007 Act s.37

GENERAL NOTE

Companies may if they wish create ranking clauses regulating the order of priority of one charge relative to another that it has granted. These provisions may override any or some of the provisions of s.40, with the exception of subs.4 (the fixed charges arising by operation of law), which will continue in all circumstances to override the floating charge. Any charge-holder who is adversely affected by the rearrangement of the order of the priority of charges must consent to such rearrangement. It is not, however, at this stage necessary for the document that indicates the consent to be registered in the Register of Floating Charges, though there is nothing to prevent such registration.

42. Assignation of floating charges

(1) A floating charge may be assigned (and the rights under it vested in the assignee) by the registration in the Register of Floating Charges of a document of assignation subscribed by the holder of the charge.

(2) An assignation under subsection (1) above may be in whole or to such extent as may be specified in the document of assignation.

(3) This section is without prejudice to any other enactment, or any rule of law, by virtue of which a floating charge may be assigned.

DEFINITIONS
"Floating charge": 2007 Act s.38
"Register of Floating Charges": 2007 Act s.37

GENERAL NOTE
A floating charge-holder may wish to assign, sell or otherwise transfer the floating charge to another person. Since the change of ownership needs to be registered there will no doubt be some special form to indicate this. The case *Libertas-Kommerz v Johnson*, 1977 SC 191 is authority to the effect that even though there was no special wording to permit or refuse assignation in the Floating Charges (Scotland) Act 1961 there was no reason why floating charges should not be assignable, and that no special words were required for the intimation of the assignation provided intimation to the company was made. This section permits partial assignation and also is relevant where a floating charge is assigned by operation of law, as when, say, it is transferred on death to the executors of the charge-holder's estate.

43. Alteration of floating charges

(1) A document of alteration may alter (whether by addition, deletion or substitution of text or otherwise) the terms of a document granting a floating charge.

(2) If (and in so far as) an alteration to the terms of a document granting a floating charge concerns-
   (a) the ranking of the charge with any other floating charge or any fixed security; or
   (b) the specification of-
      (i) the property that is subject to the charge; or
      (ii) the obligations that are secured by the charge,
   the alteration is not valid unless subsection (3) below is satisfied.

(3) This subsection is satisfied if the alteration is made by a document of alteration which is-
   (a) subscribed by-
      (i) the company which granted the charge;
      (ii) the holder of the charge; and
      (iii) the holder of any other subsisting floating charge, or any subsisting fixed security, which would be adversely affected by the alteration; and
   (b) registered in the Register of Floating Charges.

(4) But paragraph (a)(i) of subsection (3) above does not apply in respect of an alteration which-
   (a) relates only to the ranking of the floating charge first-mentioned in that subsection with any other floating charge or any fixed security; and
   (b) does not adversely affect the interests of the company which granted the charge.

(5) The granting, by the holder of a floating charge, of consent to the release from the scope of the charge of any particular property, or class of property, which is subject to the charge is to be treated as constituting an alteration-
   (a) to the terms of the document granting the charge; and
   (b) as to the specification of the property that is subject to the charge.

(6) For the purpose of subsection (5) above, property is not to be regarded as released from the scope of a floating charge by reason only of its ceasing to be the property of the company which granted the charge.

DEFINITIONS
"Fixed security": 2007 Act s.47
"Floating charge": 2007 Act s.38
"Register of Floating Charges": 2007 Act s.37

GENERAL NOTE
It is permissible to alter a floating charge by means of a document of alteration. If so, the document must be subscribed by the company itself, the holder of the floating charge, and the holder of any other floating charge or any existing fixed charge adversely affected by the alteration. It must also be registered in the new Register (subs.(3)(b)). If it is not registered, then it will not be valid against a third party (subs.(2)). However, if the secured creditors between themselves are merely rearranging their priorities, with no adverse effect on the company, it will still be possible to register the document of alteration but it will not be obligatory (subs.(4)). Subsection (5) addresses the situation where a floating charge holder agrees to release an asset from the floating charge but the company, instead of immediately selling the asset, continues to retain ownership of the asset, as happened in *Scottish & Newcastle plc v Ascot Inns Ltd*, 1994 SLT 1140. Unless there were some means of showing that the asset had been released from the floating charge, an outside creditor would be unaware that the asset was not potentially liable to be caught by the attachment (crystallisation) of the floating charge. Subsection (5) therefore treats such circumstances as constituting an alteration and requiring the registration of a document of alteration. Subsection (6) clarifies the point that a company is still free to dispose of all its assets subject to the floating charge up to the point that the charge attaches (crystallises) but that for the purposes of subs.(5), where an item of property of the company's ceases to belong to the company, by being sold or given away, such sale or donation, even where there is a floating charge in place, is not an alteration which requires to be documented by means of a document of alteration.

44. Discharge of floating charges

(1) A floating charge may be discharged by the registration in the Register of Floating Charges of a document of discharge subscribed by the holder of the charge.

(2) A discharge under subsection (1) above may be in whole or to such extent as may be specified in the document of discharge.

(3) This section is without prejudice to any other means by which a floating charge may be discharged or extinguished.

DEFINITIONS
"Fixed security": 2007 Act s.47
"Floating charge": 2007 Act s.38
"Register of Floating Charges": 2007 Act s.37

GENERAL NOTE
It is good practice but not obligatory to discharge a floating charge once the charge is no longer needed. It is also permissible partially to discharge the floating charge. The advantage of having the floating charge discharged is that any future lender to the company will be able to see immediately that there are potentially no outstanding and unredeemed floating charges still in existence.

45. Effect of floating charges on winding up

(1) Where a company goes into liquidation, a floating charge created over property of the company attaches to the property to which it relates.

(2) But, in a case mentioned in subsection (7)(a) below, there is no attachment under subsection (1) above until such time as a notice of attachment is registered in the Register of Floating Charges on the application of the holder of the charge.

(3) The attachment of a floating charge to property under subsection (1) above is subject to the rights of any person who-

    (a) has effectually executed diligence on the property to which the charge relates or any part of it;

    (b) holds over that property or any part of it a fixed security ranking in priority to the floating charge; or

    (c) holds over that property or any part of it another floating charge so ranking.

(4) Interest accrues in respect of a floating charge which has attached to property until payment is made of any sum due under the charge.

(5) Part IV, except section 185, of the Insolvency Act 1986 has (subject to subsection (1) above) effect in relation to a floating charge as if the charge were a fixed security over the property to which it has attached in respect of the principal of the debt or obligation to which it relates and any interest due or to become due on it.

(6) Subsections (1) to (5) above do not affect the operation of-

    (a) sections 53(7) and 54(6) (attachment of floating charge on appointment of receiver) of the Insolvency Act 1986;

    (b) sections 175 and 176A of that Act; or

    (c) paragraph 115(3) of Schedule B1 (attachment of floating charge on delivery of a notice by an administrator) to that Act.

(7) For the purposes of this section, reference to a company going into liquidation-

    (a) in a case where a court of a member State has under the EC Regulation jurisdiction as respects the company which granted the relevant floating charge, means the opening of insolvency proceedings in that State;

    (b) in any other case, is to be construed in accordance with section 247(2) and (3) of the Insolvency Act 1986 (c.45).

(8) In subsection (7)(a) above-

    "the EC Regulation" is the Regulation of the Council of the European Union published as Council Regulation (EC) No 1346/2000 on insolvency proceedings;

    "court" is to be construed in accordance with Article 2(d) of that Regulation;

    "insolvency proceedings" is to be construed in accordance with Article 2(a) of that Regulation;

    "member State" means a member State of the European Union apart from the United Kingdom.

DEFINITIONS
"Fixed security": 2007 Act s.47
"Floating charge": 2007 Act s.38
"Register of Floating Charges": 2007 Act s.37

GENERAL NOTE

The normal practice of a floating charge, whether a pre-Enterprise Act floating charge or post-Enterprise Act qualifying floating charge is that if the company, over whose assets the floating charge has been granted, is put into liquidation, the floating charge attaches to such of the company's assets as are subject to the floating charge, and with the liquidator has to take account of the floating charge holder's interest in the assets encompassed by the floating charge.

The effect of either of this practice is that there may in reality be very little left over for a liquidator to divide up between the unsecured creditors.

Subsection (3) states that when a floating charge (of either type) attaches to a company's property, the attachment is subject to the rights of anyone who has "effectually executed diligence" on the property, has a prior-ranking fixed security, or has a prior-ranking floating charge. While there are no difficulties with the latter two items, there are some difficulties with the term "effectually executed diligence". The term "effectually executed diligence" appears in the Insolvency Act 1986 s.55(3) on which this subsection (s.45(3) of the 2007 Act) is clearly based. It has been discussed in two cases. Where a creditor arrested an item of a company's property and the company subsequently granted a floating charge, a receiver later appointed by the floating charge holder was unable to seize that item since it was litigious (see *Iona Hotels Ltd*, 1991 S.L.T. 11); on the other hand, where a company had granted a floating charge, and a creditor later arrested in the hands of a third party an asset of that company's, but failed to carry out an action of furthcoming before the appointment of a receiver under the floating charge, the receiver successfully took possession of the asset on the grounds that an arrestment not followed up by an action of furthcoming was not effectually executed diligence (see *Lord Advocate v Royal Bank of Scotland*, 1977 S.C. 155). This would seem to suggest that the words "effectually executed diligence" require the completion of the entire procedure for diligence for each type of diligence. Whether or not this is a correct interpretation of the words has been open to doubt for some time, and there is a powerful argument adumbrated by Scott Wortley in *Squaring the circle: revisiting the receiver and "effectually executed diligence"*, Jur. Rev. 2000, 5, 325-346 that the courts have completely mistaken what was properly meant by "effectually executed diligence".

Having said this, s.206 of the 2007 Act inserts a new s73J in the 1987 Act. This allows for automatic furthcoming, and if it is automatic it is hard to see what further steps need to be taken to "effectually execute" the arrestment. Section 73B refers to a schedule of arrestment in terms that suggest that serving of the schedule amounts to execution and that no further procedure is required to execute an arrestment. It is therefore important to note Sch.5 para.14 to the 2007 Act. This inserts a new subs.(1B) into s.61 of the Insolvency Act 1986. Its wording is as follows: "For the purposes of subsection (1) above, an arrestment is an effectual diligence only where it is executed before the floating charge, by virtue of which the receiver was appointed, attached to the property comprised in the company's property and undertaking." Note that it says "effectual diligence", not an "effectually executed diligence". Was this deliberate or a drafting oversight? Who knows?

The upshot of all this is that it would appear, though it is not beyond doubt, that as far as arrestment is concerned, the decision in *Lord Advocate v Royal Bank of Scotland* will not apply, and that the final step now as regards effectual execution of arrestment (though not arrestment on the dependence of an action) is the service of the schedule in terms of s.73B.

It is on occasions such as these one could wish that the legislation either spelled out exactly what was required, or that the Government's own notes explained what the legislation was trying to achieve and why it was doing so.

Subsection (2) deals with the situation where a company with its main centre of main interests in an EU State is put into liquidation in that country or elsewhere in the European Union, the crystallisation of the Scottish floating charge will only take place if the Scottish floating charge has previously been registered in the Register of Floating Charges and a notice of attachment (yet to be designed) is registered in the Register on the application of the holder of the charge.

46. Repeals, savings and transitional arrangements

(1) Part XVIII (floating charges: Scotland) of the Companies Act 1985 (c.6) is repealed.

(2) Nothing in this Part (except sections 40 and 41 so far as they concern the ranking of floating charges subsisting immediately before the coming into force of this section) affects the validity or operation of floating charges subsisting before the coming into force of this section.

(3) So, despite the repeal of Chapters I and III of Part XVIII of that Act by subsection (1) above, the provisions of those Chapters are to be treated as having effect for the purposes of floating charges subsisting immediately before the coming into force of this section.

(4) In particular-

    (a) floating charges subsisting immediately before the coming into force of this section rank with each other as they ranked with each other in accordance with section 464 of the Companies Act 1985 immediately before that section was repealed by subsection (1) above; and

(b) a floating charge subsisting immediately before the coming into force of this section ranks with a fixed security so subsisting as it ranked with the security in accordance with section 464 of the Companies Act 1985 immediately before that section was repealed by subsection (1) above.

(5) Section 140 (floating charges (Scotland)) of the Companies Act 1989 (c.40) is repealed (but, despite being repealed, is to be treated as having effect for the purposes of subsections (3) and (4) above).

DEFINITIONS

"Fixed security": 2007 Act s.47

"Floating charge": 2007 Act s.38

"Register of Floating Charges": 2007 Act s.37

GENERAL NOTE

Subsection (1) repeals ss.410-424 of the Companies Act 1985. These same provisions may also be found in the Companies Act 2006 Pt 25 Ch.2 (ss.878-892).

It is fortunate in some respects that at the time of writing this section 46 is not yet in force, because the sections in the Companies Act 2006 dealing with the registration of Scottish charges are not yet in force either.

Subsection (2) clarifies the point that existing floating charges and their ranking arrangements remain unaltered and as far as they are concerned there is no change. Only floating charges created after the bringing into force of these provisions are affected by the 2007 Act, and pre-commencement floating charges will be able to alter their ranking by continuing to refer to the provisions of the Companies Act 1985. Even if a company creates a new floating charge after commencement, its presence will not automatically disturb existing arrangements, though it is open to the parties to effect a new ranking arrangement if they wish to do so. In essence, the 2007 Act is not retrospective.

47. Interpretation

In this Part-

"company" means an incorporated company (whether or not a company within the meaning of the Companies Act 1985 (c.6));

"fixed security", in relation to any property of a company, means any security (other than a floating charge or a charge having the character of a floating charge) which on the winding up of the company in Scotland would be treated as an effective security over that property including, in particular, a heritable security (within the meaning of section 9(8) of the Conveyancing and Feudal Reform (Scotland) Act 1970 (c.35)).

GENERAL NOTE

As the notes to the legislation indicate, this section defines "company" in a way which includes an overseas company. Limited liability partnerships do not come within this definition but community interest companies would do so. It defines "fixed security" in the same manner as in s.486 of the Companies Act 1985.

48. Formalities as to documents

(1) In section 6 (registration of documents) of the Requirements of Writing (Scotland) Act 1995 (c.7), after subsection (1)(a), insert-

"(aa) to register a document in the Register of Floating Charges;".

(2) In section 46 (extract decree of reduction to be recorded) of the Conveyancing (Scotland) Act 1924 (c.27)-

(a) in subsection (2), for the words "This section" substitute "Subsection (1) above"; and

(b) after subsection (2), insert-

"(3) This section shall apply in relation to a document registered in the Register of Floating Charges as it applies in relation to a deed or other document pertaining to a heritable security which is recorded in the Register of Sasines (and the references to recording are to be read accordingly).".

(3) In section 8 (rectification of defectively expressed documents) of the Law Reform (Miscellaneous Provisions) (Scotland) Act 1985 (c.73), after subsection (5), insert-

"(5A) Subsection (5) above applies in relation to document registered in the Register of Floating Charges as it applies in relation to a document recorded in the Register of Sasines (and the references to recording are to be read accordingly).".

GENERAL NOTE

The point of this section is to ensure consistency in the manner in which documents are subscribed. The Requirements of Writing (Scotland) Act 1995 provides for a form of subscription of documents whereby it is presumed that the document has been validly subscribed by the signatory. This Act states that only documents with such presumed authenticity may be registered in the Register of Sasines. The same principle applies to documents presented to the Land Register. Section 48(1) applies the same principle to documents registrable in the Register of Floating Charges. This should ensure uniform treatment of applications to the Registers of Scotland.

Subsections (2) and (3) deal with the following situations: (a) where a document registered in the Register of Floating Charges has been reduced as a result of an application to the court for a decree of reduction and (b) where something has been inaccurately expressed in a document registered in the Register of Floating Charges but the court has subsequently granted an order for rectification. Although these may both be uncommon, any third party, such as a person to whom a floating charge is being assigned, should be able to rely on the Register. The effect of these provisions is that no decree of reduction nor order of rectification will affect the rights of the third party unless the decree of reduction or the order has been duly registered in the Register of Floating Charges.

49. Industrial and provident societies

(1) For section 3 (application to registered societies of provisions relating to floating charges) of the Industrial and Provident Societies Act 1967 (c.48) substitute-

"3. Application to registered societies of provisions relating to floating charges

(1) The provisions of Part 2 of the Bankruptcy and Diligence etc. (Scotland) Act 2007 (asp 3) (in this section referred to as the "relevant provisions") shall apply to a registered society as they apply to an incorporated company.

(2) Where, in the case of a registered society-
  (a) there are in existence-
    (i) a floating charge created under the relevant provisions (as applied by this section), and
    (ii) an agricultural charge created under Part II of the Agricultural Credits (Scotland) Act 1929 (c.13), and
  (b) any assets of the society are subject to both charges,

sections 40(1) to (3) (including as subject to section 41(1) to (4)) and 45(3)(c) of the Bankruptcy and Diligence etc. (Scotland) Act 2007 shall have effect for the purposes of determining the ranking with one another of those charges as if the agricultural charge were a floating charge created under the relevant provisions on the date of creation of the agricultural charge.".

(2) Section 4 (filing of information relating to charges) of that Act is repealed.

(3) In section 5 (supplemental provisions) of that Act-
  (a) for paragraph (b) of subsection (1) substitute-
    "(b) any security, except a floating charge, granted by a registered society over any of its assets," ; and
  (b) the references to section 4 of that Act are to be treated as references to that section as it had effect immediately before its repeal by subsection (2) above.

GENERAL NOTE

This extends to industrial and provident societies the same provisions for floating charges as are extended to ordinary companies.

PART 3

ENFORCEMENT

Scottish Civil Enforcement Commission

50. Scottish Civil Enforcement Commission

(1) There is established a body corporate to be known as the Scottish Civil Enforcement Commission (in this Act, the "Commission") having the functions conferred on it by virtue of this Act and any other enactment.

(2) The Commission must, in the exercise of its functions, act-
  (a) in a manner that encourages equal opportunities and in particular the observance of the equal opportunity requirements; and
  (b) in accordance with any directions given to it by the Scottish Ministers.

(3) In subsection (2)(a) above, "equal opportunities" and "equal opportunity requirements" have the same meanings as in Section L2 of Part II of Schedule 5 to the Scotland Act 1998 (c.46).

(4) The Scottish Ministers may, by regulations-
  (a) confer functions on;
  (b) remove functions from; or
  (c) otherwise modify the functions of,

the Commission.

(5) Regulations made under subsection (4) above may-

    (a) transfer a function to the Commission which is conferred on another person by virtue of any other enactment; and

    (b) make such modifications to any other enactment which the Scottish Ministers consider necessary or expedient in consequence of transferring the function.

(6) The Advisory Council on Messengers-at-Arms and Sheriff Officers is abolished.

(7) Schedule 2 to this Act makes further provision about the Commission.

GENERAL NOTE

At the time of writing, it has been decided not to implement Part 3 because of the cost of setting up the new Commission. Another consideration may have been that the proposed procedure was unnecessarily complex for regulating a profession of about 200 members, especially given that the fact that there was no particular evidence that the profession was poorly regulated to begin with. Nevertheless, the following notes on the legislation, written at the time when Part 3 looked as though it be brought into force, have been retained here in the event that the proposals for the Commission are ever resuscitated.

The profession of sheriff officer, and his senior brother, messenger at arms, has great antiquity, and for many centuries they have been the "enforcers" for Lord Lyon King of Arms. Indeed, his duty to enforce good order on messengers at arms and "officiares of arms" is specifically referred to in the Act *Concerning the Office of Lyoun King-of-Armes and brether Herauldis*, 1592, c.125. Lord Lyon still presides over their investiture and keeps a register of members of the profession. Over time, the role of sheriff officer and messenger at arms has developed, so that now they act in various capacities related to the courts, from the serving of summons and writs, to effecting diligence, the retrieving of children following court orders, receiving payment for debts, providing debt advice and advising creditors on the likelihood of creditors receiving payments from their debtors. Trainee sheriff officers have to sit examinations on basic Scots law, and in particular the law of debt and of civil procedure. Firms of sheriff officers and messengers at arms often also act as investigation agents. It is not a wholly enviable role: although sheriff officers and messengers at arms work in pairs, and commonly are recruited from the ranks of former policemen or ex-service personnel, those whom they visit are not always pleased to see them, and the practicalities of carrying out their duties may not always be easy and on occasion may be dangerous.

Although sheriff officers and messengers at arms had an Advisory Council which met regularly to review the practice of their profession, as part of the general review of bankruptcy and diligence it was felt suitable that the profession should have a new, more accountable body put in charge of it, this body being known as the Scottish Civil Enforcement Commission, set up by s.50 of the 2007 Act. This is, in effect, a quango, and being a quango, there has been much concern in Holyrood about the existence and cost of yet another quango. At the time of writing there is much talk of bonfires of quangos, and if so, this may be one of the quangos that is duly burnt. This would presumably mean that the current arrangements would remain in place, which would be ironic, given that part of the purpose of this Act was to improve the current arrangements in the belief that they were archaic and unaccountable.

The second important change to the profession was that it was felt sensible to change the name of the profession. What was finally approved, with some regrets from traditionalists, was the term "judicial officer".

The Scottish Civil Enforcement Commission, if it is ever set up, must exercise its functions in accordance with any directions given to it by the Scottish Ministers and in a way which encourages equal opportunities and, in particular, complies with the equal opportunity requirements referred to in the Scotland Act 1998 Sch.5.

Subsection (4) gives the Scottish Ministers power, by regulations, to confer functions on the Commission, take functions away from the Commission or to otherwise modify the functions of the Commission. These regulations are subject to affirmative resolution procedure in the Scottish Parliament by virtue of s.224(4)(b)(i) of this Act. "Functions" in this context includes powers and duties (by virtue of s.127 of the Scotland Act 1998 and para.6(3) of the Scotland Act 1998 (Transitory and Transitional Provisions) (Publication and Interpretation etc. of Acts of the Scottish Parliament) Order 1999 (SI 1999/1379). These enable the Scottish Ministers to impose duties on the Commission as well as conferring powers on the Commission.

Subsection (5) provides that the regulations under subs.(4) may transfer a function conferred on another person (including the Scottish Ministers) by another enactment to the Commission. Those regulations may also amend regulations or Acts as a consequence of transferring the function where this is considered necessary or expedient.

Subsection (6) abolishes the Advisory Council on Messengers-at-Arms and Sheriff Officers. The Advisory Council had been set up by Pt V of the 1987 Act, to advise the Court of Session on Acts of Sederunt to regulate the profession.

Schedule 6 to this Act repeals Pt V of the 1987 Act in its entirety and is replaced by Pt 3 of this Act.

Subsection (7) refers to Sch.2. This makes further provision about the make-up of the Commission.

51. Information and annual report

(1) The Commission must provide the Scottish Ministers with information relating to the exercise of the Commission's functions as the Scottish Ministers consider appropriate.

(2) The Commission must prepare a report on its activities during the whole of each financial year as soon as practicable after the end of the period to which the report relates.

(3) A report prepared under subsection (2) above-

    (a) must include a statement of accounts, prepared in accordance with paragraph 33 of schedule 2 to this Act, for the period to which the report relates; and

    (b) may include a statistical analysis of the performance by judicial officers of their functions and the undertaking by officers of activities during the period to which the report relates or any other period specified by the Commission in the report.

(4) The Commission may, in preparing the report under subsection (2) above, require a judicial officer to provide any information it considers necessary or proper for the purposes of preparing the report.

(5) The Commission must-

    (a) send a copy of each report prepared under subsection (2) above to the Scottish Ministers; and

    (b) publish the report.

(6) The Scottish Ministers must lay a copy of a report sent to them under subsection (5)(a) above before the Scottish Parliament.

GENERAL NOTE

This section ensures that each year a report on the Commission's functions is prepared, sent to the Scottish Ministers, published and laid before the Scottish Parliament. Any judicial officer may be required to provide any necessary information for it, and refusal or delay to do so may be "misconduct" in terms of s.67(9)(b).

52. Publication of guidance and other information

(1) The Commission may-

    (a) prepare and publish information and other materials; and

    (b) carry on any other activities,

that it considers appropriate for the purposes of informing and educating the public about the matters mentioned in subsection (2) below.

(2) Those matters are-

    (a) the Commission's functions;

    (b) the functions and, subject to section 56(1) of this Act, the activities of judicial officers; and

    (c) the law of and procedures and practice relating to diligence.

GENERAL NOTE

This section enables the Commission to publicise its activities and in particular to inform and educate the public about the Commission's functions, the functions of judicial officers and the law, procedure and practice of diligence.

53. Published information not to enable identification

Information-
  (a) contained in a report prepared under section 51(2); or
  (b) published under section 52(1) or 56(1),
of this Act must not be in a form which identifies or enables the identification of judicial officers or persons against whom diligence has been executed.

GENERAL NOTE

Since the publicity afforded some matters in either the annual report or the information promulgated under s.52 could be unwelcome either for judicial officers or debtors, the information in the annual report or under s.52 must not lead to individual identification of judicial officers or debtors.

54. Register of judicial officers

(1) The Commission must keep a register of judicial officers, which is to be open to public inspection at reasonable times determined by the Commission.
(2) The Commission may make rules-
  (a) prescribing the particulars and other information to be recorded in the register;
  (b) regulating the procedure by which a judicial officer must intimate such particulars and other information to the Commission;
  (c) requiring the notification to the Commission of changes in the particulars and other information.

GENERAL NOTE

The Commission will keep a register of judicial officers, accessible to the public.

55. Code of practice

(1) The Commission-
  (a) must prepare and publish a code of practice in relation to the exercise of the functions of; and
  (b) may, subject to section 56(2)(a) of this Act, prepare and publish such a code in relation to the undertaking of activities by,
  judicial officers.
(2) The Commission may-
  (a) revise the whole or any part of a code published under this section; and
  (b) publish the revised code.
(3) The Commission must send a copy of each code of practice published under this section to-
  (a) the Scottish Ministers; and
  (b) the association designated as the professional association for judicial officers under section 63(1) of this Act (in this Part, the "professional association").
(4) The Scottish Ministers must lay a copy of a code of practice sent to them under subsection (3)(a) above before the Scottish Parliament.

GENERAL NOTE

The Commission must prepare a code of practice for judicial officers. This code of practice need not necessarily involve the code of practice referred to in s.56(2) which deals with a code of practice for people involved in informal debtor collection.

Judicial officers are expected to adhere to the code of practice (s.77) though failure to do so does not necessarily mean that criminal proceedings against the judicial officer will take place.

56. Publication of information relating to informal debt collection

(1) The Commission may publish information and other materials for the purposes of-
  (a) promoting good practice in; and
  (b) informing the public about,
  informal debt collection.

(2) Information published under subsection (1) above may take the form of-
  (a) a code of practice for persons undertaking informal debt collection; or
  (b) guidance for those persons.

(3) Where the information published under subsection (1) above takes the form of a code of practice for persons undertaking informal debt collection, subsections (2), (3)(a) and (4) of section 55 of this Act apply as they apply to a code of practice published under that section.

(4) In this section, "informal debt collection" means the collection of debts (including debts which are not constituted by decrees or documents of debt) by methods other than diligence.

(5) In subsection (4) above, "decrees" and "documents of debt" are to be construed in accordance with section 221 of this Act.

GENERAL NOTE

This permits the Commission to draw up a code of practice for informal debt collection. Informal debt collection is the process of recovering debt other than through the formal process of diligence, and may be done by writing to or visiting the debtor. It will not cover consumer debt under the Consumer Credit Act 1974 since that is already regulated by the Office of Fair Trading. Section 56 therefore covers informal debt collection for such matters such as commercial debt and public debt. The Commission may publish information and other materials promoting good practice.

Judicial officers

57. Judicial officers

(1) There is established an office to be known as judicial officer and any person who holds a commission as officer has the functions conferred by virtue of this Act and any other enactment.

(2) A person may be granted a commission as a judicial officer by the Lord President of the Court of Session but only on the recommendation of the Commission under section 58(1) of this Act.

(3) Where the Lord President grants a person a commission as a judicial officer, the Commission must intimate that decision to-
  (a) the person who applied for the commission; and
  (b) the professional association.

(4) A judicial officer who holds a commission granted under subsection (2) above may carry out that officer's functions in the whole of Scotland.

(5) Subject to section 60(2) of this Act, any person who wishes to be a judicial officer must apply to the Commission.

(6) A judicial officer may be deprived of office by the Lord President but only where-

(a) the disciplinary committee of the Commission (in this Part, the "disciplinary committee") recommends under section 72(5)(a)(ii) or (6)(b) of this Act that the officer be deprived of office;

(b) any time limit within which the officer may appeal under section 74 of this Act has expired; and

(c) no such appeal has been made.

(7) Where the Lord President deprives a judicial officer of office, the Commission must intimate that decision to-

(a) the judicial officer;

(b) the Court of Session;

(c) every sheriff principal; and

(d) the professional association.

GENERAL NOTE

What were formerly sheriff officers and messengers at arms will henceforth be known as judicial officers. Section 60 abolishes those two former offices, although anyone already qualified as a sheriff officer or messenger at arms as at the day before this part of the Act is brought into force will be deemed to be a judicial officer with effect from the date the part of the Act is brought into force. A judicial officer will need a commission from the Lord President but only where the Commission has recommended his commission under s.58 following an application to the Commission. Once commissioned, he may carry out his duties throughout Scotland, unlike the present situation where sheriff officers may only act within their sheriffdom. He may be relieved of his commission by the Lord President but only where the disciplinary committee of the Commission has recommended that this take place, where the time limit for any appeal to the Inner House has expired, or where no appeal has been lodged. The time limit is yet to be established. Where the judicial officer is deprived of office, this must be duly intimated to the judicial officer himself, the Court of Session, each sheriff principal and the judicial officers' own professional association referred to in s.63.

58. Appointment of judicial officer

(1) Where the Commission is satisfied-

(a) that a person who applies to it is a fit and proper person to be appointed as a judicial officer; and

(b) having regard to-

(i) the number of persons already holding commission as officers; and

(ii) any other matters the Commission considers relevant,

that the appointment is appropriate,

the Commission must, subject to section 63(3) of this Act, recommend that the Lord President of the Court of Session grants that person a commission as an officer.

(2) The Commission must send a copy of its decision on an application for a commission as a judicial officer to the person who applied for the commission.

(3) Where the Lord President grants a person a commission as a judicial officer under section 57(2) of this Act, the Commission must issue an official identity card, in a form determined by the Commission, to the officer.

(4) A judicial officer carrying out an officer's functions must, on being requested to do so, exhibit the official identity card issued under subsection (3) above.

(5) The Commission may make rules about-

(a) the procedure for applications for a commission as a judicial officer;

(b) the qualifications that a person must have before that person may be granted a commission under section 57(2) of this Act;

(c) the examinations that a person may be required to undertake in pursuance of a qualification prescribed by rules made under paragraph (b) above;

(d) the training that a person must undertake before that person may be granted a commission; and

(e) any other matters in relation to applications as it considers appropriate.

GENERAL NOTE

The Commission is empowered to draw up rules and qualifications for admission as a judicial officer, and to set up training for future judicial officers. The Commission will recommend suitable persons to be judicial officers, taking into account the current number of judicial officers. Judicial officers will have an official identity card which must be exhibited on request. The proposed judicial officer must be a member of the judicial officers' professional association (s.63).

59. Annual fee

(1) The Commission may make rules requiring every judicial officer holding a commission to pay an annual fee to the Commission.

(2) Rules made under subsection (1) above may include provision-

    (a) specifying the date by which the fee must be paid each year;

    (b) specifying the manner in which it must be paid; and

    (c) about any other matters in relation to the fee that the Commission considers appropriate.

(3) Anything done by the Commission under this section must be approved by the Scottish Ministers.

GENERAL NOTE

The Commission may draw up rules for the payment of an annual fee to the Commission. These must be approved by the Scottish Ministers.

Abolition of offices of messenger-at-arms and sheriff officer

60. Abolition of offices of messenger-at-arms and sheriff officer

(1) The offices of messenger-at-arms and sheriff officer are abolished.

(2) Any person who, immediately before the day on which this section comes into force, holds a commission as a messenger-at-arms or sheriff officer is deemed, from that day, to hold a commission as a judicial officer as if granted under section 57(2) of this Act.

(3) Notwithstanding subsection (1) above and subject to subsection (4) below, a judicial officer may carry out any function which, under any rule of law, it was competent for a messenger-at-arms or sheriff officer to carry out.

(4) Subsection (3) above applies only in so far as the function is not inconsistent with any provision of this Act or any other enactment.

(5) References in any enactment (other than the references in the enactments mentioned in subsection (6) below) to-

    (a) a "messenger-at-arms";

    (b) a "sheriff officer"; and

    (c) an "officer of court",

are to be construed as references to a judicial officer.

(6) Those enactments are-

    (a) section 18 of the Confirmation of Executors (Scotland) Act 1858 (c.56) (power to make Acts of Sederunt for the purposes of the Act);

    (b) section 13 of the Heritable Securities (Scotland) Act 1894 (c.44) (trustees or others to have powers conferred by the Act where debtor incapacitated);

    (c) section 18(1) of the Company Directors Disqualification Act 1986 (c.46) (Secretary of State's power to require particulars of disqualification orders or undertakings); and

    (d) section 127(1) of the Criminal Procedure (Scotland) Act 1995 (c.46) (Clerk of Justiciary to furnish forms etc. relating to appeals).

GENERAL NOTE

Sheriff officers and messengers at arms are to be abolished, though existing sheriff officers and messengers at arms will be "grandfathered" into the their new office of judicial officer. The current seniority of messenger at arms to sheriff officer disappears. All references in legislation to messengers at arms, sheriff officer and officer of court are henceforth to be deemed to refer to judicial officers, except in the particular circumstances indicated in subs.6 where the term "officer of court" is being used in a different manner, completely unrelated to the process of debt enforcement or diligence.

Regulation of judicial officers

61. Regulation of judicial officers

(1) The Scottish Ministers may, by regulations-

    (a) confer functions on;

    (b) remove functions from; or

    (c) otherwise modify the functions of,

judicial officers.

(2) The Scottish Ministers may, by regulations-

    (a) prescribe the types of business association which judicial officers may form in order to carry out their functions;

    (b) make provision about the ownership, membership, management and control of those business associations;

    (c) prescribe conditions which must be satisfied by those business associations;

    (d) make provision regulating the fees and charges which may be levied by an officer in the performance of the officer's functions.

(3) Before making regulations under subsection (1) or (2) above, the Scottish Ministers must consult the Commission.

(4) The Commission may make rules-

    (a) regulating, without prejudice to sections 67 to 73 of this Act, the conduct of judicial officers;

    (b) prohibiting the undertaking by officers of activities which appear to the Commission to be incompatible with their functions;

    (c) permitting, subject to any conditions the Commission provides for in the rules, the undertaking by officers for remuneration of activities, not appearing to the Commission to be incompatible with their functions;

    (d) which make provision-

        (i) about the accounts and finances of officers, including the keeping and auditing of officers' accounts;

        (ii) for the keeping of records by officers and the inspection of those records; and

        (iii) about the finding of caution by officers; and

    (e) regulating other matters in relation to officers that the Commission considers appropriate.

(5) A judicial officer must not undertake any activity which is not connected with the officer's functions for remuneration unless the officer obtains the permission of the Commission.

(6) The Commission must not withhold permission under subsection (5) above unless it appears to the Commission that the undertaking by the judicial officer of the activity would be incompatible with the officer's functions.

(7) The Commission may-

    (a) attach conditions to; or

    (b) revoke,

any permission granted under subsection (5) above.

GENERAL NOTE

This section allows the Scottish Ministers to regulate the profession of judicial officer. The regulations which the Scottish Ministers may use for this purpose are subject to the negative resolution procedure before the Scottish Parliament as indicated in s.224(3). The Scottish Ministers will be able to control not only the activities that judicial officers may undertake, but also what type of business organisation may be used by judicial officers and what fees they may charge. Before the regulations are made, the Scottish Ministers must consult the Commission. The Commission in its own right may make rules that both permit judicial officers from carrying out activities which are connected with their profession (such as unofficial debt advice) and also prohibit judicial officers from carrying out any activity which appears to the Commission to be incompatible with judicial officers' professional functions, such as, say, pawnbroking or estate agency. The Commission may also produce rules relating to the keeping of proper financial records by judicial officers.

Concerns have been expressed about the regulations that the Ministers may introduce concerning the ownership of judicial officers' firms and the manner in which the firms may be set up. It was felt that it was important that judicial officers should have some degree of personal interest in their firms and that ideally judicial officers should be partners in a partnership of judicial officers or members of a limited liability partnership, as is broadly the case throughout Scotland at present. These two types of business vehicles are referred to in s.62, but there is so far nothing positively denying the ownership of a judicial officers' business by a limited liability company. There were worries that a judicial officers' business, owned by a company, or owned by a non-UK company, would be subject to commercial pressures to drive up its business and turnover at the expense of debtors. A limited liability company might also become insolvent, potentially leading debtors and indeed creditors in the lurch. This may be partially resolved by the requirement that judicial officers provide caution for their actions (see subs.(4)(d)(iii)) and possibly by having one bank account for the judicial officers' firms' own funds and entirely separate bank accounts for the funds held on trust for their clients (i.e. the creditors) and funds held on trust from the debtors and due to be made over to their creditors.

It is also suggested that the legislation in this section or in s.62 has not really addressed the issue of whether or not judicial officers may run their business as a limited liability company.

Since there is reference to a limited liability partnership, the concept of the separate legal personality of the firm from the actual judicial officers seems to have been accepted, but if this is the case, it would seem surprising if judicial officers could not run their business as a limited liability company, with the possibility of the shares in that company being owned by those who had no particular connection with the underlying business or indeed the debtors in the area where the firm was working. The same would be true of a limited liability partnership, since the members of a limited liability partnership would not necessarily have to be the actual judicial officers who were carrying out the firm's business. Indeed, the members of a limited liability partnership could perfectly well be limited companies in their own right. If the Scottish Ministers or the Commission wish to ensure that judicial officers could only practise their profession through the medium of a partnership or sole trader, (or possibly an unlimited company) and therefore be personally liable, such a provision would probably require an amendment to the Companies Act 2006, specifically to prevent judicial officers incorporating. Such a move would be a deterrent to anyone setting up a new firm of judicial officers, and would be at odds with the position in England and Wales where bailiffs (other than the ones specifically employed by Her Majesty's Court Service) are allowed to incorporate.

It therefore remains to be seen what regulations and rules are drawn up in the light of ss.61 and 62 but careful consideration will need to be given to the drafting of those regulations and rules.

62. Duty to notify Commission of bankruptcy etc

(1) Where, in relation to a judicial officer, any of the events mentioned in subsection (2) below occurs, the officer must, before the expiry of the period of 28 days beginning with the occurrence of the event, notify the Commission in writing of it.

(2) The events referred to in subsection (1) above are-
   (a) the sequestration of the judicial officer;
   (b) the granting by the officer of a trust deed for creditors;
   (c) the making of a bankruptcy restrictions order in respect of the officer;
   (d) the acceptance by the Accountant in Bankruptcy of a bankruptcy restrictions undertaking made by the officer;
   (e) the making, under the Company Directors Disqualification Act 1986 (c. 46), of a disqualification order against the officer;
   (f) where the officer is a partner in a partnership the sole or main business of which is the provision of judicial officer services-
      (i) the granting by the partnership of a trust deed for creditors; or
      (ii) the sequestration of the partnership;
   (g) where the officer is a member in a limited liability partnership the sole or main business of which is the provision of judicial officer services, the commencement of the winding up of that partnership on the ground of insolvency.

(3) In subsection (2) above, "trust deed" has the meaning given by section 5(4A) of the 1985 Act.

GENERAL NOTE

This section is applicable when a judicial officer or his firm is subject to various insolvency events or insolvency-related proceedings. The judicial officer is required to notify the Commission of any of these events or proceedings within 28 days. There seems to be no requirement that a company that carries on a business involving the use and employment of suitably qualified judicial officers should intimate its winding up to the Commission. Section 67(9)(d) provides that failure to notify is misconduct. Notification may be given electronically under s.78(b).

63. Judicial officers' professional association

(1) The Scottish Ministers, by regulations-
    (a) must designate an association as the professional association for judicial officers; and
    (b) may make provision in relation to the functions, constitution and procedures of the professional association.

(2) The Scottish Ministers may not make regulations under subsection (1) above without first consulting-
    (a) the Commission;
    (b) representatives of the professional association or, as the case may be, proposed professional association; and
    (c) such other bodies or persons who appear to the Scottish Ministers to have an interest.

(3) A person may not hold a commission as a judicial officer unless that person is a member of the professional association.

GENERAL NOTE

The Scottish Ministers are obliged to designate an association as the professional association of judicial officers, and to make provision for its operation. They must consult with interested parties first. No-one may act as a judicial officer without being a member of that association.

64. Duty of professional association to forward complaints to Commission

Where the professional association receives a complaint about a judicial officer or any services provided by the officer, the association must send details of the complaint and any material which accompanies it to the Commission.

GENERAL NOTE

Any complaint received by the association about a judicial officer or the services he provided must be forwarded to the Commission.

65. Information from professional association

The Commission may require the professional association to provide any information the Commission considers necessary or proper for the purposes of-
    (a) any inspection under section 66 of this Act;
    (b) any investigation under section 67 of this Act; or
    (c) the consideration by the disciplinary committee of any matter under section 71 of this Act.

GENERAL NOTE

The Commission may require the association to provide such information as it needs for the inspection, the investigation or the potential disciplining of any judicial officer.

66. Inspection of judicial officer

(1) The Commission may appoint a person to inspect the work or particular aspects of the work of a judicial officer.

(2) A person appointed under subsection (1) above must, if required to do so by the Commission, inquire into any activities undertaken for remuneration by the judicial officer.

(3) A person appointed under subsection (1) above must submit a report of the inspection and of any inquiry under subsection (2) above to the Commission.

(4) The Commission must pay a person appointed under subsection (1) above-

    (a) a fee, unless the person is employed in the civil service and the person carries out the inspection in that person's capacity as a civil servant; and

    (b) any outlays reasonably incurred by the person,

in connection with an inspection, inquiry and report under this section.

GENERAL NOTE

The person whom the Commission appoint to inspect the judicial officer must inquire into the officer's activities and prepare a report. He is entitled to his fees (unless he is carrying out the inspection as part of his civil service duties) and expenses. He is to prepare a report for the Commission. He may be the same person as the investigator referred in the next section (see s.67(8)).

67. Investigation of alleged misconduct by judicial officer

(1) This section applies where-

    (a) a person appointed under section 66(1) of this Act submits a report to the Commission disclosing that a judicial officer may have been guilty of misconduct;

    (b) a sheriff or a Senator of the College of Justice (other than the Lord President) makes a report to the Commission alleging misconduct by an officer;

    (c) the professional association sends, under section 64 of this Act, details of a complaint about an officer to the Commission;

    (d) any other person complains to the Commission alleging misconduct by an officer; or

    (e) the Commission otherwise has reason to believe that an officer may have been guilty of misconduct.

(2) The Commission may disregard a report or complaint under subsection (1) above if the Commission considers it to be frivolous or vexatious.

(3) The Commission, after giving the judicial officer an opportunity to admit or deny the misconduct or to give an explanation of the matter, may appoint a person to investigate the matter.

(4) But the Commission may not appoint a person under subsection (3) above if the judicial officer-

    (a) admits the misconduct in writing; or

    (b) gives a satisfactory explanation of the matter.

(5) The person appointed under subsection (3) above, after carrying out the investigation-

    (a) must report to the Commission; and

    (b) may, if of the opinion that there is-

        (i) a probable case of misconduct; and

        (ii) evidence sufficient to justify disciplinary proceedings,

make a recommendation that the matter be referred to the disciplinary committee.

  (6) The Commission must, where it receives a recommendation under subsection (5)(b) above, refer the matter to the disciplinary committee to be dealt with under section 71 of this Act.

  (7) The Commission must pay the person appointed under subsection (3) above-

    (a) a fee, unless the person is employed in the civil service and the person carries out the investigation in that person's capacity as a civil servant; and

    (b) any outlays reasonably incurred by the person,

in connection with an investigation under this section and any hearing under section 71 of this Act.

  (8) In a case to which subsection (1)(a) above applies, the person appointed under subsection (3) above may be the same person as was appointed under section 66(1) of this Act.

  (9) In this Part, "misconduct" includes-

    (a) conduct tending to bring the office of judicial officer into disrepute;

    (b) failure to comply with a requirement imposed under section 51(4) of this Act;

    (c) where a fee is due by virtue of rules made under subsection (1) of section 59 of this Act and a date has been specified by rules made under subsection (2)(a) of that section, failure to pay the fee within 3 months of that date; and

    (d) failure to notify the Commission under subsection (1) of section 62 of this Act of the occurrence of an event mentioned in subsection (2) of that section.

GENERAL NOTE

Where the various circumstances in subs.(1) disclose that a judicial officer may have been guilty of misconduct, the officer will be given an opportunity to present his side of the story, and the Commission may, if necessary, appoint someone to investigate the matter. No investigation is necessary if the officer admits his misconduct in writing (though only in writing-an oral admission would be insufficient). The person appointed may in turn, if necessary, recommend to the Commission that the matter be referred to the disciplinary committee if he is of the opinion that there is a probable case of misconduct and sufficient evidence to justify disciplinary proceedings. If the Commission receives such a recommendation, it must refer the matter to the disciplinary committee (see s.71). Misconduct is stated to include conduct tending to bring the office of judicial officer into disrepute, failure to comply with the providing of information for the preparation of the Commission's annual report (s.51(4), the failure by the office to pay his annual fee to the Commission within three months of the due date (s.59(1)), and the failure to tell the Commission within 28 days of an event of insolvency event or disqualification as a director all in terms of s.62(1).

68. Suspension of judicial officer pending outcome of disciplinary or criminal proceedings

  (1) This section applies-

    (a) in any of the circumstances mentioned in section 67(1) of this Act;

    (b) where section 70 of this Act applies; or

(c) where a judicial officer has been charged with an offence.

(2) The disciplinary committee may make an order suspending the judicial officer from practice for a period specified in the order.

(3) The disciplinary committee may-

    (a) extend the period specified in the order; or

    (b) revoke the order.

GENERAL NOTE

During the period during which the judicial officer is awaiting disciplinary or criminal proceedings and is being inspected or investigated, he may be suspended by order of the disciplinary committee, as he may also be if the Commission becomes aware that the judicial officer is subject to an insolvency event or disqualification under s.62(1), and, while not necessarily guilty of misconduct, that insolvency event or disqualification nevertheless gives cause for concern about his conduct, the exercise of his function or any "activities" that he carries out. For the meaning of activities, see the note to s.70.

69. Commission's duty in relation to offences or misconduct by judicial officer

(1) This section applies where-

    (a) the Commission becomes aware that a judicial officer has been convicted by a court of any offence; or

    (b) an officer admits misconduct under section 67(4)(a) of this Act.

(2) The Commission must refer the matter to the disciplinary committee to be dealt with under section 71 of this Act.

(3) Subsection (1)(a) above and section 72(4) of this Act are without prejudice to section 4(3)(b) of the Rehabilitation of Offenders Act 1974 (c.53) (non-disclosure no grounds for dismissal etc.); and in those provisions "offence" means any offence of which the judicial officer has been convicted before or after that person was granted a commission as an officer, other than any offence disclosed in that person's application for such a commission.

GENERAL NOTE

This deals with the situation where a judicial officer is convicted by a court of any offence, or admits in writing his misconduct (see s.67(4)(a)). Although there is a proviso that spent offences in terms of the Rehabilitation of Offenders Act 1974 s.4(3)(b) which permits past convictions within the relative time spans need not be disclosed in job applications and the failure not to disclose past convictions may not be used as grounds for dismissal, the purpose of this provision is that if the Commission becomes aware that judicial officer has committed any offence, the matter must be referred to the disciplinary committee. Any offence or conviction that was disclosed in the applicant's application to become a judicial officer is not relevant in this context.

What is slightly surprising is the wideness of the rule: while it is clearly desirable that a judicial officer should, like Caesar's wife, be beyond reproach, the wording clearly says "any offence", which would include the most trivial traffic offence or even some offence such as dropping litter. It is perhaps the case that the Commission needs to become aware of the conviction first, which may not always happen. One might have expected the wording to be less wide.

70. Commission's power in relation to judicial officer's bankruptcy etc

(1) This section applies where the Commission-

    (a) becomes aware (whether by the judicial officer notifying it under section 62(1) of this Act or otherwise) that an event mentioned in subsection (2) of that section has occurred; and

(b) considers that the occurrence of that event or circumstances surrounding it, although falling short of misconduct and not involving the commission of an offence, give rise to concerns about-

    (i) the officer;

    (ii) the exercise by the officer of that officer's functions; or

    (iii) the undertaking by that officer of activities.

(2) The Commission may refer the matter to the disciplinary committee to be dealt with under section 71 of this Act.

GENERAL NOTE

Where the Commission becomes aware of any insolvency event or disqualification, and considers that the event or disqualification, while not of itself a matter of misconduct, nevertheless causes concern about the officer, the exercise of his functions as an officer, or the undertaking by that officer of activities, the matter may be referred to the disciplinary committee.

The wording in the statute "the undertaking by that officer of activities" at s.70(1)(b)(iii) is perhaps unfortunate and it is possible that originally there were supposed to be further parts to this sentence, thereby tying in the word "activities" with the use of the same word in ss.61(4)(b), (c) and 61(5) and (6). Presumably the activities that are intended to be referred to are ones that are either part of the judicial officer's professional business, or any other, perhaps more questionable, activities in which he is involved but which are not entirely suitable for a judicial officer to be involved in.

Disciplinary proceedings

71. Referrals to the disciplinary committee

(1) In dealing with any matter referred to the disciplinary committee under section 67(6), 69(2) or 70(2) of this Act, the committee-

(a) must consider-

    (i) any report made to the Commission under section 67(5)(a) of this Act; and

    (ii) any other relevant information held by the Commission; and

(b) may, if it considers it appropriate, hold a hearing.

(2) Where the judicial officer to whom a referred matter relates requests a hearing before the disciplinary committee, the committee must hold one.

(3) The disciplinary committee must, when holding a hearing, afford the persons mentioned in subsection (4) below the opportunity to-

(a) make representations (whether orally or in writing); and

(b) lead, or produce, evidence.

(4) Those persons are-

(a) the judicial officer to whom the hearing relates;

(b) where there was an investigation under section 67 of this Act, the person who carried it out; and

(c) any other person the committee considers appropriate.

(5) The disciplinary committee may award expenses in any hearing in favour of or against the judicial officer to whom the hearing relates.

(6) The Commission's expenses in any hearing include any payments made under section 66(4) and 67(7) of this Act.

(7) Where expenses are awarded under subsection (5) above-

     (a) in favour of the judicial officer, the expenses are recoverable by the officer from the Commission; or

     (b) against the officer, the expenses are recoverable by the Commission from the officer.

(8) The Commission may make rules in relation to the procedures, including the procedures to be followed during a hearing, of the disciplinary committee.

(9) Any rules made under subsection (8) above must be approved by the Scottish Ministers.

GENERAL NOTE

This explains the procedure for the holding of disciplinary committee hearings. The judicial officer is entitled to demand a hearing. The provisions for expenses are dealt with. The Commission may make further rules for the conduct of hearings. The rules must be approved by the Scottish Ministers.

72. Disciplinary committee's powers

(1) This section applies where, after dealing with a matter referred to the disciplinary committee under section 67(6), 69(2) or 70(2) of this Act, the committee is satisfied that it is appropriate to take further action under this section.

(2) Where the disciplinary committee is satisfied that—

     (a) the judicial officer is guilty of misconduct; or

     (b) the officer has admitted misconduct under section 67(4)(a) of this Act,

the committee may make one or more of the orders mentioned in subsection (5) below.

(3) Where the matter referred to the disciplinary committee is one to which section 70 of this Act applies, the committee may make an order under paragraph (a) or (c) of subsection (5) below.

(4) Where the judicial officer has been convicted of an offence, the disciplinary committee may make an order under paragraph (a), (b) or (c) of subsection (5) below.

(5) Those orders are—

     (a) an order—

          (i) suspending the judicial officer from practice for a period specified in the order; or

          (ii) recommending that the Lord President of the Court of Session deprives the officer of office;

     (b) an order censuring the officer;

     (c) an order restricting—

          (i) the functions which the officer may exercise; or

          (ii) the activities which the officer may undertake,

for such period as the committee considers appropriate;

     (d) an order imposing a fine on the officer not exceeding level 4 on the standard scale;

     (e) if the misconduct consists of or includes the charging of excessive fees or outlays, an order requiring the officer to repay so much of those fees or outlays as is excessive together with such interest as the disciplinary committee considers appropriate.

(6) Where a judicial officer fails to comply with an order under subsection (5)(d) above the disciplinary committee may, if it has not already done so, make an order—

(a) suspending the officer from practice for a period specified in the order; or

(b) recommending that the Lord President of the Court of Session deprives the officer of office.

(7) The disciplinary committee must send a copy of any decision it makes under this section to the judicial officer to whom that decision relates.

GENERAL NOTE

This section outlines the powers of the disciplinary committee and what sanctions it may impose as a result of the orders it gives. There are slightly different sanctions imposed depending on which sections of this Act are being used as the grounds for the disciplining. Where the judicial officer is guilty of misconduct or has admitted misconduct, he is open to any of the penalties under subs.(5). Where the officer's conduct has given cause for concern under s.70, but misconduct as such has not taken place, the penalties are restricted to paras (a) (suspension for a period or deprival of office) or (c) (restriction on the officer's functions or the activities he may undertake (for "activities" see ss.61(4)(b), (c) and 61(5) and (6))). Where the judicial officer has been convicted of an offence, he may suffer the penalties of subss.(5)(a) and (c) (as just indicated) or (b) (censure).

The penalty under subs.5(d) is to suffer a fine not exceeding level 4 on the standard scale. The standard fines are derived from the Criminal Justice Act 1991 and at the time of writing a level 4 fine is £2,500. Where the fine is not paid, there are further sanctions under subs.6 to have the officer suspended from practice or deprived of office.

If the officer has charged excessive fees and outlays, under the penalty under subs.5(e) he will be required to repay those fees and outlays with interest at such rate as the committee sees appropriate.

There is a right of appeal from these orders under s.74.

73. Orders under sections 68 and 72: supplementary provision

(1) An order mentioned in section 72(5)(d) of this Act is enforceable as if it were an extract registered decree arbitral bearing a warrant for execution issued by the sheriff.

(2) The Commission may recover any fine imposed by such an order.

(3) The Commission must intimate any order made by the disciplinary committee under section 68(2) or (3) or 72 (other than an order under section 72(5)(a)(ii) or (6)(b)) of this Act to-

(a) the Court of Session;

(b) every sheriff principal; and

(c) the professional association.

GENERAL NOTE

Any order issued under ss.68 or 72 is directly enforceable as if it were a decree arbitral, with a warrant for execution thereby allowing, ironically, a judicial officer to enforce diligence against the judicial officer found guilty under ss.68 and 72. The Commission must intimate any order to the Court of Session, each sheriff principal and the professional association.

Appeals

74. Appeals from decisions under sections 58, 68 and 72

(1) Where the Commission decides under section 58(1) of this Act not to recommend that the Lord President grants a person a commission as a judicial officer, the person who applied may appeal to the Inner House against that decision.

(2) Where the disciplinary committee makes an order under-

(a) section 68(2) or (3)(a); or

(b) section 72(2), (3), (4) or (6),

of this Act, the judicial officer to whom the order relates may appeal to the Inner House against that order.

(3) The decision of the Inner House on an appeal under subsection (1) or (2) above is final.

(4) The Court of Session may, by Act of Sederunt, prescribe the procedure in relation to an appeal under subsection (1) or (2) above.

GENERAL NOTE

An applicant for a commission to be a judicial officer may appeal to the Inner House against the Commission's recommendation not to admit him as an officer under s.58. A judicial officer who has been subject to a disciplinary order under ss.68 (suspension) or 72 (orders following misconduct, offences, failure to pay fines) may appeal to the Inner House. There is no further appeal after the Inner House. Court of Session rules for the procedure will in due course be drafted.

Miscellaneous

75. Judicial officer's actions void where officer has interest

(1) Anything done by a judicial officer in exercising or purporting to exercise a prescribed function in relation to a matter in which the officer has an interest is void.

(2) A judicial officer has an interest in a matter where the matter-
  (a) is one in which the officer has an interest as an individual; or
  (b) consists of or includes a debt in relation to which any of the circumstances mentioned in subsection (3) below apply.

(3) The circumstances referred to in subsection (2)(b) above are that the debt is due to or by-
  (a) a business associate of the judicial officer;
  (b) a member of the officer's family; or
  (c) a company or firm, and the officer, a business associate of the officer or a member of the officer's family-
    (i) is a director or partner of that company or firm;
    (ii) holds, either alone or along with an other person, a controlling interest in that company or firm; or
    (iii) has a pecuniary interest in that company or firm and the sole or main business of the company or firm is the purchase of debts for enforcement.

(4) Any reference in subsection (3) above to-
  (a) a business associate of a judicial officer is to be construed as a reference to a co-director, partner, employer, employee, agent or principal of the officer;
  (b) a controlling interest in a company is to be construed as a reference to an interest giving a person control of a company within the meaning of section 840 of the Income and Corporation Taxes Act 1988 (c.1) (meaning of "control").

(5) Any reference in subsection (3) above to a member of a judicial officer's family is to be construed as a reference to-
  (a) the spouse of the officer;
  (b) a person living together with the officer as husband and wife;
  (c) a civil partner of the officer;
  (d) a person living with the officer in a relationship which has the characteristics of the relationship between a husband and wife except that the person and the officer are of the same sex;
  (e) a parent of the officer;
  (f) a brother or sister of the officer;

  (g) a child of the officer, including-
    (i) a stepchild; and
    (ii) any child brought up or treated by the officer or any person mentioned in paragraph (b), (c) or (d) above as a child of the officer or, as the case may be, of that person;
  (h) a grandchild of the officer,
  and any relationships of the half blood or by affinity are to be construed as relationships of the full blood.

(6) In subsection (4)(a) above, "principal" does not include a principal in a contract for the carrying out by the judicial officer of the prescribed function in relation to the debt concerned.

(7) In subsections (1) and (6) above, "prescribed function" means any function conferred on a judicial officer by virtue of this Act or any other enactment which the Scottish Ministers by regulations specify for the purposes of this section.

GENERAL NOTE

This deals with the situation where a judicial officer has an interest in the matter that he is supposed to be dealing with in his capacity as a judicial officer. So, for example, if the judicial officer were told to collect a debt due to a creditor from a member of the officer's close family, ideally he should not act; but if he did help that family member in any way in his capacity as a judicial officer, any help he provided (such as giving the debtor extra time to pay) would be void and of no effect. This section presumably still applies in the, admittedly unlikely, situation where the judicial officer correctly carries out the required diligence in the proper manner against a family member or business in which he or his family has an interest. It is little surprising that there is no use of the word "knowingly" in the section, for it would not be completely impossible for an officer to be required to carry out diligence against, say, a stepson of whom he had no knowledge. This section defines the word interest to cover not only close family relationships but business relationships, include that of employee, controlling interest in a company and business associate.

76. Measure of damages payable by judicial officer for negligence or other fault

For the avoidance of doubt, nothing in this Part-
  (a) revives any rule of law whereby, if a messenger-at-arms or a sheriff officer has been found liable to a creditor for negligent delay or failure to execute diligence, or for other fault in the execution of diligence, the damages payable by the messenger or, as the case may be, officer are determined solely by reference to the amount of the debt; or
  (b) applies any such rule of law to a judicial officer.

GENERAL NOTE

Formerly where a sheriff officer or messenger at arms acted negligently in the execution of his duties, under the common law the damages payable were relative to the debt he was supposed to be recovering. This rule was abolished by s.85 of the DSA 1987, but as that too is being abolished, it was necessary to restate s.85 in the 2007 Act to prevent the common law reviving. Consequently the normal rules for assessing damages apply.

77. Effect of code of practice

(1) A judicial officer must, in exercising the officer's functions or undertaking any activities, have regard to the provisions (so far as they are applicable) of any code of practice published under section 55 or 56 of this Act.

(2) A failure on the part of a judicial officer to comply with any provision of a code of practice does not of itself render the officer liable to any criminal or civil proceedings.

(3) A code of practice is admissible in evidence in any criminal or civil proceedings.

(4) If any provision of a code of practice appears to-

    (a) the court or tribunal conducting any civil or criminal proceedings; or

    (b) the disciplinary committee holding a hearing under section 71 of this Act,

to be relevant to any question arising in the proceedings, that provision of the code may be taken into account in determining that question.

GENERAL NOTE

Judicial officers are expected to adhere to the Code of Practice published under ss.55 and 56 of the 2007 Act. Failure to adhere to it is not a civil or criminal offence, but, as with the Highway Code, a failure to follow it weakens the judicial officer's position, and the code itself will be admissible in evidence in criminal or civil proceedings against the judicial officer.

78. Electronic publications and communications

In this Part-

    (a) references to "publishing" include publishing by electronic means and cognate expressions are to be construed accordingly; and

    (b) any reference to a notification, admission or representation being in writing includes a reference to that notification, admission or representation being an electronic communication.

GENERAL NOTE

All the references to notification and publishing referred in this part, dealing with judicial officers, may be carried out by means of electronic communication.

PART 4

LAND ATTACHMENT AND RESIDUAL ATTACHMENT

CHAPTER I

ABOLITION OF ADJUDICATION FOR DEBT

GENERAL NOTE

Land attachment is designed to replace adjudication for debt. Adjudication for debt is a very old procedure, dating from the Adjudication Act 1621, which enables a creditor effectively to seize a debtor's heritage in satisfaction of his debt following a decree (or other document of debt enforceable by diligence). It is a cumbersome process, little used, and requires an application to the Court of Session and a potential wait of up to 10 years, known as the "legal" before the creditor (the "adjudger") can obtain the debtor's heritage. In the meantime, he is able to remove the debtor from the property and to take the rents from the debtor's property, and carry out any necessary repairs.

Because it is so cumbersome and time-consuming, and generally more appropriate for an agricultural economy than a modern commercial one, few creditors will use it unless they are prepared to take a very long term view on the desirability of the debtor's property. This places Scotland in the relatively unusual position that there has been no straightforward and easily used method of enforcing payment by debtors by the compulsory sale of their heritable property. Most other developed economies have a system, sometimes in principle similar to adjudication but without the ten year period, whereby a debtor's heritage can if necessary be sold effectively over the debtor's head. Alternatively, the decree or other instrument of debt is registered as a form of mortgage against the debtor's property which will need to be discharged before the property can be sold.

In practice in Scotland most creditors have to rely on inhibition which has the effect of ensuring that the debtor cannot sell his property without the consent of the creditor, and this is reasonably effective — but it does not prevent a debtor holding on to his property until he chooses to sell, and if the rise in value of his property is greater than the cost of interest on the debt, he may be tempted not to sell the property and thereby continue to delay payment on the debt.

Alternatively, if a creditor does not wish to wait until the debtor chooses to put his property on the market, or adjudicate for debt, a creditor may sequestrate the debtor, or put a debtor company into compulsory liquidation. This may be more than the situation requires, for a creditor might well be content with forcing a "won't pay" debtor to sell one of his houses rather than sequestrating the debtor with all the extra inconvenience that might cause. Sequestrating the debtor or having a debtor company wound up might cause the debtor's business to collapse, cause debtor's employees to lose their jobs and attract obloquy to the creditor, even where the original delay in payment or the reason for non-payment was occasioned by the debtor's behaviour.

In order to have a slightly quicker method of extracting payment out of heritage-owning debtors than adjudication for debt or inhibition, and a less drastic sanction than sequestration or liquidation, land attachment has been invented. It is not in its own right particularly complicated, and does not require applications to the Court of Session. The only really complex area is ensuring that the sale of the debtor's property does not cause undue harshness to the debtor (where the debtor is not a business) and that the needs of the debtor's family are taken into account. However, from a political point of view, there is a concern that the legislation, as framed, could potentially allow a debtor to have his home sold over his head for the relatively small sum of £3,000, and thus increase homelessness. This is where the difficulty lies, and why at the time of writing the legislation has not been brought into force.

The legislation tries to take into account the fact that the debtor's property may be his dwelling-house, and thus to some extent takes some consideration for the indigent "can't pay" debtor. At the same time the legislation also tries to allows for the situation where the debtor could perfectly well pay but refuses or delays in doing so (the "won't pay" debtor or sometimes a corporate debtor). Satisfying these two requirements is a familiar problem with any form of civil enforcement: if the legislation is too merciful towards the "can't pay" debtors, there will then be those who "play the system" in the hope that their creditors will give up. The legislation inevitably has difficulty coping with the feckless or greedy debtor who foolishly runs up more debt than he can repay, the genuine debtor who is desperate to feed his family and turns to any source of funds to put food on the table for his family, and the habitual renegade who never pays any bills.

As a further political issue, in many areas of Scotland the creditors who are owed most are local authorities. Many local authorities have trouble collecting their council tax - council tax which is collectively used for the benefit of the local communities and indeed for the local authority's citizens - but given the general unpopularity of the tax, and the distaste many councillors and MSPs have for levying the tax on those who can least afford it, it will be seen why there is a concern that council tax payers will end up homeless, thus being a further burden on the local authority which then has to house them.

These are politically difficult areas, which is probably why so far the legislation has not been brought into force. Allan Wilson, the then Minister who spoke to the legislation at the Culture and Enterprise Committee on September 26, 2006, was well aware of these difficulties and aware of the English equivalent of land attachment, known as a "charging order" which was apparently being increasingly used. He was aware of the concern that land attachment might similarly be used unscrupulously or indiscriminately in Scotland, causing much hardship. He believed that it would be unlikely that land attachment would be used much:

> "My information is that in 2004 there were 45,562 applications for charging orders in England and Wales, which related to the attachment of all types of properties, including homes, but that there were fewer than 500 sale orders, not all of which turned into sales. Extrapolating from the English figures-I acknowledge that doing so is not a precise science-would suggest equivalent figures for Scotland of about 4,500 land attachments and fewer than 50 sales. That is the scale and nature of the issue that we are discussing."

There may be some difference in practice between the two legislations, since under the Charging Orders Act 1979 s.1(5) the court, in deciding whether or not to grant a charging orders, must take into account all the circumstances of the case and the personal circumstances of the debtor. Meanwhile, the perhaps less generous (to the debtor) Scottish procedure, as to when an order for the warrant of sale of attached land, and in particular a dwellinghouse, is refused, may be found in the 2007 Act s.97(3) (the unduly harsh test), and in s.97(6) (the procedural invalidity or practical invalidity of the order). In addition, the sheriff is to have regard to the debtors' circumstances under s.98(5) and may delay the sale for up to a year (s.97(3)(a)). A further stop to land attachment is the application for a time to pay order under the 1987 Act s.5, a time order under the Consumer Credit Act 1974 s.129 or a successful application for a Debt Arrangement Plan which will stop any diligence under the 2002 Act s.4.

It remains to be seen how creditors will in practice use land attachment, though it is anticipated that the more responsible creditors will be reluctant to use it, both because it may be oppressive and because using land attachment may bring bad publicity for the creditor. It is also a very cumbersome procedure (probably deliberately so) with many opportunities for error and oversight by the creditor's agents.

For an informed discussion of adjudication for debt and for the thinking behind land attachment, see the Scottish Law Commission's Report on Diligence (SLC Report 207, May 2001).

Land attachment and sequestration

Paragraph 13(3)(e) and (f) of Sch.5 of the 2007 Act (minor and consequential amendments) contain various provisions for the ineffectuality of any land attachment in the context of sequestration. Because these provisions are contained in this schedule, the reader's attention is drawn to them at this stage, since there is no mention of this matter within this chapter otherwise. In essence, the new s.37(5B) of the 1985 Act states that where a land attachment is created within the period of six months before the date of a debtor's sequestration, the land attachment will not be effectual in creating a preference for the land attaching creditor. New s.37(5C) states that the creditor is entitled to the expenses of the land attachment out of the proceeds of sale of the attached land. New s.37(8A) states that a land attachment created after the date of sequestration is of no effect. New s.37(8B) states that where a land attachment has been created (see s.81) over the heritable estate of the debtor before the beginning of the six month period referred to in s.37(5B), and is still subsisting at the time of the sequestration, the creditor will lose his opportunity to insist on the land attachment — thus effectively saying that his delay makes him lose his chance to enforce the land attachment.

However, under s.37(8C), where there is a land attachment created over the debtor's heritable estate, and following the execution of a warrant of sale (as later explained (see s.92)) where a contract for the sale of the land is concluded, the trustee in sequestration must concur in and ratify the deed implementing the contract and the solicitor dealing with the sale must make over to the trustee the proceeds of sale after satisfaction of the land-attaching creditor's debt in terms of s.116 of the 2007 Act.

Section 37(8C) will not apply unless, under s.37(8D), the deed is registered within 28 days of either the recording of the certified copy of the warrant for sequestration was recorded in the Register of Inhibitions in accordance with s.14(1)(a) of the 1985 Act, or of the recording of the award of sequestration in a debtor application in the same Register in accordance with subs.1A (see Sch.1 para.12(3)).

Where a decree of foreclosure is granted (see s.117) but an extract is not yet registered (see s.118) the creditor may complete title by registration provided this is done within the 28 day period indicated in s.37(8D).

79. Abolition of adjudication for debt

(1) The diligence of adjudication for debt is abolished and any enactment or rule of law enabling an action of adjudication for debt to be raised ceases to have effect.

(2) Subsection (1) above does not affect an action of adjudication for debt-

   (a) raised before; and

   (b) in which decree of adjudication is granted no later than 6 months after,

the day this section comes into force.

GENERAL NOTE

Adjudication for debt is abolished, but any current actions of adjudication raised before the commencement of this section, and in which decree in granted with six months of that date, will still be validly undertaken.

80. Renaming of the Register of Inhibitions and Adjudications

(1) The Register of Inhibitions and Adjudications is renamed the Register of Inhibitions.

(2) Any reference in an enactment to-

    (a) the Register of Inhibitions and Adjudications;

    (b) the General Register of Inhibitions; or

    (c) the Register of Adjudications,

is to be construed as a reference to the Register of Inhibitions.

GENERAL NOTE

  Since adjudication is abolished, the Register of Inhibitions and Adjudications needs to be re-named the Register of Inhibitions.

CHAPTER 2

ATTACHMENT OF LAND

Land attachment

81. Land attachment

(1) There is to be a form of diligence over land to be known as land attachment.

(2) Land attachment is competent to enforce payment of a debt but only if-

    (a) the debt is constituted by a decree or document of debt;

    (b) the debtor has been charged to pay the debt;

    (c) the period for payment specified in the charge has expired without payment being made; and

    (d) where the debtor is an individual, the creditor has, no earlier than 12 weeks before registering the notice of land attachment, provided the debtor with a debt advice and information package.

(3) A land attachment is, subject to sections 83(6) and 121(1) of this Act, created at the beginning of the day which falls immediately after the expiry of the period of 28 days beginning with the day or, as the case may be, the last day on which a notice of land attachment in relation to the land is registered.

(4) During the period of 28 days referred to in subsection (3) above, the notice has effect as if it were an inhibition-

    (a) registered against the debtor in the Register of Inhibitions; and

    (b) restricted to the land described in the notice.

(5) A land attachment-

    (a) confers on the creditor a subordinate real right over the land described in the notice (in this Chapter, the "attached land"); and

    (b) secures the sum (in this Chapter, the "sum recoverable by the land attachment") mentioned in subsection (6) below.

(6) That sum is-

    (a) the sum for the payment of which the charge was served, together with any interest accruing after such service and before the attachment ceases to have effect; and

   (b) all expenses which are chargeable against the debtor by virtue of the attachment.

(7) The Scottish Ministers may, by regulations-

   (a) substitute for the period of 28 days referred to in subsection (3) above such other period; and

   (b) make such amendment of enactments (including this Act) in consequence of such a substitution,

as they think fit.

(8) In this Act, "debt advice and information package" means the debt advice and information package referred to in section 10(5) of the Debt Arrangement and Attachment (Scotland) Act 2002 (asp 17) (in this Act, the "2002 Act").

DEFINITIONS

"Creation of land attachment": 2007 Act s.81(3)

"Creditor": 1987 Act s.88 and the 2007 Act s.88 (for the purposes of this chapter only)

"Debt advice and information package": 2002 Act s.10(5)

"Decree": 2007 Act s.221 (and see also s.128)

"Document of debt": 2007 Act s.221 "Land": 2007 Act s.82

"Notice of land attachment": 2007 Act s.83

GENERAL NOTE

This institutes the new diligence of land attachment over land. It may only be used to enforce payment of a debt provided the requirements of subs.(2) are satisfied, namely that the debt has been established by decree or document of debt, the debtor has been charged to pay, payment has not taken place within the required period (normally 14 days but 28 days if the debtor is outside of Scotland) and if the debtor is a natural person, the debtor has been served a debt advice and information package no earlier than 12 weeks before the registration of the notice of land attachment.

Subsection (3) indicates when the land attachment is created, provided:

i   the notice of the land attachment has been properly registered in both the appropriate property register (i.e. the Register of Sasines or the Land Register) and the Register of Inhibitions (s.83(1));

ii   service of that notice has been made on the debtor, any other person who owns the land and any tenant under a long lease of the land (s.83(5);

iii the certificate of that service has been properly registered within the 28 day period aftermentioned in both the appropriate property register (i.e. the Register of Sasines or the Land Register) and the Register of Inhibitions (see s.83(7)); and

iv that the debtor (or someone on his behalf) has not paid the full sum due within the 28 day period aftermentioned (see s.121(1)),

The land attachment is said to be created at the beginning of the next day after the completion of that 28 day period.

The 28 day period, during which the debtor may redeem the potential land attachment, begins on two possible dates.

Date 1 is the day that the creditor registers the notice of the land attachment in both the appropriate property register and in the Register of Inhibitions on the same day. The 28 day period runs from that day.

Date 2 is where the creditor registers the notice of the land attachment on the debtor in the same registers as in Date 1 but registers the notice in one register on one day and the notice in the other register on a later day. In that event, the date of the latter of the two registrations is deemed to be the day from which the 28 day period runs. It makes no difference which register was the one that the notice was registered in first: the important date is the latter of the two dates.

Within the 28 day period, the creditor must register the certificate of service on the debtor (s.83(6)) in the same two Registers (s.83(7)), without which the notice of land attachment will be void (s.81(6)).

The next day after the expiry of the 28 day period is the date of creation of the land attachment (s.81(3)).

The wording of this subsection of the statute is unfortunate. This is partly because the words "last day" are used in the subsection when what is actually meant is "latter of the two days"; and partly because the phrase "beginning with the day" is used in two different contexts.

During the 28 day period, the notice acts as if it were an inhibition restricted to the litigious land, thus preventing the owner selling that particular land though not necessarily preventing him selling any other land he may own (subs.(4)).

Subsection (5) indicates that the creditor receives a subordinate real right in the land: the creditor's right is subordinate to the debtor's real right and to any pre-existing standard security. The "real" right means that the right is over the land and does not apply to the debtor personally, so the land cannot be sold without the consent of the creditor. The land attachment secures the sum recoverable by land attachment (which at present must be at least £3,000) together with interest running from the date of the charge until the attachment is no longer effective (either because it is discharged for some reason or because the land is finally sold) and expenses. The Scottish Ministers have power to vary the period of 28 days if necessary.

For any potential interaction with sequestration, see para.13(3)(e) and (f) of Sch.5 of the 2007 Act (minor and consequential amendments) and the note at the end of Ch.1 of this Part.

82. Attachable land

(1) In this Chapter, "land" means-
    (a) land (including buildings and other structures and land covered with water) owned by the debtor; and
    (b) a long lease of land in relation to which the debtor is the tenant.

(2) It is not competent to create a land attachment over-
    (a) land-
        (i) to which a title has never been registered; or
        (ii) to which the debtor does not have a registered title;
    (b) a proper liferent in relation to which the debtor is the liferenter; or
    (c) a long lease which is not assignable.

(3) Subsection (2)(c) above does not apply to a lease which is assignable only with the consent of the landlord, whether or not it is a condition of the lease that consent must not be withheld unreasonably.

DEFINITIONS
"Long lease": Land Registration (Scotland) Act 1979 s.28(1)

GENERAL NOTE
Subsection (1) defines "land" as land, including buildings, land covered by water, and long leases where the debtor is tenant. A long lease is one that is over twenty years in duration. Subsection (2)(a)(i) states that is not competent to create a land attachment over land to which a title has never been recorded. Although there is not very much land in Scotland which has not had a title recorded or registered over it, there are apparently a few such places: these include the Faculty of Advocates, and certain ecclesiastical buildings (The High Kirk of St Giles, Paisley Abbey, etc.) and presumably some large estates that have, somehow, managed to stay in the same family for generations. Subsection (2)(a)(ii) applies where the debtor does not have a registered title. If the debtor does not have title to the land, he can hardly have it attached. However, this is subject to s.125 of the 2007 Act which does allow land attachment where a debtor has granted a deed in favour of a third party despite the debtor being inhibited, and where that deed is subsequently reduced by the inhibiting creditor.

A liferenter cannot have his interest in the land attached, since his interest is qualified anyway.

A long lease which is not assignable may perhaps be rare, but subs.(3) clarifies that the prohibition on creating a land attachment over a long lease is not meant to include a long lease that is not assignable except with the consent of the landlord. What is meant here is a long lease that is not assignable under any circumstances.

83. Notice of land attachment

(1) A notice of land attachment must-

(a) be in (or as nearly as may be in) the form prescribed by Act of Sederunt;

(b) describe the land to be attached; and

(c) be registered in both-

   (i) the property register in which title to the land is registered (in this Chapter, the "appropriate property register"); and

   (ii) the Register of Inhibitions.

(2) It is not competent to register a notice of land attachment unless the sum which the debtor has been charged to pay exceeds the sum mentioned in subsection (3) below.

(3) That sum is-

(a) £3,000; or

(b) such other sum as may be prescribed by the Scottish Ministers by regulations.

(4) It is competent to register a single notice of land attachment in relation to two or more sums which, under separate warrants for diligence in execution, the debtor has been charged to pay.

(5) The judicial officer must, on or as soon as is reasonably practicable after the day or, as the case may be, the last day on which the notice of land attachment is registered, serve a copy of the notice on-

(a) the debtor;

(b) any person who owns the land (whether solely or in common with the debtor); and

(c) any tenant under a long lease of the land.

(6) If, before the expiry of the period of 28 days referred to in section 81(3) of this Act, the creditor does not register a certificate of service on the debtor, the notice of land attachment is, and is deemed always to have been, void.

(7) Subsection (1) above applies to a certificate of service as it applies to a notice of land attachment.

DEFINITIONS

"Debtor": 2007 Act s.125 (5) (for the purposes of this chapter only)

"Judicial officer": 2007 Act s.57

"Land": 2007 Act s.82

GENERAL NOTE

This section explains the procedure for the process of land attachment. As indicated in the notes to s.81, the notice of land attachment must be registered in two places, the first being in the appropriate register where the land is registered (i.e. the Register or Sasines or the Land Register) and the second being in the Register of Inhibitions. The registration of the notice in the two different registers may take place on the same day, but it is of course possible that this will not happen, and s.81(3) takes account of this possibility. See also the note above to s.81.

At the time of writing we await the design of the forms that will be used for this. It will not be competent to register a notice of land attachment unless the debt which the debtor has been charged to pay is greater than £3,000, though that sum may be subsequently varied by the Scottish Ministers. It will be acceptable to have two or more debts subsumed in the one land attachment. As soon as possible after the land attachment is registered in the two different registers, the judicial officer must serve a copy of the notice on the debtor himself, on any other person who owns the land and on any tenant under a long lease of the land.

The judicial officer will produce a certificate of service of the notice on the debtor (though there appears to be no requirement to produce a certificate of service on the other two persons referred to in s.83(5), namely a person who owns the land, or any tenant under a long lease of the land) and this must be registered in the same two Registers (i.e. the Register of Sasines/Land Register and the Register of Inhibitions) within 28 days of: (i) the registration of the notice in the two Registers (if the notice was registered on the same day for both Registers) or (ii) the latter of the two dates of registration in the two Registers (if the notice was registered in the two Registers on different days).

If the certificate of registration of the service is not registered as stated above, the notice of land attachment is void and the entire procedure stops (subs.(6)).

Consequences of land attachment

84. Debts secured by land attachment not rendered heritable

The creation of a land attachment does not convert any moveable debt, in relation to the enforcement of which the notice of land attachment was registered, into a heritable one.

GENERAL NOTE

This section is designed to ensure that even if the creditor dies, while his estate will take over the debt, the debt, as an asset of the late creditor's, will be treated as moveable estate, and so subject to the relevant laws of succession for moveable estate, rather than heritable estate, in terms of the Succession (Scotland) Act 1964.

85. Restriction on priority of ranking of certain securities

After section 13 of the Conveyancing and Feudal Reform (Scotland) Act 1970 (c.35), insert-

"**13A** **Effect of subsequent land attachment on ranking of standard securities**

(1) This section applies where-

    (a) a notice of land attachment, relating to land (or any part of it) which is subject to an existing standard security duly recorded, is registered in accordance with section 83(1)(c) of the Bankruptcy and Diligence etc. (Scotland) Act 2007 (asp 3);

    (b) a copy of that notice is served on the creditor in that existing standard security; and

    (c) a land attachment is subsequently created on the expiry of the period of 28 days mentioned in section 81(3) of that Act.

(2) Section 13(1) of this Act shall apply in relation to the effect on the preference in ranking of that existing standard security from the day on which the period referred to in subsection (1)(c) above expires.".

DEFINITIONS

"Notice of land attachment": 2007 Act s.83(1)

GENERAL NOTE

This inserts a new s.13A in the Conveyancing and Feudal Reform (Scotland) Act 1970. Provided a land attachment has been properly intimated to the creditor with a pre-existing standard security over the land over which the notice of land attachment has been registered (in terms of s.83(1)(c)), and the land attachment is subsequently created on the expiry of the 28 day period referred to in s.81(3), any preference the creditor with the pre-existing standard security may have in ranking as against the creditor with the land attachment is restricted to the sums already advanced and the sums that that creditor has already contracted to make. This puts the creditor with the land attachment in the same position as a postponed standard security holder.

86. Lease granted after registration of notice of land attachment

(1) This section applies where-

(a) a notice of land attachment is registered;

(b) during the period of 28 days mentioned in section 81(3) of this Act-

    (i) the debtor; or

    (ii) a tenant of the debtor,

grants a lease of land (or a part of it) specified in the notice; and

(c) a land attachment is, on the expiry of that period, created.

(2) Subject to section 163(2) to (4) of this Act (restriction on reduction of leases granted in breach of inhibition), any such lease is reducible at the instance of the creditor.

(3) In subsection (1)(b) above, "tenant" includes any subtenant of the tenant and "lease" includes a sublease.

DEFINITIONS

"Debtor": 2007 Act s.125 (5) (for the purposes of this chapter only)

"Land": 2007 Act s.82

"Notice of land attachment": 2007 Act s.83(1)

GENERAL NOTE

This applies where a notice of a land attachment is registered and within the 28 day period referred to in s.83(1) either the debtor, or a tenant of the debtor's, grants a lease of some or all of the land in question. Such a lease may be reduced at the land attaching creditor's instance provided the lease itself is for a term greater than five years. Subsection (2) states that there is a qualification to this rule, to be found at s.163(2)-(4). This indicates that if there is a lease the unexpired portion of which is for a period less than five years, and the creditor is seeking to reduce that lease, the creditor must petition the Court of Session for an order of reduction. The order will only be granted if it would be fair and reasonable in all the circumstances to do so.

As part of the mechanism for establishing whether the unexpired portion of the lease is for a period less than five years, any provision within the lease for enabling the lease to be terminated earlier than the normal termination date should be ignored, and should the lease have a provision requiring the landlord to renew the lease, the period of the renewed lease should be added to the period of the original lease.

87. Assignation of title deeds etc

(1) A land attachment assigns to the creditor the title deeds, including searches and all unregistered conveyances, affecting the attached land or any part of it.

(2) The creditor is, in the event of a sale of the attached land (or part of it) in pursuance of a warrant under section 97(2) of this Act, entitled to-

(a) deliver the title deeds (so far as in the creditor's possession and subject to the rights of any person holding prior rights to their possession) to the purchaser; and

(b) assign to the purchaser any right the creditor has to have the title deeds made forthcoming.

DEFINITIONS

"Land": 2007 Act s.82

GENERAL NOTE

This assigns to the creditor all the title deeds and other documentation affecting the attached land or part of it, and permits him to deliver the title deeds (subject to anyone else's right in them) to the purchaser following the sale of the attached land. This section echoes s.10(4) of the Conveyancing and Feudal Reform (Scotland) Act 1970, whereby a heritable creditor has similar rights.

88. Acquisition of right to execute land attachment

(1) This section applies where-

    (a) a person acquires a right as mentioned in section 88(1) (acquisition of right to decree, document, order or determination authorising diligence) of the Debtors (Scotland) Act 1987 (c.18) (in this Act, the "1987 Act"); and

    (b) a notice of land attachment has, before that acquisition, been registered in pursuance of that right.

(2) The person acquiring the right may, by registering a notice such as is mentioned in subsection (3) below, take or continue to take any steps necessary to enforce the debt by land attachment as if the appropriate clerk had, under section 88(4) of the 1987 Act, granted warrant authorising the person to do so.

(3) The notice referred to in subsection (2) above must-

    (a) be in (or as nearly as may be in) the form prescribed by Act of Sederunt; and

    (b) be registered in-

        (i) the appropriate property register; and

        (ii) the Register of Inhibitions.

(4) References in this Chapter to a "creditor" include, unless the context otherwise requires, references to a person who registers a notice under subsection (2) above.

DEFINITIONS

"Appropriate property register": 2007 Act s.83(1)(c)(i)

"Notice of land attachment": 2007 Act s.83

GENERAL NOTE

A creditor may, if he wish, assign or sell his right to execute land attachment to another person ("the assignee") particularly if he neither wishes to have the inconvenience nor bad publicity of being seen to execute a land attachment. The proposed assignee must obtain warrant from the court to have the right to execute the land attachment made over to him (1987 Act s.88(1)). Where: (i) this warrant has been obtained and (ii) where a notice of land attachment was registered before the assignation of the right to execute the land attachment, the assignee will need to register the notice in subs.3 of this section (on a form yet to be devised) in the appropriate property register and in the Register of Inhibitions if he wishes to continue with his execution of the land attachment. Providing the subs.3 notice is duly registered, the assignee may enforce the land attachment as if he were the original creditor.

Subsection 4 clarifies the point that throughout this particular chapter, the word "creditor" includes the assignee.

89. Effect of debtor's death before land attachment created

(1) This section applies where-

    (a) a debtor, in relation to whose land a creditor has taken steps to commence or execute a land attachment, dies; and

    (b) a land attachment has not, before the date of death of the debtor, been created.

(2) Any steps taken as mentioned in subsection (1)(a) above cease to have effect and any charge relating to the debt is, from the date of death of the debtor, void.

(3) Nothing in subsection (2) above stops the creditor from subsequently proceeding to raise against any executor or other representative of the debtor an action to constitute the debt.

(4) Any warrant for diligence in an extract of a decree in such an action authorises land attachment.

DEFINITIONS

"Creation of land attachment": 2007 Act s.81(3)

"Decree": 2007 Act s.221.

GENERAL NOTE

This deals with the situation where a creditor has taken steps to commence or execute a land attachment against a debtor's land, and the debtor dies before the land attachment can actually be created. In these circumstances, any steps taken towards the commencement or execution of the land attachment are void with effect from the date of death of the debtor. It is difficult to see how it would be possible to execute a land attachment without the land attachment having been created first, unless "execute" is here given a wide meaning, such as "carry out" that suggests the process of obtaining a land attachment. The more normal meaning of the word "execute" in this Act would, it is submitted, suggest that the creditor, having already created his land attachment order, proceed to the next stage of enforcing it, such as obtaining a warrant for sale. It is perhaps important to concentrate on the word "commence" rather than "execute".

Also slightly confusingly, subs.(2) refers to any "charge" relating to the debt being void. The previous use of the word "charge" in this chapter is in the context of serving a charge on the debtor, and what is probably meant is that on the debtor's death, the charge that had been served upon him is void with effect from the date of death. If that had been the case, the subsection might have referred back to s.81(2) and (6), but it does not do this. If the word "charge" is meant to mean "security" it might suggest that the land attachment was void, if the word "charge" could be taken to mean land attachment. It might even mean that any standard security granted by the debtor to the creditor, provided it related to the debt in question, would be void. It may that this confusing wording is tidied up in subsequent legislation.

Even if the debtor has died, the creditor may nevertheless subsequently proceed against the executor of the debtor in an action to constitute the debt though no doubt that would incur further expense. If the decree grants warrant for diligence the creditor may then effect land attachment against the land in question. The section is silent on the situation where no action is normally required since the debt had been constituted by a document of debt (see 2007 Act s.81(2)(a)). Presumably a prudent creditor would still have to raise an action. Equally, it may be that the power given to the Court of Session, or the sheriff, in the next section, will deal with this anomaly.

90. Effect of debtor's death after land attachment created

(1) For the avoidance of doubt, where a debtor, whose land is subject to a land attachment, dies, the land attachment continues to have effect in relation to the attached land.

(2) The Court of Session may, by Act of Sederunt, provide for the operation of this Chapter in a case to which this section applies and may, in particular-

   (a) modify the provisions about service of notices of applications for warrant for sale and foreclosure; and

   (b) confer power on the sheriff to dispense with or modify procedures under this Chapter.

GENERAL NOTE

In contrast to s.89, where a land attachment has been created, and the creditor subsequently dies, the land attachment continues to have effect. This section confers on the Court of Session the power to draw up further rules of court to deal with this particular situation and to produce special provisions for warrant for sale and foreclosure, or to allow the sheriff to modify or dispense with certain parts of the procedure for sale or foreclosure. These have yet to be produced.

91. Caveat by purchaser under missives

(1) This section applies where-

   (a) a person has entered into a contract to purchase land from a debtor; and

   (b) ownership has not been transferred to that person.

(2) The person may, for the purpose of receiving intimation of any application, under section 92(1) of this Act, for a warrant for sale

of the land, register in the Register of Inhibitions a notice in (or as nearly as may be in) the form prescribed by Act of Sederunt.

DEFINITIONS

"Debtor": 2007 Act s.125 (5) (for the purposes of this chapter only)

"Land": 2007 Act s.82

"Appropriate property register": 2007 Act s.83(1)(c)(i)

GENERAL NOTE

This section deals with the situation where a purchaser from a debtor is concerned that the debtor's land may be subject to land attachment before the title to the debtor's land is transferred to the purchaser. The purchaser may accordingly register a notice known as a "caveat" in the Register of Inhibitions in a form yet to be devised. This will cause any application by the creditor to sell the land to be intimated to the purchaser in terms of s.92(5)(b). The creditor is expected (in terms of s.92(4)) to carry out a search in the appropriate property register (the Register of Sasines or the Land Register) and in the Register of Inhibitions against the debtor and any one else who owns the land in common with the debtor. Once the purchaser has had the application for warrant to sell intimated to him, he may, within 14 days of intimation, raise objections to the application (s.92(6)). As a result of ss.99 (protection of the purchaser under contract where the creditor applies for warrant for sale) and 100 (protection of the purchaser under contract where the warrant for sale is granted) the purchaser may complete title to the land. The word "caveat" is only used in the title and not used in the subsequent sections of the 2007 Act, though for the purposes of these notes, the word "caveat" will continue to be used.

Preparations for sale of attached land

92. Application for warrant to sell attached land

(1) Where-

    (a) a land attachment is in effect;

    (b) the period of 6 months, beginning with the day or, as the case may be, the last day on which the notice of land attachment is registered, has expired;

    (c) the sum recoverable by the land attachment exceeds the sum mentioned in subsection (3) below (in this Chapter, the "prescribed sum"); and

    (d) the sum recoverable has not been paid,

the creditor may, subject to subsection (2) below, apply to the sheriff for a warrant for sale of the attached land or such part of it as may be specified in the application.

(2) The Scottish Ministers may by regulations provide that where attached land, or any part of it, is-

    (a) a dwellinghouse; or

    (b) a dwellinghouse of such description or class as may be specified in the regulations,

an application under subsection (1) above may be made only in relation to such part of the attached land which is not a dwellinghouse or, as the case may be, such a dwellinghouse.

(3) The prescribed sum is-

    (a) £3,000; or

    (b) such other sum as may be prescribed by the Scottish Ministers by regulations.

(4) An application under subsection (1) above must-

    (a) be in (or as nearly as may be in) the form prescribed by Act of Sederunt;

    (b) specify-

      (i) the attached land (or part of it) in relation to which the warrant for sale is sought; and

      (ii) a solicitor who is willing to execute any warrant for sale granted; and

  (c) be accompanied by-

      (i) a report on a search in the appropriate property register in respect of the land specified in the application;

      (ii) a report on a search in the Register of Inhibitions in respect of the debtor and any person who owns the attached land in common with the debtor;

      (iii) a copy of the notice of land attachment;

      (iv) a copy of the certificate of service of that notice on the debtor;

      (v) a declaration signed by the solicitor mentioned in paragraph (b)(ii) above; and

      (vi) any other document prescribed by Act of Sederunt.

(5) An application under subsection (1) above must be intimated to-

  (a) the debtor;

  (b) if the report mentioned in subsection (4)(c)(ii) above discloses that a notice has been registered under section 91 of this Act, the person at whose instance the notice was registered;

  (c) any person holding any security or diligence ranking prior to or *pari passu* with the land attachment;

  (d) any occupier of the land;

  (e) any person who owns the land in common with the debtor; and

  (f) any other person belonging to a class of persons prescribed by the Scottish Ministers by regulations.

(6) A person who receives intimation under subsection (5) above may, before the expiry of the period of 14 days beginning with the day on which intimation is made, lodge objections to the application.

(7) The Scottish Ministers may, by regulations, make further provision about the reports on searches mentioned in subsection (4)(c)(i) and (ii) above which are to accompany an application under subsection (1) above.

(8) Where provision is made by virtue of this Chapter or by any other enactment permitting the application under subsection (1) above to be an electronic communication-

  (a) the requirement in paragraph (c) of subsection (4) above that the application be accompanied by the documents mentioned in that paragraph is satisfied by the provision of electronic communications; and

  (b) the requirement that the declaration mentioned in sub-paragraph (v) of that paragraph be signed is satisfied by a certified electronic signature.

(9) In this section, "sheriff" means a sheriff of the sheriffdom in which the attached land or any part of it is situated.

DEFINITIONS
"Debtor": 2007 Act s.125(5) (for the purposes of this chapter only)

"Electronic signature": 2007 Act s.221
"Notice of land attachment": 2007 Act s.83
"Appropriate property register": 2007 Act s.83(1)(c)(i)
"Caveat": 2007 Act s.91

GENERAL NOTE

This section explains the procedure for applying for a warrant to sell the attached land.

Under subs.(1), the creditor may apply to the sheriff for a warrant for sale if certain conditions are satisfied. These are that a land attachment over the debtor's land is in effect, that a period of six months from the day the notice of land attachment was registered (see the note to s.81 above for more details of the precise day) has elapsed, that the sum due to the creditor exceeds the "prescribed sum" (subsequently referred to in subs.(3) as being £3,000, although at the time of writing this figure has not been conclusively decided upon) and that the sum due has not been paid. The figure of £3,000 may be changed by regulations subject to affirmative resolution procedure (see s.224(4)(b)(i)).

The significance of the six month period is that within that time, the debtor could apply to have a Debt Arrangement Scheme put in place, which would act as a "diligence stopper" and prevent the land being sold. It is worth noting that if the debtor is sequestrated within that six month period, the land attachment does not create any preference for the creditor, though he will be entitled to the expenses of obtaining the land attachment. See s.37(5B), (5C) and (8A)-(8F) of the 1985 Act as inserted by Sch.5 para.13 of the 2007 Act.

Under subs.(2), if the attached land, or part of it, is a dwellinghouse, or a dwellinghouse of a particular type within the terms of regulations yet to be drawn up by the Scottish Ministers (and subject to affirmative resolution procedure (see s.224(4)(b)(i)), an application for warrant to sell may only be made in respect of that part of the land that is not the dwellinghouse or the particular type of dwellinghouse.

This could mean that some of the debtor's land (for example, farmland) could be sold, but not the debtor's dwellinghouse itself.

The sale of a dwellinghouse ultimately depends on what is meant by the word "dwellinghouse". This is a particularly contentious issue, politically, since any definition of dwellinghouse which is too wide could possibly have severe consequences for social welfare and homelessness, while too narrow (as, for example, restricting the enforceability of warrants for sale of dwellinghouses to dwellinghouses worth more than, say, £500,000) might be unduly restrictive to creditors or unduly beneficial to debtors who might arrange to let their houses deteriorate in order to keep their value low. It is understandable that no politician wishes to be seen to be the one that promulgates a definition of "dwellinghouse" that might adversely affect his own constituents or affect his party's chances of re-election, whatever creditors might think. When the matter was being discussed in the Culture and Enterprise Committee, there were various proposals for removing dwellinghouses entirely from land attachment, but at the end of the day, dwellinghouses were not removed from land attachment. This was because without such a rule, there would be a temptation for some debtors, in particular "won't pay" debtors, to remain in substantial homes, with plenty of equity available to pay their debts, while refusing to pay those debts — which, it is thought, is unfair on those creditors (in particular small tradesmen without much commercial clout (as opposed to banks and HMRC)) who might justifiably be due their money, but be unable any other way to make their debtors take the creditors' claims seriously.

It is to be noticed, however, that subs.2 only applies where the land attachment is over a dwellinghouse. It does not apply to commercial or industrial premises, nor to separate garages, lock-ups, farmland, property that is rented out and not lived in by the debtor or his family (subject to any tenants' rights) or offices owned by the debtor.

Under subs.(4), the application for warrant to sell must be on a form yet to be devised. The form will need to specify the attached land itself (or a part of it). The form will need to indicate the name of the solicitor willing to execute the warrant for sale. This will generally be the creditor's law agent. That solicitor is later on (in s.97(2)) referred to as the "appointed person". The form must also be accompanied by a search against the land in the Register of Sasines or the Land Register (as appropriate) and in the Register of Inhibitions against the debtor and anyone owning the land in common with the debtor, and by a copy of the notice of the land attachment, a copy of the certificate of service of the notice on the debtor, a declaration by the solicitor that he is willing to execute the warrant, and any other documentation yet to be prescribed by Act of Sederunt. It is possible that the Scottish Ministers may, by regulations yet to be promulgated, indicate other searches that need to take place before the application may be considered (subs.(7)).

Under subs.(5), the application must be intimated to the debtor, anyone registering a caveat, a holder of a prior or *pari passu* security over the land, a person entitled to execute any diligence ranking prior to or *pari passu* with the attaching creditor, any occupier of the land, any person who owns the land in common and any other person within a class of person yet to be prescribed by the Scottish Ministers. Under subs.(6), any of those persons may object to the application within 14 days of intimation.

Under subs.(8), the application and the accompanying documentation may be sent in electronically and the declaration by the solicitor may also be supplied by a certified electronic signature as defined in s.221.

For any potential interaction with sequestration, see para.13(3)(e) and (f) of Sch.5 of the 2007 Act (minor and consequential amendments). See the note at the end of Ch.1 of this Part.

93. Notice to local authority of application for warrant for sale

(1) Where a creditor (other than a local authority) applies under section 92(1) of this Act for a warrant for sale of attached land which comprises or includes a dwellinghouse, the creditor must give notice of that fact to the local authority in whose area the dwellinghouse is situated.

(2) A notice under subsection (1) above must be given in the form and manner prescribed under section 11(3) of the Homelessness etc. (Scotland) Act 2003 (asp 10).

GENERAL NOTE

This requires any creditor, other than a local authority, to inform the local authority that he has applied for a warrant for sale of attached land including a dwellinghouse. The notice is in the form prescribed under the Homelessness etc. (Scotland) Act 2003 s.11(3).

94. Preliminary hearing on application for warrant to sell

(1) The sheriff must, on receiving an application under section 92(1) of this Act and after expiry of the period mentioned in subsection (6) of that section-

   (a) hold a hearing; and

   (b) give the persons mentioned in subsection (5) of that section the opportunity of making representations.

(2) The creditor must attend the hearing whether or not the application is opposed.

(3) The sheriff must, if satisfied that the application is in order, make an order-

   (a) fixing a date for a hearing on the application under section 97 of this Act;

   (b) requiring the creditor to intimate that date to the persons mentioned in section 92(5) of this Act;

   (c) appointing a chartered surveyor or other suitably qualified person to report on the open market value of the land specified in the application (that surveyor or other person, and their report, being referred to in this Chapter as the "valuer" and the "valuation report" respectively); and

   (d) where any security or diligence is held in relation to the land specified in the application and the creditor has been unable to ascertain the amount of the sums secured by that other security or diligence, requiring the holder of that security or diligence to disclose to the creditor-

      (i) the amount of the sums secured; and

      (ii) where the security holder is obliged to pay any other sums which would be secured by that security to the debtor, the amount of such sums.

GENERAL NOTE

Where the creditor has made an application to the sheriff in terms of s.92(1), the sheriff, after the expiry of the 14 day period during which objections to the application for warrant may be lodged (in terms of s.92(6)) must hold a preliminary hearing at which all those referred to in s.92(5) may have the opportunity to make their representations. The creditor must attend the preliminary hearing even if it is unopposed. If the sheriff is satisfied that the application is in order, he may fix a date for the hearing of the application itself, require the creditor to intimate the date of the hearing to all those referred to in s.92(5), appoint a chartered surveyor (or similar) (hereafter known as the "valuer") to report on the open market value of the land specified in the application, that report being known as the "valuation report", and, should the creditor be unable to find the information himself, require the holder of any security or diligence over the land to disclose the amount secured by that security or diligence and any other sums that that holder might be obliged to pay in respect of that security or diligence.

95. Valuation report

    (1) The valuer appointed under section 94(3)(c) of this Act-
      (a) may take all steps which are reasonably necessary (including inspecting the attached land) to produce a valuation report; and
      (b) must send a copy of the report to-
        (i) the creditor; and
        (ii) the persons mentioned in section 92(5) of this Act.
    (2) The debtor and any other person in occupation of attached land must allow the valuer to inspect the land and carry out any other steps which are necessary to produce the valuation report.
    (3) The creditor is liable for the valuer's reasonable remuneration and outlays incurred in exercising functions under this section.
    (4) Such remuneration and outlays are expenses incurred by the creditor in executing the land attachment.

DEFINITIONS

"Debtor": 2007 Act s.125(5) (for the purposes of this chapter only)
"Valuer": 2007 Act s.94
"Valuation report": 2007 Act s.94

GENERAL NOTE

The valuer must be allowed access by the debtor to the debtor's premises in order to prepare his valuation report. The report must be sent to the creditor and all those people referred to in s.92(5). The creditor is liable for the valuer's fees and outlays, but those fees and expenses are treated as expenses of the land attachment and therefore (assuming the land attachment is successful) ultimately payable out of the sums recovered by the land attachment.

96. Creditor's duties prior to full hearing on application for warrant for sale

    (1) The creditor must, no later than 7 clear days before the date fixed for the hearing under section 97 of this Act, lodge-
      (a) the valuation report;
      (b) a continuation of the report on the search in the appropriate property register mentioned in section 92(4)(c)(i) of this Act;

     (c) a continuation of the report on the search in the Register of Inhibitions mentioned in section 92(4)(c)(ii) of this Act; and

     (d) a note specifying the amount outstanding under any security or diligence over the land specified in the application.

(2) Where a report lodged under subsection (1)(b) or (c) above reveals a deed registered since the date of the report mentioned in section 92(4)(c)(i) of this Act or, as the case may be, a notice under section 91 of this Act registered since the date of the report mentioned in section 92(4)(c)(ii) of this Act, the sheriff-

     (a) must make an order requiring-

          (i) the application; and

          (ii) the date fixed for the hearing,

to be intimated to the person who registered that deed or, as the case may be, that notice; and

     (b) may, if it appears necessary to do so, make an order-

          (i) postponing the hearing to a later date; and

          (ii) requiring the creditor to intimate that date to that person and to the persons mentioned in section 92(5) of this Act.

(3) Where the sheriff makes an order under subsection (2)(b)(i) above postponing the hearing, the sheriff may make such ancillary orders as the sheriff thinks fit including, without prejudice to that generality, an order requiring fresh continuations of the reports on searches mentioned in subsection (1)(b) and (c) above to be lodged.

(4) Subsection (6) of section 92 of this Act applies to a person who receives intimation under subsection (2) above as it applies to a person who receives intimation under subsection (5) of that section.

(5) The Scottish Ministers may, by regulations, make further provision about the continuations of the reports on searches mentioned in subsection (1)(b) and (c) above which are to be lodged under that subsection.

DEFINITIONS

"Appropriate property register": 2007 Act s.83(1)(c)(i)
"Caveat": 2007 Act s.91
"Valuation report": 2007 Act s.94

GENERAL NOTE

The creditor must not less than seven days before the full hearing on the application for the warrant for sale lodge with the court the valuation report and continuations of the searches referred to in s.92(4)(c)(i), being the searches in the appropriate property register and the Register of Inhibitions, and a note indicating the amount secured by a holder of a security or diligence over the land (this having been established by means of s.94(3)(d)).

Under subs.(2), should the search in the appropriate property register disclose a deed (such as a disposition) registered since the first search under s.92(4)(c)(i) or a caveat registered since the first search in the Register of Inhibitions, the sheriff must order that the application and the date of the hearing are to be intimated to the person who registered the deed or entered the notice of caveat (as the case may be). He may also order the date of the hearing for the application to be postponed, although in that case all those referred to in s.92(5) would need to have the new date intimated to them. Where the hearing is postponed, the sheriff may make such other orders as may be necessary, including further continuations of the searches.

There may be further regulations produced in due course by the Scottish Ministers dealing with the continuation of the searches. This will be subject to the negative resolution procedure under s.224(3).

97. Full hearing on application for warrant for sale

(1) At the hearing on an application under section 92(1) of this Act, the sheriff must not make any order without first giving any person who has lodged objections under section 92(6) of this Act an opportunity to be heard.

(2) Subject to subsections (3) and (5) below and to sections 98, 99 and 102 of this Act, the sheriff may, if satisfied that the application is in order, make an order-

    (a) subject to subsection (4) below, granting a warrant for sale of the attached land; and

    (b) authorising the solicitor specified in the application (or such other solicitor the sheriff specifies) to execute that warrant (in this Chapter, that solicitor being referred to as the "appointed person").

(3) The sheriff may, if satisfied that granting a warrant for sale would be unduly harsh to the debtor or any other person having an interest-

    (a) make an order under subsection (2) above but suspend its effect for a period not exceeding 1 year beginning with the date on which the order is made; or

    (b) make an order refusing to grant such a warrant.

(4) The sheriff-

    (a) must specify in the warrant granted the period within which the attached land is to be sold; and

    (b) may grant warrant-

        (i) to sell only part of the attached land;

        (ii) to sell the attached land by lots.

(5) The sheriff must make an order refusing the application for a warrant for sale if satisfied that any of the grounds mentioned in subsection (6) below apply.

(6) The grounds referred to in subsection (5) above are that-

    (a) the land attachment is invalid;

    (b) the land attachment has ceased to have effect;

    (c) the attached land (or any part of it) is not capable of being sold;

    (d) the sum recoverable by the land attachment does not exceed the prescribed sum;

    (e) a warrant for sale of the attached land (or any part of it) has been granted to another creditor of the debtor;

    (f) a heritable creditor of the debtor is exercising that creditor's right to sell the attached land (or any part of it) under the security;

    (g) if the attached land (or any part of it) were sold, the likely net proceeds of the sale would not exceed the sum mentioned in subsection (7) below.

(7) The sum referred to in subsection (6)(g) above is the aggregate of-

    (a) the expenses of the land attachment chargeable against the debtor; and

    (b) whichever is the lesser of-

        (i) the sum of £1,000; and

> (ii) the sum equal to 10 per cent of the sum mentioned in section 81(6)(a) of this Act or so much of that sum as is outstanding,
>
> or such other sum or percentage as may be prescribed by the Scottish Ministers by regulations.
>
> (8) In subsection (6)(g) above, "likely net proceeds" means the sum likely to be raised by the sale of the attached land less any sums that would be due to a creditor holding a security or diligence over the attached land which ranks prior to or *pari passu* with the land attachment.

DEFINITIONS

"Land": 2007 Act s.82

"Prescribed sum": 2007 Act s.83(3)

GENERAL NOTE

When the full hearing finally takes place, the sheriff may not make any order without allowing all those who have lodged objections (including those who have registered a deed or a caveat under s.96(2), who are now treated as if they were objectors in terms of s.92(5) and (6)) the opportunity to be heard. The sheriff must also take account of any application for a time to pay order by the debtor (see new s.5(c) of the 1987 Act as amended by Sch.5 para.(4)(b) of the 2007 Act).

If the application is in order, and there are no objections in terms of ss.98, 99 and 102, or the sheriff does not sustain such objections as there are, the sheriff may make the order granting the warrant for sale of the land (or part of it), the period within which the attached land is to be sold (subs.(2)). The order will also specify the solicitor referred to in s.92(4)(b), the solicitor being now known as the "appointed person". He will be authorised to execute the warrant for sale. The creditor should send a copy of the order to the debtor and to the appointed person (s.103).

However, should the land include a dwellinghouse (see the notes to s.92 above)), where that dwellinghouse is the debtor's sole or main residence, before making an order under subs.(2) the sheriff must first have regards to the matters in s.98(5), these being:

- the nature of and reasons for the debt secured by the land attachment;
- the debtor's ability to pay the debt if the payment of the debt were suspended for a year;
- any action taken by the creditor to assist the debtor in paying the debt; and
- the ability of the debtor and others in the dwellinghouse to secure reasonable alternative accommodation.

If the attached land does not include a dwellinghouse, these matters do not need to be considered. Section 98(8) and (9) define a dwellinghouse as being a sole or main residence, even if a business is run from it and including any yard, garden, outbuilding or other pertinents).

In addition, should the sheriff be satisfied that the granting a warrant for sale for any land would be "unduly harsh" to the debtor, or anyone else having an interest, he may either make the order but suspend its operation for up to a year, or make an order refusing to grant the warrant at all (subs.(3)). The words "unduly harsh" have occasioned some concern. Some would say that removing a debtor's home from the debtor by definition is unduly harsh. Others would say that the words "unduly harsh" were used in the old legislation relating to poinding without noticeable effect. The cynic might say that the words "unduly harsh" are inherently subjective, and would almost certainly vary from one sheriff to another.

If the land is to be sold, the sheriff must specify in the warrant the period within which the land is to be sold, and may indicate that the warrant is for only part of the land or that it is to be sold in lots (subs.(4).

Subsection (5) gives the sheriff power to refuse the grant of an order, provided the refusal is in terms of one or more of the seven grounds in subs.(6). These are that the land attachment is invalid (in terms of the required procedure by the creditor); that the land attachment has expired; that the land itself is not capable of being sold (perhaps because it is worthless, or because no one would want it anyway, perhaps because it is polluted, or has been washed away in a flood); that the sale would not generate the "prescribed sum" (i.e. £3,000 or such other figure as is ultimately chosen); that some other creditor is already selling the land under a warrant for sale; that a heritable creditor is exercising his right of sale; or that the likely net proceeds of sale would not exceed the sum referred to in subs.(7). Should the sheriff refuse a warrant for sale under the last four of those grounds, the land attachment of itself still has effect and the creditor may at a later date apply again for another warrant (s.105).

Subsection 7 explains the sum as being the lesser of £1,000 or the sum equal to 10 per cent of the sum referred to in s.81(6)(a), this being 10 per cent of the actual sum being sought (assuming it is above £3,000) plus interest but not expenses, or so much of that sum as is still outstanding. The Scottish Ministers may alter the figure of £1,000 and the figure of 10 per cent. They may do so by regulations subject to affirmative resolution procedure (see s.224(4)(b)(i)).

Subsection (8) defines "net likely proceeds" as the proceeds of sale less any sums due to other creditors who rank before or equally with the attaching creditor.

98. Application for warrant for sale of sole or main residence

(1) This section applies where-
(a) the creditor applies under section 92(1) of this Act for a warrant for sale of attached land which comprises or includes a dwellinghouse; and
(b) that dwellinghouse is the sole or main residence of-
(i) the debtor;
(ii) where the owner of the dwellinghouse is not the debtor, that owner; or
(iii) any person mentioned in subsection (2) below.
(2) Those persons are-
(a) a non-entitled spouse of the debtor or the owner;
(b) a person living together with the debtor or the owner as husband and wife;
(c) a civil partner of the debtor or the owner;
(d) a person living together with the debtor in a relationship which has the characteristics of the relationship between a husband and wife except that the person and the debtor or the owner are of the same sex;
(e) a person to whom subsection (3) below applies.
(3) This subsection applies to a person where-
(a) the debtor or the owner does not reside in the dwellinghouse;
(b) a child of the debtor or the owner, who is also a child of the person, does so reside; and
(c) the person has lived together with the debtor or the owner as is mentioned in paragraph (b) or (d) of subsection (2) above throughout the period of 6 months ending with the day on which the debtor or the owner ceased to so reside.
(4) Before making, under section 97(2) of this Act, an order granting a warrant for sale, the sheriff must have regard to the matters mentioned in subsection (5) below.
(5) Subject to subsection (6) below, those matters are-
(a) the nature of and reasons for the debt secured by the land attachment;
(b) the debtor's ability to pay, if the effect of the warrant for sale were suspended by an order under subsection (7) below, the debt outstanding (including any interest and expenses chargeable against the debtor);
(c) any action taken by the creditor to assist the debtor in paying that debt;

    (d) the ability of those occupying the dwellinghouse as their sole or main residence to secure reasonable alternative accommodation.

(6) The Scottish Ministers may by regulations modify subsection (5) above to-

    (a) add to;

    (b) remove from; or

    (c) vary,

the matters mentioned there.

(7) Where the sheriff makes, under section 97(2) of this Act, an order granting a warrant for sale, the sheriff may suspend the effect of the warrant for a period not exceeding 1 year beginning with the day on which the order is made.

(8) For the purposes of subsection (1) above, a dwellinghouse may be a sole or main residence irrespective of whether it is used, to any extent, by the debtor or a person mentioned in subsection (2) above for the purposes of any profession, trade or business.

(9) In this section-

"child" means-

    (a) a child under the age of 16 years; and

    (b) includes-

        (i) a stepchild; and

        (ii) any child brought up or treated by any person to whom subsection (3) above applies or by the debtor or the owner as a child of that person, of the debtor or of the owner;

"dwellinghouse" includes any yard, garden, outbuilding or other pertinents; and

"non-entitled spouse" is to be construed in accordance with section 1(1) of the Matrimonial Homes (Family Protection) (Scotland) Act 1981 (c.59).

DEFINITIONS

"Debtor": 2007 Act s.125 (5) (for the purposes of this chapter only)

"Non-entitled spouse": Matrimonial Homes (Family Protection) (Scotland) Act 1981 s.1(1)

GENERAL NOTE

This section is designed to protect a debtor, to some extent, where a warrant for sale of attached land, granted under s.97(2) includes a dwellinghouse which is the sole or main residence of: (a) the debtor; (b) where the owner of the dwellinghouse is not the debtor, the owner or (c) anyone mentioned in subs.(3). The persons mentioned in subs.(3) are:

- the non-entitled spouse of the debtor;
- anyone living with the debtor as husband or wife;
- the civil partner of the debtor or the owner;
- a same-sex co-habitee of the debtor;
- a child of the debtor or owner (even if the debtor or owner does not reside in the dwellinghouse); and
- a former co-habitee (same-sex or otherwise) or civil partner within a period of six months before the debtor or owner ceased to live in the dwellinghouse.

Before the sheriff grants an order for sale, under subs.(5) he must "have regard" to the matters in subs.(6). The words "have regard" which increasingly appear in legislation, are renowned both for their convenience (from the politicians' point of view) and lack of clarity (from the lawyers' point of view), but appear to mean that the sheriff should at least consider the matter seriously even if he finally decides that those matters are not in any particular case significant. The matters referred to in subs.(5) are:

- the nature of and reasons for the debt secured by the land attachment;
- the debtor's ability to pay the debt if the payment of the debt were suspended for a year;
- any action taken by the creditor to assist the debtor in paying the debt; and
- the ability of the debtor and others in the dwellinghouse to secure reasonable alternative accommodation.

Presumably what the legislation is getting at is that a creditor acting reasonably, who has done his best to accommodate the debtor, will stand a better chance of success than an unreasonable and grasping creditor who has made the debtor's situation worse by unwise lending. Likewise a debtor who has been acting prodigally at creditors' expense, and with no-one but himself to blame for his spendthrift ways, may be less likely to receive much sympathy. As for the ability of the debtor to secure reasonable alternative accommodation, presumably the local authority, already alerted under s.93, would need to be contacted (perhaps by the creditor, but possibly by the debtor) to state what other accommodation would be available.

The matters in subs.(5) may be modified by regulation, subject to affirmative resolution procedure (see s.224(4)(b)(i)).

A dwellinghouse is to some extent defined for the purposes of this section (and by reference, s.97) in subss.(8) and (9) where a dwellinghouse is said to be a sole or main residence, even if a business is run from it, and includes a yard, garden, outbuilding or any other pertinents. The word "child" is also defined for the purposes of this section only.

99. Protection of purchaser under contract where creditor applies for warrant for sale

(1) This section applies where-
  (a) the creditor applies under section 92(1) of this Act for a warrant for sale of attached land; and
  (b) a person, at whose instance a notice was, by virtue of section 91 of this Act, registered (in this section, a "prospective purchaser"), has lodged objections to the application.
(2) At the hearing under section 97(1) of this Act, the sheriff may, if satisfied as to the matters mentioned in subsection (3) below, make an order-
  (a) sisting the application;
  (b) requiring the prospective purchaser to pay the price under the contract to the creditor; and
  (c) making such other incidental or consequential provision as the sheriff thinks fit.
(3) The matters are that-
  (a) the prospective purchaser did not, in entering into the contract for the purchase of the land, seek to defeat the rights of creditors of the debtor; and
  (b) both the prospective purchaser and the debtor will proceed with the purchase under the contract without undue delay.
(4) Section 116 of this Act applies to the proceeds of sale paid to the creditor in pursuance of an order under subsection (2) above as it applies to a sale in pursuance of a warrant for sale subject to the modification that references to the "appointed person" are references to the "creditor".

DEFINITIONS
"Appointed person": 2007 s.97(2)
"Caveat": 2007 Act s.91
"Debtor": 2007 Act s.125(5) (for the purposes of this chapter only)

GENERAL NOTE

This section is designed to protect an innocent purchaser where a creditor is applying for a warrant for sale. Where a creditor has applied for a warrant to sell attached land, and the prospective purchaser has lodged a caveat in terms of s.91, and lodged objections to the sale, there will be a hearing for those objections (s.97(1)). The sheriff, having heard the prospective purchasers may sist (i.e. suspend) the creditor's application (so that the order is not actually granted), make the prospective purchaser pay the purchase price for the land directly to the creditor, and make such other order as he thinks fit. He will only do this if he is satisfied that the purchaser is not in league or colluding with the debtor to defeat the rights of the creditors, and that the purchase will be effected without delay.

Subsection (4) ensures that the proceeds of sale from this sale are treated as if they were a sale by the appointed person under s.116.

For any potential interaction with sequestration, see para.13(3)(e) and (f) of Sch.5 of the 2007 Act (minor and consequential amendments).

100. Protection of purchaser under contract where warrant for sale granted

(1) This section applies where-
    (a) a warrant for sale has been granted under section 97(2) of this Act; and
    (b) a person (in this section, the "prospective purchaser") had, before the notice of land attachment was registered, entered into a contract to purchase attached land from the debtor.

(2) The sheriff may, on the application of the prospective purchaser and if satisfied as to the matters mentioned in section 99(3) of this Act, make an order-
    (a) suspending the warrant for sale for a period not exceeding 1 year from the day on which the order is made;
    (b) requiring the prospective purchaser to pay the price under the contract to the appointed person; and
    (c) making such other incidental or consequential provision as the sheriff thinks fit.

(3) Section 116 of this Act applies to the proceeds of sale paid to the appointed person in pursuance of an order under subsection (2) above as it applies to a sale in pursuance of a warrant for sale.

DEFINITIONS

"Appointed person": 2007 Act s.97(2)
"Debtor": 2007 Act s.125(5) (for the purposes of this chapter only)
"Notice of land attachment": 2007 Act s.83

GENERAL NOTE

Whereas the previous section had dealt with the position where a creditor was applying for a warrant for sale, this section deals with the position where a creditor already has been granted a warrant for sale.

If the warrant for sale has been granted, and the prospective purchaser had entered into a contract to purchase the attached land from the debtor before the notice of land attachment had been registered (see s.83), the sheriff, if satisfied that there was no collusion, and no likelihood of delay (both in terms of s.99 above), may order that the warrant for sale be suspended for up to a year, making the prospective purchaser pay the purchase price of the land to the appointed person, and do anything else the sheriff sees fit. While this may not be wholly satisfactory for the purchaser, at least he will be able to get the land eventually, while the year's delay allows the debtor or his family to find alternative accommodation.

Section 116 applies to the proceeds of such a sale.

101. Provision supplementary to sections 99 and 100

(1) This section applies where an order is made under section 99(2) or 100(2) of this Act.

(2) The sheriff may, on the application of the creditor or the appointed person, as the case may be, if satisfied as to the matters mentioned in subsection (3) below, revoke the order under section 99(2) or, as the case may be, section 100(2) of this Act.

(3) The matters are that-

    (a) the prospective purchaser and the debtor entered into the contract for the purchase of the land in order to defeat the rights of creditors of the debtor; or

    (b) there has been undue delay in completing the purchase.

DEFINITIONS

"Debtor": 2007 Act s.125(5) (for the purposes of the first reference in subs.(3)(a) only)

GENERAL NOTE

This deals with the situation where a debtor has been colluding with the debtor to defeat the rights of the creditors, or there has been undue delay in dealing with the purchase, in terms of the two previous sections. In either or both cases, the sheriff may revoke the order suspending the application or suspending the warrant for sale, requiring the prospective purchaser to pay the purchase price or doing anything else that the sheriff had previously required.

102. Warrant for sale of attached land owned in common

(1) This section applies where attached land specified in an application under section 92(1) of this Act is a pro indiviso share owned in common by the debtor and a third party.

(2) Subject to subsection (3) below, the sheriff may, under section 97(2) of this Act, make an order granting a warrant for sale of the land specified in the application.

(3) The sheriff must specify in the order whether the warrant-

    (a) authorises-

        (i) division of the land owned in common; and

        (ii) sale of the part, specified in the warrant, which, after such division, would belong to the debtor as sole owner (in this section, the "debtor's part"); or

    (b) sale of the land owned in common and, subject to subsection (5) below, division of the proceeds.

(4) Where the warrant authorises division of the land owned in common-

    (a) with effect from the day on which the order granting the warrant is made-

        (i) the debtor's part is subject to the land attachment; and

        (ii) the remaining land is disburdened of the land attachment; and

    (b) this Chapter applies as if the warrant for sale granted were a warrant for sale of the debtor's part only.

(5) Where the warrant authorises sale of the land owned in common and division of the proceeds, the appointed person must-

    (a) subject to the rights of any creditor of the third party holding a security over the third party's pro indiviso share of the land,

119

pay to the third party the share of the proceeds of sale due to that person; and

(b) deal, under section 116 of this Act, with the share of the proceeds that is attributable to the debtor's share in the land as if those proceeds were proceeds from the sale of land owned by the debtor as sole owner.

(6) Where land to which this section applies is divided and sold, or sold, in pursuance of a warrant for sale, the third party who, immediately before that warrant is granted, owned the land in common with the debtor may purchase the debtor's part or, as the case may be, the land.

(7) Where the third party purchases land which is sold under a warrant authorising sale and division of the proceeds-

(a) the third party need pay to the appointed person only the share of the price attributable to the debtor's share in the land; and

(b) subsection (5)(a) above does not apply.

DEFINITIONS

"Appointed person": 2007 Act s.97(2)

GENERAL NOTE

This section deals with the situation where the debtor owns a *pro indiviso* share of the attached land in common with a third party. The physical division of the attached land may in some cases be possible, though generally, as with a house, it will not be.

The order for the warrant for sale must specify whether the warrant authorises the physical division of the land and the sale of that part of it which belongs to the debtor as sole owner, or authorises sale of the land owned in common, and division of the sale proceeds between the debtor and the third party, with the portion for the debtor going to the debtor's creditor.

There are provisions that take account of each option, in each case so that the other person's interest is safeguarded, and is not subject to the land attachment, and the warrant for sale is only for the debtor's interest in the land.

Where the attached land is owned in common, and the warrant for sale provides for division of the proceeds, the appointed person must pay to the third party (subject to any heritable creditor's interest or the interest of any creditor effecting diligence) the third party's share of the proceeds.

The section also provides for the fairly common situation where the third party, commonly the debtor's spouse, buys out the debtor's part of the land owned in common or the debtor's interest in the attached land.

103. Intimation of sheriff's decision at full hearing

(1) Where a warrant for sale is granted under section 97(2) of this Act, the creditor must, as soon as is reasonably practicable, send a copy of the warrant to-

(a) the debtor; and

(b) the appointed person.

(2) Where a warrant for sale is refused under section 97(3)(b) or (5) of this Act, the sheriff clerk must, as soon as is reasonably practicable, send a copy of the order to the debtor and to any other person appearing to the sheriff clerk to have an interest.

DEFINITIONS

"Appointed person": 2007 Act s.97(2)

"Debtor": 2007 Act s.125(5) (for the purposes of this chapter only)

GENERAL NOTE

Once the warrant for sale is granted, the creditor must send a copy of the order to both the debtor and the appointed person. If it is refused under s.97(3)(b) or (5), the sheriff clerk must tell the debtor and anyone else having an interest in the matter.

104. Supplementary orders as respects sale

(1) The sheriff may, either when making an order granting a warrant for sale or subsequently, make such order as appears to the sheriff to be appropriate in connection with the sale of the attached land.

(2) In particular, the sheriff may, on the application of the appointed person-

    (a) extend the period specified in the warrant granted under section 97(2) of this Act within which the land is to be sold;

    (b) remove that appointed person and appoint another solicitor as the appointed person; and

    (c) on the application of the creditor, the debtor or any other person appearing to the sheriff to have an interest-

        (i) in a case where the appointed person has died, appoint another solicitor as the appointed person;

        (ii) in a case where the appointed person is unable to carry out the appointed person's functions due to ill health or incapacity, remove that person and appoint another solicitor as appointed person;

        (iii) in any other case, on cause shown, so remove and appoint.

(3) An order made under this section after the grant of a warrant for sale must be intimated by the creditor-

    (a) in such form and manner;

    (b) before the expiry of such period; and

    (c) to the debtor and such other persons,

as the sheriff may direct.

DEFINITIONS

"Appointed person": 2007 Act s.97(2)

"Debtor": 2007 Act s.125(5) (for the purposes of this chapter only)

GENERAL NOTE

This section gives the sheriff certain useful extra powers such as extending the period during which the land may be sold (the statute refers to s.97(2) when it should be s.97(4)) and replacing the appointed person.

105. Effect of certain refusals of application for warrant for sale under section 97(5)

Where, under section 97(5) of this Act, an order is made refusing an application for a warrant for sale by virtue of a ground mentioned in paragraph (d), (e), (f) or (g) of subsection (6) of that section-

    (a) the land attachment does not, by reason only of that refusal, cease to have effect; and

    (b) it is competent for the creditor to make a further application under section 92(1) of this Act.

GENERAL NOTE

This provides that should an application for warrant of sale be unsuccessful in terms of s.97(5)(d)-(g), the land attachment itself is still valid and the creditor may reapply at a later date for another warrant of sale under s.92(1).

106. Termination of debtor's right to occupy land

(1) Where an order is made granting a warrant for sale, the creditor may, by notice served on-

    (a) the debtor; and

    (b) any other person having a right, derived from the debtor, to occupy the land to which the warrant relates,

terminate, with effect from such day as the creditor specifies in the notice (being a day not less than 7 days after the date of service), any right of the debtor (or other person) to occupy that land.

(2) A notice under subsection (1) above must be-

    (a) in (or as nearly as may be in) the form prescribed by Act of Sederunt; and

    (b) served on the debtor or, as the case may be, other person.

(3) Any right of a person (other than the debtor) to occupy land which, before a notice of land attachment relating to the land was registered, would have been binding on a singular successor of the debtor is not affected by subsection (1) above.

(4) A certificate, in (or as nearly as may be in) the form prescribed by Act of Sederunt, of service of a notice such as is mentioned in subsection (1) above may be registered.

DEFINITIONS

"Debtor": 2007 Act s.125(5) (except for the reference in subs.(1)(a))

GENERAL NOTE

This section provides that a creditor may serve a notice, on a form yet to be devised, requiring the debtor, or anyone obtaining right from the debtor (unless that right predates the registration of notice of land attachment and would have been binding on a singular successor of the debtor) to vacate the land to which the warrant relates within seven (or more, if so stated) days of the service of the notice.

107. Consequences of giving notice under section 106(1)

(1) From the date on which the creditor gives notice under section 106(1) of this Act until the land attachment ceases to have effect the creditor (in place of the debtor) has the rights and obligations of a heritable creditor in lawful possession of the land.

(2) Without prejudice to the generality of subsection (1) above, those rights and obligations-

    (a) include any rights and obligations under any lease, or under any permission or right of occupancy, granted in respect of the land, including the right to receive rent from any tenant;

    (b) do not include the power to grant a lease.

(3) Subsection (2)(a) above applies only as respects rent payable on or after the date on which the creditor intimates in writing to the tenant that the notice has been given.

(4) A creditor who has given notice under section 106(1) of this Act-

    (a) may apply to the sheriff for an order-

       (i) authorising the carrying out of works of reconstruction, alteration or improvement if they are works reasonably required to maintain the market value of the land; and

      (ii) to recover from the debtor any expenses and outlays reasonably incurred in so doing;

  (b) may bring an action of ejection against the debtor; and

  (c) has title to bring any action of removing, intrusion or ejection which the debtor might competently have brought in respect of the land.

(5) Any-

  (a) expenses or outlays incurred as mentioned in subsection (4)(a)(ii) above; and

  (b) expenses of any action of removing, intrusion or ejection brought by virtue of subsection (4)(b) or (c) above,

are expenses incurred in executing the land attachment.

(6) The reference in subsection (3) above to intimation in writing includes a reference to intimation by electronic communication.

DEFINITIONS

"Debtor": 2007 Act s.125(5) (for the purposes of this chapter only)

GENERAL NOTE

Once the notice under s.106 has been given, the creditor is able to act as if he were a heritable creditor over the property, acting in terms of s.20(5) of the Conveyancing and Feudal Reform (Scotland) Act 1970. This means that he has all the rights and obligations of the debtor, including the right to receive rent or other payments, but not the right to grant a lease. He may only receive the rents once he has intimated in writing (which may be done electronically) to the tenant that the notice under s.106 has been given. The creditor, on application to the sheriff, may carry out certain works on the attached land subject to the warrant for sale, including altering or improving it if necessary to maintain the market value of the land, while recovering the expenses and outlays of so doing from the debtor (or, in practice, out of the sale proceeds of the land). He has the right to bring an action of ejection of the debtor and to raise an action of removing, ejection, etc. against anyone else whom the debtor might have brought on his land.

The sale

108. Appointed person

(1) The appointed person-

  (a) is an officer of the court; and

  (b) must act independently of the creditor, the debtor and any other interested person.

(2) Before exercising any functions conferred by virtue of this Chapter, the appointed person must lodge a bond of caution for such amount as may be prescribed by Act of Sederunt.

(3) The appointed person may apply to the sheriff who granted the warrant for sale under section 97(2) of this Act for directions as to how to exercise any of that person's functions.

(4) In executing a warrant for sale granted under section 97(2) of this Act, the appointed person must-

  (a) exercise the functions conferred-

      (i) by this Chapter; and

      (ii) by the Scottish Ministers under subsection (8) below; and

  (b) comply with any directions made under subsection (3) above.

(5) The appointed person is liable to the creditor, the debtor, any person who owns the attached land in common with the debtor and any secured creditor for any patrimonial loss caused as a result of the appointed person's negligence in executing the warrant for sale.

(6) The creditor is liable for the appointed person's reasonable remuneration and outlays incurred in exercising functions conferred by virtue of this Chapter.

(7) Such remuneration and outlays are expenses incurred by the creditor in executing the land attachment.

(8) The Scottish Ministers may, by regulations-
   (a) confer functions on;
   (b) remove functions from; or
   (c) otherwise modify the functions of,
   appointed persons.

DEFINITIONS
   "Appointed person": 2007 Act s.97(2)
   "Debtor": 2007 Act s.125(5) (for the purposes of this chapter only)

GENERAL NOTE
   This section explains certain duties and functions of the appointed person. He is an officer of the court (which he would be anyway, given that he is a solicitor) and this places him in a position of greater responsibility and requires him to act with the utmost probity in his dealings, since he is effectively deemed to be part of the official judicial system. He must not be personally interested in the creditor, the debtor or anyone else involved in the land attachment. He must lodge caution for his actions (i.e. lodge in court a bond or other sum which would make good any loss to the creditor should the appointed person default in some way). Should occasion require, he may apply to the sheriff for directions on how to exercise his functions, and those duties are themselves circumscribed by the 2007 Act itself and by any other regulations yet to be produced by the Scottish Ministers. The power to produce the regulations must be exercised subject to negative resolution procedure (see s224(3)). Should there be any patrimonial loss arising out of the appointed person's negligence in carrying out the sale, he (or presumably his professional insurers) will be liable for that loss to the creditor, to anyone who owns the land in common with the debtor, to any heritable creditor, and to the debtor. The creditor is responsible for his fees and outlays but they are an expense of the land attachment.

109. Method of sale

(1) The land in relation to which a warrant for sale is granted under section 97(2) of this Act must be sold in execution of that warrant by the appointed person.

(2) The land may, unless the sheriff otherwise directs, be sold by private bargain or at auction.

(3) The appointed person must consult the creditor before determining which of the methods of sale mentioned in subsection (2) above is to be used.

(4) The appointed person must-
   (a) advertise the sale of the attached land; and
   (b) ensure that the price at which the land is sold is the best that can reasonably be obtained.

DEFINITIONS
   "Appointed person": 2007 Act s.97(2)

GENERAL NOTE
   The appointed person must sell the land for which the warrant has been granted by private bargain or auction, unless directed otherwise by the sheriff and following consultation with the creditor. The sale price must be the best that can reasonably be obtained.

110. Legal incapacity or disability of debtor not to affect title of purchaser

Any legal incapacity or disability of a debtor has no effect on the title passed to a purchaser of attached land which has been sold in execution of a warrant for sale.

GENERAL NOTE

The legal capacity of the debtor does not affect the validity of the title of land passed to the purchaser following the sale of the attached land in execution of a warrant for sale.

111. Title of purchaser not to be affected by certain irregularities

(1) Where a disposition bearing to be granted in execution of a warrant for sale is registered in the appropriate property register, the validity of that disposition is not, if the conditions mentioned in subsection (2) below are satisfied, challengeable on the ground-

(a) that the land attachment was irregularly executed; or

(b) that, before the date of settlement of the sale, the land attachment had ceased to have effect.

(2) The conditions are that-

(a) the purchaser acted in good faith in relation to the purchase of the land; and

(b) the appointed person grants a certificate, in (or as nearly as may be in) the form prescribed by Act of Sederunt, to the purchaser confirming that the land attachment was regularly executed.

(3) In subsection (2)(a) above, a purchaser is deemed to have acted in good faith where, immediately before the date of settlement, the purchaser was not aware and could not reasonably have become aware that the land attachment was irregularly executed or, as the case may be, that it had, before that date, ceased to have effect.

DEFINITIONS

"Appointed person": 2007 Act s.97(2)

"Appropriate property register": 2007 Act s.83(1)(c)(i)

GENERAL NOTE

This section explains that provided the purchaser acted in good faith in relation to the purchase of the land, and that the appointed person provided a certificate in the required form (yet to be devised) to the purchaser confirming that the land attachment was properly executed, any disposition, which on the face of it was granted in execution of a warrant for sale and registered in the appropriate register, will not be challengeable on the grounds that the land attachment was irregularly executed or that before the date of settlement of the sale, the land attachment had ceased have effect.

The purchaser's good faith is deemed to be established by his lack of awareness (or where he could not reasonably have become aware) that the execution was irregular or that the land attachment had ceased to have effect.

112. Effect of registration of disposition on securities

Where a disposition of attached land is granted in execution of a warrant for sale to a purchaser, then, on the registration of the disposition, the land is disburdened of-

(a) the land attachment; and

(b) any-
    (i) heritable security; or
    (ii) diligence,
ranking *pari passu* with, or after, the land attachment.

DEFINITIONS
"Land": 2007 Act s.82

GENERAL NOTE
Where the disposition in execution of a warrant of sale to a purchaser is registered, the land becomes free of the land attachment and of any heritable security or diligence ranking *pari passu* with or after the land attachment.

113. Report of sale

(1) Where attached land is sold in execution of a warrant for sale, the appointed person must, before the expiry of the period of 28 days beginning with the day on which the sale price is paid, lodge with the sheriff clerk for the court which granted the warrant a report of the sale.

(2) A report lodged under subsection (1) above must-
    (a) be in (or as nearly as may be in) the form prescribed by Act of Sederunt; and
    (b) contain-
        (i) a description of the land (or part) sold and the sale price;
        (ii) a description of any land which is unsold and the price at which it was last offered for sale (or, if offered for sale at auction, the reserve price);
        (iii) a statement of the expenses incurred by the creditor in executing the land attachment;
        (iv) a statement of the amount due under any security or diligence ranking on the proceeds of sale prior to, or *pari passu* with, the land attachment;
        (v) a statement of the amount due under any security or diligence ranking on the proceeds of sale after the land attachment;
        (vi) a note of the amount of any surplus of the sale proceeds payable to the debtor; and
        (vii) a note of any balance of the debt due by the debtor to the creditor.

(3) If the appointed person-
    (a) without reasonable excuse makes a report of sale after the expiry of the period mentioned in subsection (1) above; or
    (b) wilfully refuses to make, or delays making, a report after the expiry of that period,
the sheriff may make an order providing that the appointed person is not entitled to payment from the creditor of the reasonable remuneration and outlays incurred in executing the warrant for sale or so much of such remuneration and outlays as the sheriff specifies.

DEFINITIONS
"Appointed person": 2007 Act s.97(2)
"Debtor": 2007 Act s.125(5) (for the purposes of this chapter only)
"Land": 2007 Act s.82

GENERAL NOTE

Within 28 days of the payment of the sale price, the appointed person must lodge a report with the sheriff clerk. The report will be in a form yet to be devised but will contain information about the price, the land sold, any unsold land, the creditor's expenses, the amount due to any prior or *pari passu* heritable creditors or other creditors effecting diligence, the amount (if any) due to any subsequent heritable creditors or other creditors effecting diligence, the amount (if any) of any surplus of the sale proceeds to the debtor and the amount (if any) of any balance of debt due to the debtor.

If the appointed person fails or delays to lodge this report, without good cause, the sheriff may order that he loses some or all of his entitlement to be paid by the creditor.

114. Audit of report of sale

(1) Where a report is lodged under section 113(1) of this Act, the sheriff must remit it to the auditor of court for the auditor to report on it within such time as the sheriff may specify.

(2) The auditor must—

    (a) tax the expenses of the land attachment chargeable against the debtor;

    (b) certify the balance due to or by the debtor following the sale; and

    (c) submit a report to the sheriff.

(3) The auditor is not entitled to charge a fee in respect of the report submitted under subsection (2)(c) above.

(4) The report of sale and the auditor's report must be retained by the sheriff clerk for such period as may be prescribed by Act of Sederunt and during that period must be available for inspection by any interested person on payment of such fee as may be prescribed in an order made under section 2 of the Courts of Law Fees (Scotland) Act 1895 (c.14).

GENERAL NOTE

Once the report in the above section is lodged, the sheriff must forward it to the auditor of court for audit. The auditor will tax the expenses of the land attachment, certify any balance due to or from the debtor, and submit his own report to the sheriff. The auditor may not charge a fee for his own report. The two reports will be retained by the sheriff clerk for such period as is yet to be specified and the public may inspect them on payment of the appropriate fee.

In the event that s.125 applies (namely, that a debtor has granted to a third party a deed in breach of any inhibition and that deed has been reduced) the auditor will certify any balance due to the debtor or the third party, or from the debtor or the third party.

115. Sheriff's consideration of report

(1) Where the auditor has submitted a report to the sheriff under section 114(2)(c) of this Act, the sheriff may, after considering that report and the report on sale lodged under section 113(1) of this Act—

    (a) make an order approving the report of sale subject to such amendments (if any) made—

        (i) following a hearing under subsection (2) below, by the sheriff; or

        (ii) by the auditor,

    as may be specified in the order;

    (b) if the sheriff is satisfied that there has been a substantial irregularity in the land attachment, make an order—

        (i) declaring the land attachment to be void; and

        (ii) making such consequential order as appears to the sheriff to be necessary in the circumstances.

(2) The sheriff may not make an order under subsection (1) above without first giving all interested persons an opportunity to be heard.

(3) The sheriff clerk must intimate the order of the sheriff under subsection (1) above to the debtor and any other person appearing to the sheriff clerk to have an interest.

(4) Any order under subsection (1)(b) above does not affect the title of any person to land sold in execution of the warrant for sale to which the report relates.

GENERAL NOTE

The sheriff will consider the auditor's report and the sale report and may, if he wishes, make an order approving the report of sale, subject to any amendments made by the auditor or following a hearing from any interested persons (subs.(1)(a)). If the sheriff is satisfied that there has been a material irregularity in the land attachment, he may declare the land attachment void, and make any necessary consequential order (subs.(1)(b)). In that latter event, the purchaser's title is still valid.

116. Proceeds of sale

(1) Where attached land is sold in execution of a warrant for sale, the proceeds of the sale must be disbursed by the appointed person in the following order-

  (a) subject to subsection (2) below, any expenses due to the creditor by virtue of section 114(2)(a) of this Act;

  (b) any sums due to any other creditor holding a security or diligence over the land which ranks prior to the land attachment;

  (c) any sums due to-

      (i) the attaching creditor in respect of the sum recoverable by the land attachment (other than any such expenses as are mentioned in paragraph (a) above); and

      (ii) any creditor under a security or diligence which ranks *pari passu* with the land attachment;

  (d) any sums due to any other creditor under any security or diligence which ranks after the land attachment; and

  (e) subject to section 37(8C)(b) of the 1985 Act, any balance due to the debtor.

(2) Subject to section 113(3) of this Act, the appointed person may deduct and retain from the sum mentioned in subsection (1)(a) above such remuneration and outlays incurred by the appointed person in executing the warrant for sale.

(3) Where there is a balance due to the debtor, the appointed person must pay it to the debtor or any person authorised to give a receipt for the balance on the debtor's behalf.

(4) Where, by virtue of subsection (1) above, a creditor receives the sums due to the creditor under a security or diligence, that creditor must grant a discharge of that security or diligence.

(5) If the appointed person is unable to obtain from-

  (a) the debtor; or

  (b) any creditor of the debtor;

a receipt or discharge in respect of the disbursement of the proceeds of sale, the appointed person may consign the amount due in the sheriff court for the person having right to it.

(6) Any such consignation discharges the obligation to pay the amount due; and a certificate of the sheriff clerk is sufficient evidence of the discharge.

DEFINITIONS
"Appointed person": 2007 Act s.97(2)
"Land": 2007 Act s.82
"Sum recoverable by land attachment": 2007 Act s.81(5)(b)

GENERAL NOTE
This section explains the order in which the proceeds of sale should be disbursed by the appointed person.

In essence, under subs.(1), the order is as follows:

(a) any expenses due to the creditor (less the appointed person's permitted remuneration and outlays, which may be deducted from the sale proceeds);
(b) any sums due to any prior-ranking creditor holding security or diligence over the land;
(c) any sums due to the attaching creditor in respect of the sum recoverable by the land attachment, and any sums due to any other creditor *pari passu* with the attaching creditor;
(d) any sums due to any creditor holding security or diligence ranking after the land attachment; and
(e) any balance due to the debtor, unless the debtor is sequestrated, in which case, under the 1985 Act s.37(8C)(b), the balance is paid to the trustee in sequestration.

Under subs.(2), the appointed person is entitled to be paid his fees and outlays by the creditor, but may deduct them from the sums due to the creditor (unless the sheriff has directed otherwise under s.113(3)).

The appointed person must pay any balance due to the debtor to the debtor or the debtor's authorisee.

Where a creditor receives the sums due to him by way of his security or diligence, he must grant a discharge of that security or diligence.

If the appointed person cannot obtain a receipt or discharge from the debtor or any creditor of the debtor in respect of the sale proceeds, he may consign the funds into the sheriff court for the benefit of the person entitled to it. The sheriff clerk will then certificate the discharge.

In the event that s.125 applies (namely, that a debtor has granted to a third party a deed in breach of any inhibition and that deed has been reduced), the reference to any payment of the balance to the debtor should be preceded by a further paragraph (da) indicating the payment of any balance to the third party (see s.125(9)).

Foreclosure

117. Foreclosure

(1) This section applies where the appointed person-
    (a) has exposed to sale the land specified in the warrant for sale; and
    (b) has-
        (i) failed to find a purchaser; or
        (ii) succeeded in selling only part of the land, and that at a price which is less than the sum secured by the land attachment and by any security or diligence ranking prior to, or *pari passu* with, the land attachment.

(2) The appointed person may apply, in (or as nearly as may be in) the form prescribed by Act of Sederunt, to the sheriff who granted the warrant for sale for a decree of foreclosure.

(3) The application under subsection (2) above must be accompanied by-

    (a) a statement setting out the whole amount secured-
       (i) by the land attachment; and
       (ii) by any other security or diligence ranking prior to or
          pari passu with the land attachment; and
    (b) where part of the land has been sold, a report on that sale
      under section 113(1) of this Act.
(4) A copy of an application under subsection (2) above must be
    served by a judicial officer on-
    (a) the debtor;
    (b) where the debtor does not own the land, the owner;
    (c) any occupier of the land specified in the warrant for sale;
    (d) any creditor in a heritable security affecting the land, as
      disclosed in a report of a search in the appropriate property
      register brought down to a date no later than 3 clear days
      before the day on which the application is made; and
    (e) any other person having a land attachment or other diligence
      over the land.
(5) The sheriff, after affording any person on whom a copy of the
    application was served under subsection (4) above an opportu-
    nity to make representations, may-
    (a) grant the decree of foreclosure applied for;
    (b) sist the application for a period not exceeding 3 months to
      allow the debtor to pay the sum recoverable by the land
      attachment; or
    (c) appoint a valuer to fix a reserve price at which the land (or
      remaining part of that land) must be-
       (i) auctioned; or
       (ii) advertised for sale and if unsold auctioned.
(6) The debtor may-
    (a) bid and purchase at any auction under subsection (5)(c)(i) or
      (ii) above; or
    (b) purchase at the price advertised under subsection (5)(c)(ii)
      above.
(7) Where an order has been made under subsection (5)(c) above
    and the appointed person-
    (a) produces an auctioneer's certificate that the land in question
      has been duly exposed to sale at the reserve price but is
      unsold; or
    (b) certifies in (or as nearly as may be in) the form prescribed by
      Act of Sederunt that the land has been advertised at the
      reserve price but is unsold,
    the sheriff may, without further intimation, grant decree of fore-
    closure.
(8) A decree of foreclosure granted under this section must-
    (a) be in (or as nearly as may be in) the form prescribed by Act
      of Sederunt;
    (b) describe the land in relation to which it is granted; and
    (c) contain a declaration of the price at which, on registration of
      an extract of the decree, the creditor is deemed to have
      acquired the land.
(9) Where provision is made by virtue of this Chapter or by any
    other enactment permitting the application under subsection (2)
    above to be an electronic communication, the requirement in
    subsection (3) above that the application be accompanied by the

statement and report mentioned in that subsection is satisfied by the provision of electronic communications.

DEFINITIONS
"Appointed person": 2007 Act s.97(2)
"Debtor": 2007 Act s.125(5) (for the purposes of this chapter only)
"Judicial officer": 2007 Act s.57
"Land": 2007 Act s.82

GENERAL NOTE
This section deals with foreclosure, which is where the creditor is unable to have the land sold, or sold at the right price, and eventually obtains the land himself.

Under subs.(1), if the appointed person is unable to find a purchaser, or succeeds only in selling part of the land at a price which is less than the sum secured by the land attachment plus the sums dues under any security or diligence ranking ahead of or *pari passu* with the land attachment, he may apply to the original sheriff who granted the warrant for sale for a decree of foreclosure, using a form yet to be devised. This may be done by electronic means (subs.(9)).

Under subs.(3), the application will need to be accompanied by a statement showing the amounts due in terms of subs.(1), and a report on the sale, as in s.113(1). This too may be done by electronic means (subs.(9)).

A copy of the application under subs.(2) must be served by judicial officer on the debtor, the owner of the land (if not the debtor), any occupier of the land indicated in the warrant for sale, any heritable creditor (as revealed by searches in the appropriate property register no later than three clear days before the application date) and anyone else having a land attachment or other diligence over the land (subs.(4)).

The sheriff, having allowed the persons in subs.(4) to have the opportunity to make representations, may grant the decree of foreclosure or may sist the application for three months to allow the debtor a further chance to pay the sums recoverable by the land attachment. As a further option the sheriff may appoint a valuer to fix a reserve price for the land (or the remaining part of the land) for the purpose of an auction, or for advertisement for sale and auction if the land remains unsold (subs.(5)).

The debtor himself may bid at the auction or try to buy the land following advertisement (subs.(6)).

Where an auction is ordered and takes place but the land remains unsold at the reserve price (as evidenced by an auctioneer's certificate to that effect), or the appointed person certifies (in a form yet to be devised) that the sale of the land was advertised at the reserve price but no sale took place, the sheriff, under subs.(7), may grant decree of foreclosure.

The decree itself will be in a form yet to be devised, and will describe the land subject to the foreclosure and contain a statement of the price at which the creditor will be deemed to have acquired the land. This will be necessary both for registration purposes and for stamp duty land tax purposes, as well as the next section.

For any potential interaction with sequestration, see para.13(3)(e) and (f) of Sch.5 of the 2007 Act (minor and consequential amendments). See the notes at the end of Ch.1 of this Part.

118. Registration of decree of foreclosure

(1) On registration of an extract of the decree of foreclosure in the appropriate property register–

(a) any right to discharge the land attachment by payment is extinguished;

(b) the creditor has right to, and is vested in, the land as if an irredeemable disposition of the land, granted in favour of the creditor by the debtor, had been delivered to the creditor and, on the date of registration of the extract of the decree, duly registered;

(c) the land is disburdened of the land attachment and of any security or diligence ranking after the land attachment; and

(d) the creditor has the like right as the debtor to redeem or as the case may be to discharge by payment any security or diligence ranking prior to, or pari passu with, the land attachment.

(2) Notwithstanding the registration of an extract of a decree of foreclosure, any personal obligation of the debtor under any security remains in full force and effect in so far as not extinguished by the price for which the creditor is deemed to have acquired the land and the price for which any part of the land has been sold.

(3) Title acquired by virtue of a decree of foreclosure under this section is not challengeable on the ground of any irregularity in the proceedings for, or in any diligence which preceded, foreclosure.

(4) Notwithstanding subsection (3) above, nothing in this section affects the competency of any claim for damages in respect of such proceedings or diligence as are mentioned in that subsection.

DEFINITIONS
"Appropriate property register": 2007 Act s.83(1)(c)(i)
"Foreclosure": 2007 Act s.117
"Land": 2007 Act s.82

GENERAL NOTE
Under subs.(1), once the decree of foreclosure is registered in the appropriate property register, the debtor has no further opportunity to discharge the land attachment by payment. The creditor is vested in the land as if the debtor had granted and delivered to him a disposition of the land, with the date of registration of the extract decree being the date of registration for that land. The land itself is disburdened of any security or diligence ranking after the land attachment, and the creditor takes over the debtor's position in respect of the debtor's right to discharge any security or diligence raking prior to or *pari passu* with the land attachment. The creditor effectively will own the land, or in the case of a long lease, will be the tenant in place of the debtor.

Under subs.(2), even after foreclosure, the debtor may still be due sums to the attaching creditor (or any postponed creditor) if the price for which the land was deemed to be transferred to the attaching creditor does not discharge the debtor's debt or other obligation.

Under subs.(3), the creditor's title is not challengeable because of any irregularity in the foreclosure or diligence proceedings, though under subs.(4), the debtor retains a right to claim damages for wrongful diligence.

Payments to account and expenses

119. Ascription

(1) This section applies where any sums are-
   (a) recovered by a land attachment; or
   (b) paid to account of the sum recoverable by the land attachment while it is in effect.

(2) Such sums must be ascribed to the following in the order in which they are mentioned-
   (a) the expenses which are chargeable against the debtor incurred in the land attachment;
   (b) any interest which has accrued, at the day or, as the case may be, the last day on which the notice of land attachment was registered, on the sum for payment of which the charge was served;
   (c) any sum for payment of which that charge was served together with such interest as has accrued after the day mentioned in paragraph (b) above.

DEFINITIONS
"Notice of land attachment": 2007 Act s.83
"Sum recoverable by land attachment": 2007 Act s.81(5)(b)

GENERAL NOTE
This section deals with ascription, which explains how any payments recovered by the land attachment, or made by the debtor (or others on his behalf), are to be used towards the paying off of the sums recoverable under the land attachment. They are first to be paid: (a) towards the expenses chargeable against the debtor arising out of the land attachment, then (b) towards the interest accruing since the day of the registration of the notice of land attachment (or the latter of the two days of registration of that notice) and finally (c) towards the sums due under the charge (under s.81(2)(b)) together with interest arising from the day (or latter day) in (b) above.

120. Expenses of land attachment

(1) The expenses incurred by the creditor in executing a land attachment are chargeable against the debtor.

(2) Expenses which, in accordance with subsection (1) above, are chargeable against the debtor are recoverable from the debtor by the land attachment but not by any other legal process.

(3) Where any expenses such as are mentioned in subsection (2) above have not been recovered by the time the land attachment is completed, or otherwise ceases to have effect, they cease to be so recoverable.

(4) In subsection (2) above, the reference to expenses does not include a reference to the expenses of service of a charge.

(5) The sheriff may, if satisfied that the debtor has objected on frivolous grounds to-

(a) an application for a warrant for sale; or

(b) an application for a decree of foreclosure,

award expenses, not exceeding such amount as may be prescribed by the Scottish Ministers by regulations, against the debtor.

DEFINITIONS
"Debtor": 2007 Act s.125(5) (for the purposes of this chapter only)

GENERAL NOTE
This section follows the usual practice throughout this Act of ensuring that although the expenses of land attachment are chargeable to the debtor, the expenses of any one diligence are only recoverable by that form of diligence. Consequently the expenses of the land attachment may only be recovered by land attachment and not by any other diligence - with the exception of the expenses of the service of the original charge (see s.81(2)(b)), which may be recovered by any other diligence. Where the expenses are not recovered by the time of completion of the land attachment, or where the land attachment ceases to have effect, the creditor may not attempt to recover them.

The debtor may also be liable for the expenses of any frivolous objection to the application for warrant for sale or the application for foreclosure: the amount of such expenses is yet to be established by regulations produced by the Scottish Ministers, such regulations being subject to negative resolution procedure (see s.224(3)).

Termination, discharge etc. of land attachment

121. Termination by payment etc.

(1) If the full sum for payment of which the charge was served is, before the expiry of the period of 28 days mentioned in section 81(3) of this Act, either paid or tendered to the

creditor, to a judicial officer or to any other person who has authority to receive payment on behalf of the creditor-

(a) the land attachment is not created; and

(b) the notice of land attachment ceases to have effect.

(2) Subject to subsection (3) below, if the full sum recoverable by a land attachment is either paid or tendered to-

(a) any of the persons mentioned in subsection (1) above; or

(b) the appointed person,

the land attachment ceases to have effect.

(3) Subsection (2) above does not apply unless the sum is paid before-

(a) where a warrant for sale of the attached land (or part of it) is granted, a contract of sale of the attached land is concluded; or

(b) an extract of a decree of foreclosure in relation to the attached land (or part of it) is registered.

DEFINITIONS

"Appointed person": 2007 Act s.97(2)
"Appropriate property register": 2007 Act s.83(1)(c)(i)
"Foreclosure": 2007 Act s.117
"Judicial officer": 2007 Act s.57
"Notice of land attachment": 2007 Act s.83
"Sum recoverable by land attachment": 2007 Act s.81(5)(b)

GENERAL NOTE

This deals with termination of the land attachment. Under subs.(1), if the full sum for which the charge was served under s.81(2)(b) was paid or tendered to the creditor, a judicial officer or anyone authorised to receive payment on behalf of the creditor within the 28 day period referred to in s.81(3) (being the 28 day period starting with the day, or the latter of the two days, of the registration of the notice of land attachment), the land attachment is not created and the notice of land attachment ceases to have any effect.

Under subs.(2), if the full sum recoverable is paid or tendered to the creditor, a judicial officer, anyone authorised to receive payment on behalf of the creditor, or the appointed person, after the land attachment is in place, the land attachment ceases to have effect. However, under subs.(3), this will only be the case where the debtor pays the sum before a contract of sale of the attached land (or part of it) to a purchaser (under ss.108-116) is concluded (notwithstanding the fact that an order for the warrant for sale had been granted), or an extract of the decree of foreclosure (under ss.117-118) is registered in the appropriate property register. So in the unlikely event that the debtor pays the sum after the appointed person has concluded a sale of the attached land (or part of it) or the creditor has obtained the land (or part of it) by foreclosure, the land attachment remains in place. This is to protect the position of the purchaser or the creditor to ensure that their title is secure. Nevertheless, it is possible that the debtor would erroneously pay the full sum, perhaps unaware of the contract for sale or the foreclosure. If the contract for sale, or the value placed on the land for foreclosure purposes, was equal to the full sum, there would be no occasion for the creditor to keep it and he would have to return it to the debtor, but to the extent that the sale price or foreclosure value was less than the full sum, he presumably could retain that part of the full sum that represented the shortfall in his recovery of the sums due to him, and return the balance to the debtor. Equally, the creditor might have only been able to sell or foreclose on a part of the attached land, so the land attachment would remain in place for the remaining part of the attached land. Payment of the outstanding sum would then render the land attachment of the remaining part of the attached land ineffective in terms of subs.(2).

122. Discharge

(1) This section applies where-

(a) under section 121(1)(b) of this Act, a notice of land attachment ceases to have effect; or

(b) under subsection (2) of that section, a land attachment ceases to have effect.

(2) The creditor must discharge-
    (a) the notice of land attachment; or
    (b) the land attachment,
      provided that the expenses of discharge are paid or tendered to any of the persons mentioned in section 121(1) of this Act.
(3) It is competent to register any such discharge.

DEFINITIONS
"Judicial officer": 2007 Act s.57
"Notice of land attachment": 2007 Act s.83

GENERAL NOTE
Where under s.121 a land attachment ceases to have effect, the creditor must discharge the notice of land attachment or the land attachment (as appropriate) provided that the expenses of the discharge are met by the debtor and paid to the creditor, a judicial officer or anyone authorised to receive payment on behalf of the creditor. Although the wording says that it is competent to register the discharge, which suggests that it is not obligatory to do so, it would be in his interest to have it registered in order to save any difficulty when he tries to sell his property at a later date. The section does not say so, but it is presumed that registration would take place in the appropriate property register.

123. Recall and restriction of land attachment

(1) The debtor or any other person having an interest may apply to the sheriff for an order-
    (a) recalling a land attachment; or
    (b) restricting such an attachment.
(2) An application under subsection (1) above must-
    (a) be in (or as nearly as may be in) the form prescribed by Act of Sederunt; and
    (b) be intimated to the creditor.
(3) The sheriff must, if satisfied-
    (a) that the land attachment-
        (i) is invalid;
        (ii) has been executed incompetently or irregularly; or
        (iii) has ceased to have effect; or
    (b) that the creditor is, under section 122(2)(b) of this Act, obliged to discharge it,
    make an order declaring that to be the case and recalling the land attachment.
(4) The sheriff may, if satisfied that a land attachment is valid but-
    (a) having regard to the sum recoverable by the land attachment, that significantly more land is attached than need be; and
    (b) that it is reasonable to do so,
    make an order restricting the effect of the land attachment to part only of the land to which it relates.
(5) An order of recall or restriction must be in (or as nearly as may be in) the form prescribed by Act of Sederunt.
(6) It is competent for a person who obtains an order of recall or restriction to register that order in the appropriate property register.

DEFINITIONS
"Appropriate property register": 2007 Act s.83(1)(c)(i)

GENERAL NOTE

This permits a debtor or anyone else with an interest to apply to the sheriff for an order to recall the land attachment or restrict it. The form in which this is to be done is yet to be devised, but must be intimated to the creditor. If the sheriff is satisfied that the land attachment is invalid, was executed incompetently or irregularly, or has ceased to have effect, or that the creditor under the previous section should discharge the land attachment, he may make an order recalling the land attachment. Under subs.(4), the sheriff may also restrict a valid land attachment if it attaches more land than is necessary for the sum to be recovered and where it is reasonable to do so.

The order of recall or restriction are in forms yet to be devised. It is competent for the orders to be registered in the appropriate property register.

124. Duration of land attachment

(1) Subject to sections 121 to 123 of this Act and to subsection (2) below, a land attachment ceases to have effect on the expiry of the period of 5 years beginning with the day or, as the case may be, the last day on which the notice of land attachment is registered.

(2) The creditor may extend the period mentioned in subsection (1) above for a further period of 5 years.

(3) Such an extension is effected by the creditor registering, during the period of 2 months ending with the day on which the period mentioned in subsection (1) above ends, a notice of extension in (or as nearly as may be in) the form prescribed by Act of Sederunt.

(4) The creditor may extend the period for which a land attachment has effect on more than one occasion and subsections (1) to (3) above apply as if for the reference in subsection (1) above to the day on which the notice of land attachment is registered there were substituted a reference to the day or, as the case may be, the last day on which the notice of extension is last registered.

DEFINITIONS

"Notice of land attachment": 2007 Act s.83

GENERAL NOTE

In common with the usual rules in Scotland for prescription, the land attachment remains in place for five years from the date on which the notice of the land attachment was registered. The land attachment may be extended by a further period of five years by registering a form (yet to be devised) within two months of the end of each five year period.

Land attachment subsequent to reduction of deed granted in breach of inhibition

125. Land attachment subsequent to reduction of deed granted in breach of inhibition

(1) Notwithstanding section 82(2)(a)(ii) of this Act, where-

(a) a debtor has granted a deed to a person (in this section, a "third party") in breach of an inhibition; and

(b) the deed has been reduced by the inhibiting creditor on the ground that it breached the inhibition,

it is competent for the inhibiting creditor to register a notice of land attachment in relation to land to which the reduced deed relates.

(2) A land attachment created following registration of a notice of land attachment in the circumstances mentioned in subsection (1) above enjoys preference in ranking in any competition with-
   (a) a security granted over any land described in the notice in favour of; and
   (b) a land attachment over any such land executed by,
a creditor of the third party

(3) Where a notice of land attachment is registered in the circumstances mentioned in subsection (1) above, this Chapter applies with the following modifications (and in those modifications "third party" means a third party within the meaning given by subsection (1) above).

(4) The references mentioned in subsection (5) below to the "debtor" are to be read as references to the debtor and the third party.

(5) Those references are the references in sections 83(5)(a), 92(4)(c)(iv) and (5)(a), 103(1)(a), 104(3)(c), 106(1)(a), 108(5) and 117(4)(a).

(6) The references mentioned in subsection (7) below to the "debtor" are to read as references to the debtor or the third party.

(7) Those references are-
   (a) the references in sections 86(1)(b), 91(1)(a), 95(2), 98(1)(b), (2), (3), (8) and (9)(b)(ii), 99(3)(b), 100(1)(b), 106(1) (except the reference in paragraph (a)), 107(1) and (4)(b) and (c), 113(2)(b)(vi), 116(3) and (5), 117(4) and (6) and 120(5); and
   (b) the first reference in section 101(3)(a).

(8) In section 114(2)(b), after "to" insert "the debtor or third party".

(9) In section 116(1), after paragraph (d) insert-
   "(da) any balance due to the third party;".

DEFINITIONS
"Notice of land attachment": 2007 Act s.83

GENERAL NOTE
This deals with the situation where: (i) a debtor grants a deed (in practice, a disposition or standard security) to a purchaser or creditor from the debtor (the purchaser or creditor being known as the "third party") even though the debtor has already been inhibited and (ii) where the inhibiting creditor has obtained a decree of reduction of the deed because the debtor had breached the inhibition. This particular decree of reduction is *ex capite inhibitionis*, which means that the debtor still retains title to the property as far as any other creditors are concerned, and, as far as anyone other than the inhibiting creditor is concerned, the title could (in theory if not in practice) be transferred. The transfer of the property to a third party would be valid as far as the debtor and the purchaser are concerned, but nevertheless subject to the overriding interest of the inhibiting creditor, so the inhibiting creditor can reduce the title of the third party. However, until the title is reduced, the purchaser has title to the property, the debtor does not, and therefore s.82(2), which states that it is not possible to create a land attachment over land to which a title has never been registered, or land to which the debtor has no registered title, would apply.

Consequently, this section (i.e. s.125) begins with the words "Notwithstanding section 82(2)(a)(ii) of this Act" and continues, "it is competent for the inhibiting creditor to register a notice of land attachment in relation to the land to which the reduced deed relates." This section is saying that even though the inhibited debtor does not have title to the land, and the third party does, the attaching creditor may still attach the land. In effect, what is happening is that the inhibiting creditor is being given much the same rights as the inhibiting creditor under adjudication, without having to wait for the expiry of the legal.

Under subs.(2), a land attachment created after the reduction of the deed in favour of the third party, and following the registration of the notice of land attachment, will rank in priority to any security (over land) granted by the third party to any creditor of the third party, and in priority to any land attachment over the land executed by a creditor of the third party. This prevents the third party's own creditors having an advantage over the inhibiting/attaching creditor.

As has been previously noted, the 2007 Act has been careful to ensure that an, as it were, "innocent" prospective purchaser of land from a debtor in the process of suffering a land attachment is given some degree of protection. The protection is in the form of allowing the prospective purchaser the right of notification of the land attachment and the right to a hearing on any objections he may have to the warrant for sale (see, for example, ss.99 and 100). Subsection (5) is a list of the occasions when the third party should receive notification of steps being taken by the creditor to enforce the land attachment, so that the word "debtor" in those occasions is deemed to include either the debtor or the third party.

Subsection (7) is a list of the occasions where the third party is required to be involved in the process of the land attachment and so may obtain the benefits, or suffer the consequences, that would apply to the debtor, and therefore on the occasions within the list the word "debtor" again includes either the debtor or the third party.

The remainder of this section has similar consequential changes.

General and miscellaneous

126. Land attachment as heritable security

For the avoidance of doubt, a land attachment is not a heritable security for the purposes of the Heritable Securities (Scotland) Act 1894 (c.44).

GENERAL NOTE

This confirms, for the avoidance of doubt, that a land attachment is not a heritable security and so the creditor may not use the remedies that are available to a heritable creditor under the Heritable Securities (Scotland) Act 1894.

127. Statement on impact of land attachment

(1) The Scottish Ministers must, within 15 months of the commencement of this Chapter, prepare, publish and lay before the Scottish Parliament a statement setting out the impact of land attachment on debt recovery and homelessness.

(2) The statement must specify-
  (a) the number of land attachments registered;
  (b) the number of warrants for sale-
    (i) granted;
    (ii) refused; or
    (iii) suspended,
  under section 97;
  (c) the number of persons made homeless as a consequence of this Chapter;
  (d) the mean and median sums recovered by land attachment; and
  (e) the effect which land attachment appears to have had on debtors' abilities to meet ongoing financial obligations and repay other debts.

(3) In this section, "homeless" has the meaning given in section 24 of the Housing (Scotland) Act 1987 (c.26).

GENERAL NOTE

The Scottish Ministers must, within 15 months of the commencement of this particular chapter, present a statement setting out the impact of land attachment upon land attachment and homelessness. This requirement was suggested in order to allow the Scottish Parliament to review the effect of land attachment on debt recovery and homelessness. As there was much concern in the Scottish Parliament that this chapter could, or would, lead to homelessness, the statement may enable the Scottish Parliament to have an informed view of the impact of the chapter. "Homeless" is defined in terms of the Housing (Scotland) Act 1987 s.24. Under s.31 of that Act, and provided the debtor has not become homeless deliberately, the local authority is under a duty to house the debtor if he is a priority need, or at the very least provide advice and assistance towards his obtaining accommodation. It is therefore ironic that it is quite likely that local authorities may well (if this chapter is brought into force) be using land attachment as a means of forcing debtors to pay outstanding council taxes, which in turn will be used to provide accommodation for those made homeless by land attachment.

128. Interpretation

(1) In this Chapter, unless the context otherwise requires-

"appointed person" has the meaning given by section 97(2)(b) of this Act;

"appropriate property register" has the meaning given by section 83(1)(c)(i) of this Act;

"attached land" has the meaning given by section 81(5)(a) of this Act;

"decree" has the meaning given in section 221 of this Act (except that paragraphs (c), (g) and (h) of the definition of "decree" in that section do not apply) being a decree which, or an extract of which, authorises land attachment;

"document of debt" has the meaning given in section 221 of this Act, being a document which, or an extract of which, authorises land attachment;

"judicial officer" means the judicial officer appointed by the creditor;

"land" has the meaning given by section 82(1) of this Act;

"long lease" has the same meaning as in section 28(1) of the Land Registration (Scotland) Act 1979 (c. 33);

"notice of land attachment" has the meaning given by section 83(1) of this Act;

"prescribed sum" has the meaning given by section 92(1)(c) of this Act;

"property register" means the Land Register of Scotland or, as the case may be, the General Register of Sasines;

"registering", in relation to any document, means, unless the context otherwise requires, registering an interest in land or information relating to an interest in land (being an interest or information for which that document provides) in the Land Register of Scotland or, as the case may be, recording the document in the Register of Sasines (cognate expressions being construed accordingly);

"sum recoverable by the land attachment" has the meaning given by section 81(5)(b) of this Act; and

"warrant for sale" means a warrant granted under section 97(2) of this Act.

(2) In this Chapter-

(a) any reference to a purchase, sale, conveyance or disposition is, in a case where the attached land is a lease, to be construed as a reference to an assignation; and

(b) any reference to the ownership of land in such a case is to be construed as a reference to the right of lease,

and cognate expressions are to be construed accordingly.

(3) The Scottish Ministers may by order modify the definitions of "decree" and "document of debt" in subsection (1) above by-
   (a) adding types of decree or document to;
   (b) removing types of decree or document from; or
   (c) varying the description of,
the types of decree or document to which those definitions apply.

GENERAL NOTE

This section contains a number of definitions used throughout this particular chapter. The definitions referring to ownership and transfer of land may be read as covering the equivalent definitions appropriate to the land attachment of a long lease.

The Scottish Ministers are given powers to vary the definitions of certain terms, exercisable by order subject to negative resolution procedure (see s.224(3)).

CHAPTER 3

RESIDUAL ATTACHMENT

GENERAL NOTE

Residual attachment is a new form of diligence, expressly designed to catch articles of worth or property that other forms of attachment were not designed or unable to catch. The draughtsman appears to have been unwilling, at least at the stage the bill went through Holyrood, to be too specific as to what sort of property is meant to be caught, as s.129(2) carefully says that residual attachment may be used to attach property (heritable or moveable) only of such description or class as may be specified by the Scottish Ministers by regulation. It is suggested that the sort of property that could be caught by residual attachment would be assets such as, say, the right to charge entrance charges to a building or land, the right to charge fishermen the right of access to water or over land, the right of copyright in a book the debtor had written (and similar other intellectual property rights), the right to hold a valuable but short-term lease and a right to charge guests in a hotel for accommodation. As may be seen, these rights are heritable and moveable.

Much of this chapter will be supplemented by Scottish Statutory Instruments which at the time of writing are not available. These should provide the detail which is not present in this Act.

In essence, the creditor applies for a residual attachment order; provided it is not successfully objected to, the court makes an order for the residual attachment. The creditor then serves a schedule of the residual attachment order on the debtor, which attaches the property. The creditor may then apply for a "satisfaction" order which in due course will allow the creditor to sell the attached property to repay the debt owed to him, with any surplus, after interest and expenses being returned to the debtor.

It should be noted that there is no opportunity for residual attachment on the dependence of an action, and that time to pay directions and time to pay orders in terms of ss.2 and 5 of the 1987 Act may prevent the residual diligence taking place, especially, in the case of s.5, where no satisfaction order has been obtained (see Sch.5 para.16(4)(b)).

Residual attachment

129. Residual attachment

(1) There is to be a form of diligence over property of a debtor to be known as residual attachment.
(2) Residual attachment may be used to attach property (heritable or moveable) only of such description or class as may be specified by the Scottish Ministers by regulations.
(3) The Scottish Ministers may specify any property but only if-
   (a) it is transferable; and
   (b) it is not-
      (i) attachable by; or
      (ii) exempt from,

any other diligence.

(4) The Scottish Ministers may not specify-

    (a) a right of a debtor as tenant of a dwellinghouse which is the debtor's sole or main residence; or

    (b) a right of a debtor as tenant of a croft.

(5) Property which is owned in common by a debtor and a third party may be attached by residual attachment in satisfaction of the debts of the debtor.

(6) Regulations under subsection (2) above may-

    (a) vary the description of; or

    (b) remove property of such description or class from,

the property which may be attached by residual attachment.

(7) Regulations under subsection (2) above may make further provision, in the case of property of a particular description or class, about-

    (a) the content and effect of an application for an order under section 132(2) of this Act (in this Chapter, a "residual attachment order");

    (b) the effect of such an order;

    (c) the content and effect of an application for an order under section 136(2) of this Act (in this Chapter, a "satisfaction order");

    (d) the effect of such an order and, in particular-

        (i) the methods for and procedures involved in satisfying the sum recoverable by the residual attachment out of the attached property which such an order may authorise;

        (ii) the duration of such an order; and

        (iii) the disbursement of any sums recovered by such an order;

    (e) the powers of the court in relation to residual attachment orders, satisfaction orders and other orders made by virtue of this Chapter; and

    (f) the termination of residual attachment.

(8) Regulations under subsection (2) above may make further provision-

    (a) about the effect of the making of time to pay directions and time to pay orders on residual attachment; and

    (b) about the effect of sequestration on residual attachment including, without prejudice to that generality, provision-

        (i) that a residual attachment created during such period before the date of sequestration as may be prescribed is not to be effectual to create a preference for the creditor;

        (ii) about the effect of sequestration on the rights of a creditor to insist in a residual attachment created before any such period; and

        (iii) about the effect of sequestration on the rights of a creditor to create a residual attachment on or after the date of sequestration.

GENERAL NOTE

This states that there will be a new type of attachment known as residual attachment. As indicated above, the Scottish Ministers by regulations will specify the property, heritable or moveable, that may be attached by this new diligence, and much of this section describes what further powers the Ministers may exercise if necessary in respect of these regulations (e.g. variation or removal of attachable assets), the procedure, the duration of the procedure, how funds arising out of the residual attachment are dealt with, the court's powers relative to the procedure and the termination of the residual attachment.

The Scottish Ministers are also given power to provide for the use of time to pay directions and time to pay orders on residual attachment, and the interaction between sequestration and residual attachment (subs.8). This may already have been done, at least in respect of time to pay directions and time to pay orders (see Sch.5 paras 16(2)(a)(vii) and 16(4)(b)).

In order to be liable to residual diligence, the property must be transferable and must not be capable of attachment by any other type of diligence. The Scottish Ministers will not be able to specify that residual attachment may attach the right of a debtor to the tenancy of his dwellinghouse if that dwellinghouse is his sole or main residence, or the right of a debtor as a tenant of a croft (subs.4). It will be permissible to attach property that is held in common with another person (subs.5).

Application for residual attachment order

130. Application for residual attachment order

(1) A creditor may apply to the court for a residual attachment order but only if-

(a) the debt is constituted by a decree or document of debt;

(b) the debtor has been charged to pay the debt;

(c) the period for payment specified in the charge has expired without payment being made; and

(d) where the debtor is an individual, the creditor has, no earlier than 12 weeks before applying for the residual attachment order, provided the debtor with a debt advice and information package.

(2) An application for a residual attachment order, must-

(a) be in (or nearly as may be in) the form prescribed by Act of Sederunt;

(b) specify the property which it is sought to attach;

(c) state-

(i) how, were a satisfaction order made, the value of that property would be realised; and

(ii) that doing so would result in the sum mentioned in section 134(3) of this Act being paid off or reduced; and

(d) be intimated to-

(i) the debtor; and

(ii) any other person having an interest.

(3) A person who receives intimation of the application may, before the expiry of the period of 14 days beginning with the day on which that intimation is made, lodge objections to the application.

DEFINITIONS

"Croft": Crofters (Scotland) Act 1993 s.3

"Debt advice and information package": 2002 Act s.10(5)

"Decree": 2007 Act s.221 (omitting paras (c), (g) and (h), and see s.145)

"Document of debt": 2007 Act s.221 (though see s.145)

"Court": 2007 Act s.145 (for the purposes of this chapter only)

"Residual attachment order": 2007 Act s.132(2)

GENERAL NOTE

This explains that a creditor may apply to the court (this being either the sheriff court or the Court of Session) for a residual attachment order provided the debt has been constituted by the normal methods indicated throughout this Act, namely by a decree or a document of debt, the debtor has been charged to pay the debt, the debt remained unpaid during the period specified for the charge, and where the debtor is an individual, the debtor has received a debt advice and information package.

The application will be in a form yet to be devised, will specify the property to be attached, state how it is to be realised, will state that it should cover the sum that was the subject of the charge, and must be intimated to the debtor and any else with an interest. The debtor or the other person with an interest then must raise any objections with 14 days.

131. Effect of application for residual attachment order

(1) Where an application for a residual attachment order is intimated to a debtor, the debtor must not, during the period mentioned in subsection (2) below, take any of the steps mentioned in subsection (3) below in relation to the property specified in the application.

(2) The period referred to in subsection (1) above is the period-

    (a) beginning with the day on which the application is intimated to the debtor; and

    (b) ending with the day on which the court-

        (i) makes a residual attachment order; or

        (ii) dismisses the application.

(3) The steps referred to in subsection (1) above are-

    (a) transferring or otherwise disposing of the property;

    (b) burdening the property;

    (c) granting any licence or sub-licence in relation to the property; or

    (d) entering into any agreement to do anything mentioned in paragraph (a), (b) or (c) above in relation to the property.

(4) Any step mentioned in subsection (3) above which is taken in breach of subsection (1) above is void.

(5) Breach by the debtor or any other person of subsection (1) above may be dealt with as a contempt of court.

GENERAL NOTE

Once the application has been intimated to the debtor, the debtor must not dispose of the property, burden it, grant a licence over it or agree to do any of these prohibited actions between the date of intimation to the debtor and the date on which the court either grants the application for the residual attachment or dismisses it. Any attempt to do any of the prohibited actions would be void and would be deemed to be contempt of court. The sanctions for contempt of court include admonition, fine and, in extreme cases, imprisonment. See the Contempt of Court Act 1981.

Residual attachment order

132. Residual attachment order

(1) At the hearing on an application under section 130(1) of this Act, the court must not make any order without first giving any person who has lodged objections under subsection (3) of that section an opportunity to be heard.

(2) Subject to subsection (4) below, the court may, if satisfied that the application is in order, make-

(a) a residual attachment order; and

(b) any other order which the court thinks fit in consequence of the residual attachment order.

(3) A residual attachment order must-

(a) specify the property to be attached;

(b) require the creditor to intimate the order to-

(i) the debtor; and

(ii) any other person the court specifies; and

(c) state on whom the schedule of residual attachment must be served.

(4) The court must make an order refusing the application for a residual attachment order if satisfied-

(a) that the property specified in the application (or any part of it) is not capable of being attached by residual attachment; or

(b) that-

(i) were the satisfaction order proposed in the application made, it would not result in the value of that property being realised; or

(ii) were that order made and the value of that property realised, it would not result in the sum recoverable by the residual attachment being paid off or reduced.

(5) Without prejudice to the generality of subsection (2)(b) above, an order under that paragraph may-

(a) prohibit a specified person from acting so as to defeat the residual attachment in whole or in part;

(b) prohibit a specified person from making payments due to the debtor in respect of the property to be attached;

(c) appoint a judicial factor to ingather and manage that property;

(d) require a specified person to produce to the court documents relating to the debtor's right to that property;

(e) authorise the creditor to complete title in the name of the debtor to that property; and

(f) authorise the creditor to take specified action to preserve the value of that property.

DEFINITIONS

"Court": 2007 Act s.145 (for the purposes of this chapter only)

"Schedule of residual attachment": 2007 Act s.133

GENERAL NOTE

Where a creditor has applied to court for a residual attachment order, he should have intimated the application to the debtor and anyone else with an interest, as indicated in s.130(2)(d), and under s.130(3), the debtor and anyone else with an interest may lodge objections to the residual attachment. Subsection (1) provides that the objectors must be given the opportunity to be heard. If the objections are overruled, or there are no objections, and provided the application is not refused under subs.(4), the court may make a residual attachment order or any other order which the court thinks fit as a result of the residual attachment order. Possible orders that the court might consider are indicated in subs.(5). The order must specify the property to be attached, require the creditor to intimate the order to the debtor and any other person the court specifies, and state on whom the "Schedule of residual attachment" (referred to in the next section) should be served.

The court may refuse the order where it is satisfied that: (a) the property is not capable of being attached by residual attachment or (b) that even if it were granted it would not result in the value in the property being realised, or the sum recoverable by the residual attachment would not reduce or pay off the debt being recovered.

133. Schedule of residual attachment

(1) Where the court grants a residual attachment order, the creditor may serve a schedule of residual attachment.

(2) A schedule of residual attachment must-
  (a) be in (or as nearly as may be in) the form prescribed by Act of Sederunt;
  (b) be served on-
    (i) the debtor; and
    (ii) any person specified in the residual attachment order; and
  (c) specify the property which is being attached.

GENERAL NOTE

This explains what needs to be in the "Schedule of residual attachment". The form itself is yet to be devised. It will nevertheless need to say what the property is to be attached, and to be served on the debtor and anyone else specified in the residual attachment order.

134. Creation and effect of residual attachment

(1) A residual attachment is, subject to section 142(1) of this Act, created over the property specified in the schedule of residual attachment (in this Chapter, the "attached property") at the beginning of the day after the day on which that schedule is served on the debtor.

(2) A residual attachment-
  (a) confers on the creditor a right in security over the attached property; and
  (b) secures the sum mentioned in subsection (3) below (in this Chapter, the "sum recoverable by the residual attachment").

(3) That sum is-
  (a) the sum for the payment of which the charge was served, together with any interest accruing after such service and before the residual attachment ceases to have effect; and
  (b) all expenses which are chargeable against the debtor by virtue of the attachment.

GENERAL NOTE

The residual attachment is created at the beginning of the day after the day that the schedule is served on the debtor. It gives a right in security over the attached property and secures the "Sum recoverable by residual attachment", this being (under subs.3) the sum for which the charge was served (see s.130(1)(b)) plus interest from the date of service from the charge up to the date that the residual attachment ceases to have effect (see. s.139), plus all expenses of the attachment chargeable against the debtor.

Satisfaction order

135. Application for satisfaction order

(1) The creditor may, where a residual attachment is in effect, apply to the court for a satisfaction order authorising the satisfaction of the sum recoverable by the residual attachment out of the attached property.

(2) An application under subsection (1) above must-
  (a) be in (or as nearly as may be in) the form prescribed by Act of Sederunt;

(b) specify the attached property (or part of it) in relation to which the application is made;

(c) state-
   (i) how, were a satisfaction order made, the value of that property would be realised; and
   (ii) that doing so would result in the sum recoverable by the residual attachment being paid off or reduced; and

(d) be accompanied by-
   (i) a copy of the schedule of residual attachment; and
   (ii) any other document prescribed by Act of Sederunt.

(3) An application under subsection (1) above must be intimated to-
   (a) the debtor;
   (b) any person to whom the residual attachment order was intimated; and
   (c) any other person having an interest.

(4) A person who receives intimation under subsection (3) above may, before the expiry of the period of 14 days beginning with the day on which intimation is made, lodge objections to the application.

(5) Where provision is made by virtue of this Chapter or by any other enactment permitting the application under subsection (1) above to be an electronic communication, the requirement in paragraph (d) of subsection (2) above that the application be accompanied by the documents mentioned in that paragraph is satisfied by the provision of electronic communications.

DEFINITIONS
"Residual attachment order": 2007 Act s.132(2)
"Satisfaction order": 2007 Act s.136
"Schedule of residual attachment": 2007 Act s.133
"Sum recoverable by residual attachment": 2007 Act s.134(3)

GENERAL NOTE
Once the residual attachment order is in place, the creditor may apply for a satisfaction order which would authorise the payment of the sum recoverable by the residual attachment out of the attached property. Under subs.(2), the application must be in a form yet to be devised, but should specify the attached property, how the value from it is to be realised, that the value should result in the sum recoverable by the residual attachment being paid off or reduced, and be accompanied by a copy of the schedule and any other document required.

The application must be intimated to the debtor, anyone to whom the residual attachment order was intimated, and anyone else with an interest (subs.(4)). Any of these may within 14 days of intimation lodge objections to the application (subs.(5)).

Intimation may be made by electronic means (subs.(5)).

136. Satisfaction order

(1) At the hearing on an application under section 135(1) of this Act, the court must not make any order without first giving any person who has lodged objections under subsection (4) of that section an opportunity to be heard.

(2) Subject to subsection (6) below, the court may, if satisfied that the application is in order, make-
   (a) a satisfaction order authorising the satisfaction of the sum recoverable by the residual attachment out of the attached property (or part of it) specified in the order; and

(b) any other order which the court thinks fit in consequence of the satisfaction order.

(3) A satisfaction order must-
    (a) specify the attached property to which it applies; and
    (b) require the creditor to intimate the order to-
        (i) the debtor; and
        (ii) any other person the court specifies.

(4) Without prejudice to the generality of subsection (2) above, a satisfaction order may authorise-
    (a) the creditor to sell the attached property;
    (b) the transfer of ownership of the property to the creditor;
    (c) the transfer of income derived from the property to the creditor; or
    (d) the creditor to lease or licence the property.

(5) Where the court makes a satisfaction order-
    (a) authorising the sale of attached property, it must-
        (i) appoint a suitably qualified person (in this Chapter, the "appointed person") who is willing to execute the order; and
        (ii) specify in the order the period within which the attached property is to be sold;
    (b) it may appoint a suitably qualified person to report on the market value of the attached property.

(6) The court must make an order refusing the application for a satisfaction order if satisfied that any of the grounds mentioned in subsection (7) below apply.

(7) The grounds referred to in subsection (6) above are-
    (a) the residual attachment is invalid;
    (b) the residual attachment has ceased to have effect; or
    (c) that-
        (i) were the satisfaction order proposed in the application made, it would not result in the value of that property being realised; or
        (ii) were that order made and the value of that property realised, it would not result in the sum recoverable by the residual attachment being paid off or reduced.

(8) The court may, if satisfied that making a satisfaction order would be unduly harsh to the debtor or any other person having an interest-
    (a) make a satisfaction order but suspend its effect for a period not exceeding 1 year beginning with the day on which the order is made; or
    (b) make an order refusing the application.

DEFINITIONS
"Court": 2007 Act s.145 (for the purposes of this chapter only)
"Sum recoverable by residual attachment": 2007 Act s.134(3)

GENERAL NOTE
    Where the creditor has applied for a satisfaction order, the court must hear any objections raised by those to whom the application was intimated in terms of s.135(4). Assuming the order is not refused under subs.(6), the court will make the order authorising the satisfaction of the sum recoverable by the residual attachment out of the attached property or a part of it, and any other necessary order the court sees fit. The order must specify the actual property to which the order applies, and require the creditor to intimate it to the debtor and any other person the court requires.

The order itself may permit the creditor, amongst other options, to sell, to take for himself, or to "lease or licence" the property. It is submitted that the draftsman meant to say "let" the property since it is generally the tenant of a property who leases it: the ambiguous use of the word "lease" could suggest that the creditor was taking a lease of the property from the debtor, when it is more likely that what was intended was that the creditor, standing in the shoes of the debtor, could let the property to a tenant, who would thereby lease the property from the creditor.

In addition the creditor could be authorised to have the income derived from the property to be transferred to him.

Under subs.(5), where the court makes an order authorising the sale of the attached property, it must appoint someone suitable, known as the appointed person, to execute the order by selling the property within the time the court specifies, and may appoint someone suitably qualified to report on the market value of the property.

The court may refuse the order under subs.(6) if one of the grounds of subs.(7) applies, namely, that the residual attachment is invalid, that it has ceased to have effect, or that even if it were granted it would not result in the value in the property being realised, or the sum recoverable by the residual attachment would not reduce or pay off the debt being recovered.

There is protection, to some extent, for the debtor, in that if the court, under subs.(8), thinks that a satisfaction order would be unduly harsh, it may grant the order but suspend its operation for up to a year, or even refuse the order. It remains to be seen what degree of harshness constitutes "unduly harsh".

137. Intimation of court's decision

(1) Where a satisfaction order is made, the creditor must, as soon as is reasonably practicable, send a copy of the order to-
   (a) the debtor;
   (b) where the satisfaction order authorises the sale of the attached property, the appointed person; and
   (c) any other person the court specifies in the order.

(2) Where the court refuses to make a satisfaction order, the court must, as soon as is reasonably practicable, send a copy of the order to the debtor and to any other person appearing to the court to have an interest.

DEFINITIONS
"Court": 2007 Act s.145 (for the purposes of this chapter only)

GENERAL NOTE
Once the satisfaction order is made, the creditor must send a copy of it to the debtor, the appointed person where appropriate, and any other person specified in the order. Where the court refuses to make an order, the court must send a notice of the fact to the debtor and anyone else appearing to have an interest.

138. Effect of certain refusals of application for satisfaction order

Where, under section 136(6) of this Act, an order is made refusing an application for a satisfaction order by virtue of the ground mentioned in paragraph (c) of subsection (7) of that section-
   (a) the residual attachment does not, by reason only of that refusal, cease to have effect; and
   (b) it is competent for the creditor to make a further application under section 135(1) of this Act.

DEFINITIONS
"Satisfaction order": 2007 Act s.136
"Sum recoverable by residual attachment": 2007 Act s.134(3)

GENERAL NOTE

Where the application for the satisfaction order is refused on the grounds that even if it were granted it would not result in the value in the property being realised, or the sum recoverable by the residual attachment would not reduce or pay off the debt being recovered (see s.136(7)(c)), the residual attachment does not by virtue of that refusal cease to have effect and the creditor is free to make a further application for another satisfaction order under s.135.

Termination, discharge etc. of residual attachment

139. Termination by payment etc.

(1) Subject to subsection (2) below, if the full sum recoverable by the residual attachment is either paid or tendered to-

    (a) the creditor;

    (b) where one has been appointed, the appointed person; or

    (c) a judicial officer or any other person who has authority to receive payment on behalf of the creditor,

the residual attachment ceases to have effect.

(2) Subsection (1) above does not apply unless the sum is paid or tendered before-

    (a) where a satisfaction order authorising sale of the attached property is made, a contract of sale of the attached property is concluded; or

    (b) in any other case, the attached property is otherwise disposed of.

DEFINITIONS

"Judicial officer": 2007 Act s.57

"Sum recoverable by residual attachment": 2007 Act s.134(3)

GENERAL NOTE

Under subs.(1), if the full sum recoverable is paid or tendered to the creditor, a judicial officer, anyone authorised to receive payment on behalf of the creditor, or the appointed person, after the residual attachment is in place, the residual attachment ceases to have effect. However, under subs.(2) this will only be the case where, following a satisfaction order authorising sale of the property, the debtor pays the sum before a contract of sale of the attached property (or part of it) to a purchaser is concluded, or, in any other case, before the attached property is disposed of.

140. Recall

(1) The debtor or any other person having an interest may apply to the court for an order-

    (a) recalling a residual attachment; or

    (b) restricting such an attachment.

(2) An application under subsection (1) above must-

    (a) be in (or as nearly as may be in) the form prescribed by Act of Sederunt; and

    (b) be intimated to the creditor.

(3) The court must, if satisfied that the residual attachment-

    (a) is invalid;

    (b) has been executed incompetently or irregularly; or

    (c) has ceased to have effect,

make an order declaring that to be the case and recalling the residual attachment.

(4) The court may, if satisfied that the residual attachment is valid but-

    (a) having regard to the sum recoverable by the residual attachment, that significantly more property is attached than need be; and

    (b) that is it reasonable to do so,

make an order restricting the effect of a residual attachment to part only of the property to which it relates.

(5) An order of recall or restriction must be in (or as nearly as may be in) the form prescribed by Act of Sederunt.

DEFINITIONS

"Court": 2007 Act s.145 (for the purposes of this chapter only)

GENERAL NOTE

This permits a debtor or anyone else with an interest to apply to the court for an order to recall the residual attachment or restrict it. The form in which this is to be done is yet to be devised, but must be intimated to the creditor. If the court is satisfied that the land attachment is invalid, was executed incompetently or irregularly, or has ceased to have effect, it may make an order recalling the land attachment.

Under subs.(4), the court may also restrict a valid residual attachment if it attaches more property than is necessary for the sum to be recovered and where it is reasonable to do so.

The order of recall or restriction is in a form yet to be devised.

141. Duration of residual attachment

(1) Subject to sections 139 and 140 of this Act and to subsection (2) below, a residual attachment ceases to have effect on the expiry of the period of 5 years beginning with the day on which the schedule of residual attachment is served on the debtor.

(2) The court may, on the application of the creditor during the period of 2 months ending with the day on which the period mentioned in subsection (1) above ends, extend the period during which a residual attachment has effect.

(3) The court may extend the period for which a residual attachment has effect on more than one occasion and subsections (1) and (2) above apply as if for the reference in subsection (1) above to the day on which the schedule of residual attachment is served on the debtor there were substituted a reference to the day on which the court last extended that period.

DEFINITIONS

"Court": 2007 Act s.145 (for the purposes of this chapter only)
"Schedule of residual attachment": 2007 Act s.133

GENERAL NOTE

The residual attachment remains in place for five years from the date on which the schedule was served on the debtor. The residual attachment may be extended by a further unspecified period by application to court within two months of the end of the initial five year period and thereafter within two months of each further period.

142. Effect of death of debtor

(1) Where, in relation to a debt-

    (a) the creditor has taken any steps towards obtaining a residual attachment order against the debtor; but

(b) has not, before the date of death of the debtor, served a schedule of residual attachment on the debtor,

any such steps cease to have effect; and accordingly any residual attachment order relating to that debt becomes, on that date, void.

(2) Where a residual attachment is created before the death of the debtor, it continues to have effect in relation to the attached property after that death.

(3) The Court of Session may, by Act of Sederunt, provide for the operation of this Chapter in a case to which this section applies and may, in particular-

    (a) modify the provisions about intimation of applications for satisfaction orders; and

    (b) confer power on the sheriff to dispense with or modify procedures under this Chapter.

DEFINITIONS

"Court": 2007 Act s.145 (for the purposes of this chapter only)
"Residual attachment order": 2007 Act s.132(2)
"Schedule of residual attachment": 2007 Act s.133

GENERAL NOTE

Subsection (1) deals with the situation where a creditor has started to apply for or obtain a residual attachment order against the debtor, but the debtor dies before the schedule of residual attachment has been served upon him in terms of s.133. In these circumstances, any steps taken towards applying for or obtaining a residual attachment order cease to have effect, and any residual attachment order is void with effect from the date of death of the debtor.

There is a slight ambiguity here, because subs.(1)(a) refers to the taking of steps towards obtaining the order. The phrase "taking of steps towards obtaining the residual attachment order" would normally suggest that the order has not actually been obtained. If this is the case, where it later says that any residual attachment order is void on the death of the debtor, it would be difficult to make that order void when it has yet to be obtained. It is submitted that what the draftsman was trying to say was that any steps taken towards obtaining the residual attachment order, including successfully obtaining the order, would cease to have effect and be void, unless the schedule had actually been served on the debtor before his death. The difficulty lies in the phrase "taking of steps".

Where a residual attachment (i.e. the schedule was successfully served on the debtor before his death) is created before the death of the debtor, it remains in place in relation to the attached property.

Rules of court may in due course provide further rules relating to this matter.

General and miscellaneous

143. Expenses of residual attachment

(1) The expenses incurred by the creditor in executing a residual attachment are chargeable against the debtor.

(2) Expenses which, in accordance with subsection (1) above, are chargeable against the debtor are recoverable from the debtor by the residual attachment but not by any other legal process.

(3) Where any expenses such as are referred to in subsection (2) above have not been recovered by the time the residual attachment is completed, or otherwise ceases to have effect, they cease to be so recoverable.

(4) In subsection (2) above, the reference to expenses does not include a reference to expenses of service of a charge.

(5) The court may, if satisfied that the debtor has objected to an application for a satisfaction order on frivolous grounds, award expenses, not exceeding such amount as may be prescribed by the Scottish Ministers by regulations, against the debtor.

DEFINITIONS
"Court": 2007 Act s.145 (for the purposes of this chapter only)

GENERAL NOTE
This section follows the usual practice throughout this Act of ensuring that although the expenses of diligence are chargeable to the debtor, the expenses of the actual method of diligence used may only be recoverable by that particular diligence and no other. Consequently the expenses of residual attachment may only be recovered by residual attachment and not by any other diligence — with the exception of the expenses of the service of the original charge, which may be recovered by any diligence (subs.(4)). Where the expenses are not recovered by the time of completion of the residual attachment, or where the land attachment ceases to have effect, the creditor may not further attempt to recover them (subs.(3)).

Under subs.(5), there is also the opportunity for the debtor to be liable for the expenses of any frivolous objection to the application for a satisfaction order: the amount of such expenses is yet to be established by regulations produced by the Scottish Ministers, such regulations being subject to negative resolution procedure (see s.224(3)).

144. Ascription

(1) This section applies where any sums are-
   (a) recovered by a residual attachment; or
   (b) paid to account of the sum recoverable by the residual attachment while it is in effect.

(2) Such sums must be ascribed to the following in the order in which they are mentioned-
   (a) the expenses which are chargeable against the debtor incurred in the residual attachment;
   (b) any interest which has accrued, at the date of the making of the residual attachment order, on the sum for payment for which the charge was served;
   (c) any sum for payment of which that charge was served together with such interest as has accrued after the day mentioned in paragraph (b) above.

DEFINITIONS
"Residual attachment order": 2007 Act s.132(2)

GENERAL NOTE
This section deals with ascription, which explains how any payments recovered by the land attachment, or made by the debtor (or others on his behalf), are to be used towards the paying off of the sums recoverable under the residual attachment. They are first to be paid: (a) towards the expenses chargeable against the debtor arising out of the residual attachment, then (b) towards the interest, accruing since the day of the making of the residual attachment order, on the sum for which the charge (see s.130(1)(b)) was served and finally (c) towards the sums due under the charge together with interest arising from the day in (b) above.

145. Interpretation

(1) In this Chapter-
   "appointed person" has the meaning given by section 136(5)(a)(i) of this Act;
   "attached property" has the meaning given by section 134(1) of this Act;

"court" means-
(a) the Court of Session; or
(b) the sheriff,

and references to applying to the court are references to applying by petition or, as the case may be, by summary application;

"croft" has the meaning given by section 3 of the Crofters (Scotland) Act 1993 (c.44);

"decree" has the meaning given in section 221 of this Act (except that paragraphs (c), (g) and (h) of the definition of "decree" in that section do not apply) being a decree which, or an extract of which, authorises residual attachment;

"document of debt" has the meaning given in section 221 of this Act, being a document which, or an extract of which, authorises residual attachment;

"dwellinghouse" includes any yard, garden, outbuilding or other pertinents;

"judicial officer" means the judicial officer appointed by the creditor;

"residual attachment order" means an order under section 132(2) of this Act;

"satisfaction order" means an order under section 136(2) of this Act; and

"sum recoverable by the residual attachment" has the meaning given by section 134(2)(b) of this Act.

(2) The Scottish Ministers may by order modify the definitions of "decree" and "document of debt" in subsection (1) above by-
(a) adding types of decree or document to;
(b) removing types of decree or document from; or
(c) varying the description of,

the types of decree or document to which those definitions apply.

GENERAL NOTE

This section contains a number of definitions used throughout this particular chapter.

The Scottish Ministers are given powers to vary the definitions of certain terms, including the terms "decree" and "document of debt", exercisable by order subject to negative resolution procedure (see s.224(3)).

PART 5

INHIBITION

GENERAL NOTE

Inhibition is a method of preventing a debtor from selling or burdening any land that he owns until he has paid the creditor his debt. Most of the time it is a very effective diligence, since the creditor effectively has a security over all of the debtor's heritable property in Scotland. No purchaser will buy land from an inhibited debtor, and no lender will take a security over any land owned by the inhibited debtor, because the inhibiting creditor may reduce any deed granted by the debtor.

What inhibition does not do is to give the inhibiting creditor any real right in the debtor's heritage. The debtor, even though inhibited, is in practice merely prevented from selling his land, and so his land is preserved for the benefit of his creditors. The debtor continues to have title to the land, and in theory could still transfer it to a purchaser, were it not that the deed could be reduced. If the debtor repays the debt for which the inhibition was granted, the inhibition may be discharged and the debtor is free to sell his property again.

Inhibition normally lasts for five years.

The changes under this Act are designed to make the process of obtaining an inhibition simpler and easier, by putting on a statutory basis what has hitherto been covered under a confusing mixture of the common law and statute. No longer will there be the arcane ritual of having letters of inhibition signeted at the Court of Session: instead inhibition will be available from the sheriff court. In addition, there are provisions to protect a purchaser where he obtains property from an inhibited debtor but without, in good faith, being aware that the debtor is inhibited and while having taken all reasonable steps to discover the existence of any inhibition. Although such an event is unlikely to occur, it is always possible that searchers might fail to notice an extant inhibition, or the Register of Inhibitions itself might be inaccurate.

A further change is that while hitherto inhibition applied to the debtor, to prevent him disposing of property, henceforth diligence applies both to the debtor and to any property of which he is trying to dispose (see ss.150, 153, 155, 159, 160 and 167). This changes it to a hybrid diligence that is simultaneously *in personam* and *in rem*, a concept that would probably not have appealed to Roman law purists. It should be noted that, although the 2007 Act does make a number of practical changes to the law relating to inhibition, much of the old law remains in place, so that recall of inhibition may still take place where the creditor's behaviour is nimious and oppressive, and a creditor's refusal to discharge the inhibition when called upon to do so, despite payment of all sums due to him by the debtor, may still result in the creditor being liable for all the expenses of the application for recall (*Robertson v Park, Dobson & Co* (1896) 24 R. 30; *Milne v Birrell* (1902) 4 F. 879).

It will remain possible to carry out inhibition on the dependence, but the law on this has also been updated and is now to be found in Pt 6 of the 2007 Act, introducing a new Pt 1A to the 1987 Act.

Creation

146. Certain decrees and documents of debt to authorise inhibition without need for letters of inhibition

(1) Inhibition in execution is competent to enforce-

    (a) payment of a debt constituted by a decree or document of debt;

    (b) subject to subsection (2) below, an obligation to perform a particular act (other than payment) contained in a decree.

(2) Inhibition under subsection (1)(b) above is competent only if the decree is a decree-

    (a) in an action containing an alternative conclusion or crave for payment of a sum other than by way of expenses; or

    (b) for specific implement of an obligation to convey heritable property to the creditor or to grant in the creditor's favour a real right in security, or some other right, over such property.

(3) In section 3 of the Writs Execution (Scotland) Act 1877 (c.40) (warrant in extract writ to authorise diligence), after paragraph (b) insert-

        "(ba) in relation to an ordinary debt within the meaning of the Debtors (Scotland) Act 1987, inhibition against the debtor;".

(4) In section 7(1) of the Sheriff Courts (Scotland) Extracts Act 1892 (c.17) (warrant in extract decree to authorise diligence), after paragraph (b) insert-

        "(ba) in relation to an ordinary debt within the meaning of the Debtors (Scotland) Act 1987, inhibition against the debtor;".

(5) In section 87(2) of the 1987 Act (warrant in extract decree to authorise diligence), after paragraph (b) insert-

"(ba) in relation to an ordinary debt, inhibition against the debtor;".

(6) It is not competent for the Court of Session to grant letters of inhibition.

(7) In a case where inhibition is executed under subsection (1)(b) above-

(a) sections 165 and 166 of this Act do not apply; and

(b) sections 158, 159, 160 and 163 of this Act have effect as if references to a "debtor" or "creditor" were references to the debtor or creditor in the obligation.

(8) In this Part-

"decree" has the meaning given by section 221 of this Act, except that paragraphs (c), (g) and (h) of the definition of "decree" in that section do not apply; and

"document of debt" has the meaning given by section 221 of this Act.

(9) The Scottish Ministers may by order modify the definitions of "decree" and "document of debt" in subsection (8) above by-

(a) adding types of decree or document to;

(b) removing types of decree or document from; or

(c) varying the description of,

the types of decree or document to which those definitions apply.

DEFINITIONS

"Decree": 2007 Act s.221 (omitting paras (c), (g) and (h), though see s.146(9))

"Document of debt": 2007 Act s.221 (though see s.146(9))

GENERAL NOTE

Subsection (1) explains that inhibition is competent to enforce payment of a debt constituted by decree or by a document of debt, or to enforce an obligation to perform some act (commonly known as *ad factum praestandum*) other than payment. However, under subs.(2)(a), the enforcement of the performance of that act may only be carried out if the decree itself was the result of an action in which the pursuer's or petitioner's crave had a requirement to pay money other than by way of expenses as an alternative to the requirement that the defender or respondent perform the act. If the pursuer had only sought to have a particular act being performed, as opposed to receiving the monetary equivalent of the performance of the act, inhibition would not be competent (unless it were for the conveyance of heritable property). Prudent pursuers would therefore generally be wise to insert such an alternative crave if they wish to enforce their claim through inhibition.

What this also means is that if a document of debt (as opposed to a decree) contained an obligation to perform some act, it would not be permissible to inhibit the debtor on the strength of the document of debt to force performance. Documents of debt may only use inhibition where the aim is to get paid (subs.(1)(a)).

Under subs.(2)(b), inhibition is competent where there is a decree (but not a document for debt) for specific implement of an obligation to convey heritable property to the creditor, or to grant a creditor a real right in security (effectively a standard security) or some other right over that property. So if a debtor has undertaken to sell some land to a purchaser and is taken to court to force him to do so, but still fails to do so despite a decree to that effect, the purchaser could effect an inhibition on the debtor to prevent him transferring any property to anyone.

Subsection (2)(b) confusingly uses the word "creditor". It would be possible for a defender or respondent not actually to be indebted in financial terms to the pursuer or petitioner, but merely be required to do something which he has failed to do. In this case the pursuer or petitioner would not be a creditor in the normal sense of the word. The draftsman has anticipated this in subs.(7)(b) by saying that references to debtor and creditor are deemed to include debtor and creditor in the actual obligation, thereby widening the meanings of the words to something approaching the words obligant and obliger.

Subsections (3)-(5) insert provisions relating to an inhibition for ordinary debt into the Writs Execution (Scotland) Act 1877, the Sheriff Courts (Scotland) Extracts Act 1892 and the 1987 Act.

This means that extract decrees, including extracts of decrees granted in the sheriff court, or documents for payment, will automatically carry a warrant for inhibition. Previously, a creditor wishing to inhibit in execution of a sheriff court decree had to apply by letters of inhibition to the Court of Session and a sheriff could not grant warrant for inhibition in execution. A sheriff may now grant such warrants. This means that there is now no need to apply for letters of inhibition and subs.(6) abolishes the Court of Session procedure.

Subsection (7)(a) deals with the situation referred to in subs.(1)(b) (see above) where the decree is for the performance of a particular act and inhibition is executed. Where this takes place, s.165, which deals with the expenses of inhibition, and s.166 which deals with ascription (payments to account), will not apply, because there should be no principal sum with which to claim expenses, and without a principal sum there could be no payment to account. It would appear, therefore, that where the pursuer is insisting upon performance of a certain act (such as is envisaged under subs.(2)(b), the conveyance of heritable property to the creditor) and where inhibition is successfully executed, the pursuer will be unable to claim his expenses of the inhibition from the debtor. It would appear that even if there were an alternative crave for payment, expenses would still not be payable by the defender because of the explicit exclusion of s.166 where inhibition is executed under subs.1(b).

Parts (8) and (9) explain the meaning of the words "decree" and "document of debt" and permits the Scottish Ministers to further refine and define the meanings of those words by regulations, subject to the negative resolution procedure (see s.224(3)).

147. Provision of debt advice and information package when executing inhibition

Where the debtor is an individual, a schedule of inhibition served in execution of an inhibition under section 146(1) of this Act (other than an inhibition such as is mentioned in section 146(2)(b)) must be accompanied with a debt advice and information package.

DEFINITIONS
"Debt advice and information package": 2002 Act s.10
"Schedule of inhibition": 2007 Act s.148

GENERAL NOTE
If the debtor is an individual, as opposed to a corporate entity, and when the individual is served a schedule of inhibition, he must be given a debt information advice package. Failure to deliver the package would render the inhibition incompetent. This is not necessary where the debtor is being required by specific implement to convey heritable property to the creditor or grant in favour of the creditor a real right in the debtor's property in terms of s.146(2)(b).

148. Registration of inhibition

(1) An inhibition is registered only by registering-
    (a) the schedule of inhibition; and
    (b) the certificate of execution of the inhibition,
in the Register of Inhibitions.
(2) References in any enactment to registering or, as the case may be, recording an inhibition must, unless the context otherwise requires, be construed as references to registration in accordance with subsection (1) above.
(3) The-
    (a) schedule of inhibition; and
    (b) certificate of execution of the inhibition,
must be in (or as nearly as may be in) the form prescribed by the Scottish Ministers by regulations.

GENERAL NOTE

This section provides that an inhibition is registered by registering in the Register of Inhibitions the schedule of inhibition and the certificate of execution of the inhibition. These two documents are in forms yet to be devised by the Scottish Ministers in regulations subject to the negative resolution procedure (see s.224(3)). The date of the registration is explained in the next section.

149. Date on which inhibition takes effect

In the Titles to Land Consolidation (Scotland) Act 1868 (c.101) (in this Chapter, the "1868 Act"), for section 155 (date on which inhibitions take effect) substitute-

"155. Date on which inhibition takes effect

(1) An inhibition has effect from the beginning of the day on which it is registered unless the circumstances referred to in subsection (2) below apply.

(2) Those circumstances are-

    (a) a notice of inhibition is registered in the Register of Inhibitions;

    (b) the schedule of inhibition is served on the debtor after that notice is registered; and

    (c) the inhibition is registered before the expiry of the period of 21 days beginning with the day on which the notice is registered.

(3) In those circumstances the inhibition has effect from the beginning of the day on which the schedule of inhibition is served.

(4) A notice of inhibition must be in (or as nearly as may be in) the form prescribed.".

GENERAL NOTE

Section 155 of the Titles to Land Consolidation (Scotland) Act 1868 is replaced by a new s.155, which takes account of the changes under the 2007 Act. An inhibition is effectual from the beginning of the day on which it is registered in the Register of Inhibitions unless a notice of inhibition is registered in that Register, the schedule of inhibition is served upon the debtor after the registration of the notice, and the inhibition itself is registered within 21 days of the registration of the notice. Under these circumstances, the inhibition takes effect from the date of service of the schedule. This could be a date earlier than the date of registration of the inhibition. The notice of inhibition is in a form yet to be devised.

Effect

150. Property affected by inhibition

(1) Subject to section 153 of this Act, inhibition may affect any heritable property.

(2) Any enactment or rule of law by virtue of which inhibition may affect other property ceases to have effect.

(3) For the purposes of subsection (1) above and section 157 of the 1868 Act, a person acquires property at the beginning of the day on which the deed conveying or otherwise granting a real right in the property is delivered to that person.

GENERAL NOTE

Subsection (1) alters the previous view of inhibition which was that inhibition affected the debtor's ability to convey property, not the property itself. This section quite categorically changes the meaning of inhibition to convert it to a diligence that affects heritable property itself, not just the debtor.

Subsection (2) states that inhibition may no longer affect any other property other than heritable property. This raises the question as to whether inhibition ever did affect any property other than heritable property: although the notes to the legislation, as prepared by the then Scottish Executive, suggest that inhibition may be executed against property subject to adjudication, and that adjudication is not limited to heritable property, the occasions where it was ever used must be few and far between. It is true that there was an instance where adjudication was used on bank stock (see *Royal Bank v Fairholm* (1770) Mor. App. Adjudication No.3) but the general view is that inhibition is only for heritable property (see Wilson, *Debt*, Greens, 2nd edn, 19.1).

If inhibition is said to affect both debtor and his property, it is important to know when a person acquires property. In order to put the matter beyond doubt, it is expressly stated in subs.(3) that for the purposes of this section and s.157 of the Titles to Land Consolidation (Scotland) Act 1868, a person acquires property at the beginning of the day when a person has delivered to him a deed conveying a real right in the property. It is not the date of registration, but the date of delivery that is significant. This means that if a deed of conveyance is delivered to an acquirer of heritage, and later that day the acquirer is inhibited, the newly acquired heritage is caught by the inhibition and any deed granting by the acquirer conveying the heritage could be reduced. However, if a debtor is already inhibited, but receives property (*acquirenda*) after he is inhibited, s.157 of the Titles to Land Consolidation (Scotland) Act 1868 expressly states that he is not inhibited in respect of that newly acquired property, since the inhibition is effectively retrospective not prospective.

151. Effect on inhibition to enforce obligation when alternative decree granted

Where-

    (a) an inhibition is executed to enforce a decree such as is mentioned in section 146(2)(a) of this Act; and

    (b) decree is subsequently granted in terms of the alternative conclusion or crave mentioned in that section,

the inhibition continues to have effect for the purposes of enforcing payment of the debt constituted by that subsequent decree.

GENERAL NOTE

This deals with the situation referred to in s.146(2)(a) above where inhibition is executed to enforce a decree in an action containing an alternative crave or conclusion for payment of a sum other than by way of expenses. If decree is at a later date granted for that alternative crave or conclusion, perhaps because the debtor failed to comply with the initial decree, the inhibition remains in place and in effect for the purpose of enforcing payment constituted by the later decree.

The virtue of this section is that it avoids the need to go back to court to get a second inhibition, this time to enforce payment.

152. Effect of conversion of limited inhibition on the dependence to inhibition in execution

Where-

    (a) a creditor obtains a decree for payment of all or part of a principal sum concluded or craved for in proceedings on the dependence of which warrant for inhibition was granted; and

    (b) the warrant was limited to specified property by virtue of section 15J(b) of the 1987 Act (property affected by inhibition on dependence),

any inhibition in execution of the decree is not limited to that property.

GENERAL NOTE

When a creditor seeks an inhibition on the dependence of an action (see Pt 6 of the 2007 Act), the warrant for inhibition on the dependence will be limited to a specific heritable property if the action is brought for specific implement of an obligation to convey that particular property, or grant in the creditor's favour a real right in that property, or grant some other right over that property (see the 1987 Act s.15J, as inserted by s.169 of the 2007 Act). Should this be the case, any inhibition in execution of the decree itself (as opposed to the warrant for inhibition on the dependence) is not limited to that property and may be extended to any property of the debtor's. Effectively a limited inhibition is converted into a wide inhibition.

153. Property affected by inhibition to enforce obligation to convey heritable property

Where a decree such as is mentioned in section 146(2)(b) of this Act is granted, any inhibition executed to enforce that decree is limited to the property to which the decree relates.

GENERAL NOTE

Where a creditor obtains a decree under s.146(2)(b), following an action for specific implement of an obligation to convey a particular heritable property, or grant in the creditor's favour a real right in that property, or grant some other right over that property, any inhibition executed to enforce the decree will be restricted to that particular property. This qualifies the wide effect of s.150(1).

154. Inhibition not to confer a preference in ranking

(1) An inhibition does not confer any preference in any-
    (a) sequestration;
    (b) insolvency proceedings; or
    (c) other process in which there is ranking.
(2) Subsection (1) above does not affect any preference claimed in-
    (a) a sequestration;
    (b) insolvency proceedings; or
    (c) any other process,
where the inhibition has effect before this section comes into force.
(3) For the avoidance of doubt, in this section, "other process" includes the process, under section 27(1) of the Conveyancing and Feudal Reform (Scotland) Act 1970 (c.35), of applying the proceeds of sale where a creditor in a standard security has effected a sale of the security subjects.
(4) In this section, "insolvency proceedings" means-
    (a) winding up;
    (b) receivership;
    (c) administration; and
    (d) proceedings in relation to a company voluntary arrangement,
within the meaning of the Insolvency Act 1986 (c.45).

GENERAL NOTE

Formerly, inhibition gave a preference by exclusion if the inhibition took place at least 60 days before sequestration (see 1985 Act s.37(2)). Although this section does not specifically disapply section s.37(2) of the 1985 Act it clearly indicates that an inhibition gives the inhibiting creditor no preference in the event of the debtor's sequestration, insolvency proceedings or any other process in which there may be ranking. Insolvency proceedings are stated in subs.(3) to cover winding up, receivership, administration or a company voluntary arrangement.

Under subs.(2), where the inhibition is in place before this section comes into force, it will retain such preference as it has relative to any of these proceedings.

155. Power of receiver or liquidator in creditors' voluntary winding up to dispose of property affected by inhibition

(1) The Insolvency Act 1986 (c.45) is amended as follows.
(2) After section 61(1) (which sets out the process by which a receiver may dispose of property subject to both the floating

charge and to another security, other encumbrance or diligence) insert-

> "(1A) For the purposes of subsection (1) above, an inhibition which takes effect after the creation of the floating charge by virtue of which the receiver was appointed is not an effectual diligence.".

(3) After section 166(1) (which applies the provisions of that section to a liquidator nominated by the company in a creditors' voluntary winding up) insert-

> "(1A) The exercise by the liquidator of the power specified in paragraph 6 of Schedule 4 to this Act (power to sell any of the company's property) shall not be challengeable on the ground of any prior inhibition.".

DEFINITIONS

"Creation of floating charge": 2007 Act s.38(3)

GENERAL NOTE

This section makes changes to the Insolvency Act 1986, by inserting a new s.61(1A) which provides that an inhibition taking effect after the creation of the floating charge by which a receiver is appointed is not an effectual diligence. The date of creation of the floating charge will, in the case of a floating charge created before the coming into force of the parts of this Act that relate to floating charges and the new Register of Floating Charges, be the date of execution, whereas after the Register of Floating Charges is operational, the date of creation will be the date of registration (2007 Act s.38(3)). This means that the receiver may still dispose of the property notwithstanding the presence of the inhibition, and the inhibitor's interest will be postponed to the receiver's prior interest. See also the note to s.45 of the 2007 Act.

As pre-Enterprise Act 2002 floating charges are gradually reducing in number and being replaced by qualifying floating charges (entitling the floating charge holder to appoint an administrator), and as many floating charge holders, even with old-style floating charges, are reluctant to use receivership, this section will probably fall into disuse over time.

Similar provisions apply to a liquidator nominated by the company in a creditors' voluntary winding up under s.166 of the Insolvency Act 1986. A new subs.(1A) is inserted to the effect that the liquidator's power in these circumstances to sell the company's heritable property will not be challengeable by the existence of any prior inhibition. The inhibitor's interest is still maintained but only in his capacity as one of the company's unsecured creditors.

Termination

156. Termination of effect of inhibition

In section 44(3) of the Conveyancing (Scotland) Act 1924 (c.27) (limitation of effect of certain entries in the Register of Inhibitions and Adjudications)-

> (a) in paragraph (a), the word "inhibitions,", where it second occurs, is repealed; and
> (b) after that paragraph insert-
>> "(aa) all inhibitions shall cease to have effect on the lapse of five years from the date on which they take effect.".

DEFINITIONS

"Take effect": 2007 Act s.149 (inserting new s.155 of the Titles to Land Consolidation (Scotland) Act 1868)

GENERAL NOTE

The effect of this section is that the excision of the word "inhibitions" and the new paragraph inserted in s.44(3) of the Conveyancing (Scotland) Act 1924 ensure that henceforth inhibitions cease to have effect five years from the date on which they take effect. This means that unlike land attachment the same inhibition may not be renewed and there is no opportunity to "pause" the inhibition and restart it. It is nevertheless possible to obtain a brand new inhibition in relation to the same debt as the first inhibition, but it would require a new decree to obtain it. In that event, the debtor is only liable for the expenses of the first inhibition and the second, but no more (see the 2007 Act s.165(3)).

157. Inhibition terminated by payment of full amount owing

(1) This section applies where-
  (a) an inhibition executed to enforce payment of a debt has effect; and
  (b) a sum is paid, in respect of the debt constituted by the decree or document of debt authorising the inhibition, to the creditor, a judicial officer or any other person who has authority to receive payment on behalf of the creditor.
(2) Where the sum paid amounts to the sum of-
  (a) the debt (including any interest due under the decree or document of debt);
  (b) the expenses incurred by the creditor in executing an inhibition (referred to in this section and in sections 165 and 166 as the "inhibition expenses"); and
  (c) the expenses of discharging the inhibition,
the inhibition ceases to have effect.
(3) Any rule of law to the effect that an inhibition ceases to have effect on payment or tender of the debt constituted by the decree or document of debt is abolished.
(4) This section and sections 165 and 166 of this Act do not apply to an inhibition on the dependence of an action.

DEFINITIONS
  "Judicial officer": 2007 Act s.57

GENERAL NOTE
  Common law states that tender of the principal sum, without expenses or interest, was sufficient to discharge an inhibition where an inhibition was being used to enforce payment, as opposed to enforce the performance of some act. This section overrules any such common law rules (see subs.(3)). If there is an inhibition being used to enforce payment of a debt, and a sum, representing the debt itself, interest thereon, the expenses of creating the inhibition and the expenses of discharging the inhibition, is paid to the creditor, a judicial officer or anyone else authorised to receive payment for the creditor, the inhibition will cease to have effect. If the sum is insufficient to pay the debt itself and the other items, the inhibition will remain in place.
  This rule will not, however, apply to an inhibition on the dependence of an action (subs.(4)).

158. Inhibition terminated by compliance with obligation to perform

Where-
  (a) an inhibition executed to enforce an obligation to perform a particular act (other than payment) contained in a decree has effect; and
  (b) the debtor has complied with the decree,
the inhibition ceases to have effect.

GENERAL NOTE

Whereas s.157 deals with payment, this section deals with the performance of the act (*ad factum praestandum*) that was the subject of the original action. Where the act is performed so that the debtor has complied with the decree, the inhibition ceases to have effect. There is no provision for expenses nor, obviously, for interest.

159. Termination of inhibition when property acquired by third party

(1) Notwithstanding section 160 of this Act, an inhibition ceases to have effect (and is treated as never having had effect) in relation to property if a person acquires the property (or a right in the property) in good faith and for adequate consideration.

(2) For the purposes of subsection (1) above, a person acquires property (or a right in the property) when the deed conveying (or granting the right in) the property is delivered to the person.

(3) An acquisition under subsection (1) above may be from the inhibited debtor or any other person who has acquired the property or right (regardless of whether that person acquired in good faith or for value).

(4) For the purposes of subsection (1) above, a person is presumed to have acted in good faith if the person-

(a) is unaware of the inhibition; and

(b) has taken all reasonable steps to discover the existence of an inhibition affecting the property.

GENERAL NOTE

This section deals with the (one hopes) unlikely situation where a purchaser, in good faith and for adequate consideration, buys property from an inhibited debtor unaware of the inhibition and having taken all reasonable steps to discover the existence of the inhibition affecting the property. Such a situation might arise where the Register of Inhibitions is inaccurate or a search was improperly carried out. While this might give rise to a claim against the Keeper, or indeed the purchaser's agents, this section gives redress to a purchaser who through no fault of his own acquires property, either from the debtor, or from any other person who has acquired the property or right in question (irrespective of whether that person himself had acquired it in good faith and for value), and finds that there is an inhibiting creditor ready to reduce his newly delivered (not registered) deed. In such circumstances, the "innocent" purchaser is protected as the inhibition ceases to have effect.

The unhappy inhibiting creditor presumably will have in turn a claim against the Keeper if the Register is inaccurate.

Breach

160. Breach of inhibition

An inhibited debtor breaches the inhibition when the debtor delivers a deed-

(a) conveying; or

(b) otherwise granting a right in,

property over which the inhibition has effect to a person other than the inhibiting creditor.

GENERAL NOTE

The inhibition is breached when the inhibited debtor delivers to a third party the deed conveying or granting a right in the property over which the inhibition has effect. It is significant that, as in the previous section, it is the date of delivery that is of import, not the date of registration of the deed (if, indeed, it ever were registered).

161. Prescription of right to reduce transactions in breach of inhibition

For the avoidance of doubt, section 8(1) of the Prescription and Limitation (Scotland) Act 1973 (c.52) (extinction of certain rights relating to property by prescriptive period of 20 years) applies to the right of an inhibitor to have a deed granted in breach of an inhibition reduced.

GENERAL NOTE

This section removes any doubt that the 20 year period of long negative prescription (as set out in s.8(1) of the Prescription and Limitation (Scotland) Act 1973) applies to the right of an inhibitor to obtain the reduction of any deed granted in breach of the inhibition.

162. Registration of notice of litigiosity and discharge of notice

After section 159 of the 1868 Act insert-

"**159A Registration of notice of summons of action of reduction**

(1) This section applies where a pursuer raises an action of reduction of a conveyance or deed of or relating to lands granted in breach of an inhibition.

(2) The pursuer shall, as soon as is reasonably practicable after the summons in the action is signeted-

  (a) register a notice of that signeted summons in accordance with section 159 of this Act; and

  (b) register in the Land Register of Scotland or, as the case may be, record in the Register of Sasines a copy of that notice.

(3) Where a decree of reduction is not obtained in the action to which the notice relates, the pursuer shall, as soon as is reasonably practicable-

  (a) register in the Register of Inhibitions; and

  (b) register in the Land Register of Scotland or, as the case may be, record in the Register of Sasines,

a discharge of that notice in (or as nearly as may be in) the form prescribed.".

DEFINITIONS

"1868 Act": Titles to Land Consolidation (Scotland) Act 1868

GENERAL NOTE

This section inserts a new s.159A into the 1868 Act. When a pursuer wishes to reduce a deed granted in breach of an inhibition by raising an action of reduction, he must, as soon as possible after the signeting of the summons, register a notice of that signeted summons in accordance with s.159 of the 1868 Act, and register in the Register of Sasines or the Land Register (as the case may be) a copy of that notice. Such a notice is known as a notice of litigiosity. If the action of reduction is unsuccessful he must register in the Register of Inhibition and the Register of Sasines or the Land Register (as the case may be) a discharge of the notice. The forms for these notices have yet to be devised, but there is power given to the Scottish Ministers under s.164 of the 2007 Act to have them devised.

163. Reduction of lease granted in breach of inhibition

(1) This section applies where an inhibited debtor grants a lease of property affected by the inhibition.

(2) A lease which, on the date an action of reduction of the lease is raised, has an unexpired duration of not less than 5 years is reducible.

(3) A lease which, on the date an action of reduction of the lease is raised, has an unexpired duration of less than 5 years may be reduced only if the Court of Session is satisfied that it would be fair and reasonable in all the circumstances to do so.

(4) In calculating the unexpired duration of a lease for the purposes of subsections (2) and (3) above-

    (a) any provision in the lease (however expressed) enabling the lease to be terminated earlier than the date on which the lease would otherwise terminate must be disregarded; and

    (b) where the lease includes provision (however expressed) requiring the landlord to renew it, the duration of any such renewed lease must be added to the duration of the original lease.

GENERAL NOTE

This deals with the situation where an inhibited debtor, in breach of his inhibition, grants a lease of property that is affected by the inhibition. If the lease has more than five years to run before its expiry date, it may be reduced (subs.(2)). If the unexpired portion of the lease is less than five years, it may only be reduced where the Court of Session believes if would be fair and reasonable to do so. When calculating the unexpired portion of the lease with less than five years remaining, one should not take account of any early termination clause, and where there is a clause indicating that the landlord must renew the lease, the duration of the renewed lease must be added to the duration of the original lease.

General and miscellaneous

164. Power to prescribe forms in the 1868 Act

(1) In section 159 of the 1868 Act (no litigiosity before date notice of summons is registered), for the words from "set" to "annexed" substitute "be in (or as nearly as may be in) the form prescribed.".

(2) After section 159A of that Act (which is inserted by section 162 of this Act) insert-

"159B Power of the Scottish Ministers to prescribe forms

(1) In sections 155, 159 and 159A of this Act, "prescribed" means prescribed by the Scottish Ministers by regulations.

(2) The power conferred on the Scottish Ministers to make regulations under subsection (1) above is exercisable by statutory instrument.

(3) A statutory instrument containing regulations made under subsection (1) above is subject to annulment in pursuance of a resolution of the Scottish Parliament.".

GENERAL NOTE

This section gives the Scottish Ministers powers to devise new forms to deal with the registration of inhibitions (see the 2007 Act s.149), notices of action of reduction and notices of discharge of the action for reduction of a deed (see the 2007 Act s.162). These forms will be in statutory instruments which will be subject to the negative resolution procedure.

165. Expenses of inhibition

(1) Subject to subsection (3) below, the inhibition expenses are chargeable against the debtor.

(2) Inhibition expenses are recoverable from the debtor by land attachment or residual attachment executed for the purpose of enforcing payment of the debt to which the inhibition relates but not by any other legal process.

(3) Where a creditor has executed an inhibition, the expenses of only one further inhibition in relation to the debt to which the first inhibition relates are chargeable against the debtor as inhibition expenses.

(4) For the purposes of a sequestration or other process in which there is ranking, the inhibition expenses must be treated as part of the debt constituted by the decree or document of debt authorising the inhibition.

GENERAL NOTE

The expenses of the inhibition are chargeable against the debtor. However, the actual expenses are not recoverable from the inhibition itself since the inhibition does not actually ensure payment into the creditor's hands. All the inhibition does is to prevent the sale or burdening of the debtor's property, unless the creditor chooses, in terms of s.157, to pay the full sum owing. In practice, paying the full sum owing is generally what happens, since the creditor will only discharge the inhibition if the full sum is paid, or arranged to be paid. Should the creditor wish to recover the inhibition expenses, the expenses will need to be recovered (if not proferred by the debtor) by carrying out a land attachment or residual attachment (subs.(2)). Neither ordinary attachment nor arrestment may be used to recover the expenses of the inhibition. It is difficult to see why these have been excluded unless it is to favour the debtor's position. From the creditor's point of view it would be extremely laborious to embark upon a land attachment to recover any expenses, and while less laborious to use residual attachment, residual attachment, as has been previously indicated, is not a diligence that can easily be used since it only applies where no other diligence is suitable. From the debtor's point of view, this arrangement is advantageous indeed, since many creditors will just wait until the debtor tries to sell his property and finds that he cannot do so until the inhibition is discharged, whereupon the creditor will be able to claim his expenses.

Where the creditor has obtained an inhibition, and it has expired after its duration of five years (see s.161), the creditor may apply for another inhibition. Subsection (3) permits the creditor to recover the expenses of a second inhibition from the debtor by land attachment or residual attachment, but will not permit the recovery of the expenses of any further inhibitions.

In the event of the debtor being sequestrated or becoming insolvent (see s.154) the inhibition expenses are deemed to be treated as part of the debt constituted by the decree or the document of debt which authorised the inhibition. The debt has no longer any preference in sequestration (or other insolvency proceedings), and so neither do the expenses of the inhibition.

It should be noted that where the creditor has used inhibition as a method of enforcing the performance of an obligation in terms of s.146(1)(b) above, this particular section (i.e. s.165) does not apply and the creditor may not obtain the expenses of the inhibition and must bear his own expenses (see s.146(7)(a) above).

166. Ascription

(1) This section applies where-
  (a) an inhibition has effect; and
  (b) any sums are paid to account of the sums recoverable from the debtor by virtue of the decree or document of debt authorising the inhibition.

(2) Such sums must be ascribed to the following in the order in which they are mentioned-
  (a) the expenses which are chargeable against the debtor incurred in respect of any diligence (other than the inhibition) authorised by the decree or document of debt;

(b) the inhibition expenses;

(c) any interest which has accrued, at the date on which the inhibition takes effect, on the debt constituted by the decree or document of debt;

(d) the debt constituted by the decree or document of debt together with such interest as has accrued after the date on which the inhibition takes effect.

DEFINITIONS

"Decree": 2007 Act s.221

"Document of debt": 2007 Act s.221

"Takes effect": 2007 Act s.149 (inserting new s.155 of the Titles to Land Consolidation (Scotland) Act 1868)

GENERAL NOTE

This deals with ascription, or payments to account. Where a inhibited debtor makes payments to account for a debt due to the creditor, they must be used to pay off (in the following order) the expenses of any diligence (other than the inhibition itself) authorised by the decree or instrument of debt, the inhibition expenses, interest on the debt up to the date of the inhibition taking effect and interest on the debt from the date of the inhibition taking effect.

167. Keeper's duty to enter inhibition on title sheet

In section 6 of the Land Registration (Scotland) Act 1979 (c.33) (content of title sheet)-

(a) in subsection (1)(c), at the beginning insert "subject to subsection (1A) below,"; and

(b) after subsection (1) insert-

"(1A) The Keeper shall enter an inhibition registered in the Register of Inhibitions in the title sheet only when completing registration of an interest in land where the interest has been transferred or created in breach of the inhibition.".

GENERAL NOTE

This inserts a new subs.(1A) into s.6 of the Land Registration (Scotland) Act 1979. This indicates that the only occasion that the Keeper must enter on a property's title sheet the existence of an inhibition duly registered in the Register of Inhibitions is when he is completing the registration of an interest in land where that interest has been transferred or created in breach of the inhibition.

In practice this is likely to be a very rare occurrence, but might arise under s.159.

168. Inhibition effective against judicial factor

(1) Notwithstanding the appointment of a judicial factor on a debtor's estate, an inhibition has effect.

(2) But subsection (1) above does not apply in a case where-

(a) a judicial factor is appointed under section 11A of the Judicial Factors (Scotland) Act 1889 (c.39) (application for judicial factor on deceased person's estate); and

(b) the inhibition was effective against the debtor prior to the debtor's death.

GENERAL NOTE

An inhibition remains in effect even if the debtor's affairs have been taken over by a duly appointed judicial factor. This will not, however, apply where a judicial factor is appointed under s.11A of the Judicial Factors (Scotland) Act 1889 (which provides for the appointment of a judicial factor on someone's death) and the inhibition was effective against the debtor before his death.

PART 6

DILIGENCE ON THE DEPENDENCE

169. Diligence on the dependence

After section 15 of the 1987 Act, insert-

"PART 1A

DILIGENCE ON THE DEPENDENCE

Availability of diligence on the dependence

15A Diligence on the dependence of action

(1) Subject to subsection (2) below and to sections 15C to 15F of this Act, the Court of Session or the sheriff may grant warrant for diligence by-

(a) arrestment; or

(b) inhibition,

on the dependence of an action.

(2) Warrant for-

(a) arrestment on the dependence of an action is competent only where the action contains a conclusion for payment of a sum other than by way of expenses; and

(b) inhibition on the dependence is competent only where the action contains-

(i) such a conclusion; or

(ii) a conclusion for specific implement of an obligation to convey heritable property to the creditor or to grant in the creditor's favour a real right in security, or some other right, over such property.

(3) In this Part of this Act, "action" includes, in the sheriff court-

(a) a summary cause;

(b) a small claim; and

(c) a summary application,

and references to "summons", "conclusion" and to cognate expressions shall be construed accordingly.

15B Diligence on the dependence of petition

(1) Subject to subsection (2) below and to sections 15C to 15F of this Act, the Court of Session may grant warrant for diligence by-

(a) arrestment; or

(b) inhibition,

on the dependence of a petition.

(2) Warrant for-

(a) arrestment on the dependence of a petition is competent only where the petition contains a prayer for payment of a sum other than by way of expenses; and

(b) inhibition on the dependence is competent only where the petition contains-

    (i) such a prayer; or

    (ii) a prayer for specific implement of an obligation to convey heritable property to the creditor or to grant in the creditor's favour a real right in security, or some other right, over such property.

(3) The provisions of this Act (other than section 15A), of any other enactment and of any rule of law relating to diligence on the dependence of actions shall, in so far as is practicable and unless the contrary intention appears, apply to petitions in relation to which it is competent to grant warrant for such diligence and to the parties to them as they apply to actions and to parties to them.

15C Diligence on the dependence to secure future or contingent debts

(1) It shall be competent for the court to grant warrant for diligence on the dependence where the sum concluded for is a future or contingent debt.

(2) In this section and in sections 15D to 15M of this Act, the "court" means the court before which the action is depending.

Application for diligence on the dependence

15D Application for diligence on the dependence

(1) A creditor may, at any time during which an action is in dependence, apply to the court for warrant for diligence by-

(a) arrestment; or

(b) inhibition,

on the dependence of the action.

(2) An application under subsection (1) above shall-

(a) be in (or as nearly as may be in) the form prescribed by Act of Sederunt;

(b) subject to subsection (3) below, be intimated to and provide details of-

    (i) the debtor; and

    (ii) any other person having an interest;

(c) state whether the creditor is seeking the grant, under section 15E(1) of this Act, of warrant for diligence on the dependence in advance of a hearing on the application under section 15F of this Act; and

(d) contain such other information as the Scottish Ministers may by regulations prescribe.

(3) An application under subsection (1) above need not be intimated where the creditor is seeking the grant, under section 15E(1) of this Act, of warrant in advance of a hearing on the application under section 15F of this Act.

(4) The court, on receiving an application under subsection
(1) above, shall-

    (a) subject to section 15E of this Act, fix a date for a
hearing on the application under section 15F of this Act;
and

    (b) order the creditor to intimate that date to-

        (i) the debtor; and

        (ii) any other person appearing to the court to have
an interest.

15E   Grant of warrant without a hearing

(1) The court may, if satisfied as to the matters mentioned in
subsection (2) below, make an order granting warrant for
diligence on the dependence without a hearing on the application under section 15F of this Act.

(2) The matters referred to in subsection (1) above are-

    (a) that the creditor has a *prima facie* case on the merits of
the action;

    (b) that there is a real and substantial risk enforcement of
any decree in the action in favour of the creditor would
be defeated or prejudiced by reason of-

        (i) the debtor being insolvent or verging on
insolvency; or

        (ii) the likelihood of the debtor removing, disposing
of, burdening, concealing or otherwise dealing with
all or some of the debtor's assets,

were warrant for diligence on the dependence not granted
in advance of such a hearing; and

    (c) that it is reasonable in all the circumstances, including
the effect granting warrant may have on any person
having an interest, to do so.

(3) The onus shall be on the creditor to satisfy the court that
the order granting warrant should be made.

(4) Where the court makes an order granting warrant for
diligence on the dependence without a hearing on the
application under section 15F of this Act, the court shall-

    (a) fix a date for a hearing under section 15K of this Act;
and

    (b) order the creditor to intimate that date to-

        (i) the debtor; and

        (ii) any other person appearing to the court to have
an interest.

(5) Where a hearing is fixed under subsection (4)(a) above,
section 15K of this Act shall apply as if an application had
been made to the court for an order under that section.

(6) Where the court refuses to make an order granting a
warrant without a hearing under section 15F of this Act
and the creditor insists in the application, the court shall-

    (a) fix a date for such a hearing on the application; and

    (b) order the creditor to intimate that date to-

        (i) the debtor; and

        (ii) any other person appearing to the court to have
an interest.

15F   Hearing on application

(1) At the hearing on an application for warrant for diligence on the dependence, the court shall not make any order without first giving-

   (a) any person to whom intimation of the date of the hearing was made; and

   (b) any other person the court is satisfied has an interest,

an opportunity to be heard.

(2) The court may, if satisfied as to the matters mentioned in subsection (3) below, make an order granting warrant for diligence on the dependence.

(3) The matters referred to in subsection (2) above are-

   (a) that the creditor has a *prima facie* case on the merits of the action;

   (b) that there is a real and substantial risk enforcement of any decree in the action in favour of the creditor would be defeated or prejudiced by reason of-

      (i) the debtor being insolvent or verging on insolvency; or

      (ii) the likelihood of the debtor removing, disposing of, burdening, concealing or otherwise dealing with all or some of the debtor's assets,

   were warrant for diligence on the dependence not granted; and

   (c) that it is reasonable in all the circumstances, including the effect granting warrant may have on any person having an interest, to do so.

(4) The onus shall be on the creditor to satisfy the court that the order granting warrant should be made.

(5) Where the court makes an order granting or, as the case may be, refusing warrant for diligence on the dependence, the court shall order the creditor to intimate that order to-

   (a) the debtor; and

   (b) any other person appearing to the court to have an interest.

(6) Where the court makes an order refusing warrant for diligence on the dependence, the court may impose such conditions (if any) as it thinks fit.

(7) Without prejudice to the generality of subsection (6) above, those conditions may require the debtor-

   (a) to consign into court such sum; or

   (b) to find caution or to give such other security,

as the court thinks fit.

Execution before service

15G   Execution of diligence before service of summons

(1) This section applies where diligence by-

   (a) arrestment; or

   (b) inhibition,

on the dependence of an action is executed before service of the summons on the debtor.

(2) Subject to subsection (3) below, if the summons is not served on the debtor before the end of the period of 21 days beginning with the day on which the diligence is executed, the diligence shall cease to have effect.

(3) The court may, on the application of the creditor, make an order extending the period referred to in subsection (2) above.

(4) In determining whether to make such an order the court shall have regard to-

(a) the efforts of the creditor to serve the summons within the period of 21 days; and

(b) any special circumstances preventing or obstructing service within that period.

Restriction on property attached

15H   Sum attached by arrestment on dependence

(1) The court may, subject to subsection (2) below, when granting warrant for arrestment on the dependence, limit the sum which may be attached to funds not exceeding such amount as the court may specify.

(2) The maximum amount which the court may specify under subsection (1) above shall be the aggregate of-

(a) the principal sum concluded for;

(b) a sum equal to 20 per cent of that sum or such other percentage as the Scottish Ministers may, by regulations, prescribe;

(c) a sum equal to 1 year's interest on the principal sum at the judicial rate; and

(d) any sum prescribed under subsection (3) below.

(3) The Scottish Ministers may, by regulations, prescribe a sum which appears to them to be reasonable having regard to the expenses likely to be-

(a) incurred by a creditor; and

(b) chargeable against a debtor,

in executing an arrestment on the dependence.

(4) For the avoidance of doubt, section 73F of this Act applies to any sum attached under this section.

15J   Property affected by inhibition on dependence

Where the court grants warrant for diligence by inhibition on the dependence-

(a) in a case where the action is brought for specific implement of an obligation-

(i) to convey heritable property to the creditor;

(ii) to grant in the creditor's favour a real right in security over such property; or

(iii) to grant some other right over such property,

the court shall limit the property inhibited to that particular property; and

(b) in any other case, the court may limit the property inhibited to such property as the court may specify.

15K   Recall or restriction of diligence on dependence

(1) This section applies where warrant is granted for diligence on the dependence.

(2) The debtor and any person having an interest may apply to the court for an order-

    (a) recalling the warrant;

    (b) restricting the warrant;

    (c) if an arrestment or inhibition has been executed in pursuance of the warrant-

        (i) recalling; or

        (ii) restricting,

    that arrestment or inhibition;

    (d) determining any question relating to the validity, effect or operation of the warrant; or

    (e) ancillary to any order mentioned in paragraphs (a) to (d) above.

(3) An application under subsection (2) above shall-

    (a) be in (or as nearly as may be in) the form prescribed by Act of Sederunt; and

    (b) be intimated to-

        (i) the creditor; and

        (ii) any other person having an interest.

(4) At the hearing on the application under subsection (2) above, the court shall not make any order without first giving-

    (a) any person to whom intimation of the application was made; and

    (b) any other person the court is satisfied has an interest,

an opportunity to be heard.

(5) Where the court is satisfied that the warrant is invalid it-

    (a) shall make an order-

        (i) recalling the warrant; and

        (ii) if an arrestment or inhibition has been executed in pursuance of the warrant, recalling that arrestment or inhibition; and

    (b) may make an order ancillary to any order mentioned in paragraph (a) above.

(6) Where the court is satisfied that an arrestment or inhibition executed in pursuance of the warrant is incompetent, it-

    (a) shall make an order recalling that arrestment or inhibition; and

    (b) may make an order ancillary to any such order.

(7) Subject to subsection (8) below, where the court is satisfied that the warrant is valid but that-

    (a) an arrestment or inhibition executed in pursuance of it is irregular or ineffective; or

    (b) it is reasonable in all the circumstances, including the effect granting warrant may have had on any person having an interest, to do so,

the court may make any order such as is mentioned in subsection (2) above.

(8) If no longer satisfied as to the matters mentioned in subsection (9) below, the court-

   (a) shall make an order such as is mentioned in subsection (5)(a) above; and

   (b) may make an order such as is mentioned in subsection (5)(b) above.

(9) The matters referred to in subsection (8) above are-

   (a) that the creditor has a *prima facie* case on the merits of the action;

   (b) that there is a real and substantial risk enforcement of any decree in the action in favour of the creditor would be defeated or prejudiced by reason of-

      (i) the debtor being insolvent or verging on insolvency; or

      (ii) the likelihood of the debtor removing, disposing of, burdening, concealing or otherwise dealing with all or some of the debtor's assets; and

   (c) that it is reasonable in all the circumstances, including the effect granting warrant may have had on any person having an interest, for the warrant or, as the case may be, any arrestment or inhibition executed in pursuance of it to continue to have effect.

(10) The onus shall be on the creditor to satisfy the court that no order under subsection (5), (6), (7) or (8) above should be made.

(11) In granting an application under subsection (2) above, the court may impose such conditions (if any) as it thinks fit.

(12) Without prejudice to the generality of subsection (11) above, the court may impose conditions which require the debtor-

   (a) to consign into court such sum; or

   (b) to find such caution or to give such other security,

as the court thinks fit.

(13) Where the court makes an order under this section, the court shall order the debtor to intimate that order to-

   (a) the creditor; and

   (b) any other person appearing to the court to have an interest.

(14) This section applies irrespective of whether warrant for diligence on the dependence is obtained, or executed, before this section comes into force.

15L Variation of orders and variation or recall of conditions

(1) Where-

   (a) an order restricting warrant for diligence on the dependence is made under section 15K(7); or

   (b) a condition is imposed by virtue of-

      (i) section 15F(6); or

      (ii) section 15K(11),

of this Act, the debtor may apply to the court for variation of the order or, as the case may be, variation or removal of the condition.

(2) An application under subsection (1) above shall-

    (a) be in (or as nearly as may be in) the form prescribed by Act of Sederunt; and

    (b) be intimated to-

        (i) the creditor; and

        (ii) any other person having an interest.

(3) At the hearing on the application under subsection (1) above, the court shall not make any order without first giving-

    (a) any person to whom intimation of the application was made; and

    (b) any other person the court is satisfied has an interest,

an opportunity to be heard.

(4) On an application under subsection (1) above, the court may if it thinks fit-

    (a) vary the order; or

    (b) vary or remove the condition.

(5) Where the court makes an order varying the order or, as the case may be, varying or removing the condition, the court shall order the debtor to intimate that order to-

    (a) the creditor; and

    (b) any other person appearing to the court to have an interest.

General and miscellaneous

15M Expenses of diligence on the dependence

(1) Subject to subsection (3)(a) below, a creditor shall be entitled to such expenses as the creditor incurs-

    (a) in obtaining warrant for diligence on the dependence; and

    (b) where an arrestment or inhibition is executed in pursuance of the warrant, in so executing the arrestment or inhibition.

(2) Subject to subsection (3)(b) below, a debtor shall be entitled, where-

    (a) warrant for diligence on the dependence is granted; and

    (b) the court is satisfied that the creditor was acting unreasonably in applying for it,

to the expenses incurred in opposing that warrant.

(3) The court may modify or refuse-

    (a) such expenses as are mentioned in subsection (1) above if it is satisfied that-

        (i) the creditor was acting unreasonably in applying for the warrant; or

        (ii) such modification or refusal is reasonable in all the circumstances and having regard to the outcome of the action; and

    (b) such expenses as are mentioned in subsection (2) above if it is satisfied as to the matter mentioned in paragraph (a)(ii) above.

(4) Subject to subsections (1) to (3) above, the court may make such finding as it thinks fit in relation to such expenses as are mentioned in subsections (1) and (2) above.

(5) Expenses incurred as mentioned in subsection (1) and (2) above in obtaining or, as the case may be, opposing an application for warrant shall be expenses of process.

(6) Subsections (1) to (5) above are without prejudice to any enactment or rule of law as to the recovery of expenses chargeable against a debtor as are incurred in executing an arrestment or inhibition on the dependence of an action.

15N   Application of this Part to admiralty actions

This Part of this Act (other than sections 15H, 15J and 15M) shall apply, in so far as not inconsistent with the provisions of Part V of the Administration of Justice Act 1956 (c.46) (admiralty jurisdiction and arrestment of ships), to an arrestment on the dependence of an admiralty action as it applies to any other arrestment on the dependence.".

GENERAL NOTE

Part 6 of the 2007 Act (with the exception of s.172) came into force on April 1, 2008. S.169 inserts new ss.15A-N into a new Pt 1A of the 1987 Act, and what it effectually does is to codify and set out in statutory form a revised version of some of the common law on the diligences of arrestment and inhibition on the dependence of an action or a petition. S.169 came into force on April 1, 2008, with the exception of s.15H(4) which has not yet been brought into force.

For a further discussion on arrestment generally, see the notes to Pt 10 of this Act.

Arrestment on the dependence is a method whereby a pursuer (in an action) or a petitioner (in a petition) may "freeze" an asset in the hands of a third party (arrestment), before any summons, petition or initial writ has been served on the defender or respondent. Likewise inhibition on the dependence prevents the defender/respondent attempting to dispose of his heritage (inhibition) before the summons, petition or initial writ has been served on the defender or respondent. In each case, the appropriate diligence requires a warrant from the court before the action or petition has actually started. It gives the pursuer/petitioner an effective security over the debtor's property for any sum for which the defender/respondent may ultimately be liable. It is extremely effective from the pursuer's/petitioner's point of view. It is also particularly useful when there is a danger that the defender/respondent would try to dispose of his assets if he knew that litigation was about take place against him.

This Part also deals with admiralty arrestments on the dependence. These work on broadly the same basis, save that ships are not generally in the hands of a third party, and ships may as a result of an admiralty arrestment on the dependence be prevented from leaving harbour until the arrestment is lifted.

In each case, the relevant diligence on the dependence may be converted into a normal diligence once decree is given in favour of the pursuer/petitioner.

A similar process for attachment of assets in the debtor's own premises on the dependence of an action or petition, known as interim attachment, is to be found in Pt 7 of the 2007 Act, introducing a new Pt 1A9 into the 2002 Act.

The draftsman, in preparing the legislation, had to take account of three important issues. One was that arrested assets or inhibited heritable property may not necessarily be in the sole ownership or possession of the defender/respondent, and account should be taken of other owners' or possessors' interests. Secondly, the amount arrested should not cause hardship for the defender's/respondent's family. Thirdly, the Human Rights Act 1998 entitles citizens to the peaceful enjoyment of their property, and arrestment and inhibition on the dependence clearly prevent this. So a defender/respondent is allowed an opportunity (under the new s.15F and K of the 2002

Act) to say why the warrant for diligence on the dependence should not be granted. This takes account of the difficulties that arose in *Karl Construction Ltd v Palisade Properties Plc* 2002 S.C. 270; 2002 S.L.T. 312. As a result of that case the Court of Session Rules of Court take account of the need for intimation to the defender/respondent (see Rules of Court 13.6A, 13.8A) and give him the opportunity to seek recall of the diligence on the dependence. This is echoed in the new s.15K of the 2002 Act.

The legislation in this section refers to various forms which must be used. For the procedure to be followed, see the Act of Sederunt (Sheriff Court Rules Amendment) (Diligence) 2008 (SSI 2008/121) and the Act of Sederunt (Rules of the Court of Session Amendment No.3) (Bankruptcy and Diligence etc (Scotland) Act 2007) 2008 (SSI 2008/122). These indicate the various forms and statements required for the interim diligence and inhibition. The two Acts of Sederunt came into force on April 1, 2008.

Section 15A (of the 1987 Act)

Both the Court of Session and the sheriff court may grant warrant for arrestment or inhibition on the dependence of an action. However, subject to s.15C-F, arrestment on the dependence is competent only where the action seeks payment of a sum other than expenses, and inhibition on the dependence is competent only where the action seeks payment of a sum other than expenses or specific implement for the conveyance of heritable property, or a right in that property, to the creditor (subs.(2)).

Hitherto it has not been possible to obtain an inhibition on the dependence of an action from the sheriff court. This is now available. This ties in with s.146 of the 2007 Act which both disapplies the old procedure of obtaining letters of inhibition and allows warrant for inhibition to be granted in the sheriff court.

For the purposes of this Part, sheriff court does not just mean the ordinary court: it also includes summary causes, small claims and summary applications (subs.(3)).

Section 15B

This section permits the Court of Session to grant warrant for arrestment or inhibition on the dependence of a petition. However, subject to s.15C-F, arrestment on the dependence is competent only where the action seeks payment of a sum other than expenses, and inhibition on the dependence is competent only where the action seeks payment of a sum other than expenses or specific implement for the conveyance of heritable property, or a right in that property, to the creditor.

Subsection (2) explains that references to diligence on the dependence of actions is deemed also to mean reference to diligence on the dependence of petitions, in order to avoid unnecessary repetition, unless the contrary intention is evident.

Section 15C

It is competent for the court to grant warrant for diligence on the dependence where the sum being sought is a future or contingent debt. This covers such debts as aliment, maintenance and capital sums payable on divorce. These were formerly dealt with by s.19 of the Family Law (Scotland) Act 1985, which is repealed in Sch.6 of the 2007 Act. There is further reference to arrestment on the dependence of an action for a future or contingent debt at s.95A of the 1987 Act (as inserted by s.170 of the 2007 Act).

Subsection (2) explains that the word "court" in s.15D-M hereafter means the court before which the action is taking place. This may be either the sheriff court or the Court of Session, but in the case of petitions, it will only be the Court of Session.

Section 15D

In this and the succeeding sections in this Part, the word "creditor" is deemed to mean the pursuer or petitioner (as the case may be) even if the subject matter of the action or petition is not necessarily involving the payment of money, since it may include the conveying of property or the granting of security in favour of the creditor. Likewise "debtor" means the defender or respondent. Where the word "diligence" is used in these notes to this Part, it will mean both arrestment and inhibition unless the contrary is indicated.

A creditor may apply for a warrant for diligence by arrestment or inhibition on the dependence, and must do so on the relevant form (in the Court of Session, Form 14AZ; in the sheriff court, both Form G4A and the necessary accompanying statement on Form 15a). A copy of the application will normally be sent to the applicant and anyone else having an interest, and must state whether or not the creditor is seeking a grant of warrant for diligence on the dependence before any preliminary hearing under s.15F takes place (subs.(2)). Although normally a preliminary hearing under s.15F would take place, it is possible that a creditor may seek to obtain a warrant ahead of a preliminary hearing if s.15E applies, in which case the appropriate hearing would in fact be under s.15K. As will be seen, s.15E applies where the creditor both has a *prima facie* case on the merits of the action, and where the creditor is able to persuade the court that there is a danger of the debtor's assets being dissipated or the debtor becoming insolvent. Under these circumstances, the creditor may need to act swiftly, and so subs.(3) of s.15D enables the creditor to dispense with intimation to the debtor and anyone else with an interest, and obtain under s.15E(1) from the court a warrant for diligence on the dependence.

Where a warrant under s.15E is not sought, a preliminary hearing under s.15F will take place (subs.(4)).

Section 15E

This applies where a creditor is seeking warrant for diligence on the dependence and the creditor wishes to dispense with intimation to the debtor and anyone else with an interest, usually in the interest of speed. This may only be done if the court is satisfied that the warrant should be so granted. In order to satisfy the court, it must be persuaded (and it is for the creditor to convince the court of this (subs. (3)) that the creditor has a *prima facie* case and that there is a real and substantial risk that any attempt to enforce any subsequent decree in the action about to be raised would be defeated or be less effective because of the debtor being insolvent or being about to become insolvent, or because of the likelihood that the debtor would remove or dissipate his assets in order to place them out of the reach of creditors. In addition it must be reasonable in all the circumstances to grant the order for the warrant (subs.(2)). It will be seen that these terms mirror the old common law requirements of *vergens ad inopiam* and *in meditatione fugae*.

Since it would be unjust, for the reasons indicated in the introduction to this Part, to deny the debtor his day in court, where a warrant without a preliminary hearing has been granted in terms of this section, a hearing nevertheless is available under s.15K, which deals with recall or restriction of diligence on the dependence. The court must automatically fix a hearing under s.15K if it has granted a warrant without a preliminary hearing under s.15F (see subs.(4)). Section 15K(10) puts the onus on the creditor to show why the diligence on the dependence should be allowed to take place and a recall or restriction order not made.

However, the court may decline to grant a s.15E warrant without a preliminary hearing, so that the s.15E application warrant fails, whereupon a hearing under s.15F should take place. In that event, assuming the creditor still insists on his application for a warrant for diligence on the dependence, the hearing under s.15 must be intimated to the debtor and anyone else having an interest (subs.(6)).

Section 15F

This section gives the debtor and anyone else with an interest the opportunity to put his case as to why diligence on the dependence should not be granted, and so they must receive notice of the hearing (subs.(1)). The court may grant the order for the warrant if satisfied that the creditor has a *prima facie* case and that there is a real and substantial risk that any attempt to enforce any subsequent decree in the action about to be raised would be defeated or be less effective because of the debtor being insolvent or being about to become insolvent, or because of the likelihood that the debtor would remove or dissipate his assets in order to place them out of the reach of creditors. In addition it must be reasonable in all the circumstances to grant the order for the warrant (subs.(3)). As in s.15E it is for the creditor to satisfy the court that the order should be granted (subs.(4)). If the order is granted, or indeed refused, the creditor must intimate the order for the warrant, or the order for the refusal of warrant, to the debtor and anyone else with an interest (subs.(5)). If the order is refused, it may nevertheless be refused on condition that the debtor carry out some other act, such as finding caution or consigning some money into court (subs.(6)).

Section 15G

This section deals with the requirement that the summons for the action must be served on the debtor within 21 days of the date of the execution of the diligence on the dependence. If the summons is not served, the diligence will have no effect, unless the creditor applies to court for an extension to that period, particularly where there may be difficulty in serving the summons on the debtor. The word "summons" is deemed to cover all court-case initiating claims, in order to avoid the unnecessary reiteration of summons, petitions and initial writs (see ss.15A(3) and 15B(3)).

Section 15 H

Note that subsection (4) of this section has not at the time of writing been brought into force. This section restricts the amount of money (since it uses the word "funds") that may be arrested by virtue of the warrant for diligence on the dependence. That amount is not to be more than the principal sum sued for in the action, plus 20 per cent or such amount as the Scottish Ministers decide, one year's interest at the judicial rate and the reasonable expenses of the arrestment. Subsection (4) refers to s.73F of the 1987 Act. This is to be found in s.206 of the 2007 Act, and it refers to the preservation of a minimum unarrestable balance in a debtor's bank account, at the time of writing being £370. If the debtor's bank account is in credit, only the sums in excess of that figure may be arrested.

"Judicial rate" is a matter that is being discussed by the Scottish Government with a view to having a more settled policy. See their Consultation and Draft Bill 2008 on judicial interest.

Where the items arrested are not funds, the above restrictions on what is arrestable do not apply.

Although it is not mentioned at this stage, s.73G of the 1987 Act (as inserted by the 2007 Act s.206) requires the arrestee to send to the creditor and the debtor information about what has been arrested on the dependence of the action. This must be done within three weeks of the arrestment.

There does not appear to be a requirement for the judicial officer arresting the assets in the hands of the arrestee to tell the debtor, by means of a schedule, about the execution of the arrestment on the dependence, or indeed how much or what has been arrested. This is curious because s.73B of the 1987 Act requires the creditor to use a schedule (in a form yet to be prescribed) when executing an arrestment not on the dependence. Section 73D also refers to a schedule being served (presumably on the debtor, though it does not so explicitly say so) at the same time as a debt advice and information package is provided to the debtor.

It may be that this is an oversight: it may be that this was deliberate. It may be that it is thought that the ensuing summons, and the information from the arrestee should suffice. Nevertheless it is submitted that it might be a good idea for some form of schedule to be sent to the debtor, especially since the whole point of much of the 2007 Act is to improve the position of the debtor and to give the chance to object if he feels he is being treated harshly. In order to object, he needs to know fully what has been done to him by the creditor.

Section 15 J

Whereas the previous section dealt with arrested funds, this section deals with inhibited property. Where warrant for inhibition on the dependence has been granted, and where the action for which the warrant was granted was in connection with specific implement of an obligation to convey heritable property to the creditor, or to grant the creditor a real right in the debtor's heritable property, the inhibition on the dependence is only in respect of that heritable property and no other.

Where warrant for inhibition on the dependence has been granted, but the action is not one of specific implement as just explained, the court has wider discretion and may limit, or not, the inhibition to such property as the court may see fit.

This section ties in with s.152. This states that, notwithstanding the limited nature of an inhibition on the dependence relating to a particular heritable property, the conversion of the inhibition on the dependence to an ordinary post-decree inhibition lifts the limitation to the one particular heritable property, and the post-decree inhibition may be extended to all of the debtor's property.

Section 15 K

This section gives the debtor the opportunity to apply to have recalled or restricted both the warrant for diligence on the dependence and the diligence itself, or to question the procedural or other validity of the warrant (subs.(2)). The debtor, or anyone else with an interest in the recall or restriction, must apply by incidental application, and intimate the application to the creditor or anyone else having an interest (subs.(3)). At the ensuing hearing, the creditor and anyone else having an interest must be given his opportunity to put his case forward (subs.(4)).

If the warrant is held to be invalid, the court will recall the warrant and any diligence flowing from it (subs.(5)). If the actual arrestment on the dependence or the inhibition on the dependence executed following the grant of the warrant is incompetent, the arrestment or inhibition must be recalled (subs.(6)).

If the warrant itself was valid, but the arrestment or inhibition was irregular or ineffective, or if recall or restriction is reasonable under all the circumstances, the arrestment or inhibition may be recalled or restricted as in subs.(2) above (subs.(7)). "Irregular" might suggest some procedural irregularity, such as a failure to intimate a hearing or some oversight in the practicalities of effecting an arrestment or inhibition. "Ineffective" arrestment or inhibition would arise when, for example, the summons is not served on the debtor in the required period of 21 days (see s.15G(2)).

Subsection (7) is subject to subs.(8) which states that the warrant for diligence may be recalled or restricted if the court is no longer satisfied with the grounds on which the diligence was originally sought: these are, namely, that the creditor had a *prima facie* case; that there was a real and substantial risk that any attempt to enforce any subsequent decree in the action about to be raised would be defeated or be less effective because of the debtor being insolvent or being about to become insolvent, or because of the likelihood that the debtor would remove or dissipate his assets in order to place them out of the reach of creditors; and that, in addition, it was reasonable in all the circumstances to grant the order for the warrant, taking into account any effect the diligence on the dependence was having on anyone with an interest (subs.(9)).

When the debtor, or anyone having an interest, is seeking to have the diligence of the dependence recalled or restricted under subss.(5)-(8), it is for the creditor to satisfy the court that the diligence should not be recalled or restricted (subs.(10)).

The court may if it wishes impose any order under subs.(2) that it sees fit. Equally, it may require the debtor to pay into court some money or to find caution (subs.(12)).

The debtor, being the one making the application, will be the one who has to send a copy to the creditor (or anyone else with an interest) of any order made by the court under this section (subs.(13)).

This section is applicable even if the warrant for the diligence on the dependence was obtained before this particular section was brought into force (subs.14).

Section 15L

Subsection (1) permits a debtor to apply for a variation to or removal of any order granted under ss.15K(7) (recall or restriction of any diligence on the dependence proceeding from a valid warrant), 15F(6) or 15K(11) (conditions imposed on the debtor by the court when warrant for diligence is refused).

The application must be intimated to the creditor and anyone else with an interest (subs.(2)). These persons have to be given the opportunity of a hearing (subs.(3)). If an order is granted varying or removing an order or condition (subs.(4)), this must be intimated by the debtor to the creditor and anyone else with an interest (subs.(5)).

Section 15M

In this section, the creditor's and debtor's liability for expenses is explained. The creditor in a successful application for and successful execution of diligence on the dependence will be entitled to expenses from the debtor (subs.(1)), but where the court is satisfied that the creditor acted unreasonably in applying for diligence on the dependence (even when it was granted), the creditor will be liable for the expenses (subs.(2)). The court has discretion to modify or refuse an award of expenses under subss.(1) and (2) as necessary (subss.(3) and (4)). Subsection (5) states that expenses arising out of obtaining or opposing an application for warrant will be expenses of process. None of the above subsections affect any existing rules of law relating to the recovery of expenses from a debtor when executing arrestment or inhibition on the dependence of an action. Reference should be made to s.93 of the 1987 Act which provides that the recovery of expenses arising out of arrestment (whether on the dependence or otherwise) must, if they need to be enforced by diligence, by enforced by arrestment and no other source. The recovery of the expenses of inhibition would come when the creditor discharges the inhibition on payment by the debtor.

Section 15N

This provides that this new Pt 1A of the 1987 Act will apply to admiralty actions, with the exception of s.15H, J and M, since they are clearly inappropriate for arresting on the dependence of an admiralty action. Schedule 4 of the 2007 Act inserts a new s.47B into the Administration of Justice Act 1956 (admiralty jurisdiction and arrestment of ships); this new section deals with expenses.

170. Prescription of arrestment

After section 95 of the 1987 Act, insert-

"95A Prescription of arrestment

(1) Subject to subsection (2) below, an arrestment which is not insisted in prescribes-

    (a) where it is on the dependence of an action, at the end of the period of 3 years beginning with the day on which a final interlocutor is obtained by the creditor for payment of all or part of a principal sum concluded for; or

    (b) where it is in execution of an extract decree or other extract registered document relating to a due debt, at the end of the period of 3 years beginning with the day on which the arrestment is executed.

(2) Where the arrestment secures or enforces a future or contingent debt due to the creditor, it prescribes, if not insisted in, at the end of the period of 3 years beginning on the day on which the debt becomes due.

(3) In a case where-

    (a) a time to pay direction;

    (b) an interim order under section 6(3) of this Act; or

    (c) a time to pay order,

has been made, there shall be disregarded, in computing the period at the end of which the arrestment prescribes, the period during which the time to pay direction, interim order or time to pay order is in effect.

(4) Nothing in this section shall apply to an earnings arrestment, a current maintenance arrestment or a conjoined arrestment order.

(5) Subsections (1) to (3) above apply irrespective of whether the arrestment is executed, or warrant for it obtained, before this section comes into force.

(6) For the purposes of subsection (1)(a) above, a final interlocutor is obtained when an interlocutor cannot be recalled or altered and is not subject to review.".

DEFINITIONS

    "Conjoined arrestment order": 1987 Act s.60

    "Current maintenance agreement": 1987 Act s.51

    "Earnings arrestment": 1987 Act s.47

GENERAL NOTE

This section inserts a new s.95A into the 1987 Act to deal with prescription of arrestment. It is in force with effect from April 1, 2008.

Section 95A

The phrase "not insisted in" means that no action is taken by the creditor to enforce his claim. So if a creditor successfully obtained a decree for a principal sum, and there had been an arrestment on the dependence of his claim, the creditor has three years from the date of the interlocutor of the court to complete his arrestment, and if he fails to do so, it prescribes (subs.(1)(a)).

Where a creditor has a decree or a document of debt and has executed an arrestment, that too prescribes at the end of the period of three years commencing on the day of execution of the arrestment (subs.(1)(b)).

Where a creditor has executed an arrestment on the dependence of a future or contingent debt due to the creditor, the debt prescribes at the end of the three year period commencing on the day on which the debt became due (subs.(2)).

Where there has been a time to pay direction, interim order or order in terms of the 1987 Act Pt 1, the periods during which the direction, interim order or order is in place is disregarded for the purposes of the three year prescription period (subs.(3)).

Earnings arrestments, current maintenance agreements and conjoined arrestment orders are not affected by this section (subs.(4)).

The provisions in this section should be read in light of s.73J of the 1987 Act as inserted by s.206 of the 2007 Act, which provides that where there has been a final decree in an action on the dependence of which the creditor has executed an arrestment, and the arrestment has attached funds due to the debtor, the arrestee (the person holding the arrested funds, commonly a bank or insurance company) must release to the creditor the permitted arrested funds within 14 weeks of the service of the final decree relating to the action for which the arrestment on the dependence took place. This is known as "automatic release of arrested funds". The word "permitted" is relevant because it is not permissible to evacuate a debtor's funds in a bank account: only the excess over the sum of £370 (as at the time of writing) may be released (s.73F) and there are other rules restricting the amount to be released (see s.73K, L and Q).

What should be noticed about s.73J is that it only applies to arrested funds, commonly money in a bank account. However, s.95A does not restrict itself to funds. Arrested assets do not need to be funds. There are plenty of other assets that could be arrested, such as furniture stored in a depositary, livestock in the hands of an auctioneer, a partnership interest, shares in a company, or a vested right in a trust. The three year rule therefore applies to all arrestments, whatever the nature of the assets arrested.

171. Abolition of letters of loosing

(1) Subject to subsection (2) below, it is no longer competent for any court to loose an arrestment.

(2) Subsection (1) above does not affect-

    (a) any enactment or rule of law relating to the loosing of an arrestment of a ship or its cargo; or

    (b) the exercise of any other power of the court to recall or restrict an arrestment.

GENERAL NOTE

Loosing is a procedure whereby an arrestment is lifted by the release of property from the arrestee without the debt being extinguished. The property itself was uplifted and put into the hands of the debtor who was then able to regain the arrested property. It required signeted letters of loosing and is little, if at all, used. In any event, it is now abolished, except in the context of the loosing of a ship or its cargo. Notwithstanding the abolition, the court still retains its inherent power to recall or restrict an arrestment generally. This section is in force with effect from April 1, 2008.

172. Abolition of adjudication in security

Any enactment or rule of law enabling adjudication in security to be used ceases to have effect.

GENERAL NOTE

Adjudication in security is a little known and less used method of obtaining security for a future or contingent debt. It is now abolished.

PART 7

INTERIM ATTACHMENT

GENERAL NOTE

This section inserts a new Pt 1A into the 2002 Act, and came into force on April 1, 2008.

Interim attachment is effectively attachment on the dependence of an action, and in many respects resembles arrestment and inhibition on the dependence, but taking account of the special nature of attachment and the desire not to cause distress to the debtor or his family by attaching assets in his dwellinghouse. Attachment, the replacement for the former diligence of poinding, is a method of seizing a debtor's corporeal moveables and if necessary selling them to recover the debt due to a creditor. It was introduced by Pt 2 of the 2002 Act. Attachment, broadly speaking, is initially to be carried out at the debtor's business premises and only if that fails to generate sufficient funds to repay the creditor may attachment be carried out against the debtor's assets in his dwellinghouse, such attachment being known as "exceptional attachment". It is uncommon for exceptional attachments to be carried out. This is for a variety of reasons, these being the bad publicity for the creditor, the laborious procedure involved, the debtor somehow finding the money to pay the creditor, and more pragmatically, the fact that it is often not worth the creditor's while proceeding to exceptional attachment in the light of the low anticipated value or quantity of the attachable assets. Exceptional attachment is nevertheless a useful sanction for creditors when dealing with "won't pay" as opposed to "can't pay" debtors.

While arrestment and inhibition on the dependence of an action may never be welcome to a debtor, they possibly do not perhaps have the same emotional charge as interim attachment which permits the creditors' agents, judicial officers, to come to the debtor's home, to tell the debtor not to remove his belongings, and in some cases, to take his belongings away pending the resolution of any court action. For this reason, there may be some political resistance to the bringing of this new Pt 1A to the 2002 Act. At the same time, if arrestment and inhibition may take place on the dependence of an action, it would be consistent if interim attachment could also be carried out on the dependence of an action.

The draftsman, in preparing the legislation, had to take account of three important issues. One was that attached assets may not necessarily be in the sole ownership or possession of the debtor, and account should be taken of other owners' or possessors' interests. Secondly, the amount attached should not cause hardship for the debtor's family's wellbeing. Thirdly, the Human Rights Act 1998 entitles citizens to the peaceful enjoyment of their property, and interim attachment clearly prevents this. So a debtor is allowed an opportunity (under new s.9E and M of the 2002 Act) to say why the warrant for interim attachment should not be granted. This takes account of the difficulties that arose in *Karl Construction Ltd v Palisade Properties Plc* 2002 S.C. 270; 2002 S.L.T. 312.

The various forms, statements and schedules referred to will be found in the Rules of the Court of Session and the Sheriff Court Rules.

173. Interim attachment

After section 9 of the 2002 Act, insert-

"PART 1A

INTERIM ATTACHMENT

Interim attachment

9A Interim attachment

(1) Subject to sections 9B to 9E below, the court may grant warrant for diligence by attachment of corporeal moveable property owned (whether alone or in common) by the debtor on the dependence of an action (such attachment is to be known as interim attachment).

(2) Warrant for interim attachment is competent only where an action contains a conclusion for payment of a sum other than by way of expenses.

(3) This Part of this Act shall apply to petitions in the Court of Session and to parties to them as it applies to actions and to parties to them.

(4) In this Part of this Act-
"action" includes, in the sheriff court-
    (a) a summary cause;
    (b) a small claim; and
    (c) a summary application,

and references to "summons", "conclusion" and to cognate expressions shall be construed accordingly;

"court" means-

    (a) the court before which the action is in dependence; or

    (b) where, by virtue of section 9L(1)(a) below, the interim attachment has effect after the creditor obtains a final interlocutor for payment, the court which granted that interlocutor;

"creditor" means the party who concludes for payment and who seeks, obtains or executes warrant for interim attachment;

"debtor" means the party against whom the conclusion for payment is addressed; and

expressions used in this Part of this Act have, unless the context otherwise requires, the same meanings as those expressions have in Part 2 of this Act.

9B   Articles exempt from interim attachment

It is not competent to attach by interim attachment-

    (a) any article within a dwellinghouse;

    (b) any article which, by virtue of section 11 below, it is not competent to attach;

    (c) a mobile home which is the only or principal residence of a person other than the debtor;

    (d) any article of a perishable nature or which is likely to deteriorate substantially and rapidly in condition or value; or

    (e) where the debtor is engaged in trade, any article acquired by the debtor-

        (i) to be sold by the debtor (whether or not after adaptation); or

        (ii) as a material for a process of manufacturing for sale by the debtor,

in the ordinary course of that trade.

Application for interim attachment

9C   Application for warrant for interim attachment

(1) A creditor may, at any time during which an action is in dependence, apply to the court for warrant for interim attachment.

(2) An application under subsection (1) above shall-

    (a) be in (or as nearly as may be in) the form prescribed by Act of Sederunt;

    (b) subject to subsection (3) below, be intimated to and provide details of-

        (i) the debtor; and

        (ii) any other person having an interest;

    (c) state whether the creditor is seeking the grant, under section 9D(1) below, of warrant for interim attachment

in advance of a hearing on the application under section 9E below; and

(d) contain such other information as the Scottish Ministers may by regulations prescribe.

(3) An application under subsection (1) above need not be intimated where the creditor is seeking the grant, under section 9D(1) below, of warrant in advance of a hearing on the application under section 9E below.

(4) The court, on receiving an application under subsection (1) above, shall-

    (a) subject to section 9D below, fix a date for a hearing on the application under section 9E below; and

    (b) order the creditor to intimate that date to-

        (i) the debtor; and

        (ii) any other person appearing to the court to have an interest.

9D Grant of warrant without a hearing

(1) The court may, if satisfied as to the matters mentioned in subsection (2) below, make an order granting warrant for interim attachment without a hearing on the application under section 9E below.

(2) The matters referred to in subsection (1) above are-

    (a) that the creditor has a *prima facie* case on the merits of the action;

    (b) that there is a real and substantial risk enforcement of any decree in the action in favour of the creditor would be defeated or prejudiced by reason of-

        (i) the debtor being insolvent or verging on insolvency; or

        (ii) the likelihood of the debtor removing, disposing of, burdening, concealing or otherwise dealing with all or some of the debtor's assets,

were warrant for interim attachment not granted in advance of such a hearing; and

    (c) that it is reasonable in all the circumstances, including the effect granting warrant may have on any person having an interest, to do so.

(3) The onus shall be on the creditor to satisfy the court that the order granting warrant should be made.

(4) Where the court makes an order granting warrant for interim attachment without a hearing on the application under section 9E below, the court shall-

    (a) fix a date for a hearing under section 9M below; and

    (b) order the creditor to intimate that date to-

        (i) the debtor; and

        (ii) any other person appearing to the court to have an interest.

(5) Where a hearing is fixed under subsection (4)(a) above, section 9M (except subsection (11)) below shall apply as if an application had been made to the court for an order under that section.

(6) Where the court refuses to make an order granting warrant without a hearing under section 9E below and the creditor insists in the application, the court shall-

    (a) fix a date for such a hearing on the application; and

    (b) order the creditor to intimate that date to-

        (i) the debtor; and

        (ii) any other person appearing to the court to have an interest.

9E Hearing on application

(1) At the hearing on an application for warrant for interim attachment, the court shall not make any order without first giving-

    (a) any person to whom intimation of the date of the hearing was made; and

    (b) any other person appearing to the court to have an interest,

an opportunity to be heard.

(2) The court may, if satisfied as to the matters mentioned in subsection (3) below, make an order granting warrant for interim attachment.

(3) The matters referred to in subsection (2) above are-

    (a) that the creditor has a *prima facie* case on the merits of the action;

    (b) that there is a real and substantial risk enforcement of any decree in the action in favour of the creditor would be defeated or prejudiced by reason of-

        (i) the debtor being insolvent or verging on insolvency; or

        (ii) the likelihood of the debtor removing, disposing of, burdening, concealing or otherwise dealing with all or some of the debtor's assets,

were warrant for interim attachment not granted; and

    (c) that it is reasonable in all the circumstances, including the effect granting warrant may have on any person having an interest, to do so.

(4) The onus shall be on the creditor to satisfy the court that the order granting warrant should be made.

(5) Where the court makes an order granting or, as the case may be, refusing warrant for interim attachment, the court shall order the creditor to intimate that order to-

    (a) the debtor; and

    (b) any other person appearing to the court to have an interest.

(6) Where the court makes an order refusing warrant for interim attachment, the court may impose such conditions (if any) as it thinks fit.

(7) Without prejudice to the generality of subsection (6) above, those conditions may require the debtor-

    (a) to consign into court such sum; or

    (b) to find caution or to give such other security,

as the court thinks fit.

9F   Execution of interim attachment

(1) Sections 12, 13, 15 and (subject to subsection (6) below) 17 below apply to execution of an interim attachment as they apply to execution of an attachment.

(2) The officer shall, immediately after executing an interim attachment, complete a schedule such as is mentioned in subsection (3) below (in this Part of this Act, a "schedule of interim attachment").

(3) The schedule of interim attachment-

   (a) shall be-

      (i) in (or as nearly as may be in) the form prescribed by Act of Sederunt; and

      (ii) signed by the officer; and

   (b) shall specify-

      (i) the articles attached; and

      (ii) their value, so far as ascertainable.

(4) The officer shall-

   (a) give a copy of the schedule of interim attachment to the debtor; or

   (b) where it is not practicable to do so-

      (i) give a copy of the schedule to a person present at the place where the interim attachment was executed; or

      (ii) where there is no such person, leave a copy of the schedule at that place.

(5) References in this Part of this Act to the day on which an interim attachment is executed are references to the day on which the officer complies with subsection (4) above.

(6) The application of section 17 below shall be subject to the following modifications-

   (a) subsections (3)(b) and (4) shall not apply;

   (b) in subsections (1), (5) and (6), the references to the sheriff shall be construed as references to the court; and

   (c) in subsection (6)(b), the reference to the sheriff clerk shall, in the case of an action in the Court of Session, be construed as a reference to the clerk of the court.

9G   Execution of interim attachment before service

(1) This section applies where an interim attachment is executed before the service of the summons on the debtor.

(2) Subject to subsection (3) below, if the summons is not served on the debtor before the end of the period of 21 days beginning with the day on which the interim attachment is executed, the attachment shall cease to have effect.

(3) The court may, on the application of the creditor, make an order extending the period referred to in subsection (2) above.

(4) In determining whether to make such an order the court shall have regard to-

    (a) the efforts of the creditor to serve the summons within
the period of 21 days; and

    (b) any special circumstances preventing or obstructing
service within that period.

Interim attachment: further procedure

9H   Order for security of attached articles

(1) The court may, on an application, at any time after articles
have been attached-

    (a) by the creditor;

    (b) the officer; or

    (c) the debtor,

make an order for the security of any of the attached articles.

(2) An application for an order under subsection (1) above
shall-

    (a) be in (or as nearly as may be in) the form prescribed by
Act of Sederunt; and

    (b) be intimated-

        (i) where it is made by the creditor or the officer, to
the debtor;

        (ii) where it is made by the debtor, to the creditor and
the officer.

(3) At the hearing on the application under subsection (1)
above, the court shall not make any order without first
giving-

    (a) any person to whom intimation of the application was
made; and

    (b) any other person the court is satisfied has an interest,

an opportunity to be heard.

Interim attachment: effects

9J   Unlawful acts after interim attachment

Section 21 (except subsections (3) and (15)) below applies to
an interim attachment as it applies to an attachment with the
following modifications-

    (a) in subsections (10) and (11), the references to the sheriff
shall be construed as references to the court; and

    (b) in subsection (12), the references to sections 51 and
54(1) below shall be of no effect.

9K   Articles belonging to or owned in common by a third party

(1) Where-

    (a) a third party claims to own an article attached by
interim attachment; and

    (b) the court, on the application of the third party, makes
an order stating that it is satisfied that the claim is
valid,

the interim attachment of that article shall cease to have effect.

(2) Where-

> (a) a third party claims to own an article attached by interim attachment in common with the debtor;
>
> (b) the court, on the application of the third party, makes an order stating that it is satisfied-
>
> > (i) that the claim is valid; and
> >
> > (ii) that the continued attachment of the article would be unduly harsh to the third party,

the interim attachment of that article shall cease to have effect.

(3) Subsection (2) of section 34 below applies where a third party makes an application for the purposes of subsection (1)(b) above as it applies where a third party makes an application for the purposes of subsection (1)(b)(ii) of that section.

(4) Where the attachment of an article ceases, by virtue of an order under subsection (1) or (2) above, to have effect, the officer may attach other articles which are owned by the debtor and kept at the place at which the original interim attachment was executed.

9L   Duration of interim attachment

(1) An interim attachment shall, unless recalled, have effect only until-

   (a) subject to subsections (2), (4) and (7) below, where-

   > (i) the creditor obtains a final interlocutor for payment of all or part of a principal sum concluded for in the action on the dependence of which warrant for interim attachment was granted;
   >
   > (ii) the creditor obtains a final interlocutor in the creditor's favour in respect of another remedy concluded for in that action; or
   >
   > (iii) the final interlocutor is of absolvitor or dismissal and the court grants decree under and for the purposes of section 9Q(1)(b) below,

   the expiry of the period of 6 months after the action is disposed of;

   (b) where-

   > (i) the final interlocutor is of absolvitor or dismissal; and
   >
   > (ii) no decree under and for the purposes of section 9Q(1)(b) below is granted,

   the granting of that interlocutor; or

   (c) the creditor consents, by virtue of subsection (3) below, to the interim attachment ceasing to have effect in relation to every article attached.

(2) An interim attachment shall have effect in relation to a specific article only until the article is attached by the creditor in execution of any such final interlocutor or decree as is mentioned in subsection (1)(a) above.

(3) The creditor may at any time consent in writing to the interim attachment ceasing to have effect in relation to a specific article attached; and the attachment shall cease to have effect when that consent is notified to the court.

(4) The court may, on an application by the creditor, extend the period mentioned in subsection (1)(a) above but only if-

    (a) the application is made before the expiry of the period mentioned in that subsection; and

    (b) the court is satisfied that exceptional circumstances make it reasonable to grant the application.

(5) An application under subsection (4) above shall-

    (a) be in (or as nearly as may be in) the form prescribed by Act of Sederunt; and

    (b) be intimated by the creditor to-

        (i) the debtor; and

        (ii) any other person having an interest.

(6) The court shall order the creditor to intimate any decision under subsection (4) above disposing of the application under that subsection to-

    (a) the debtor; and

    (b) any other person appearing to the court to have an interest.

(7) Where such an application is made but not disposed of before the date on which the interim attachment would, but for this subsection, cease to have effect, the interim attachment shall continue to have effect until the application is disposed of.

(8) In calculating the period mentioned in subsection (1)(a) above, any period during which-

    (a) a time to pay direction under section 1(1) of the Debtors (Scotland) Act 1987 (c.18); or

    (b) an order under-

        (i) section 6(3) of that Act (interim order sisting diligence); or

        (ii) section 9(4) of that Act (diligence sisted if not recalled on making of time to pay order),

is in effect shall be disregarded.

(9) For the purposes of subsection (1) above-

    (a) a final interlocutor is obtained when an interlocutor-

        (i) cannot be recalled or altered; and

        (ii) is not subject to review; and

    (b) an action is disposed of on the date on which the final interlocutor mentioned in paragraph (a) of that subsection is obtained unless, on a later date, the creditor obtains a final interlocutor for expenses in the action, in which case it is disposed of on that later date.

Recall etc. of interim attachment

9M Recall or restriction of interim attachment

(1) This section applies where warrant is granted for interim attachment.

(2) The debtor and any person having an interest may apply to the court for an order-

    (a) recalling the warrant;

    (b) restricting the warrant;

    (c) if an interim attachment has been executed in pursuance of the warrant-

        (i) recalling; or

        (ii) restricting,

  that attachment;

    (d) determining any question relating to the validity, effect or operation of the warrant; or

    (e) ancillary to any order mentioned in paragraphs (a) to (d) above.

(3) An application under subsection (2) above shall-

    (a) be in (or as nearly as may be in) the form prescribed by Act of Sederunt; and

    (b) be intimated to-

        (i) the creditor; and

        (ii) any other person having an interest.

(4) At the hearing on the application under subsection (2) above, the court shall not make any order without first giving-

    (a) any person to whom intimation of the application was made; and

    (b) any other person the court is satisfied has an interest,

an opportunity to be heard.

(5) Where the court is satisfied that the warrant is invalid it-

    (a) shall make an order-

        (i) recalling the warrant; and

        (ii) if interim attachment has been executed in pursuance of the warrant, recalling that interim attachment; and

    (b) may make an order ancillary to any order mentioned in paragraph (a) above.

(6) Where the court is satisfied that an interim attachment executed in pursuance of the warrant is incompetent, it-

    (a) shall make an order recalling the interim attachment; and

    (b) may make an order ancillary to any such order.

(7) Subject to subsection (8) below, where the court is satisfied that the warrant is valid but that-

    (a) an interim attachment executed in pursuance of it is irregular or ineffective; or

    (b) it is reasonable in all the circumstances, including the effect granting warrant may have had on any person having an interest, to do so,

the court may, subject to subsection (11) below, make any order such as is mentioned in subsection (2) above.

(8) If no longer satisfied as to the matters mentioned in subsection (9) below, the court-

    (a) shall make an order such as is mentioned in subsection (5)(a) above; and

    (b) may make an order such as is mentioned in subsection (5)(b) above.

(9) The matters referred to in subsection (8) above are-

    (a) that the creditor has a *prima facie* case on the merits of the action;

(b) that there is a real and substantial risk enforcement of any decree in the action in favour of the creditor would be defeated or prejudiced by reason of-

    (i) the debtor being insolvent or verging on insolvency; or

    (ii) the likelihood of the debtor removing, disposing of, burdening, concealing or otherwise dealing with all or some of the debtor's assets; and

(c) that it is reasonable in all the circumstances, including the effect granting warrant may have had on any person having an interest, for the warrant or, as the case may be, any interim attachment executed in pursuance of it to continue to have effect.

(10) The onus shall be on the creditor to satisfy the court that no order under subsection (5), (6), (7) or (8) above should be made.

(11) Where-

    (a) by virtue of section 9L(1)(a) above, the interim attachment continues to have effect after the creditor obtains a final interlocutor for payment; and

    (b) the period of six months mentioned in that paragraph has not expired,

the court shall not make an order under subsection (7) above.

(12) In granting an application under subsection (2) above, the court may impose such conditions (if any) as it thinks fit.

(13) Without prejudice to the generality of subsection (12) above, those conditions may require the debtor-

    (a) to consign into court such sum; or

    (b) to find such caution or to give such other security,

as the court thinks fit.

(14) Where the court makes an order under this section, the court shall order the debtor to intimate that order to-

    (a) the creditor; and

    (b) any other person appearing to the court to have an interest.

9N   Variation of orders and variation or recall of conditions

(1) Where-

    (a) an order restricting warrant for interim attachment is made under section 9M(7) above; or

    (b) a condition is imposed under-

        (i) section 9E(6) above; or

        (ii) section 9M(12) above,

the debtor may apply to the court for variation of the order or, as the case may be, variation or removal of the condition.

(2) An application under subsection (1) above shall-

    (a) be in (or as nearly as may be in) the form prescribed by Act of Sederunt; and

    (b) be intimated to-

        (i) the creditor; and

        (ii) any other person having an interest.

(3) At the hearing on the application under subsection (1) above, the court shall not make any order without first giving-

(a) any person to whom intimation of the application was made; and

(b) any other person the court is satisfied has an interest,

an opportunity to be heard.

(4) On an application under subsection (1) above, the court may if it thinks fit-

(a) vary the order; or

(b) vary or remove the condition.

(5) Where the court makes an order varying the order or, as the case may be, varying or removing the condition, the court shall order the debtor to intimate that order to-

(a) the creditor; and

(b) any other person appearing to the court to have an interest.

General and miscellaneous provisions

9P Expenses of interim attachment

(1) Subject to subsection (3)(a) below, a creditor shall be entitled to the expenses incurred-

(a) in obtaining warrant for interim attachment; and

(b) where an interim attachment is executed in pursuance of the warrant, in so executing that attachment.

(2) Subject to subsection (3)(b) below, a debtor shall be entitled, where-

(a) warrant for interim attachment is granted; and

(b) the court is satisfied that the creditor was acting unreasonably in applying for it,

to the expenses incurred in opposing that warrant.

(3) The court may modify or refuse-

(a) such expenses as are mentioned in subsection (1) above if it is satisfied that-

(i) the creditor was acting unreasonably in applying for the warrant; or

(ii) such modification or refusal is reasonable in all the circumstances and having regard to the outcome of the action; and

(b) such expenses as are mentioned in subsection (2) above if it is satisfied as to the matter mentioned in paragraph (a)(ii) above.

(4) Subject to subsections (1) to (3) above, the court may make such findings as it thinks fit in relation to such expenses as are mentioned in subsections (1) and (2) above.

(5) Expenses incurred as mentioned in subsections (1) and (2) above in obtaining or, as the case may be, opposing an application for warrant shall be expenses of process.

9Q Recovery of expenses of interim attachment

(1) Subject to subsection (4) below, any expenses chargeable against the debtor which are incurred in executing an interim attachment shall be recoverable only by attachment-

    (a) in execution of a decree granted by virtue of-

        (i) the conclusion for payment in the action on the dependence of which the warrant for interim attachment was granted; or

        (ii) another conclusion in the creditor's favour in that action; or

    (b) where the final interlocutor in the action is of absolvitor or dismissal, in execution of a decree granted under and for the purposes of this subsection.

(2) Where any such expenses cease to be recoverable in pursuance of subsection (1) above, they cease to be chargeable against the debtor.

(3) Subsection (4) below applies where interim attachment is-

    (a) recalled under section 2(3), 3(1)(b), 9(2)(cb) or 10(1)(b) of the 1987 Act in relation to a time to pay direction or order;

    (b) in effect immediately before the date of sequestration (within the meaning of the Bankruptcy (Scotland) Act 1985 (c.66)) of the debtor's estate;

    (c) in effect immediately before the appointment of an administrator under Part II of the Insolvency Act 1986 (c.45);

    (d) in effect against property of the debtor immediately before a floating charge attaches all or part of that property under section 53(7) (attachment on appointment of receiver by holder of charge) or 54(6) (attachment on appointment of receiver by court) of the 1986 Act;

    (e) in effect immediately before the commencement of the winding up, under Part IV or V of the 1986 Act, of the debtor; or

    (f) rendered unenforceable by virtue of the creditor entering into a composition contract or acceding to a trust deed for creditors or by virtue of the subsistence of a protected trust deed within the meaning of Schedule 5 to the 1985 Act.

(4) Where this subsection applies-

    (a) the expenses of the interim attachment which were chargeable against the debtor remain so chargeable; and

    (b) if the debtor's obligation to pay the expenses is not discharged under or by virtue of the time to pay direction or order, sequestration, appointment, receivership, winding up, composition contract or trust deed for creditors, those expenses are recoverable in pursuance of subsection (1) above.

9R Ascription of sums recovered while interim attachment is in effect

(1) This section applies where-
    (a) any amounts are-
        (i) secured by an interim attachment; and
        (ii) while the attachment is in effect, paid to account of the amounts recoverable from the debtor; and
    (b) that interim attachment ceases to have effect.
(2) Such amounts shall be ascribed to the following in the order in which they are mentioned-
    (a) the expenses incurred in-
        (i) obtaining warrant for; and
        (ii) executing,
   the interim attachment;
    (b) any interest which has accrued, in relation to a sum due under a decree granted by virtue of the conclusion in relation to which warrant for interim attachment was granted, as at the date of execution;
    (c) any sum due under that decree together with such interest as has accrued after that date.
(3) Where an interim attachment is followed by an attachment in execution of a decree granted by virtue of the conclusion in relation to which the warrant for the interim attachment was granted, section 41 below shall apply to amounts to which this section applies as it applies to amounts to which that section applies.

9S Ranking of interim attachment

For the purposes of any enactment or rule of law as to ranking or preference-
    (a) where-
        (i) an interim attachment has been executed; and
        (ii) the creditor has, without undue delay, obtained an interlocutor for payment of all or part of the sum concluded for,
   that interim attachment shall be treated as if it were an attachment by virtue of section 10 below of the property attached, executed when the interim attachment was executed; and
    (b) where an interim attachment has ceased to have effect in relation to any article by virtue of section 9L(2) above, the attachment of the article in question shall be taken to have been executed when the interim attachment was executed.".

GENERAL NOTE

Subsection (1) introduces interim attachment by defining it as attachment proceeding from a warrant for attachment of corporeal moveable property owned by the debtor, either by himself or in common with others, on the dependence of an action. The word "action" is used to mean both petitions in the Court of Session (subs.(3)), actions in the Court of Session and actions in the sheriff court, including ordinary actions, summary causes, small claims and summary applications (subs.(4)). "Court" is also carefully designed to include the court before which the application for interim attachment is heard and the court which grants the final interlocutor. Words and phrases that are defined and used in Pt 2 of the 2002 Act are given the same meanings for the purposes of Pt 1A.

Section 9B

DEFINITIONS
"Dwellinghouse": 2002 Act s.45
"Mobile home": 2002 Act s.45
"Money": 2007 Act s.175

GENERAL NOTE

There are various places where interim attachment may not be carried out. These include a dwellinghouse, which while not defined in its own right, is deemed not to include a garage, even if that garage is part of or attached to the dwellinghouse, nor to include any other structures used in connection with the dwellinghouse, such as a shed, or a mobile home which is not used for living in. A mobile home means a caravan, houseboat or other moveable structure used as a dwellinghouse.

Equally, there are certain articles that may not be subject to interim attachment. These include articles within a dwellinghouse, and any articles which may be attached because of s.11 of the 2002 Act (para.(b)). Section 11(1) forbids the attachment of the debtor's implements, tools of his trade or other equipment reasonably required for his trade or business and not exceeding (when aggregated together) the sum of £1,000 or such sum as may be decided upon by the Scottish Ministers from time to time. Vehicles, provided their use is reasonably required by the debtor, and not exceeding £1,000 in value, may not be attached. Garden tools may also not be attached. In practice, this will mean that nothing in the debtor's home may be attached by interim attachment, although certain assets stored in garages or other outbuildings, provided they are not connected with the tools of his trade or gardening, may be attachable. This should significantly limit the use of interim attachment, and of course prudent debtors would be wise to bring in any valuable assets from their garages or outbuildings into their homes, secure in the knowledge that s.9B(a) would apply and that only exceptional attachment could be used to force their removal from the dwellinghouse.

Section 11 of the 2002 is amended by Sch.4 para.10 of the 2007 Act, which states that it is not competent to attach cargo on board ship but it is otherwise competent to arrest cargo by virtue of s.47C of the Administration of Justice Act 1956 (which deals with the arrestment of cargo). Section 47C itself is introduced into the Administration of Justice Act 1956 by Sch.4 para.9 of the 2007 Act. The point of this provision is that attachment is not the diligence that should be used for cargo on a ship: arrestment (of the cargo on the ship) is the proper diligence.

Section 11(1) is also altered by Sch.5 para.3(a) by the insertion of the word "money" as a new paragraph (e) to that section, so that it is not competent to have interim attachment of money, the word "money" being defined in s.175 of the 2007 Act.

This section (9B) also exempts from attachment perishable articles and, where the debtor is engaged in trade, any article that he has bought in order subsequently to sell it (with or without any adaptation by the debtor) and any article bought as a material needed as stock or for the manufacture of any goods or products that the debtor sells in the ordinary course of his trade.

Section 9C

GENERAL NOTE

A creditor wishing to effect interim attachment must apply to the court for a warrant to do so. He will do so on the requisite form and will have to intimate the application to the debtor and anyone else with an interest. He will also have to indicate whether he is proposing to do this in advance of a hearing under the terms of s.9D, or whether he is applying for a warrant only after a hearing, in which case s.9E applies (subs.(2)). If the creditor seeks the warrant before the hearing (in other words, the creditor proposes to use the s.9D procedure) he is not obliged to intimate the application to the debtor, since the debtor might take the opportunity to do the very thing that s.9D is designed to obviate, namely to become insolvent or to dispose of his assets (subs.(3)).

The court, on receiving the application, will fix a hearing if the s.9E procedure is being followed, and require the creditor to intimate the date of the hearing to the debtor and anyone else with an interest (subs.4)).

It is permissible to seek interim attachment at any time while the action is in dependence (subs.(1)). Indeed, the whole process of applying for the warrant, obtaining it and executing the interim attachment may be complete before the summons is served (s.9G).

The requisite form or forms may be seen in the Schedules to the Act of Sederunt (Rules of the Court of Session Amendment No.3) (Bankruptcy and Diligence etc (Scotland) Act 2007) 2008 (SSI 2008/122), and the Act of Sederunt (Sheriff Court Amendment) (Diligence) 2008 (SSI 2008/121). Both of these came into force April 1, 2008.

Section 9D

GENERAL NOTE

This applies where the creditor wishes to obtain a warrant for interim attachment without a hearing. Since the point of this procedure is to steal a march on the debtor to prevent him becoming insolvent or disposing of his assets the moment he knows an action is being raised against him, but at the same time to ensure that such procedure should not be abused, the creditor is required to satisfy the court that he has a *prima facie* case on the merits of the action, that there is a real risk that the enforcement of any decree against the debtor would be frustrated by the debtor's insolvency or the likelihood of the debtor disposing of his assets, and that it is reasonable under all the circumstances (including the effect on anyone having an interest) for the warrant to be granted (subs.(2)). It will be seen that these terms mirror the old common law rules of *vergens ad inopiam* and *in meditatione fugae*. It is for the creditor to satisfy the court that the warrant should be granted (subs.(3)). If the court is minded to grant the warrant as requested (i.e. without a hearing) it must nevertheless fix a date for a hearing in terms of s.9M and order the creditor to intimate the date of the hearing to the debtor and anyone else with an interest (subs.(4)). This will allow the debtor and anyone else with an interest the opportunity to seek recall or restriction of the warrant for interim attachment, or, as the case may be, recall or restriction of the execution of the interim attachment. The onus will be on the creditor to satisfy the court that the warrant for or the execution of the interim attachment should remain in place (s.9M10).

Subsection (5) states that where the court fixes a hearing under s.9M, it is as if the debtor, or anyone with an interest, has applied to the court for the hearing.

It may be that the court is not willing to grant a warrant under s.9D but the creditor still wishes to proceed with his application. In this case (dealt with in subs.(6)) a hearing under s.9E will take place and the creditor will be required to intimate the date of the hearing to the debtor and anyone else with an interest.

Section 9E

GENERAL NOTE

At the hearing under s.9E, the debtor and anyone else with an interest must be given the opportunity to be heard. The court, at the hearing, must decide to grant the warrant for interim attachment (subs.(2)), but it is for the creditor to satisfy the court that it should be granted (subs.(4)) and this will only happen where the court is satisfied that he has a *prima facie* case on the merits of the action, that there is a real risk that the enforcement of any decree against the debtor would be frustrated by the debtor's insolvency or the likelihood of the debtor disposing of his assets, and that it is reasonable under all the circumstances (including the effect on anyone having an interest) for the warrant to be granted (subs.3).

Whether the order for the warrant is granted or refused, the order must be intimated by the creditor to the debtor and anyone else with an interest (subs.(5)). Where it is refused, the court may require that the debtor complies with certain conditions (subs.(6)), such conditions including consigning money into court or granting caution or other security (subs.(7)).

Section 9F

DEFINITIONS

"Officer": 2002 Act s.45

GENERAL NOTE

The process of executing an interim attachment is the same as executing an attachment under the normal provisions of the 2002 Act (see ss.12, 13, 15 and 17, subject to the further provisions of s.9F(6), which take account of the fact that some of the wording should include references to the court rather than to the sheriff, and also disapply those parts of attachment that would be inconsistent with interim attachment or are already dealt with). These indicate, respectively, the permitted times and dates of executing attachment, the presumption, (subject to inquiry) of ownership of the assets by the debtor, the power of entry and valuation by judicial officers and the requirement to make a report of the attachment by the judicial officers. As mobile homes and articles within dwellinghouses are already excluded from attachment (see s.9B) the range of attachable articles may be fairly restricted.

After executing the interim attachment, the officer must serve a schedule on the debtor. The schedule must be signed by the officer and must indicate the articles attached and their value (subs.(3)). A copy of the schedule must be given to the debtor or someone present, or left at the debtor's premises. The day of the giving (or leaving) of the schedule with or for the debtor is the day of interim execution (subs.(5)).

Section 9G

DEFINITIONS

"Summons": 2002 Act s.9A(4)

GENERAL NOTE

It is perfectly possible for the warrant for interim attachment and the execution of interim attachment to have taken place before the service of the summons. Even so, the summons must be served within 21 days of the day of execution of interim attachment (see s.9F(5)), failing which the attachment will cease to have effect. The court may, under subs.(3), extend the period of 21 days if there are difficulties serving the summons on the debtor.

Section 9H

DEFINITIONS

"Officer": 2002 Act s.45

GENERAL NOTE

It may be necessary for the attached articles to be taken into a place of safe-keeping or security. This may be done, following an application to the court by the debtor, the creditor or the officer (subs.(1)), and intimated to the debtor (where the application is made by the creditor or officer) or to the creditor and officer (where the application is made by the debtor) (subs.(2)). The court will have a hearing and will give the all those to whom the application was intimated the opportunity to be heard (subs.(3)).

Section 9J

GENERAL NOTE

This section refers to s.21 of the 2002 Act which deals with what should happen should the attached articles be moved, stolen, disposed of or destroyed. Where the articles have been deliberately moved, disposed of or destroyed, other articles of overall equal value may be attached instead, and if the articles are known to be in the hands of a third party who knows that they have been attached, and they are not returned, the third party will have to consign into court money to the value of the articles. The deliberate removal, disposition or destruction of the articles would be a breach of the attachment as such would be contempt of court and punishable accordingly. If the articles are stolen, the officer and creditor will need to be given the details of any insurance claims relating to those articles. Damaged articles will be revalued.

Section 9K

GENERAL NOTE

This deals with articles that belong to or are owned by a third party. If a third party asserts that an attached article is solely his, applies to court to press his claim, and is successful, the interim attachment becomes ineffective (subs.(1)). If an article is owned in common by the debtor and a third party, and the third party applies to court, he may have the interim attachment lifted where it is established that it would be unduly harsh to the third party were the interim attachment to remain in place. His application in respect of the article owned in common does not prevent a separate application in respect of any article under subs.(1)).

Where the third party's application is successful, the officer may attach other articles of the debtor's instead (subs.(4)).

It will be noticed that the wording of s.34 (to which the wording of s.9K is similar) gives more discretion to the officer than does s.9K, in that if the officer accepts the third party's claim as his ownership of the article, and if no one comes forward to contradict the claim, the third party may apply to have the attached article released from attachment. This not only could be beneficial to the third party, but also beneficial to an unscrupulous debtor, keen to claim that an article (in reality, his own) is owned by a third party.

Section 9L

The duration of interim attachment varies according to circumstances, assuming it is not recalled.

It remains in place for a period of six months from the date of the conclusion of the action for which the interim attachment was executed provided:

(a)   the creditor obtained a final interlocutor in his favour for all or part of the principal sum he had sued for;
(b)   the creditor obtained a final interlocutor in his favour for some other remedy sought in the conclusion or crave, such as delivery or specific performance; or
(c)   the final interlocutor was of absolvitur or dismissal but the court granted decree to the creditor for expenses (s.9Q(1)(b) refers to the expenses of interim attachment) (subs.(1)((a)).

In effect what this means is that where the creditor wins his case, or even if he does not win it, the court makes the debtor pay his expenses, the interim attachment remains in place for up to six months, but if he fails to do anything about the interim attachment within the six month period, his entitlement to execute the interim attachment lapses.

The period of six months may be extended by the court following an application by the creditor, provided the application takes place before the expiry of the six month period, there are exceptional circumstances that justify the extension (subs.(4)), and the application, on a form yet to be devised, has been intimated to the debtor and anyone else with an interest (subs.5). Any subsequent court decision on this matter must be intimated by the creditor to the debtor and anyone else with an interest (subs.(6)). Where the interim attachment would normally have expired, but the application is still before the court, the interim attachment is continued until the application is decided upon (subs.(7)). Should any time to pay direction (under s.1(1) of the 1987 Act s.1(1)) apply, or sisting of diligence (under s.6(3) of the same Act) or sisting of diligence where the diligence has not been recalled on the making of a time to pay order (under s.9(4) of the same Act) take place, any period during which this direction or the sist applies is not be included within the six month period (section (8)).

Where the final interlocutor is of absolvitur or dismissal, and the court makes no decree as to expenses (so that each side bears its own expenses), the interim attachment remains in effect only until the granting of that interlocutor (subs.(1)(b)).

Where the creditor consents in writing (as permitted in subs.(3)) to the attachment ceasing to have effect in relation to every article attached, it ceases to have effect when that consent is notified to the court (subs.(1)(c)).

An interim attachment ceases to have effect where it is effectively superseded by an attachment following an interlocutor or decree (subs.(2)).

The creditor may at any time in writing consent to the release of the interim attachment of any attached article, and the interim attachment ceases when the consent is notified to the court (subs.(3)).

Subsection (9) explains what is meant by "final interlocutor" and an action "being disposed of". Normally it will be day of the last interlocutor in the action, taking account of any appeal or, say, reference to the European Court of Justice and which has come back to Scotland for a final decision. Furthermore, there may be occasions where although the main points have been dealt with, a decree on expenses has been held over for further argument, in which case the final interlocutor, or the action being disposed of, will be the day of the interlocutor for expenses.

Section 9M

GENERAL NOTE

This section deals with the recall or restriction of interim attachment. It is used where the debtor or anyone with an interest wishes to recall or restrict a warrant (issued under s.9E or F) or, where a warrant has already been executed, to recall or restrict the interim attachment itself; and the court may grant an order to that effect (subs.(2)) under such conditions as it sees fit (subs.(11)) including requiring the debtor to consign money into court or finding caution for expenses (subs.(12)). It is also used where the debtor or any person with an interest wishes to question the validity, effect or operation of the warrant. To do this the debtor or anyone with an interest must apply to the court (subs.(2)), on a form, yet to be devised. The application must be intimated to the creditor and anyone else having an interest, say, a judicial officer (subs.(3)). Those to whom intimation has been given must be given the opportunity to be heard at the court hearing for the recall or restriction (subs.(4)).

If the court is satisfied that the warrant was invalid, it may recall both it and any ensuing interim attachment (along with any other suitable order) (subs.(5)).

If the court is satisfied that any executed interim attachment is incompetent, it may be recalled, while making any other suitable order (subs.(6)).

If the court is satisfied that the warrant was valid but the interim attachment was irregular or ineffective (perhaps because of some procedural irregularity, or because service of the summons was not carried out within the required period (see s.9G(2)), or where it would be reasonable in all the circumstances, the court may recall or restrict the warrant or the interim attachment in terms of subs.(2) (subs.(7)).

The recall or restriction available under subs.(7) is subject to subs.(8) which provides that if the court is no longer satisfied that the circumstances outlined in subs.(9) apply, the court may instead make an order in terms of subs.(5) above to recall the original warrant itself, plus any subsequent interim attachment.

The recall or restriction available under subs.(7) is also subject to the operation of subs.(11) which, by referring to s.9L(1)(a), provides that the interim attachment may stay in place for a period of up to six months but only where the creditor has effectively won his case, or obtained decree for expenses. What this means is that the recall or restriction under subs.(7) of this section (9M) is not available if the creditor has already won his case, or at least won it as regards expenses, and if the period of six months (or any permitted extension) has not elapsed.

Subsection (8), as already indicated, states that if the court is no longer satisfied as to the requirements of subs.(9), it may make an order in terms of subs.(5). Subsection (9) reiterates (with a slight amendment) the grounds under which the warrant was originally granted in s.9E(3), namely that the creditor had a *prima facie* case on the merits of the action, that there was a real risk that the enforcement of any decree against the debtor would be frustrated by the debtor's insolvency or the likelihood of the debtor disposing of his assets, and that it was reasonable under all the circumstances (including the effect on anyone having an interest) for the warrant to be granted, or, as the case may be, the interim attachment to be executed.

In each case, it is for the creditor to satisfy the court that the debtor's application should not be granted.

As already indicated, where the creditor has won his case, or won his case as regards expenses, the creditor has six months from the date of the relevant interlocutor (see s.9L) in which to execute his interim attachment. Where this is the case, subs.(7) does not apply.

Where the court makes an order under this section, it is for the debtor to intimate the order to the creditor and anyone else with an interest (subs.(13)).

Section 9N

GENERAL NOTE

Any order granted under s.9M(7) or condition imposed under ss.9E(6) or 9M(12) may be varied or removed by the court, following an application to the court by the debtor (subs.(1)). This must be intimated to the creditor and anyone else having an interest on a form yet to be devised (subs.(2)). Those to whom the application has been intimated must be given an opportunity to be heard at the hearing for the variation or removal (subs.(3)). Assuming the order for variation or removal is granted, the order must be intimated by the debtor to the creditor or anyone having an interest (subs.(5)).

Section 9P

GENERAL NOTE

In this section, the creditor's and debtor's liability for expenses for interim attachment is explained. The creditor in a successful application for the warrant of interim attachment will be entitled to expenses from the debtor for obtaining the warrant and executing the warrant (subs.(1)), but where the court is satisfied that the creditor acted unreasonably in applying for the warrant, or where the modification or refusal of the expenses is reasonable in all the circumstances, the court may modify or refuse the payment of expenses by the debtor (subs.(3)).

The debtor is entitled to the expenses of opposing a warrant where warrant for interim attachment is granted, but the court is satisfied that the creditor was acting unreasonably in applying for it (subs.(2)), though those expenses may be modified or indeed refused where it is reasonable to do so in all the circumstances and having regard to the outcome of the action. This would appear to lead to the slightly odd position of a debtor opposing a warrant, it presumably having already been granted having had regard to s.9E(3) (i.e. "reasonable under all the circumstances"), then trying to claim that the creditor was acting unreasonably in applying for it, possibly succeeding in obtaining the expenses of opposing the creditor's warrant, but in turn having those expenses modified or refused. Perhaps the important wording here is "having regard to the outcome of the action": a judge taking an overall view of the whole process of the action may be in a position to take a better view than the judge granting the initial warrant who may not have the benefit of the full picture as later revealed.

Subsection (4) provides that, subject to subss.(1)-(3), the court may make such findings as it thinks fit in relation to expenses as mentioned in subss.(1) and (2).

Subsection (5) provides that expenses incurred in obtaining or opposing a warrant are to be expenses of process.

Section 9Q

GENERAL NOTE

This deals with the recovery of expenses. This section follows the broad rule that expenses of any diligence may only be recovered, if not otherwise paid, by that diligence alone. Section 9Q(1) provides that, subject to subs.(4), any expenses chargeable against the debtor which are incurred by the creditor in carrying out an interim attachment can be recovered only by attachment of the debtor's assets where, in effect, the creditor wins the action or, even if he does not win the action, he is allowed to claim the expenses of the action from the debtor. This echoes the wording in s.9G. Subsection (2) states that where any expenses cease to be recoverable under subs.(1), they will no longer be chargeable against the debtor. Subsections (3) and (4) indicate that expenses remain chargeable against the debtor under subs.(4) where the interim attachment:

(a)   is recalled on the making of a time to pay direction, an interim order or a time to pay order under the 1987 Act;

(b)   was in effect immediately before the date of sequestration of the debtor's estate under s.12(4) of the 1985 Act or;

(c)   was in effect immediately before the appointment of an administrator under Pt II of the Insolvency Act 1986;

(d)   was in effect against property of the debtor (again, where the debtor is corporate) immediately before a floating charge attaches all or part of that property (see ss.53(7) and 54(6) of the Insolvency Act 1986);

(e)   was in effect immediately before the commencement of the winding up, under Pt IV of the 1986 Act, of the debtor; or

(f)   becomes unenforceable either because the creditor enters into a composition contract or accedes to a trust deed for creditors, or by virtue of the subsistence of a protected trust deed for creditors.

This means that, notwithstanding the events in paras (a)-(f), the debtor is still liable for the expenses incurred in obtaining the interim attachment to the extent that expenses are not discharged by the time to pay direction, time to pay order, the sequestration, the administration, the receivership, winding up, the composition contract or the trust deed.

If the expenses are not discharged under any of the above, the debtor remains liable.

Section 9R

GENERAL NOTE

This section deals with ascription, or payments to account. While an interim attachment is in effect, any payments to account are directed first towards paying the expenses of the warrant, and then to the expenses of executing the interim attachment. Thereafter they are directed to the interest on the principal sum sued for as at the date of execution and finally towards the principal sum (subss.(1) and (2)). Where the interim attachment is followed by attachment in execution of a decree in the action for which the interim attached was granted, s.41 of the 2002 Act applies, to much the same effect, namely that the payments are directed towards the expenses of the attachment, the expenses of any previous permitted diligence (such as the expenses of the interim attachment), interest and finally the principal sum.

Section 9S

GENERAL NOTE

This deals with the ranking of the interim attachment. Where there is competition between creditors, and where an interim attachment has been executed and the creditor has obtained decree for payment of the sum sued for, the interim attachment is deemed to be equivalent to a normal attachment of the attached property under s.10 of the 2002 Act, but deemed to be executed for these purposes on the day of the interim attachment (subs.(1)).

Where an interim attachment of some article of the debtor's property ceases to have effect because it is superseded, as it were, by attachment following decree, the attachment of the article is deemed to have taken place on the day of interim attachment (subs.(2)).

PART 8

ATTACHMENT OF MONEY

GENERAL NOTE

Traditionally, the main diligences have been arrestment, inhibition, adjudication and poinding. There were other certain diligences specific to certain types of debt, such as tinsel of the feu, poinding of the ground, mails and duties and so on, but none that was suitable for seizing money or instruments of debt such as cheques. As part of the general principle that everything of value ought to be capable of enforcement for debt, and given the special nature of money, it was decided that money should be given a special category of its own rather than being put in the category of residual attachment.

The main reason for having its own category lies in the liquid nature of money, the general untraceability of money and the practical problems for judicial officers of dealing with large quantities of cash. Not only is there the security problem to consider but also there is the fact that there could be significant awkwardness for judicial officers if they attempt to attach money in a till, when the employees of the business, whose till is being emptied by the judicial officers, are expecting to be paid out of the day's takings held in the till. Wisely, there is no suggestion that money attachment should take place in a debtor's dwellinghouse: although there may be some crafty debtors who would therefore keep their cash, not in a bank account where it might be arrested, but at home (or indeed in someone else's home) in cash, there is the more general point that it would be inhumane to take money from debtors in their own home, particularly if that money were desperately needed for the debtor's family.

Money for the purposes of this Part means cash (sterling and other currencies), cheques, negotiable instruments, promissory notes, money orders and postal orders. There is no mention of gift vouchers so these are presumably excluded. In view of the fact that increasingly purchases for large items are being made less and less by cash and cheques, and more and more by credit and debit cards, it may be that money attachment is not used in practice very much except in places where much cash changes hands, such as in shops, public houses and places of entertainment.

From a judicial officer's point of view money attachment may be an unwelcome task: the rules, while sensible and straightforward, must be followed to the letter in order to ensure every protection for the debtor, and any procedural mistake may invalidate the entire procedure.

It is worth noting that the wording of this Part is on the whole very straightforward and easy to follow. For that reason subsection references have generally been omitted in the notes to this Part unless any subsection is particularly significant.

Money attachment

174. Money attachment

(1) There is to be a form of diligence over money owned by a debtor to be known as money attachment.

(2) Money attachment is competent to enforce payment of a debt but only if-
  (a) the debt is constituted by a decree or document of debt;
  (b) the debtor has been charged to pay the debt;
  (c) the period for payment specified in the charge has expired without payment being made; and
  (d) where the debtor is an individual, the creditor has, no earlier than 12 weeks before executing the money attachment, provided the debtor with a debt advice and information package.

(3) Money attachment is not competent in relation to money-
  (a) kept within a dwellinghouse; or
  (b) in relation to which arrestment is competent.

DEFINITIONS
"Debt advice and information package": 2002 Act s.10(5)
"Decree": 2007 Act s.221 (see also s.128)
"Document of debt": 2007 Act s.221

GENERAL NOTE
This introduces the new diligence of money attachment. It is competent to use money attachment as a diligence to enforce a debt, but only where and when the debt has been constituted by decree or a document of debt, the debtor has been charged to pay the debt, the period allowed for the charge has expired (14 days or 28 days if the debtor is furth of Scotland) and, where the debtor is an individual, he has been served with a debt advice and information package (subs.(2)).

Money attachment may not take place within a dwellinghouse or where arrestment would be the proper diligence to use (subs.(3)).

A debtor may be able to apply for a time to pay direction to prevent the money attachment taking place (see s.2(1)(b)(v) of the 1987 Act as amended by Sch.5 para.2(a) of the 2007 Act).

175. Meaning of "money" and related expressions

(1) In this Part-
  "cash" means coins and banknotes in any currency;
  "banking instrument" means-
    (a) cheques and other instruments to which section 4 of the Cheques Act 1957 (c.36) applies;
    (b) any document (other than one mentioned in section 4(2)(c) of that Act) issued by a public officer which is intended to enable a person to obtain payment from a government department of the sum mentioned in it;

    (c) promissory notes (other than banknotes);

    (d) other negotiable instruments; and

    (e) money orders and postal orders; and

"money" means cash and banking instruments but does not include any cash or instrument which has an intrinsic value greater than any value it may have as a medium of exchange; and any reference to the value of money is, unless the context otherwise requires, a reference to-

    (a) the amount of cash;

    (b) where that cash is in a currency other than sterling, the amount in sterling which that cash would realise on its conversion under section 177(3) of this Act;

    (c) the amount in cash which would be obtained were the value of a banking instrument realised; and

    (d) in the case where money comprises both cash and instruments, the aggregate of the amounts referred to in, as the case may be, paragraphs (a) to (c) above.

(2) In the definition of "banking instrument" in subsection (1) above, "government department" includes-

    (a) any Minister of the Crown;

    (b) any part of the Scottish Administration;

    (c) the National Assembly for Wales;

    (d) the Northern Ireland Assembly, any Northern Ireland Minister or Northern Ireland junior Minister and any Northern Ireland department.

(3) The Scottish Ministers may by order modify the definition of "banking instrument" in subsection (1) above so as to-

    (a) add or remove types of instrument to or, as the case may be, from those referred to in that definition; or

    (b) vary the descriptions of the types of instrument so referred to.

GENERAL NOTE

Subsection (1) gives various definitions. Money is defined to mean cash and banknotes in any currency, but the value of the money must be its normal commercial value, not its value as, say, a collector's item (if it were a rare coin or banknote), which may be in excess of its face value. A banking instrument covers cheques, banker's drafts, any documents given to a third party by a bank's customer and permitting his bank to pay money to a third party, any government cheques (usually from the Queen's Lord Remembrancer or the Paymaster General), cheques from other government departments (as defined in subs.(2)), promissory notes, money orders and postal orders.

Where the money is in cash and not in sterling, any reference to the value of the money is to the value that the non-sterling cash would be worth on conversion into sterling.

The value of a banking instrument is the amount in cash, were the instrument to be realised. There is no requirement that the banking instrument must be in sterling.

The Scottish ministers may vary the definition of "banking instrument" if necessary (subs.(3)).

176. When money attachment not competent

(1) It is not competent to execute a money attachment on-

    (a) a Sunday;

    (b) a day which is a public holiday in the area in which the attachment is to be executed; or

    (c) such other day as may be prescribed by Act of Sederunt.

(2) The execution of a money attachment must not-

    (a) begin before 8 a.m. or after 8 p.m.; or

    (b) be continued after 8 p.m.,

unless the judicial officer has obtained prior authority from the sheriff for such commencement or continuation.

    (3) Subject to section 183(12)(b), 186(3)(b) or 191(4) of this Act, where money is attached (or is purported to be attached) at any place, it is not competent to attach other money kept at that place to enforce the same debt unless that other money is brought to that place after execution of the first money attachment.

    (4) Money which has been attached by a money attachment may not, if that money attachment ceases to have effect in relation to that money, be attached again for the same debt.

DEFINITIONS
"Judicial officer": 2007 Act s.45

GENERAL NOTE

It is incompetent to carry out money attachment on certain occasions, these being on Sundays and public holidays (or such other days as may later be decided), not between 20.00 and the following 08.00 and where a money attachment is taking place, it must not continue after 20.00. A judicial officer may, if necessary, obtain prior approval from the sheriff for executing a money attachment outside those hours (subs.(1)).

Where money has already been attached in one place, it is not competent to attach other money at the same place for the same debt unless that other money is brought to that place after the execution of the first money attachment. This is subject to various exceptions which arise when it is established that the attached money was not actually the debtor's money, or where the money is owned jointly, the other owner is allowed to keep his share, and so a debt is still standing. If this is the case, it is permissible to go back to the same place to attach other money of the debtor's (subs.(3)).

Where money has been attached, but the attachment ceases to have effect in relation to that money, that particular money may not be attached a second time (subs.(4)).

Execution of money attachment

177. Removal of money attached

    (1) The judicial officer must attach and remove, from the place in which it is found, such money, the value of which in the opinion of the officer does not exceed a sum equal to the sum mentioned in subsection (2) below (in this Part, the "sum recoverable by the money attachment").

    (2) That sum is-

      (a) the sum for the payment of which the charge was served, together with any interest accruing after such service and before the money attachment ceases to have effect; and

      (b) all expenses which are chargeable against the debtor by virtue of the money attachment.

    (3) Where cash in a currency other than sterling is attached, the judicial officer must, as soon as reasonably practicable after attaching it, convert that cash into sterling.

    (4) The judicial officer must take all reasonable steps to obtain the highest amount for such cash as is practicable.

    (5) The judicial officer must deposit any cash attached and any proceeds of converting cash in a currency other than sterling in a bank account.

    (6) The judicial officer-

      (a) need not attach any banking instruments other than cheques unless instructed to do so by the creditor; and

(b) is not liable to the creditor for any loss caused by the failure to attach any such instruments unless so instructed.

(7) The judicial officer must, subject to section 180(1) of this Act, value any instruments attached at the price which they are likely to fetch on the open market.

(8) Where any instruments are attached, the judicial officer must ensure that they are kept in a secure place.

(9) In this Part, any reference to money being attached includes a reference to it being removed under subsection (1) above.

DEFINITIONS
"Banking instrument": 2007 Act s.175(1)
"Judicial officer": 2007 Act s.45
"Money": 2007 Act s.175(1)

GENERAL NOTE
This outlines the procedure for the removal of the attached money. The judicial officer must uplift what is in his opinion the right amount that he is required to uplift, namely the sum for which the charge was served, plus interest and expenses. If the cash is foreign currency, he must as soon as possible try to obtain the best rate for conversion into sterling. He must deposit the attached cash in a bank account. The judicial officer is not obliged to attach any banking instruments unless authorised to do so by the creditor, and if he fails to attach any banking instruments unless he was positively instructed to do, he will not be liable to the creditor. The judicial officer must value any attached banking instruments at their open market value price. Section 180 provides authority for the judicial officer to have the banking instrument valued by a suitable expert. Any banking instruments must be safely lodged in a secure place.

Subsections (7) and (8) refer to "instruments": the context suggests that the defined term "banking instrument" is what is meant.

178. Presumption of ownership

(1) A judicial officer may, when executing a money attachment, assume that the debtor owns, solely or in common with a third party, any money found in the place where the attachment is executed.

(2) The judicial officer must, before attaching any money, make enquiries of any person present at the place in which it is found as to the ownership of it (and in particular must enquire as to whether there is any person who owns it in common with the debtor).

(3) The judicial officer may not make the assumption mentioned in subsection (1) above where the officer knows or ought to know that the contrary is the case.

(4) The judicial officer is not precluded from relying on that assumption by reason only that an assertion has been made that the money is not owned by the debtor.

DEFINITIONS
"Judicial officer": 2007 Act s.45
"Money": 2007 Act s.175(1)

GENERAL NOTE
The judicial officer is entitled to assume that the debtor owns the money, either solely or in common with others, if it is at the place where the money attachment is being executed. Nevertheless, he is expected to enquire as to the ownership of the money by asking anyone present who owns the money, and in particular if anyone else owns the money in common with the debtor. The

judicial officer may not make the aforementioned assumption if he knew or ought to have known that the money was not the debtor's, or not all the debtor's, but merely because someone says that the money is not the debtor's does not make the assumption invalid.

179. Schedule of money attachment

(1) The judicial officer must, immediately after executing a money attachment, complete a schedule such as is mentioned in subsection (2) below (in this Part, the "schedule of money attachment").

(2) A schedule of money attachment-
  (a) must be-
    (i) in (or as nearly as may be in) the form prescribed by Act of Sederunt;
    (ii) signed by the judicial officer; and
  (b) must specify-
    (i) the money attached; and
    (ii) the value of that money, so far as ascertainable.

(3) The judicial officer must-
  (a) give a copy of the schedule to the debtor; or
  (b) where it is not practicable to do so-
    (i) give a copy of the schedule to a person present at the place where the money attachment was executed; or
    (ii) where there is no such person, leave a copy of the schedule at that place.

(4) In this Part, any reference to the day on which a money attachment is executed is a reference to the day on which the judicial officer complies with subsection (3) above.

DEFINITIONS
"Judicial officer": 2007 Act s.45
"Money": 2007 Act s.175(1)

GENERAL NOTE
Once the judicial officer has executed his money attachment, he must complete a schedule on a form yet to be devised. This he must sign, and specify the money attached and the value of the attached money. He must give a copy to the debtor but should this not be practicable, he must give a copy to someone present at the place of the execution, or leave a copy there. The day of execution of a money attachment is the day that the schedule is given to the debtor or anyone else present, or left at the place of execution. The schedule may be in electronic form and signed by a certified electronic signature.

180. Valuation of banking instruments

(1) Where the judicial officer considers that a banking instrument attached in execution of a money attachment is such that it is appropriate for valuation of the price the instrument is likely to fetch on the open market to be carried out by a professional valuer or other suitably skilled person, the officer must arrange for such a valuation.

(2) The creditor is liable for the valuer's reasonable remuneration and outlays incurred by virtue of subsection (1) above.

DEFINITIONS
"Judicial officer": 2007 Act s.45

GENERAL NOTE
Where a judicial officer attaches a banking instrument and he considers it appropriate to have it valued, as he probably will if it is any form of banking instrument that is in a foreign currency, or drawn on an unfamiliar drawee, he may, at the creditor's expense, have it valued to establish its open market price.

181. Order for realisation of money likely to deteriorate in value

(1) The-

    (a) creditor;

    (b) judicial officer; or

    (c) debtor,

may, at any time after money has been attached, apply to the sheriff for an order that the creditor or, as the case may be, the officer make arrangements for the immediate realisation of the value of that money (or any part of it).

(2) A person applying under subsection (1) above must at the same time intimate the application to the persons mentioned in that subsection who would otherwise be entitled to apply.

(3) The sheriff may, if satisfied that the money is likely to deteriorate substantially and rapidly in value, make an order such as is mentioned in subsection (1) above.

(4) An order under subsection (3) above authorises the judicial officer-

    (a) to act as the irrevocable agent of the debtor in relation to the money; and

    (b) to take any of the steps mentioned in section 184(3) of this Act.

(5) Subsection (4) of section 184 of this Act applies to any steps taken by virtue of subsection (4) above.

(6) Any sum realised by virtue of an order under subsection (3) above must be deposited in a bank account.

(7) The sheriff's decision under subsection (3) above is final.

DEFINITIONS
"Judicial officer": 2007 Act s.45
"Money": 2007 Act s.175(1)

GENERAL NOTE
If, after the money has been attached, any of the debtor, the creditor or the judicial officer may apply to court (having intimated as much to the other two) to have the money immediately realised. The sheriff may permit this if satisfied that the value of the money is about to deteriorate substantially and rapidly. There is no appeal against the sheriff's decision. If an order is granted, the judicial officer will be authorised to act as the agent of the debtor and to carry out the requirements of s.184 (effectively presenting the banking instrument for payment or such other steps as may be necessary to obtain value). So if the attached banking instrument is a cheque made out to the debtor, the judicial officer may present the cheque for payment. This might be particularly important if the drawer of the cheque was about to become insolvent. Having done so, the funds realised must be placed in a bank account.

182. Report of money attachment

(1) The judicial officer must, before the expiry of the period of 14 days beginning with the day on which the money attachment is executed (or such longer period as the sheriff on cause shown

　　　　may, on the application of the officer, allow), make a report to
　　　　the sheriff.

(2)　A report under subsection (1) above must be-

　　(a)　in (or as nearly as may be in) the form prescribed by Act of
　　　　Sederunt; and

　　(b)　signed by the judicial officer.

(3)　The report must specify-

　　(a)　the money attached;

　　(b)　the value of that money;

　　(c)　whether any cash in a currency other than sterling was
　　　　attached and, if so-

　　　　　(i)　the exchange rate used; and

　　　　　(ii)　any commission incurred,

　　in converting it into sterling;

　　(d)　whether any person has asserted that any money attached is
　　　　not owned by the debtor (or is owned in common by the
　　　　debtor and a third party);

　　(e)　whether the value of any money has been realised under
　　　　section 181 of this Act; and

　　(f)　whether any money attached has been released by virtue of
　　　　section 185(3), 186 or 188(1) of this Act.

(4)　On making the report, the judicial officer must send a copy of
　　it to-

　　(a)　the debtor;

　　(b)　the creditor; and

　　(c)　any person such as is mentioned in subsection (3)(d) above.

(5)　The sheriff may refuse to receive a report on the ground that it
　　has not been made and signed in accordance with subsections (1)
　　and (2) above.

(6)　If the sheriff so refuses-

　　(a)　the money attachment ceases to have effect;

　　(b)　the sheriff must require the judicial officer to return the
　　　　money attached or, where the value of any such money has
　　　　been realised, a sum equivalent to that value, to the debtor;
　　　　and

　　(c)　the sheriff clerk must intimate the refusal to-

　　　　　(i)　the debtor;

　　　　　(ii)　the officer;

　　　　　(iii)　the creditor; and

　　　　　(iv)　any person the sheriff thinks has an interest.

(7)　In this Part, any reference to the day on which the report of
　　money attachment is made is a reference to the day on which the
　　sheriff receives the report under subsection (1) above.

DEFINITIONS

"Banking instrument": 2007 Act s.175(1)

"Judicial officer": 2007 Act s.45

"Money": 2007 Act s.175(1)

GENERAL NOTE

　Within 14 days (unless an extension is permitted) of the execution of the money attachment
(see s.179(4)) the judicial officer must give a duly signed report to the sheriff in a form yet to be
devised. The report must detail the various matters referred to in subs.(3), namely the money, its
value, the exchange rate and commission if any of the money were in a foreign currency, whether
anyone stated that the money did not belong to the debtor or belonged to someone else in com-

mon with the debtor (subs.(3)(d)), the sums realised under any order under s.181 and any sums released under s.185(3) (the "unduly harsh" release order), under s.186 (where the execution of the attachment is irregular) or under s.188(1) (redemption of the banking instrument within 14 days from the date the report is received by the sheriff (see subs.(3) of s.182)).

A copy of the report is sent to the debtor, the creditor and any person who had indicated that the money did not belong in whole or in part to the debtor. The sheriff may refuse the report if it is not made timeously and signed by the judicial officer.

Where the sheriff refuses the order, the money attachment ceases to have effect and the money (or if necessary, its value) must be returned to the debtor, and intimation of the refusal must be made by the sheriff clerk to the debtor, the creditor, the judicial officer (referred to in subs.6(c) as the "officer") and anyone else with an interest.

Under subs.(3), the day on which the report of the money attachment is made is the day the sheriff receives it. It may be made electronically with the required electronic signature (s.198(3)).

Release of money attached

183. Creditor's application for payment order

(1) This section applies where-
    (a) money has been attached by a judicial officer in execution of a money attachment; and
    (b) that money (or part of it) has not been released by virtue of section 182(6)(b), 185(3), 186 or 188(1) of this Act.
(2) The creditor may apply to the sheriff for an order (in this Part, a "payment order") authorising payment to the creditor out of the money attached of a sum not exceeding the sum recoverable by the money attachment.
(3) An application under subsection (2) above must be-
    (a) in (or as nearly as may be in) the form prescribed by Act of Sederunt;
    (b) made before the expiry of the period of 14 days beginning with the day on which the report of money attachment is made.
(4) On making the application, the creditor must send a copy of it to-
    (a) the debtor;
    (b) the judicial officer; and
    (c) any person such as is mentioned in section 182(3)(d) of this Act.
(5) Subject to subsections (10) and (12) below, where there is no opposition to the application, the sheriff must make a payment order.
(6) The debtor or a third party who claims ownership (whether solely or in common with the debtor) of any of the money attached may oppose the application under subsection (2) above.
(7) An opposition under subsection (6) above must be-
    (a) in (or as nearly as may be in) the form prescribed by Act of Sederunt; and
    (b) made before the expiry of the period of 14 days beginning with the day on which the application is made.
(8) Where there is opposition, the sheriff may not make a payment order without first-
    (a) giving-
        (i) the creditor;

      (ii) the debtor; and

      (iii) any third party who opposes the application,

an opportunity to make representations; or

  (b) holding a hearing.

(9) Where the debtor or, as the case may be a third party, opposes the application on the ground that money attached is not owned by the debtor, it is for the debtor or the third party to prove that fact.

(10) Where the sheriff is satisfied, after considering any opposition or on the sheriff's own initiative, that there has been a material irregularity in the execution of the money attachment, the sheriff must make an order such as is mentioned in subsection (11) below.

(11) That order is an order-

  (a) declaring that the money attachment ceases to have effect; and

  (b) requiring the judicial officer to return the money attached or, where the value of any such money has been realised, a sum equivalent to that value, to the debtor or, as the case may be, the person whose money it is.

(12) Where the sheriff is satisfied after considering any opposition or on the sheriff's own initiative, that any money attached is not owned by the debtor-

  (a) the sheriff must make an order such as is mentioned in subsection (11) above restricted to that money; and

  (b) after the order is made, the judicial officer may attach other money owned by the debtor and kept at the place at which the original money attachment was executed.

DEFINITIONS

"Banking instrument": 2007 Act s.175(1)

"Judicial officer": 2007 Act s.45

"Money": 2007 Act s.175(1)

GENERAL NOTE

Once the execution has taken place successfully, and the report has been safely lodged, the creditor's next step is to apply for a payment order. This will not be permitted if the money has been released under the provisions of s.182(6)(b), under ss.185(3) (the "unduly harsh" release order), 186 (where the execution of the attachment is irregular) or 188(1) (redemption of the banking instrument within 14 days from the date the report is received by the sheriff (see subs.(3) of s.182)).

The payment order must be applied for in a form yet to be devised and intimated to the debtor, the judicial officer and to any person stated that the money did not belong to the debtor or belonged to someone else in common with the debtor (see s.182(3)(d)). Provided there is no opposition to the application, the payment order must be made (subs.(5)). Opposition may be made by the debtor or a third party claiming ownership (either sole ownership or in common with the debtor) (subs.(6)). The opposition must be made on a form yet to be devised, and must be made within 14 days of the application for the payment order (subs.(7)). Curiously, there seems to be no requirement to intimate the opposition to the creditor or the judicial officer, although these two persons, and any third party who opposes the payment order, must be given the opportunity to make representations or to be given a hearing (subs.(8)). It is for the debtor, or the third party claiming ownership, to prove that fact (subs.(9)).

If the sheriff is satisfied, either on the basis of the opposition or on his own view, that there has been a material irregularity in the execution of the money attachment (subs.(10)) he may make an order under subs.(11) that the money attachment is to have no effect and the money or its value to be returned to the debtor or to the true owner of the money.

If the money is returned to the true owner, the judicial officer may return to the place of the original money attachment and carry out a second money attachment there (subs.12(b)).

184. Effect of payment order

(1) A payment order authorises the judicial officer-

    (a) to realise the value of money attached; and

    (b) subject to section 37 of the 1985 Act (effect of sequestration on diligence), to dispose of the proceeds of the money attachment by-

        (i) retaining such amount as necessary to meet the fees and outlays of the officer;

        (ii) paying to the creditor the remainder of those proceeds so far as necessary to meet the sum recoverable by the money attachment; and

        (iii) paying to the debtor any surplus remaining.

(2) For the purposes of subsection (1) above, the payment order authorises the judicial officer-

    (a) to act as the irrevocable agent of the debtor in relation to any banking instrument attached; and

    (b) to take any of the steps mentioned in subsection (3) below.

(3) Those steps are-

    (a) presenting the instrument for payment;

    (b) if instructed by the creditor to do so, raising any action for payment that would have been open to the debtor to raise against any person liable to honour the instrument;

    (c) except where the instrument is not negotiable, negotiating the instrument-

        (i) for value; or

        (ii) to the creditor for value credited against the sum recoverable by the money attachment;

    (d) any other steps the debtor could have taken in relation to the instrument before the money attachment was executed.

(4) The judicial officer must, in taking any of the steps referred to in subsection (3) above, obtain the highest amount for the instrument as is reasonably practicable.

(5) In subsection (1)(b) above, "proceeds of the money attachment" includes any amount-

    (a) deposited in a bank account by virtue of section 181(6) or 185(4)(b)(iii) of this Act;

    (b) obtained as a result of taking any of the steps mentioned in subsection (3) above; and

    (c) received by the judicial officer by virtue of section 191(2)(c) of this Act.

DEFINITIONS

"Banking instrument": 2007 Act s.175(1)

"Judicial officer": 2007 Act s.45

"Money": 2007 Act s.175(1)

"Payment order": 2007 Act s.183

GENERAL NOTE

The payment order allows the judicial officer to realise the money attached and to pay the money owed to the creditor, having retained enough to pay his own fees and expenses, and, where appropriate, returning any surplus to the debtor. The judicial officer is to be treated as the irrevocable agent of the debtor for any banking instruments, which means that although any cheques etc. may be made out to the debtor, the judicial officer is entitled to receive payment for them on behalf of the debtor, albeit that the judicial officer gives the money thereafter to the creditor. The judicial officer may also raise any judicial proceedings to enforce payments from any banking instruments, or negotiate the banking instrument for value (i.e. sell or transfer it to someone else or the creditor (assuming it is negotiable)). If negotiated to the creditor, the creditor may then receive payment directly from the drawee/acceptor and the sum received would be deducted from the debt that the debtor owes to the creditor. In each case, the judicial officer must try to obtain the best price possible.

This section is subject to s.37 of the 1985 Act (effect of sequestration on diligence).

This section provides that no diligence effected within 60 days prior to sequestration serves to give a preference to the creditor carrying out diligence. This section is sometimes known as the equalisation of diligence provision. Should diligence take place within this 60 day period the creditor must hand to the trustee in sequestration that part of the debtor's estate subject to the creditor's diligence, though the creditor may retain from it the expenses of the diligence.

185.   Release of money where attachment unduly harsh

(1) The debtor may, before-

    (a) a payment order is made; or

    (b) the money attachment ceases to have effect,

apply to the sheriff for an order such as is mentioned in subsection (2) below. ·

(2) That order is one-

    (a) providing that the money attachment ceases to have effect in relation to-

        (i) the money attached; or

        (ii) so much of it as the sheriff specifies; and

    (b) requiring the judicial officer to return that money or, where the value of the money has been realised, a sum equivalent to that value, to the debtor.

(3) Where the sheriff is satisfied that, in the circumstances, the money attachment is unduly harsh to the debtor, the sheriff must, subject to subsection (4) below, make an order such as is mentioned in subsection (2) above.

(4) Where the value of the money attached exceeds £1,000 or such other amount as the Scottish Ministers may by regulations prescribe, the sheriff-

    (a) may not specify money the value of which exceeds that amount; and

    (b) may, where the money attached includes or comprises a banking instrument, authorise the judicial officer to-

        (i) realise the value of the instrument;

        (ii) pay to the debtor from the money and, as the case may be, proceeds of that realisation the sum specified; and

        (iii) deposit any surplus remaining in a bank account.

(5) In a case to which subsection (4)(b) above applies, the order under subsection (3) above authorises the judicial officer-

    (a) to act as the irrevocable agent of the debtor in relation to the instrument; and

    (b) to take any of the steps mentioned in section 184(3) of this Act.

(6) Subsection (4) of section 184 of this Act applies to any steps taken by virtue of subsection (5) above.

(7) Where the amount realised under subsection (4)(b)(i) above is less than the amount specified, the order is to be deemed to have required the judicial officer to pay the amount realised only.

DEFINITIONS

"Banking instrument": 2007 Act s.175(1)

"Judicial officer": 2007Act s.45

"Money": 2007 Act s.175(1)

"Payment order": 2007 Act s.183

GENERAL NOTE

A debtor may apply to the sheriff for the release of money where he is able to persuade the sheriff that the attachment would be unduly harsh. He may do this either before the payment order is made or before the money attachment ceases to have effect. He may apply for an order asking for the money attachment not to apply to the attached money or some specified part of it, or he may apply for the return of the money (or its value) from the judicial officer (subs.(2)).

The sheriff, if satisfied that the money attachment is unduly harsh, must make one of the above orders (subs.(3)). However, if the attached money is worth more that £1,000 (or such other later prescribed figure), the sheriff may not order the release of more than that amount (subs.(4)(a)). The sheriff will thus be placed in the difficult position of having to decide between creditor and debtor: what may be unduly harsh to the debtor may also cause hardship to a creditor too.

Where again the money attached is in excess of £1,000, and comprises a banking instrument, the sheriff may order that the banking instrument be realised, that from the funds realised the sum (of £1,000 or less, as the sheriff specifies) should be extracted and paid to the debtor, with the balance remaining in a bank account (subs.(4)(b)).

Where this happens the judicial officer acts as the irrevocable agent of the debtor in the same manner as in s.184(2) and may obtain payment as in s.184(3) at the best possible price (subs.(6)).

Should the amount realised be less than the sum the sheriff specifies, the order applies only to the amount realised (subs.(7)).

186. Invalidity and cessation of money attachment

(1) Where, at any time before a payment order is made or the money attachment ceases to have effect, the sheriff is satisfied that there has been a material irregularity in the execution of the money attachment, the sheriff must make an order such as is mentioned in subsection (2) below.

(2) That order is an order-

    (a) declaring that the money attachment ceases to have effect; and

    (b) requiring the judicial officer to return the money attached or, where the value of any such money has been realised, a sum equivalent to that value, to the debtor or, as the case may be, the person whose money it is.

(3) Where, at any time before a payment order is made or the money attachment ceases to have effect, the sheriff is satisfied that any money attached is not owned by the debtor-

    (a) the sheriff must make an order such as is mentioned in subsection (2) above restricted to that money; and

    (b) after the order is made, the judicial officer may attach other money owned by the debtor and kept at the place at which the original money attachment was executed.

(4) An order under this section may be made-

    (a) on the application of-

        (i) the debtor; or

        (ii) a third party claiming an interest; or

    (b) on the sheriff's own initiative.

(5) Where such an order is made on the sheriff's own initiative, the sheriff clerk must intimate the order to-

    (a) the debtor;

    (b) the creditor;

    (c) the judicial officer; and

    (d) any other person the sheriff thinks has an interest.

(6) The sheriff may not make an order under this section without first-

    (a) giving-

        (i) the debtor;

        (ii) the creditor; and

        (iii) any other person the sheriff thinks has an interest,

    an opportunity to make representations; or

    (b) holding a hearing.

(7) The sheriff must give reasons for making, or refusing to make, an order under this section.

DEFINITIONS

"Banking instrument": 2007 Act s.175(1)

"Judicial officer": 2007 Act s.45

"Money": 2007 Act s.175(1)

"Payment order": 2007 Act s.183

GENERAL NOTE

If before the payment order is made or the money attachment ceases to have effect the sheriff is satisfied that there has been a material irregularity in the execution of the money attachment, he may grant an order declaring that the money attachment ceases to have effect, and requiring the judicial officer to return the money, or its value, to the debtor (subs.(2)). The sort of material irregularity that might be considered by the sheriff might be an unauthorised execution of the money attachment at a prohibited time under s.176, the failure by the sheriff officer to get the best possible exchange rate for foreign currency (s.177(4), or the failure to take account of any known competing interest in the money attached (s.178(3)).

Subsection (3) differs from subs.(1) in that it deals not with a material irregularity, but with the situation where the sheriff is satisfied that any money attached does not belong to the debtor. In that case any order, declaring that the money attachment ceases to have effect, that the sheriff makes, is restricted to that part of the money that belongs to the person other than the debtor. The judicial officer may then go and attach further money, belonging to the debtor and at the place of attachment.

The debtor or a third party claiming an interest may apply for this, or the sheriff may make the order *ex proprio motu*. Where the sheriff makes the order *ex proprio motu* the sheriff clerk must intimate it to debtor, the creditor, the judicial officer and anyone else the sheriff thinks may have an interest (subs.(5)). There appears to be no provision for the debtor or the third party to intimate the application to the creditor and the judicial officer, but the sheriff must not make any order, whether at the debtor's application, the third party's application, or his own instance, without giving the debtor, creditor and anyone else with an interest the opportunity to make representations, or without holding a hearing. Presumably, therefore, there will, in regulations yet to be drafted, be a mechanism for intimating the hearing to those involved.

The sheriff is required to give his reasons for any order under this section (subs.(7)).

187. Termination of money attachment

(1) A money attachment ceases to have effect on the expiry of the period of 14 days beginning with the day on which the report of money attachment is made unless, within that period, the creditor-

    (a) applies for a payment order; and

    (b) sends a copy of the application to the judicial officer under section 183(4)(b) of this Act.

(2) A money attachment ceases to have effect if the sum recoverable by the money attachment is-

    (a) paid to-

        (i) the creditor;

        (ii) the judicial officer; or

      (iii) any other person who has authority to receive payment on behalf of the creditor; or
   (b) tendered to any of those persons and the tender is not accepted within a reasonable time.

(3) Where a money attachment ceases to have affect by virtue of subsection (1) or (2) above, the judicial officer must return money attached or, where the value of any such money has been realised, a sum equivalent to that value, to the debtor.

DEFINITIONS
"Judicial officer": 2007 Act s.45
"Money": 2007 Act s.175(1)
"Payment order": 2007 Act s.183
"Day on which the report of money attachment is made": 2002 Act s.182(7)

GENERAL NOTE
Under subs.(1), a money attachment ceases to have effect 14 days after the day the report of the money attachment is made to the sheriff. Accordingly the creditor must apply swiftly for a payment order and in doing so must send a copy of the application to the judicial officer under s.183(4)(b).

A money attachment also ceases to have effect if the sum recoverable by the money attachment is paid to the creditor, the judicial officer or anyone else authorised to receive it on the creditor's behalf, or tendered to any of those people and not accepted within a reasonable time (subs.(2)).

Where the money attachment ceases to have effect as above, the judicial officer must return the money or its value to the debtor (subs.(3)).

188. Redemption of banking instrument

(1) The debtor may, before the expiry of the period of 14 days beginning with the date on which the report of money attachment is made, redeem a banking instrument attached by the money attachment.

(2) The debtor may not redeem an instrument in relation to which an order under section 181(3) of this Act has been made.

(3) The amount for which such an instrument may be redeemed is the value of the instrument specified in the report of money attachment.

(4) The judicial officer must, on receiving payment from the debtor for the redemption of an attached instrument-
   (a) grant a receipt in (or as nearly as may be in) the form prescribed by Act of Sederunt to the debtor; and
   (b) report the redemption to the sheriff as soon as is reasonably practicable.

(5) The money attachment ceases, on the grant of such a receipt, to have effect in relation to the redeemed instrument.

DEFINITIONS
"Banking instrument": 2007 Act s.175(1)
"Judicial officer": 2007 Act s.45
"Day on which the report of money attachment is made": 2002 Act s.182(7)

GENERAL NOTE
The debtor may redeem a banking instrument within 14 days of the day the report is made to the sheriff, but may not do this where an order under s.181(3) has been made. Section 181(3) deals with the situation where a banking instrument needs to be swiftly realised as it is about to deteriorate in value.

The value of the redemption will be the value of the instrument specified in the money instrument, with no discount or premium. The wording of the legislation suggests that redemption will be made to the judicial officer holding the instrument, and so, when the judicial officer is paid, it is for that judicial officer to give a receipt to the debtor and report the redemption to the sheriff as soon as reasonably possible. This also causes the money attachment to have no further effect on that particular banking instrument.

Statement of money attachment

189. Final statement of money attachment

(1) The judicial officer must, before the expiry of the period of 14 days beginning with the day mentioned in subsection (2) below, give a statement to the sheriff.

(2) The day referred to in subsection (1) above is the day on which-
   (a) the judicial officer made payment to the creditor under a payment order; or
   (b) the money attached (or the last part of it) was returned to the debtor or, as the case may be, a third party by virtue of section 182(6), 183(11), 185(3), 186, 187 or 188 of this Act,
whichever is the later.

(3) The statement mentioned in subsection (1) above must be-
   (a) in (or as nearly as may be in) the form prescribed by Act of Sederunt; and
   (b) signed by the judicial officer.

(4) The statement must specify-
   (a) any banking instruments, the values of which have been realised;
   (b) the value realised in respect of each such instrument;
   (c) any sums paid by the debtor to account of the sum recoverable by the money attachment;
   (d) any chargeable expenses;
   (e) any sums paid to the creditor;
   (f) any surplus paid or instruments returned to the debtor or, as the case may be, a third party; and
   (g) any balance due by or to the debtor.

(5) The statement must contain a declaration by the judicial officer that all the information contained within it is, to the best of the officer's knowledge, true.

(6) If the judicial officer-
   (a) without reasonable excuse gives the statement after the expiry of the period mentioned in subsection (1) above; or
   (b) wilfully refuses to make, or delays making, the statement after the expiry of that period,
the sheriff may make an order providing that the officer is liable for the chargeable expenses, either in whole or in part.

(7) An order under subsection (6) above does not prejudice the right of the sheriff to report the matter to the Commission by virtue of section 67(1)(b) of this Act (investigation into alleged misconduct by judicial officers).

DEFINITIONS
   "Judicial officer": 2007 Act s.45

"Commission": 2007 Act s.50

GENERAL NOTE

This requires the judicial officer, within 14 days of: (a) the judicial officer making payment to the creditor or (b) the attached money being returned to the debtor or any third party (whichever is the later) to give a signed statement to the sheriff in a form yet to be devised. The form should indicate all the necessary information relating to the money attachment including the sums realised, expenses, etc. The statement must be declared by the judicial officer to be true.

If the judicial officer gives the statement after the required 14 day period without reasonable excuse, or deliberately refuses or delays to make the statement, the sheriff may order the judicial officer to be liable for the chargeable expenses. Furthermore, the sheriff could report the judicial officer to the Commission.

The statement may be sent in electronically with a certified electronic signature.

190.   Audit of final statement under section 189(1)

(1) The sheriff must remit the statement under section 189(1) to the auditor of court who must-
   (a) tax the chargeable expenses;
   (b) certify any balance due by or to the debtor; and
   (c) make a report to the sheriff.
(2) The auditor of court must not alter the statement without first giving all interested persons an opportunity to make representations.
(3) The auditor of court must not charge a fee in respect of the report made under subsection (1)(c) above.
(4) On receipt of a report made under subsection (1)(c) above the sheriff must make an order-
   (a) declaring the balance due by or to the debtor, as certified by the auditor of court;
   (b) declaring such a balance after making modifications to the balance so certified; or
   (c) where the sheriff is satisfied that there has been a material irregularity in the execution of the money attachment (other than the timing of the statement under section 189(1) of this Act), declaring the attachment void.
(5) An order under subsection (4)(c) above may make such consequential provision as the sheriff thinks fit.
(6) An order under subsection (4)(c) above does not affect the title of a person to any money acquired by that person in good faith.
(7) The sheriff may not make an order under subsection (4)(b) or (c) above without first-
   (a) giving-
      (i) the debtor;
      (ii) the creditor; and
      (iii) any third party who claims ownership (whether alone or in common with the debtor or any other person) of any money attached,
   an opportunity to make representations; or
   (b) holding a hearing.
(8) The sheriff clerk must intimate the sheriff's order under subsection (4) above to the persons mentioned in subsection (7)(a) above.

GENERAL NOTE

The sheriff, having received the statement from the judicial officer, remits it to the auditor of court who will tax the chargeable expenses, certify any balance and make a report to the sheriff. If there are any errors or other matters in the statement with which the auditor is not satisfied, the auditor may wish to have the statement changed, in which case all those interested in the statement must be allowed to make representations. The auditor then prepares a report for the sheriff, who will as the case may be, declare the sums due or by the debtor (as stated in the statement and approved in the report by the auditor, or equally as revised by the auditor), or, if there has been a material irregularity in the execution of the money attachment, declare the attachment void (subs.(4)). This could mean that the creditor was unable to retain the debtor's money and would have to refund it to the debtor. In order to protect the innocent purchaser of any banking or other instrument who acquired the instrument in good faith, subs.(6) protects the purchaser and he will not be required to give up the instrument or refund anything. This would not prevent the debtor being entitled to a refund from the creditor if the sheriff had ordered a refund. If the material irregularity in the money attachment were the fault of the judicial officer, the creditor could perhaps claim against the judicial officer for his ensuing loss.

Where the sheriff makes an order under the last two parts of subs.(4), the sheriff clerk must write to the debtor, creditor and any third party claiming ownership in order to allow them the opportunity to make any representations or to have a hearing (subs.(7)).

General and miscellaneous

191. Money in common ownership

(1) Money which is owned in common by a debtor and a third party may be attached in satisfaction of the debts of the debtor.

(2) Where at any time before the disposal of attached money-

(a) a third party claims to own the money in common with the debtor;

(b) either-

(i) the judicial officer is satisfied that the claim is valid; or

(ii) the sheriff, on the third party's application, makes an order stating that the sheriff is so satisfied; and

(c) the third party pays to the officer a sum equal to the value of the debtor's interest in the money,

the debtor's interest in the money is transferred to the third party.

(3) Where the sheriff is satisfied-

(a) that money attached is owned in common by the debtor and a third party; and

(b) that the disposal of the money would in the circumstances be unduly harsh to the third party,

the sheriff may, on the third party's application made before the money's disposal, order that the money attachment is to cease to have effect in relation to that money.

(4) Where-

(a) the debtor's interest in money owned in common by the debtor and a third party is, under subsection (2) above, transferred to the third party; or

(b) the money attachment ceases, in pursuance of an order made under subsection (3) above, to have effect in relation to that money,

the judicial officer may attach other money owned by the debtor and kept at the place at which the original money attachment was executed.

(5) In this section and in section 192 of this Act, references to the "disposal" of attached money (and to cognate expressions) are to be construed as references to the value of that money being realised by virtue of-

(a) an order under section 181 of this Act; or

(b) a payment order.

DEFINITIONS
"Judicial officer": 2007 Act s.45
"Money": 2007 Act s.175(1)
"Payment order": 2007 Act s.183

GENERAL NOTE

This section deals with the situation where money is attached and the judicial officer, or subsequently the sheriff, accepts that a third party owns the money in common with the debtor. Where the third party pays the judicial officer a sum equal to the debtor's interest in the money, the third party obtains the debtor's interest in that money and, although the legislation does not specifically say so, it may be assumed that that money is no longer attached (subs.(2)). This permits the judicial officer to return to the place of the execution of the money attachment to carry out a second money attachment to replace the amount that was owned by the third party (subs.(4)).

Where the money is owned in common with a third party and the sheriff is satisfied that the realisation of the money (under the "deterioration" grounds of s.181) or the normal terms of s.183 would be unduly harsh to the third party, he can order that the money attachment should cease.

192. Procedure where money owned in common is disposed of

(1) This section applies where-

  (a) a third party claimed, before attached money was disposed of, to own the money in common with the debtor;

  (b) the debtor's interest in the money has not transferred to the third party under section 191(2) of this Act;

  (c) the money attachment has not, by virtue of an order under section 191(3) of this Act, ceased to have effect in relation to that money;

  (d) the third party's interest in the money has, on the disposal of the money, been-

    (i) transferred to another person; or

    (ii) extinguished by virtue of the disposal; and

  (e) either-

    (i) the third party's claim is, after that disposal, admitted by the creditor and the debtor; or

    (ii) where the third party's claim is not so admitted, the sheriff, on an application by the third party after that disposal, is satisfied that the claim is valid.

(2) The creditor must pay to the third party a sum equal to the fraction of the value of the money which corresponded to the third party's interest in it.

DEFINITIONS
"Money": 2007 Act s.175(1)

GENERAL NOTE

This deals with the situation where:

- the third party claimed to own the money in common with the debtor, and made the claim before the attached money was either realised (under the "deterioration" grounds of s.181) or the normal terms of s.184;
- the debtor's interest was not, as ideally it should have been, transferred in terms of the preceding section;
- the third party's interest on the realisation of the money has been transferred to another person or extinguished by that realisation; and
- either, after the realisation, debtor and creditor admit the third party's interest, or even if the third party's interest is not admitted, the sheriff is satisfied that the third party's claim is valid.

The creditor must pay to the third party an amount equivalent to the third party's interest in the money.

193. Unlawful acts after money attachment

(1) This section applies where-
    (a) a money attachment has been executed; and
    (b) the debtor-
        (i) realises (or purports to realise) the value of an attached banking instrument;
        (ii) otherwise relinquishes ownership of such an instrument; or
        (iii) obtains (or attempts to obtain), by fraud or other dishonest means, a banking instrument in place of such an instrument.
(2) The debtor is acting in breach of the money attachment.
(3) A person who-
    (a) assists a debtor to do anything mentioned in subsection (1)(b) above; and
    (b) knows (or ought reasonably to know) that a money attachment has been executed against the debtor,
is acting in breach of the money attachment.
(4) A breach of the money attachment under subsection (2) or (3) above may be dealt with as a contempt of court.

GENERAL NOTE

This deals with fraudulent acts by the debtor. A debtor who realises or tries to realise the value of an attached banking instrument, tries to give up his ownership of such of an attached instrument, or tries to obtain another one to replace the one attached, will be acting in breach of the money attachment and will render himself open to proceedings for contempt of court. Likewise anyone who helps the debtor will be liable.

A practical example of this would be where a debtor has a dividend cheque attached by money attachment. He might pretend that he had lost the dividend cheque and request a new one. This would be a breach of the attachment.

194. Appeals

(1) Subject to subsection (2) below, an appeal against any decision of the sheriff made under this Part of this Act may be made only-
    (a) to the sheriff principal;
    (b) with the leave of the sheriff; and
    (c) on a point of law.

(2) This section does not apply to decisions made under section 181(3) of this Act.

(3) The decision of the sheriff principal on such an appeal is final.

GENERAL NOTE

This deals with appeals and is self-evident. Section 181(3) refers to the need to realise a banking instrument before the money deteriorates in value. There is no appeal against the sheriff's decision on this matter.

The purpose of the rule is to prevent endless and unnecessary litigation.

195. Recovery from debtor of expenses of money attachment

(1) Expenses which, in accordance with schedule 3 to this Act, are chargeable against the debtor are to be recoverable from the debtor by the money attachment but not by any other legal process.

(2) Where any expenses such as are mentioned in subsection (1) above have not been recovered by the time the proceeds of the money attachment are disposed of under a payment order, or the money attachment otherwise ceases to have effect, they cease to be chargeable against the debtor.

(3) The sheriff must grant decree for payment of any expenses awarded by the sheriff against the debtor in favour of the creditor under paragraph 4 of schedule 3 to this Act.

(4) Subsection (5) below applies where a money attachment is-

(a) in effect immediately before the date of sequestration (within the meaning of the 1985 Act) of the debtor's estate;

(b) in effect immediately before the appointment of an administrator under Part II of the Insolvency Act 1986 (c.45), in relation to the debtor;

(c) in effect against property of the debtor immediately before a floating charge attaches to all or part of that property under section 53(7) (attachment on appointment of receiver by holder of charge) or 54(6) (attachment on appointment of receiver by court) of that Act of 1986;

(d) in effect immediately before the commencement of the winding up, under Part IV or V of that Act of 1986, of the debtor; or

(e) rendered unenforceable by virtue of the creditor entering into a composition contract or acceding to a trust deed for creditors or by virtue of the subsistence of a protected trust deed within the meaning of Schedule 5 to the 1985 Act.

(5) Where this subsection applies-

(a) the expenses of the money attachment which were chargeable against the debtor remain so chargeable; and

(b) if the debtor's obligation to pay the expenses is not discharged under or by virtue of the sequestration, administration order, receivership, winding up, composition contract or trust deed, those expenses are recoverable by further money attachment.

GENERAL NOTE

This deals with the recovery of expenses. This section follows the broad rule that expenses of any diligence may only be recovered, if not otherwise paid, by that diligence alone. So in this case, the expenses of money attachment may only be recovered by money attachment.

Subsection (2) states that where any expenses have not been recovered by the time the proceeds of the money attachment have been disposed of under a payment order or the money attachment for any other reason ceases to have effect, they will no longer be chargeable against the debtor.

Subsection (3) refers to para.4 Sch.3 of the 2002 Act. The schedule details the expenses chargeable against the debtor. Paragraph 4 explains that frivolous applications by the debtor, or as the case may be, a third party, may result in the person making the frivolous application being liable for the expenses.

Subsection (4) indicates that expenses remain chargeable against the debtor under subs.(5) where the money attachment is:

(a)   in effect immediately before the date of sequestration of the debtor's estate under s.12(4) of the 1985 Act;
(b)   in effect immediately before the appointment of an administrator (where the debtor is corporate) under Pt II of the Insolvency Act 1986;
(c)   in effect against property of the debtor (again, where the debtor is corporate) immediately before a floating charge attaches all or part of that property (see ss.53(7) and 54(6) of the Insolvency Act 1986);
(d)   in effect immediately before the commencement of the winding up, under Pts IV or V of the 1986 Act, of the debtor; or
(e)   unenforceable because the creditor enters into a composition contract or accedes to a trust deed for creditors or by virtue of the subsistence of a protected trust deed for creditors.

This means that, notwithstanding the events in paras (a)-(e), the debtor is still liable for the expenses incurred in obtaining the money attachment to the extent that expenses are not discharged by the sequestration, the administration, the receivership, winding up, the composition contract or trust deed.

If the expenses are not discharged under any of the above, the debtor remains liable.

196. Liability for expenses of money attachment

(1) Schedule 3 to this Act has effect for the purposes of determining the liability, as between the creditor and the debtor, for expenses incurred in serving a charge and in the process of money attachment.

(2) The Scottish Ministers may by order modify that schedule so as to-

(a) add or remove types of expenses to or, as the case may be, from those referred to in that schedule; or

(b) vary any of the descriptions of the types of expenses referred to in it.

GENERAL NOTE

This refers to Sch.3 of the 2007 Act which details the various expenses involved in money attachment. As indicated above, para.4 deals with the expenses of frivolous applications to the sheriff. Power is given to the Scottish Ministers to change the types of expenses if necessary.

197. Ascription

(1) This section applies where any sums are-

(a) attached by a money attachment; or

(b) paid to account of the sum recoverable by that attachment while it is in effect.

(2) Such sums are to be ascribed to the following in the order in which they are mentioned-

(a) the expenses which are chargeable against the debtor incurred in the money attachment;

   (b) any interest which has accrued, at the day on which the money attachment was executed, on the sum for payment for which the charge was served;

   (c) any sum for payment of which that charge was served together with such interest as has accrued after the day the money attachment was executed.

GENERAL NOTE

  This section deals with ascription, or payments to account. While money attachment is in effect, any payments to account are directed first towards paying the expenses of executing the money attachment. Thereafter they are directed to the interest on the principal sum sued for as at the date of execution and finally towards the principal sum and any interest arising after the date of execution (subss.(1) and (2)).

198. Interpretation

(1) In this Part-

"decree" has the meaning given by section 221 of this Act, being a decree which, or an extract of which, authorises money attachment;

"document of debt" has the meaning given by section 221 of this Act, being a document which, or an extract of which, authorises money attachment;

"dwellinghouse" has the same meaning as in section 45 of the 2002 Act;

"judicial officer" means the judicial officer appointed by the creditor;

"money" has the meaning given by section 175 of this Act;

"payment order" has the meaning given by section 183(2) of this Act;

"schedule of money attachment" has the meaning given by section 179(1) of this Act; and

"sum recoverable by the money attachment" has the meaning given by section 177(1) of this Act.

(2) The Scottish Ministers may by order modify the definitions of "decree" and "document of debt" in subsection (1) above by-

  (a) adding types of decree or document to;

  (b) removing types of decree or document from; or

  (c) varying the description of,

the types of decree or document to which those definitions apply.

(3) Where-

  (a) a schedule, report or statement under this Part of this Act requires to be signed; and

  (b) provision is made by virtue of this Part of this Act or by any other enactment permitting the schedule, report or statement to be an electronic communication,

the requirement is satisfied by a certified electronic signature.

GENERAL NOTE

  This deals with various definitions and permits the report, schedule and statement to be sent in electronically with a certified electronic signature.

PART 9

DILIGENCE AGAINST EARNINGS

GENERAL NOTE

This part came into force on April 1, 2008.

The purpose of the sections within this Part is to tidy up some anomalies that over time have become apparent within the operation of the 1987 Act. The first of these deals with the priority of an earnings arrestment over a current maintenance arrestment: the new rule is that where a debtor's net earnings are insufficient to pay both of these simultaneously, the earnings arrestment no longer has priority and both it and the current maintenance rank equally, so that the ordinary creditors do not benefit at the expense of the debtor's family.

The next deals with deductions where net earnings include holiday pay. This deals with the practice whereby workers, and particularly workers on piece work, were not given time off, but given money within their ordinary pay which represented holiday pay for holidays that they might or might not be able to take. From an employer's point of view, this saved the employer having to pay employees while they were on holiday. It was particularly convenient for employers who would hire employees for a certain period of time to complete a project, then disengage them, and then perhaps hire them again later should another project become available. From the employee's point of view it was less desirable, since he was effectively not getting any paid holiday and no time to rest, contrary to Directive 2003/88 (Working Time Directive) Art.7. See also *Robinson-Steele v RD Retail Services Ltd; Clarke v Frank Staddon Ltd; Caulfield and Others v Hanson Clay Products Ltd* [2006], ICR 932, ECJ, (Cases (C-131) and (257/04)), (2005 September 15, October 27 and 2006 March 16). As a result of this case and subsequent direction from the DBERR, rolled up holiday pay, while not completely forbidden, is really only possible where it is agreed between the employer and the employee and the arrangements are entirely transparent and comprehensible. As a result of this, it is probable that the holiday pay arrangements in the 2007 Act at s.200 will not be used much. A further reason the section will not be used much is that most debtors who are in full time employment and receiving wages or salary do not receive holiday pay anyway.

Formerly, for the purposes of an earnings arrestment, the normal earnings and holiday pay, if paid on the same day, would be aggregated, which could lead to a larger than expected amount being taken from the aggregated pay and leaving the debtor's family much less holiday money than might have been anticipated. The new arrangements change this, so that there are now separate calculations for ordinary pay and holiday pay which reduce the overall amount deducted.

There are provisions to ensure the delivery of a debt information and advice package to debtors suffering an earnings arrestment, and there are provisions to ensure that employers provide creditors and where appropriate sheriff clerks with information about any employees subject to earnings arrestments, current maintenance arrestements or conjoined arrestment orders, and also tell the creditors and sheriff clerks about any employees so subject who are leaving their employment. There are sanctions for the failure to provide this information. Where possible, the debtors should also indicate who their new employers are. There appear not to be any sanctions for the debtor's failure to provide that information.

199. Simultaneous operation of arrestments against earnings where net earnings insufficient

(1) In section 58 of the 1987 Act (simultaneous operation of earnings arrestment and current maintenance arrestment), for subsection (2) substitute-

   (2) If on any pay-day N is less than S, the employer shall operate both the earnings arrestment and the current maintenance arrestment in accordance with subsection (3) below.

   (3) The employer shall-

(a) for the purposes of section 47(1) of this Act, deduct the sum equal to-

$$N \times {}^E/_S; \text{ and}$$

(b) for the purposes of section 51(1) of this Act, deduct the sum equal to-

$$N \times {}^C/_S.$$

(4) In subsections (2) and (3) above-

N is the amount of any net earnings in so far as they exceed the sum mentioned in subsection (2)(b) of section 53 of this Act for the number of days mentioned in subsection (2)(a) of that section;

E is the sum which the employer is required to deduct under section 47(1) of this Act;

C is the sum which the employer is required to deduct under section 51(1) of this Act; and

S is the total of E and C.".

(2) In section 63(5)(b) of that Act (sum payable under conjoined arrestment order including both ordinary debts and current maintenance), for "all the debts were current maintenance" substitute "the only debts were the current maintenance debts".

(3) In Schedule 3 to that Act (disbursement under conjoined arrestment order)-

(a) in paragraph 4, for the words from "priority" to the end substitute "disbursement shall be in accordance with paragraph 4A below."; and

(b) after that paragraph, insert-

"**4A** Where-

(a) only one of the debts is an ordinary debt, the creditor in that debt shall be paid the sum equal to-

$$D \times {}^E/_S;$$

(b) more than one of the debts is an ordinary debt, each of the creditors in those debts, out of the sum mentioned in sub-paragraph (a) above, shall be paid the same proportion of the amount of that creditor's debt;

(c) only one of the debts is current maintenance, the creditor in that debt shall be paid the sum equal to-

$$D \times {}^C/_S;$$

(d) more than one of the debts is current maintenance, each of the creditors in those debts, out of the sum mentioned in sub-paragraph (c) above, shall be paid the same proportion of the amount of that creditor's debt,

where-

D is the sum deducted under subsection (5) of section 63 of this Act;

E is the sum deducted under paragraph (a) of that subsection;

C is the sum which would, if the only debts were the current maintenance debts, be deducted under subsection (3) of that section; and

S is the total of E and C.".

DEFINITIONS

"Current maintenance arrestment": 1987 Act s.46(1)(b)
"Conjoined arrestment order": 1987 Act s.46(1)9(c)
"Earnings arrestment": 1987 Act s.46(1)(a)
"Net earnings": 1987 Act s.73

GENERAL NOTE

Subsection (1) deletes the existing subs.(2) of and inserts new subss.(2), (3) and (4) into s.58 of the 1987 Act. That section provided for the priority of an earnings arrestment over a current maintenance arrestment if the debtor's earnings were insufficient to satisfy both. The new provisions, by the exercise of the formula indicated in subs.(3) of s.58, permit the two arrestments to rank equally so that they abate in proportion to each other as opposed to the earnings arrestment getting most of the net earnings and current maintenance arrestment getting whatever was left over. The previous arrangements were clearly unsatisfactory for debtors' families even if perhaps the original intention was that the debtors' debts would be cleared more quickly than otherwise might be the case.

Subsection (2) makes a minor change to the wording of s.63(5)(b) to make it clearer how the debtor's employer is to calculate the sum to be deducted where a conjoined arrestment order is in effect.

Subsection (3) makes changes to the way in which a sheriff clerk (in terms of Sch.3 of the 1987 Act) divides up the monies sent to him by way of a conjoined arrestment order. Hitherto the ordinary debts (these being the ones recoverable by earnings arrestment) had priority: now they are to be treated in the same manner with any current maintenance so that they rank equally and abate proportionally.

200. Arrestment of earnings: deductions from holiday pay

(1) In section 47(1) of the 1987 Act (general effect of earnings arrestment), after "section 49" insert "or 49A".

(2) In section 49(1) of that Act (method of calculating deduction from earnings), at the beginning insert "Subject to section 49A of this Act,".

(3) After section 49 of that Act, insert-

"49A Deductions where net earnings include holiday pay

(1) This section applies where-

(a) the debtor's earnings are paid at regular intervals; and

(b) on one pay-day (in this section, the "normal pay-day") there are paid to the debtor both-

(i) earnings normally payable on that pay-day (in this section, "normal earnings"); and

(ii) earnings such as are mentioned in subsection (2) below (in this section, "holiday pay").

(2) Holiday pay is earnings which-

(a) are paid in respect of a period of annual leave or public holiday; and

      (b) would, were they not paid in respect of such leave or holiday, have been paid on a pay-day other than the normal pay-day.

(3) In arriving at the sum to be deducted under section 47 of this Act on the normal pay-day, subsections (4) to (8) below shall apply.

(4) Calculate in accordance with section 49 of this Act the sum, if any, which would be deducted from the normal earnings if the holiday pay had no. been paid on the normal pay-day.

(5) Where-

      (a) the debtor's normal earnings are payable weekly, monthly or at regular intervals of a whole number of weeks or months; and

      (b) all of the holiday pay relates to a whole number of weeks or months,

the sum, if any, to be deducted from the holiday pay shall be the sum arrived at by applying sub-paragraphs (i) to (iii) of section 49(1)(c) of this Act to the holiday pay as if it were the net earnings mentioned in that sub-paragraph (i).

(6) Where the debtor's normal earnings are payable weekly, monthly or at regular intervals of a whole number of weeks or months but part of the holiday pay relates to a whole number of weeks or months and part does not, the sum, if any, to be deducted from the holiday pay shall be the sum arrived at by-

      (a) in relation to the part of the holiday pay which relates to a whole number of weeks or months, applying subsection (5) above to that part;

      (b) in relation to the part of the holiday pay which does not relate to a whole number of weeks or months, applying paragraphs (a) to (c) of section 49(2) of this Act to that part of the holiday pay as if it were the net earnings mentioned in that paragraph (a); and

      (c) aggregating the sums arrived at as mentioned in paragraphs (a) and (b) above.

(7) Where-

      (a) the debtor's normal earnings are payable weekly, monthly or at regular intervals of a whole number of weeks or months but none of the holiday relates to such a whole number of weeks or months; or

      (b) the debtor's normal earnings are payable at regular intervals other than at intervals to which paragraph (a) above applies,

the sum, if any, to be deducted from the holiday pay shall be arrived at by applying paragraph (b) of subsection (6) above to the holiday pay.

(8) Aggregate-

      (a) the deduction, if any, calculated under subsection (4) above; and

      (b) the deduction, if any, calculated under subsection (5), (6) or, as the case may be, (7) above.".

GENERAL NOTE

This section, which inserts a new s.49A into the 1987 Act, deals with the situation where a debtor receives, by way of his wages or salary or other earnings ("earnings"), on the one day two payments, one representing his "normal earnings" payable on that payday, and the other representing "holiday pay", which is designed to be paid in respect of public holidays or annual leave. Should his earnings be subject to deductions by his employer for, say, an earnings arrestment or a current maintenance arrestment, the normal earnings and holiday pay are aggregated and the relevant amount is deducted in accordance with the provisions of Sch.B of the 1987 Act. This indicates, broadly, that a debtor earning little has less deducted and paid towards his debts than a debtor earning a good deal, who has to pay a higher proportion towards his debts. So a debtor receiving both normal earnings and holiday pay would unexpectedly pay a higher proportion than he would if he were merely receiving his normal pay.

However, this is now changed.

What is now deducted is the amount that would normally be deducted from his normal net earnings as if there were no holiday pay (subs.(4)). To that will be added a sum, to be deducted from his holiday pay, as if the holiday pay were ordinary net earnings (subs.(5)). This means that a lower proportion of both the normal earnings and the holiday pay is deducted than would be the case if the two payments were aggregated.

The remaining subsections deal with essentially the same point, but taking account of the situation where the holiday pay relates to some but not all, of a whole number of weeks (if paid wages) or months (if paid a salary), or no whole number, in the same manner as in s.49(2), so that the appropriate deduction corresponds to the whole number of weeks or months plus the relevant proportion for the part of the week or the part of the month.

The effect of all this is that less is overall deducted from the debtor's earnings than under the previous arrangement, and he has more money for his holiday, but he takes longer to pay off his debt.

201. Provision of debt advice and information package

(1) In section 47 of the 1987 Act (general effect of earnings arrestment)-

  (a) in subsection (2)(a), after "shall" insert ", subject to subsection (3) below,"; and

  (b) after subsection (2) insert-

    "(3) An earnings arrestment shall not come into effect unless, no earlier than 12 weeks before the date on which the earnings arrestment schedule is served, the creditor has provided the debtor with a debt advice and information package.

    (4) In this section and in sections 51(2A) and 60(3A) of this Act, "debt advice and information package" means the debt advice and information package referred to in section 10(5) of the Debt Arrangement and Attachment (Scotland) Act 2002 (asp 17).".

(2) In section 51 of that Act (general effect of current maintenance arrestment)-

  (a) in subsection (2)(a), after "shall" insert ", subject to subsection (2A) below,"; and

  (b) after subsection (2) insert-

    "(2A) A current maintenance arrestment shall not come into effect unless, no earlier than 12 weeks before the date on which the current maintenance arrestment schedule is served, the creditor has provided the debtor with a debt advice and information package.".

(3) In section 60 of that Act (conjoined arrestment orders), after subsection (3) insert-

"(3A) It shall not be competent to make a conjoined arrestment order unless, no earlier than 12 weeks before the date of the application under subsection (2) above, the creditor has provided the debtor with a debt advice and information package.".

(4) In section 73(1) of that Act (interpretation), after the definition of "current maintenance" insert-

""debt advice and information package" has the meaning given by section 47(4) of this Act;".

DEFINITIONS

"Current maintenance arrestment": 1987 Act s.46(1)(b)
"Conjoined arrestment order": 1987 Act s.46(1)9(c)
"Debt advice and information package": 2002 Act s.10(5)
"Earnings arrestment": 1987 Act s.46(1)(a)

GENERAL NOTE

This inserts provisions into s.47 of the 1987 Act to the effect that not more than 12 weeks before any earnings arrestment schedule or current maintenance arrestment is served, the debtor must be given a debt advice and information package.

Likewise, not more than 12 weeks before a conjoined arrestment order is made, the debtor must receive the same package.

202. Intimation of arrestment schedule

(1) Section 70 of the 1987 Act is amended as follows.
(2) In subsection (1), for the words ", if reasonably practicable," substitute "take all reasonably practicable steps to".
(3) After subsection (4), insert-

"(4A) An employer on whom an earnings arrestment schedule or a current maintenance arrestment schedule is served shall, as soon as is reasonably practicable-

(a) intimate a copy of it to the debtor; and
(b) notify the debtor of-
    (i) the date on which the first deduction is made; and
    (ii) the sum so deducted.

(4B) An employer on whom a copy of a conjoined arrestment order is served shall, as soon as is reasonably practicable, notify the debtor of the matters mentioned in sub-paragraphs (i) and (ii) of subsection (4A)(b) above.".

GENERAL NOTE

This makes a slight change to s.70 of the 1987 Act. The judicial officer is required, not just to serve a copy of an earnings arrestment schedule or current maintenance schedule to a debtor "if reasonably practicable" but to undertake the more demanding and arguably more effective role of taking all reasonably practicable steps to provide the debtor with the copy of the appropriate schedule. This is presumably because there must have been a suspicion that some sheriff officers or messengers at arms, as they then were, were not as diligent as they might have been in intimating the copy to the debtor, so that when he founds his wages were being deducted, it came as a surprise to him. Secondly, an employer of a debtor and on whom an earnings arrestment or current maintenance arrestment has been served in respect of his debtor-employee must intimate a copy of the appropriate arrestment on the debtor and tell him when the deductions from his earnings will begin and how much will be deducted. Similar rules will apply where there is a conjoined arrestment order.

203. Provision of information

After section 70 of the 1987 Act, insert-

"70A Employer's duty to provide information

(1) Where an employer receives, in relation to a debtor-

(a) an earnings arrestment schedule;

(b) a current maintenance arrestment schedule; or

(c) a copy of a conjoined arrestment order,

the employer shall, as soon as is reasonably practicable, send to the creditor or, in the case of a conjoined arrestment order, the sheriff clerk, the information mentioned in subsection (3) below.

(2) The employer shall, provided the debt has not been extinguished, send, on or as soon as is reasonably practicable after the dates mentioned in subsection (4) below, to the creditor or, as the case may be, the sheriff clerk the information mentioned in subsection (3) below.

(3) The information referred to in subsection (1) above is-

(a) how the debtor is paid (whether weekly, monthly or otherwise);

(b) the date of the debtor's pay-day next following-

(i) where subsection (1) above applies, receipt of the schedule or order; or

(ii) where subsection (2) above applies, the date mentioned in subsection (4) below;

(c) the sum deducted on that pay-day and the net earnings from which it is so deducted; and

(d) any other information which the Scottish Ministers may, by regulations, prescribe.

(4) The dates referred to in subsection (2) above are-

(a) the later of-

(i) 6 April next following receipt of the schedule or order; or

(ii) the day falling 6 months after receiving the schedule or order; and

(b) each 6 April thereafter.

(5) Notwithstanding subsections (1) and (2) above, the employer shall, if the debtor ceases for whatever reason to be employed by the employer, give notice, as soon as is reasonably practicable, to the creditor or, as the case may be, the sheriff clerk-

(a) of that fact; and

(b) in so far as is known to the employer, the name and address of any new employer of the debtor.

(6) Where an employer sends information under subsection (1) or (2) above or gives notice under subsection (5) above, the employer shall, as soon as is reasonably practicable, send a copy of that information or notice to the debtor.

70B Failure to give notice under section 70A(5)

(1) Where an employer fails without reasonable excuse to give notice under section 70A(5) of this Act, the sheriff may, on

the application of any creditor, make an order requiring the employer-

(a) to provide such information as is known to the employer as to the debtor's employment after ceasing to be employed by that employer;

(b) to pay to the creditor an amount not exceeding twice the sum which the employer would have been required to deduct on the debtor's next payday had the debtor still been employed by that employer.

(2) Where a sum is paid by virtue of an order under subsection (1)(b) above-

(a) the debt owed by the debtor to the creditor shall be reduced by that sum; and

(b) the employer shall not be entitled to recover that sum from the debtor.

(3) An employer aggrieved by an order under subsection (1) above may, before the expiry of the period of 14 days beginning with the day on which the order is made, appeal, on point of law only, to the sheriff principal, whose decision shall be final.

70C   Creditor's duty to provide information

(1) A creditor who is receiving payment from a debtor by virtue of-

(a) an earnings arrestment;

(b) a current maintenance arrestment; or

(c) a conjoined arrestment order,

shall, provided the debt has not been extinguished, send, on or as soon as is reasonably practicable after the dates mentioned in subsection (2) below, to the employer or, in the case of a conjoined arrestment order, the sheriff clerk the information mentioned in subsection (3) below.

(2) The dates referred to in subsection (1) above are-

(a) the later of-

(i) 6 April next following service of the schedule of arrestment or, as the case may be, order; or

(ii) the day falling 6 months after the service of the schedule or order; and

(b) each 6 April thereafter.

(3) The information referred to in subsection (1) above is-

(a) the sum owed by the debtor to the creditor;

(b) the amounts received by the creditor by virtue of the arrestment or order; and

(c) the dates of payment of those amounts.

70D   Debtor's duty to provide information

Where a debtor ceases to be employed by an employer who is deducting sums under this Part of this Act, the debtor shall give notice to the creditor or, where those sums are being deducted by virtue of a conjoined arrestment order, the sheriff clerk-

(a) of that fact; and

(b) of the name and address of any new employer.".

GENERAL NOTE

This inserts new s.70A-D into the 1987 Act.

Section 70A

DEFINITIONS

"Current maintenance arrestment": 1987 Act s.46(1)(b)
"Conjoined arrestment order": 1987 Act s.46(1)9(c)
"Earnings arrestment": 1987 Act s.46(1)(a)

This requires an employer to tell a creditor (in respect of an earnings arrestment or current maintenance arrestment) or the sheriff clerk (in respect of a conjoined arrestment order) both initially straight after on receipt, and at the later of the beginning of each tax year or six months after receiving the appropriate schedule or order, and at the beginning of each tax year thereafter, the information contained in subs.(3). The information required is how the debtor is paid, his next payday, the sum deducted and his net earnings.

Should the debtor-employee leave his job, the employer is required to inform the creditor or sheriff clerk as the case may be of this fact, and pass on so far as is known the name and address of the debtor's new employer (subs.(5)). A copy of any letter to this effect must also be sent to the debtor (subs.(6)).

Section 70B

This is the sanction to be used against the employer should he not send on the required information under subs.(5) of the previous section. If the employer has no reasonable excuse for this, the sheriff, on the creditor's application, may order the employer to provide such information as he has about the debtor's new employment, if any, and to pay the creditor a sum equal to twice the normal deduction that the employer would have deducted had the debtor still been employed (subs.(1)). This reduces the debtor's debt and is not recoverable from the debtor (subs.(2)). The employer may appeal to the sheriff principal on this matter but only within 14 days, and only on a point of law (subs.(3)).

This section does not apply to the Queen (see s.105 of the 1987 Act as amended by para.16(13)(c) of Sch.5 to the 2007 Act) in her capacity as an employer.

Section 70C

DEFINITIONS

"Current maintenance arrestment": 1987 Act s.46(1)(b)
"Conjoined arrestment order": 1987 Act s.46(1)9(c)
"Earnings arrestment": 1987 Act s.46(1)(a)

The duty in s.70A is not one way. The creditor must inform the employer or as appropriate the sheriff clerk at the later of the beginning of each tax year or six months after the service of the schedule of arrestment or order, and at the beginning of each tax year thereafter, of the sum owed by the debtor, the amounts he has received and the dates of payments of those amounts.

Section 70D

The debtor also has to keep the creditor or the sheriff clerk, as the case may be, informed of any change of employment, but there are no penalties for his failure to do so.

204. Conjoined arrestment orders: jurisdiction

In section 73(1) of the 1987 Act (interpretation of Part 3 of that Act), in paragraph (c) of the definition of "sheriff", for the words from "the" where it second occurs to the end substitute-

> "(i) the place where the debtor is principally employed;
>
> (ii) where that place is outside Scotland, any other place where the debtor is employed; or
>
> (iii) where neither sub-paragraph (i) nor sub-paragraph (ii) above applies, the place where the debtor is domiciled.".

GENERAL NOTE

This section extends the jurisdiction of the sheriff referred to in s.73(1)(c) of the 1987 Act. References to the sheriff in particular sections of the 1987 Act are to the sheriff who has jurisdiction over:

(a)   the principal place of employment of the debtor;
(b)   where that principal place of employment is outwith Scotland, any other place of employment in Scotland; or
(c)   where neither of the above apply, the debtor's domicile.

205.   Arrestment of seamen's wages

In section 73 of the 1987 Act (interpretation of Part 3 of that Act), subsections (3)(c) and (4) are repealed.

GENERAL NOTE

Because of s.73(3)(c) of the 1987 Act, the wages of seamen (other than fishermen) were not treated as earnings for the purposes of earnings arrestments under the 1987 Act, though they could be subject to a current maintenance arrestment. This is now repealed and seamen are no longer exempt. As they are exempt there is no longer any need for s.73(4), so it too is repealed.

PART 10

ARRESTMENT IN EXECUTION AND ACTION OF FURTHCOMING

GENERAL NOTE

Arrestment is the diligence appropriate for seizing the debtor's assets in the hands of a third party. A more legalistic definition under the common law would be that is the diligence used by creditor (formerly known as the "arrester") to attach:

i   any obligations of a third party (the "arrestee") to account to a debtor (the "common debtor"); or
ii   any corporeal moveables in the hands of an arrestee.

In practice, the most common occasion for arrestment is the arrestment of a debtor's bank account, effectively freezing the account, so that the debtor is unable to withdraw any money from the account, and the bank, as the arrestee, is not allowed to pay any money from the account to the debtor or anyone else until the arrestment is lifted. The arrestment is generally lifted by the debtor agreeing to sign a mandate authorising the bank to pay the required amount to the creditor. This has the virtue of being cheaper for the debtor than the alternative, which is for the creditor to go to court after the successful arrestment and to raise an action of furthcoming. The decree of furthcoming allows the arrestee to pay the required amount out of the debtor's bank account to the creditor. The 2007 Act introduces a method of automatic furthcoming for arrested funds (see s.73J of the 1987 as inserted by s.206 of the 2007 Act).

The second common type of arrestment is the arrestment of corporeal moveable assets in the hands of a third party. A good example would be the arrestment of the debtor's spare furniture stored in a depositary. The judicial officers would prevent the depositary returning the furniture to the debtor, until either a mandate was signed permitting the creditor to receive such furniture as will cover the debtor's debt or a decree in an action of sale in execution was granted.

There are many other examples of assets that may be subject to arrestment, and they include such assets as the proceeds of an insurance policy arrested in the hands of the insurance company, dividends on shares, interest on deposit accounts, rent, partnership interests, any liability to account, and legitim. What are not arrestable are articles in the hands of the debtor himself (since attachment would be the proper diligence) or, at least under the common law, in the hands of those identified with him, such as his servants, his wife, his factor. A *spes successionis* is not arrestable, and neither is any payment from the Government (such as social security benefits) (Social Security Act 1975 s.87(1)). Assets that may not be attached in terms of the 1987 Act s.16 may also not be arrested (see 1987 Act s.99), namely the tools of the debtor's trade, essential items for the maintenance of his family, essential furniture, etc.

In practice, arrestment is only useful and financially worthwhile for the creditor where the creditor has:

(a) a good knowledge of the debtor's assets and where they might be (other than in the debtor's home or business premises);

(b) knowledge of the debtor's bank account (assuming it is not overdrawn, which in many cases it will be); and

(c) a debtor who is not astute enough to remove any funds from his bank account ahead of any arrestment.

The new provisions, to be discussed shortly, require a charge to be served on a debtor before execution of arrestment this may well alert a streetwise debtor to the need to empty his bank account, or at least to reduce it to the unarrestable minimum.

The 2007 Act puts on a statutory basis some parts of the common law, in particular the arrestment of the debtor's funds, and makes the law more intelligible by the use of the words "creditor" and "debtor" rather than arrester and common debtor. It protects a minimum bank balance in the debtor's account. It also introduces an opportunity to remedy the position for the debtor where the operation of arrestment would be "unduly harsh" (s.73Q). This will replace the common law rules whereby arrestments could be set aside on the grounds that the arrestments were "nimious and oppressive", "nimious" being from the Latin word *nimius* meaning "excessive". The thrust of the 2007 Act is primarily towards protecting the debtor from rapacious creditors: what is not addressed is any means of making arrestment, well known for being (from the creditor's point of view) a very hit and miss affair, a more practical and effective diligence. The Act does not deal with arrestment to found jurisdiction which is the method whereby a debtor who is not otherwise subject to the jurisdiction of the Scottish courts may arrest the debtor's assets in Scotland in order to permit the creditor to raise an action in Scotland against the debtor. The common law will continue to apply to that. The arrestment of a debtor's corporeal assets to be followed by action of sale still also remains predominantly governed by the common law.

Part 6 of this Act deals with arrestment on the dependence.

There are provisions in para.16 of Sch.5 of the 2007 Act to insert various amendments to the 1987 Act Pt 1 to permit the debtor to apply for time to pay directions and time to pay orders to stay the operation of any arrestment, particularly if the arrestment has not proceeded to furthcoming, or in the case of automatic furthcoming, within the first 8 of the 14 weeks required before automatic furthcoming.

For a useful discussion on the common law of arrestment generally, see Wilson, *Debt*, W. Green, 2nd edn, 1991, Ch.17.

206. Arrestment in execution

After section 73 of the 1987 Act, insert-

"PART 3A

ARRESTMENT AND ACTION OF FURTHCOMING

73A Arrestment and action of furthcoming to proceed only on decree or document of debt

(1) Arrestment and action of furthcoming or sale shall be competent only in execution of-

    (a) subject to subsection (2) below, a decree; or

    (b) a document of debt.

(2) Arrestment and action of furthcoming or sale in execution of a summary warrant shall be competent only if-

    (a) the debtor has been charged to pay the debt due by virtue of the summary warrant; and

(b) the period for payment specified in the charge has expired without payment being made.

(3) Any rule of law, having effect immediately before the coming into force of this section, as to the decrees or documents on which arrestment and action of furthcoming or sale can proceed shall, in so far as inconsistent with this section, cease to have effect.

(4) In this Part of this Act-

"decree" means-

    (a) a decree of the Court of Session, of the High Court of Justiciary or of the sheriff;

    (b) a decree of the Court of Teinds;

    (c) a summary warrant;

    (d) a civil judgment granted outside Scotland by a court, tribunal or arbiter which by virtue of any enactment or rule of law is enforceable in Scotland;

    (e) an order or determination which by virtue of any enactment is enforceable as if it were an extract registered decree arbitral bearing a warrant for execution issued by the sheriff;

    (f) a warrant granted, in criminal proceedings, for enforcement by civil diligence; or

    (g) a liability order within the meaning of section 33(2) of the Child Support Act 1991 (c.48),

being a decree, warrant, judgment, order or determination which, or an extract of which, authorises arrestment and action of furthcoming or sale; and

"document of debt" means-

    (a) a document registered for execution in the Books of Council and Session or the sheriff court books; or

    (b) a document or settlement which by virtue of an Order in Council under section 13 of the Civil Jurisdiction and Judgments Act 1982 (c.27) is enforceable in Scotland,

being a document or settlement which, or an extract of which, authorises arrestment and action of furthcoming or sale.

(5) The Scottish Ministers may, by order, modify the definitions of "decree" and "document of debt" in subsection (4) above so as to-

    (a) add or remove types of decree or document to or, as the case may be, from those referred to in that provision; or

    (b) vary any of the descriptions of the types of decree or document there referred to.

73B Schedule of arrestment to be in prescribed form

(1) This section applies where a creditor arrests in execution of-

    (a) a decree and the creditor has not executed an arrestment on the dependence of the action; or

    (b) a document of debt.

(2) The schedule of arrestment used in executing the arrestment shall be in (or as nearly as may be in) the form prescribed by the Scottish Ministers by regulations.

73C   Arrestment on the dependence followed by decree

(1) This section applies where a creditor obtains a decree (in this Part of this Act referred to as a "final decree") in an action on the dependence of which the creditor has executed an arrestment.

(2) The creditor shall, as soon as reasonably practicable, serve a copy of that final decree, in (or as nearly as may be in) the form prescribed by Act of Sederunt, on the arrestee.

73D   Debt advice and information

(1) This section applies where-
(a) a creditor-
   (i) obtains a final decree in an action on the dependence of which the creditor has executed an arrestment; or
   (ii) arrests in execution of a decree or document of debt; and
(b) the debtor is an individual.

(2) The creditor shall, during the period of 48 hours beginning with the time at which the copy of the final decree is served under section 73C(2) of this Act or, as the case may be, the time at which the schedule of arrestment is served, provide the debtor with a debt advice and information package.

(3) Where the creditor fails to comply with subsection (2) above, the arrestment shall cease to have effect or, as the case may be, shall be incompetent.

(4) In this section, "debt advice and information package" has the meaning given by section 47(4) of this Act.

73E   Funds attached

(1) Subsections (2) to (5) below apply-
(a) where a creditor arrests in execution of-
   (i) a decree and the creditor has not executed an arrestment on the dependence of the action; or
   (ii) a document of debt; and
(b) only to the extent that the arrestee holds funds due to the debtor the value of which, at the time the arrestment is executed, is or can be ascertained (whether or not that arrestee also holds other moveable property of the debtor).

(2) Subject to subsection (4) below and to section 73F of this Act, the funds mentioned in subsection (1)(b) above attached by the arrestment shall be the lesser of-
(a) the sum due by the arrestee to the debtor; or
(b) the aggregate of-
   (i) the principal sum, in relation to which the decree or document is executed, owed by the debtor to the creditor;

      (ii) any judicial expenses chargeable against the debtor by virtue of the decree;

      (iii) the expenses of executing the arrestment;

      (iv) interest on the principal sum up to and including the date of service of the schedule of arrestment;

      (v) the interest on the principal sum which would be accrued in the period of 1 year beginning with the day after the date mentioned in sub-paragraph (iv) above;

      (vi) any interest on the expenses of executing the arrestment which is chargeable against the debtor; and

      (vii) any sum prescribed under subsection (3) below.

(3) The Scottish Ministers may, by regulations, prescribe a sum which appears to them to be reasonable having regard to the average expenses likely to be incurred and chargeable against a debtor in a typical action of furthcoming.

(4) Where-

    (a) the arrestee holds both funds due to and other moveable property of the debtor; and

    (b) the sum mentioned in paragraph (b) of subsection (2) above exceeds the sum mentioned in paragraph (a) of that subsection,

the arrestment shall, in addition to the funds equal to the sum mentioned in that paragraph (a), attach the whole moveable property so held.

(5) Except as provided for in subsection (4) above, an arrestment to which this section applies shall not attach any moveable property of the debtor other than the sum attached under subsection (2) above.

(6) Where, in a case to which subsections (2) to (5) above apply-

    (a) in addition to the funds mentioned in subsection (1)(b) above, the arrestee holds funds due to the debtor the value of which is not or cannot be ascertained; and

    (b) the sum mentioned in paragraph (a) of subsection (2) above exceeds the sum mentioned in paragraph (b) of that subsection,

the arrestment shall not attach any of the funds mentioned in paragraph (a) above.

73F Protection of minimum balance in certain bank accounts

(1) Subject to subsection (2) below, this section applies where-

    (a) a creditor arrests-

      (i) in pursuance of a warrant granted for diligence on the dependence of an action; or

      (ii) in execution of a decree or document of debt;

    (b) the arrestment attaches funds standing to the credit of a debtor in an account held by a bank or other financial institution; and

    (c) the debtor is an individual.

(2) This section does not apply where the account is-

(a) held in the name of a company, a limited liability partnership, a partnership or an unincorporated association; or

(b) operated by the debtor as a trading account.

(3) The arrestment shall-

(a) in a case where the sum standing to the credit of the debtor exceeds the sum mentioned in subsection (4) below, attach only the balance above that sum; and

(b) in any other case, attach no funds.

(4) The sum referred to in subsection (3)(a) above is the sum first mentioned in column 1 of Table B in Schedule 2 to this Act (being the sum representing the net monthly earnings from which no deduction would be made under an earnings arrestment were such an arrestment in effect).

(5) In subsection (1) above, "bank or other financial institution" means-

(a) the Bank of England;

(b) a person who has permission under Part 4 of the Financial Services and Markets Act 2000 (c.8) to accept deposits;

(c) an EEA firm of the kind mentioned in paragraph 5(b) of Schedule 3 to that Act which has permission under paragraph 15 of that schedule (as a result of qualifying for authorisation under paragraph 12 of that schedule) to accept deposits; or

(d) a person who is exempt from the general prohibition in respect of accepting deposits as a result of an exemption order made under section 38(1) of that Act,

and the expressions in this definition shall be read with section 22 of that Act, any relevant order made under that section and Schedule 2 to that Act.

(6) The Scottish Ministers may, by regulations-

(a) modify subsection (2) above so as to-

(i) add or remove types of account to or, as the case may be, from those referred to in that paragraph; or

(ii) vary any of the descriptions of the types of account there referred to; and

(b) modify the definition of "bank or other financial institution" in subsection (5) above so as to-

(i) add or remove types of financial institution to or, as the case may be, from those referred to in that provision; or

(ii) vary any of the descriptions of the types of institution there referred to.

73G   Arrestee's duty of disclosure

(1) This section applies where a creditor arrests-

(a) in pursuance of a warrant granted for diligence on the dependence of an action; or

(b) in execution of a decree or document of debt.

(2) The arrestee shall, before the expiry of the period mentioned in subsection (3) below, send to the creditor in (or as nearly as may be in) the form prescribed by the

Scottish Ministers by regulations, the information mentioned in subsection (4) below.

(3) The period referred to in subsection (2) above is the period of 3 weeks beginning with the day on which the arrestment is executed.

(4) The information referred to in subsection (2) above is-

    (a) where any property, other than funds due to the debtor, is attached-

        (i) the nature of that property; and

        (ii) the value of it in so far as known to the arrestee; and

    (b) where any such funds are attached, the nature and value of those funds.

(5) The arrestee shall, at the same time as sending, under subsection (2) above, the information to the creditor, send a copy of it to-

    (a) the debtor; and

    (b) in so far as known to the arrestee, any person-

        (i) who owns or claims to own attached property; or

        (ii) to whom attached funds are or are claimed to be due,

solely or in common with the debtor.

73H   Failure to disclose information

(1) Where an arrestee fails without reasonable excuse to send the prescribed form under section 73G(2) of this Act, the sheriff may, on the application of the creditor, make an order requiring the arrestee to pay to the creditor-

    (a) the sum due to the creditor by the debtor; or

    (b) the sum mentioned in section 73F(4) of this Act,

whichever is the lesser.

(2) Where the arrestee fails to send the prescribed form in relation to an arrestment on the dependence of an action, the sheriff-

    (a) may not make an order under subsection (1) above until the creditor has served a copy of the final decree under section 73C(2) above; and

    (b) may deal with the failure as a contempt of court.

(3) Where a sum is paid by virtue of an order under subsection (1) above-

    (a) the debt owed by the debtor to the creditor shall be reduced by that sum; and

    (b) the arrestee shall not be entitled to recover that sum from the debtor.

(4) An arrestee aggrieved by an order under subsection (1) above may, before the expiry of the period of 2 weeks beginning with the day on which the order is made, appeal, on point of law only, to the sheriff principal, whose decision shall be final.

73J   Automatic release of arrested funds

(1) This section applies where-

    (a) a creditor-

(i) obtains a final decree in an action on the dependence of which the creditor has executed an arrestment; or

(ii) arrests in execution of a decree or document of debt; and

(b) the arrestment attaches funds which are due to the debtor (whether or not it also attaches other moveable property of the debtor).

(2) Subject to section 73L of this Act, the arrestee-

(a) shall, on the expiry of the period mentioned in subsection (3) below, release to the creditor, from the attached funds, a sum calculated in accordance with section 73K of this Act; and

(b) may, where a mandate authorises the arrestee to do so, release that sum before the expiry of that period.

(3) The period referred to in subsection (2) above is the period of 14 weeks beginning with the date of service of a copy of the final decree under section 73C(2) of this Act or, as the case may be, the date of service of the schedule of arrestment.

(4) In this section and in sections 73K to 73P of this Act, references to funds or sums due to or by any person do not include references to funds or sums due in respect of future or contingent debts.

73K   Sum released under section 73J(2)

The sum released under section 73J(2) of this Act is the lowest of-

(a) the sum attached by the arrestment;

(b) the sum due by the arrestee to the debtor; or

(c) the aggregate of-

(i) the principal sum, in relation to which the decree or document is executed or, as the case may be, which is decerned for in the final decree, owed by the debtor to the creditor;

(ii) any judicial expenses chargeable against the debtor by virtue of the decree or final decree;

(iii) the expenses of executing the arrestment;

(iv) interest on the principal sum up to and including the date of service of the schedule of arrestment or, as the case may be, the date of the final decree;

(v) the interest on the principal sum which would be accrued in the period beginning with the day after the date mentioned in sub-paragraph (iv) above and ending on the day on which the funds are released under section 73J(2) of this Act; and

(vi) any interest on the expenses of executing the arrestment which is chargeable against the debtor.

73L   Circumstances preventing automatic release

(1) No funds may be released under section 73J(2) of this Act where-

(a) a person mentioned in subsection (2) below applies, by notice of objection, to the sheriff under section 73M(1) of this Act;

(b) the debtor applies to the sheriff under section 73Q(2) of this Act;

(c) an action of multiplepoinding is raised in relation to the funds attached by the arrestment; or

(d) the arrestment is-

    (i) recalled;

    (ii) restricted; or

    (iii) otherwise ceases to have effect.

(2) The persons referred to in subsection (1)(a) above are-

(a) the debtor;

(b) the arrestee; and

(c) any other person to whom the funds are due solely or in common with the debtor (in this section and in sections 73M and 73N of this Act, the "third party").

73M   Notice of objection

(1) Where section 73J of this Act applies-

(a) the debtor;

(b) the arrestee; or

(c) a third party,

may, by notice of objection, apply to the sheriff for an order recalling or restricting the arrestment.

(2) The notice of objection referred to in subsection (1) above shall-

(a) be in (or as nearly as may be in) the form prescribed by Act of Sederunt;

(b) be given to the persons mentioned in subsection (3) below before the expiry of the period of 4 weeks beginning with the date of service of a copy of the final decree under section 73C(2) of this Act or, as the case may be, the date of service of the schedule of arrestment; and

(c) specify one or more of the grounds of objection mentioned in subsection (4) below.

(3) The persons referred to in subsection (2)(b) above are-

(a) the creditor;

(b) the sheriff clerk;

(c) the debtor or, as the case may be, the arrestee; and

(d) in so far as known to the person objecting, any third party.

(4) The grounds of objection referred to in subsection (2)(c) above are-

(a) the warrant in execution of which the arrestment was executed is invalid;

(b) the arrestment has been executed incompetently or irregularly;

(c) the funds attached are due to the third party solely or in common with the debtor.

(5) Where a person applies by notice of objection under subsection (1) above, that person may not, subject to subsection (6) below, raise-

(a) an action of multiplepoinding; or

(b) subject to subsection (7) below, any other proceedings,

in relation to the funds attached.

(6) Subsection (5) above is without prejudice to the right of the person-

(a) to enter any such action or proceedings raised by any other person; and

(b) to raise such an action or proceedings where the sheriff makes, under section 73N(5) of this Act, an order sisting the proceedings on the objection.

(7) A debtor who applies by notice of objection under subsection (1) above may apply to the sheriff under section 73Q(2) of this Act and, in such a case, the sheriff may deal with both applications at one hearing.

73N Hearings following notice of objection

(1) Subject to subsection (5) below, before the expiry of the period of 8 weeks beginning with the day on which an application by notice of objection is made under section 73M(1) of this Act, the sheriff shall hold a hearing to determine the objection.

(2) At the hearing under subsection (1) above, the sheriff shall not make any order without first giving-

(a) the creditor;

(b) the arrestee;

(c) the debtor; and

(d) any third party,

an opportunity to be heard.

(3) Where the sheriff upholds the objection, the sheriff may make an order recalling or restricting the arrestment.

(4) Where the sheriff rejects the objection, the sheriff may make an order requiring a sum determined in the order to be released to the creditor-

(a) in a case where the period mentioned in section 73J(3) of this Act has not expired, on the expiry of that period; or

(b) in any other case, as soon as reasonably practicable after the date on which the order is made.

(5) Where-

(a) the sheriff is satisfied that it is more appropriate for the matters raised at the hearing to be dealt with by-

(i) an action of multiplepoinding; or

(ii) other proceedings,

raised in relation to the funds attached; or

(b) at any time before a decision is made under subsections (3) or (4) above, such an action is or other proceedings are raised,

the sheriff shall make an order sisting the proceedings on the objection.

(6) The sheriff may make such other order as the sheriff thinks fit.

(7) Where the sheriff makes an order under this section, the sheriff shall order the person who objected to intimate that

order to such of the persons mentioned in subsection (2) above as the sheriff thinks fit.

(8) A person aggrieved by a decision of the sheriff under this section may, before the expiry of the period of 14 days beginning with the day on which the decision is made, appeal, on point of law only, to the sheriff principal, whose decision shall be final.

73P Arrestee not liable for funds released in good faith

Where an arrestee releases funds under section 73J(2) of this Act in good faith but-

(a) the warrant in execution of which the arrestment was executed is invalid; or

(b) the arrestment was incompetently or irregularly executed,

the arrestee is not liable to the debtor or to any other person having an interest in the funds for damages for patrimonial loss caused by the release of funds.

73Q Application for release of property where arrestment unduly harsh

(1) This section applies where-
    (a) a creditor-
        (i) obtains final decree in an action on the dependence of which the creditor executed an arrestment; or
        (ii) arrests in execution of a decree or document of debt; and
    (b) the arrestment attaches funds due to or other moveable property of the debtor.

(2) The debtor may apply to the sheriff for an order-
    (a) providing that the arrestment ceases to have effect in relation to-
        (i) the funds or other property attached; or
        (ii) so much of those funds or that property as the sheriff specifies; and
    (b) requiring the arrestee to release the funds or property to the debtor.

(3) An application under subsection (2) above shall be-
    (a) in (or as nearly as may be in) the form prescribed by Act of Sederunt;
    (b) made at any time during which the arrestment has effect; and
    (c) intimated to-
        (i) the creditor;
        (ii) the arrestee; and
        (iii) any other person appearing to have an interest.

73R Hearing on application under section 73Q for release of property

(1) At the hearing on an application under section 73Q(2) of this Act, the sheriff shall not make any order without first giving-
    (a) the creditor;

(b) the arrestee; and

(c) any other person appearing to the court to have an interest,

an opportunity to be heard.

(2) Subject to subsection (3) below, if the sheriff is satisfied that the arrestment is unduly harsh-

(a) to the debtor; or

(b) where the debtor is an individual, to any person such as is mentioned in subsection (4) below,

the sheriff shall make an order such as is mentioned in section 73Q(2) of this Act.

(3) Before making an order under subsection (2) above the sheriff shall have regard to all the circumstances including, in a case where the debtor is an individual and funds are attached-

(a) the source of those funds; and

(b) where the source of those funds is or includes earnings, whether an earnings arrestment, current maintenance arrestment or conjoined arrestment order is in effect in relation to those earnings.

(4) The persons referred to in subsection (2)(b) above are-

(a) a spouse of the debtor;

(b) a person living together with the debtor as husband and wife;

(c) a civil partner of the debtor;

(d) a person living with the debtor in a relationship which has the characteristics of the relationship between a husband and wife except that the person and the debtor are of the same sex;

(e) a child of the debtor under the age of 16 years, including-

(i) a stepchild; and

(ii) any child brought up or treated by the debtor or any person mentioned in paragraph (b), (c) or (d) above as a child of the debtor or, as the case may be, that person.

(5) Where the sheriff refuses to make an order under subsection (2) above, the sheriff may, in a case where funds are attached, make an order requiring a sum determined in the order to be released to the creditor-

(a) in a case where the period mentioned in section 73J(3) of this Act has not expired, on the expiry of that period; or

(b) in any other case, as soon as reasonably practicable after the date on which the order is made.

(6) Where the sheriff makes an order under this section, the sheriff shall order the debtor to intimate that order to the persons mentioned in subsection (1) above.

(7) A person aggrieved by a decision of the sheriff under this section may, before the expiry of the period of 14 days beginning with the day on which the decision is made, appeal, on point of law only, to the sheriff principal, whose decision shall be final.

73S Mandate to be in prescribed form

(1) A mandate authorising an arrestee to pay over any funds or hand over other property attached by an arrestment shall be in (or as nearly as may be in) the form prescribed by the Scottish Ministers by regulations.

(2) A mandate which is not in (or as nearly as may be in) the prescribed form is invalid.

(3) Where-

    (a) a mandate is invalid by virtue of subsection (2) above; but

    (b) the arrestee pays over funds or hands over other property in accordance with that mandate,

the arrestee is not liable to the debtor or to any other person having an interest in the funds or property for damages for patrimonial loss caused by paying over the funds or handing over the property provided the arrestee acted in good faith.

73T Arrestment of ships etc

For the avoidance of doubt, this Part of this Act does not apply to the arrestment of a ship, cargo or other maritime property.".

Section 73A

DEFINITIONS

"Decree": s.73A(4)

"Debt advice and information package": 2002 Act s.10(5)

"Document of debt": s.73A(4)

GENERAL NOTE

As with the other diligences discussed in the 2007 Act, arrestment is only competent in execution of a decree of a document of debt, the definitions of these words for the purpose of Pt 3A being given in subs.(4). Before arrestment and action of furthcoming or sale in execution of a summary warrant takes place, the debtor must be charged to pay the debt first and the period of charge must have expired (14 days if within the United Kingdom, 28 days otherwise) (subs.(2)). This is a change from the previous procedure, whereby summary warrants, which apply in the case of council tax, excise duty and tax generally, did not need a charge to be served on the debtor first. The reason for the change was that since summary warrants require no preliminary application to court, it was felt that the debtor could be taken unawares by a judicial officer arresting his bank account without, from the debtor's point of view, any prior warning. The service of a charge, it is thought, will emphasise the reality of the imminent action to be taken against him, the importance of the need to get help in dealing with his financial difficulties, and the need generally to pay his debts. In this he will be helped by the fact that the judicial officer will provide the debtor with a debt advice and information package. This should direct the debtor to useful sources of advice on how to deal with his debts. The requirement for a charge in execution of a summary warrant under s.73A(2) of the 1987 Act is the only part of this Part 10 of the 2002 Act that so far is in force (with effect from April 1, 2008).

Where there is no summary warrant (as with an ordinary decree) there is no need for a charge and arrestment may proceed forthwith.

Any rule of law concerning the type of decrees or documents of debt on which arrestment, furthcoming and sale in execution may proceed will cease to have effect if it is inconsistent with the Act (subs.(3)).

Section 73B

GENERAL NOTE

Where the creditor has obtained decree (without having executed an arrestment on the dependence of the action beforehand) and arrests the debtor's assets, or where the creditor arrests the debtor's assets in execution of an instrument of debt, a schedule of arrestment in a form yet to be devised must be used (subs.(1)(a)). This section does not make clear what is meant to be done with the schedule. This is odd, because as may be seen in the notes to the next section, generally this Act indicates who is to receive any such schedules. It is likely that the schedule is meant to be served on the debtor and possibly the arrestee, but s.73B does not state as much. Section 73D(2) implies that the schedule is served on the debtor, but there is no specific requirement to say that it must be served on the debtor. It may be that this is a matter that will have to be clarified in the regulations yet to be drafted and referred to in subs.(2), which allows the Scottish Ministers to design a new set of wording for an arrestment.

This may be all too necessary, for the current wording of arrestments is archaic in the extreme. The case of *Bremner v TSB (Scotland) Plc* 1993 SLT (Sh Ct) at p.3 refers to the wording of an arrestment as follows:

> *"... lawfully fenced and arrested in the hands of [the arrestee] the sum of [£] less or more, due and addebted by the said arrestee to [the common debtor] ... together with all horses, cattle, goods, gear, merchant-wear of all sorts, sums of money, rents of land and houses, and every other thing presently in their hands, custody and keeping pertaining and belonging to [the common debtor], all to remain in the hands of the said arrestee under sure fence and arrestment at the instance of the said pursuers, aye and until they shall be fully satisfied and paid the sums of [£], being the [details of the debt] ..."*

The schedule of arrestment, by exclusion (see subs.(1)(a)), will not be necessary where the debtor has already been subject to arrestment on the dependence of the same action.

Section 73C

GENERAL NOTE

Where the creditor has obtained a decree in an action (having previously executed arrestment on the dependence of that action), such a decree being known as a "final decree", he must serve a copy of that final decree on the debtor on a form yet to be devised. This was not required under the common law, where the previous execution of the arrestment on the dependence automatically converted into execution of the arrestment on the final decree. Under this section, there is a positive requirement to tell the debtor that the arrestment on the dependence has, as it were, been converted into arrestment on the final decree. No doubt in practice a creditor or judicial officer would then indicate to the debtor that an action of furthcoming or the automatic release of funds may follow if a mandate is not signed by the debtor - though there is no mention of that in this section.

It is possible that there is a drafting oversight here. Elsewhere in the Act, every execution of diligence over moveable property is followed up by the service of a schedule on the debtor indicating what diligence has been carried out and against what assets. See, for example, ss.133 (schedule of residual attachment), 179 (schedule of money attachment) and 202 (schedule of arrestment of earnings). However, although s.73B refers to a schedule to be served on the debtor where there has been no previous execution of arrestment on the dependence, effectively telling the debtor against what assets the arrestment has been executed, there is no mention in Pt 6 of the 2007 Act (which deals with diligence on the dependence) of any schedule of arrestment on the dependence of an action (indicating what assets have been subject to the execution of the arrestment) being served on the debtor.

As ever when scrutinising a statute, it is difficult to establish whether the omission is deliberate or an oversight. It is submitted that perhaps there ought to be some schedule of execution of arrestment on the dependence, so as at least to let the debtor what has happened and what may in future happen to his assets. The sheriff court ordinary court rules do not appear to provide for a schedule to be served on the debtor (See the Act of Sederunt (Sheriff Court Ordinary Cause Rules) 1993 No.1956 (S.223) Ch.6) and neither do the Rules of the Court of Session (see Rules of Court 16.12, 16.13).

The practical issue here is that a debtor who has had assets arrested on the dependence of an action might or might not be aware that his assets have been arrested, since there appears to be no mechanism to give him notice of what exactly happened until he receives notice from the arrestee under s.73G. Nevertheless, under this section at least he will receive intimation of the final decree.

Whether or not he receives a schedule, he will nevertheless within three weeks of any arrestment receive a copy of a form sent by the arrestee to the creditor intimating what has been arrested and its value (see s.73G).

Section 73D

DEFINITIONS

"Debt advice and information package": 2002 Act s.10(5)

GENERAL NOTE

Where the creditor obtains final decree, having previously executed an arrestment of the debtor's assets on the dependence, or where the creditor arrests in execution of a decree, and in each case where the debtor is an individual, the debtor must be provided with a debt information and advice package. This must be provided within 48 hours of the copy of final decree being served under s.73C(2) or within 48 hours of the service (presumably on the debtor, though there is no specific indication as such) of the schedule of arrestment referred to in s.73B.

Failure to provide the package means that any existing arrestment ceases to have effect or any future arrestment will be incompetent.

Section 73E

DEFINITIONS

"Decree": 1987 Act s.73(4)
"Document of debt": 1987 s.73(4)

GENERAL NOTE

This section only applies where arrestment has been executed following a decree or a document of debt, and where the value of the arrested funds is ascertainable. It does not apply where there has been a previous execution of arrestment on the dependence (see s.15H of the 1987 Act as inserted by s.169 of the 2007 Act). As will be seen shortly, it does not apply in respect of unascertainable funds.

Section 73E applies to limit the amount of the debtor's funds held by the arrestee and which are subject to the arrestment. Under the common law it was permissible to arrest more funds than were required to satisfy the sums owed to the creditor. This was made possible by inserting in the crave for the warrant to arrest the words "more or less" followed by the intended amount. This could mean that more was arrested than was strictly speaking necessary, and this could cause hardship to the debtor. In order to prevent this happening (except in the limited circumstances shown below), subs.(2) limits the extent of the arrestment under this section to the lesser of :

(a) the sum due by the arrestee to the debtor (which may be less than the sum being sued for by the creditor); or
(b) the total of the principal sum sued for, the judicial expenses payable by the debtor, the expenses of execution of the arrestment, interest on the principal sum up to the date of the service of the schedule of arrestment (see s.73B), interest on the principal sum accrued from the date of the service of the schedule of arrestment, any interest on the expenses of arrestment and a further sum (yet to be decided upon by the Scottish Ministers) representing a reasonable figure for any further expenses that may be likely to arise and payable by the debtor.

If the arrestee simultaneously holds both funds due to the debtor and other moveable property of the debtor's, and the ascertainable funds in his hands do not cover the total shown in para.(b) above, the arrestment will be deemed to apply to all the moveable property of the debtor's in the arrestee's hands (subs.(4)).

However, where the ascertainable funds arrested do cover the total in para.(b) above, it will not be permissible to arrest any other moveable property of the debtor's (subs.(5)).

Even if the arrestee holds funds, the value of which is not ascertained (because they are uncertain future or contingent debts due by the arrestee to the debtor), and the sum due by the arrestee to the debtor (i.e. para.(a) above) is greater than the total shown in para.(b) above, the arrestment *under this section* still will not cover any of the funds whose value is not ascertainable (subs.(6)).

Unascertainable funds would be, in general, future debts which are uncertain (because, say, there is a danger that the arrestee due to pay the future debt might become insolvent, or because the amount payable might fluctuate because of interest rates) and debts that are contingent on some other eventuality.

Since this section deals only with ascertainable funds, the common law is left to deal with any unascertainable funds. Therefore, if after the operation of this section the funds arrested (being ascertainable funds) are insufficient to discharge the total liability under para.(b) above, in order to cover the shortfall it will be necessary to use the common law crave for arrestment of a sum "more or less" the intended amount, since arrestment at common law may attach the funds not caught by s.73E, in other words the unascertainable funds.

Although this section is undoubtedly ingenious, what it gains by succinctness and compression it loses in intelligibility. It is not immediately obvious that the common law continues to apply to unascertainable debts to the extent that arrestment under the section is insufficient to cover the total sum owed to the creditor. It would not have been difficult to insert a subsection explaining this point, instead of requiring those who use the legislation having to puzzle it out. Given that the debtors increasingly seek the help of Consumer Advice Bureaux and other organisations where the staff does not necessarily have the benefit of legal training, it is unfortunate that this section, which will directly affect debtors' interests, is not easier to understand.

All this is subject to s.73F.

Section 73F

DEFINITIONS
    "Decree": 1987 Act s.73A(4)
    "Document of debt": 1987 Act s.73A(4)

GENERAL NOTE
    This section is designed to protect a minimum bank balance for the debtor, provided the debtor is an individual and the account in question is not a business or trading account.

    This section applies both to arrestment on the dependence of an action, and to arrestment in execution of a decree or document of debt.

    Where the debtor's account is in the name of a company, a limited liability partnership, a limited partnership or an unincorporated association, this section will not apply (subs.(2)).

    Nor will it apply where the debtor's account is not with a bank or other financial institution (subs.(1)(b)), banks and financial institutions being defined in subs.(5) but broadly encompassing banks and building societies.

    Under subs.(3), the arrestment of the debtor's bank account may only arrest sums in excess of a minimum protected balance, this balance being referred to in subs.(4) and at the time of writing being £370. This figure was set at £370 by the Diligence against Earnings (Variation) (Scotland) Regulations 2006 (SSI 2006/116). This figure may be varied by the Scottish Ministers under the power given to them in s.49(7)(a) of the 1987 Act. The functions of the Lord Advocate in the 1987 Act were transferred to the Secretary of State by the Transfer of Functions (Lord Advocate and Secretary of State) Order 1999 (SI 1999/678) and to the Scottish Ministers by s.53 of the Scotland Act 1998.

    If the debtor's account has less than £370 in it, it may not be arrested.

Section 73G

DEFINITIONS
    "Decree": 1987 Act s.73A(4)
    "Document of debt": 1987 Act s.73A(4)

GENERAL NOTE
    Where a debtor's property and/or funds have been successfully arrested (whether on the dependence of the action or in execution of the decree or document of debt), and having taken account of s.73F, the arrestee must within three weeks of the date of execution of the arrestment inform the creditor as much in a form yet to be devised. The form will indicate what property and funds have been arrested, and their value. A copy must be sent to the debtor and, so far as is known by the arrestee, to any person who owns or claims to own the property or to anyone to

whom the attached funds may be due or claimed to be due, in each case solely or in common with the debtor (subs.(5)).

If nothing is attached, the bank or other financial institution is not required to make a nil return. This is also not stated in the legislation. While this is undoubtedly beneficial for the bank or other potential arrestee, it is not particularly helpful for the creditor, who may have to wait for three weeks to see if the arrestment has been successful. One would imagine that a debtor would also benefit from knowing that an attempt had been made to arrest his bank account. The reason that the bank is not required to make a nil return is probably to save the bank the cost and inconvenience of writing, which given that it has to bear some of the cost and inconvenience of having to deal with arrestments generally, is no doubt a fair recompense.

Section 73H

DEFINITIONS
"Final decree": 1987 Act s.73C(1)

GENERAL NOTE
The arrestee must send in the form in s.73G within the required period of three weeks and if he does not do so, the creditor may apply to the sheriff for an order making the arrestee pay to the creditor the lesser of the sum due to the creditor or the sum in s.73F(4), being the amount in the debtor's account in excess of the protected amount (at the time of writing, £370) (subs.(1)).

If the arrestee fails to send in the form in s.73G the sheriff may not make the order in subs.(1) until the creditor has served a copy of the final decree on the arrestee (subs.2(a)). The debtor's failure to send in the form may be treated as contempt of court (subs.(2)(b)).

Where the arrestee is required to pay a sum to the creditor under subs.(1) the debtor's debt to the creditor is reduced by that amount and the arrestee may not recover the sum from the debtor.

If the arrestee is aggrieved by this matter, he may appeal to the sheriff principal within a period of two weeks of the date of the sheriff's order. There is no further appeal.

Section 73J

DEFINITIONS
"Final decree": 1987 Act s.73C(2)
"Schedule of arrestment": 1987 Act s.73B

GENERAL NOTE
This section allows for the automatic release of any arrested funds (but not other moveable property, for which an action of furthcoming coupled with a warrant for sale, is required, nor for unascertainable debts, which will require an action of furthcoming). Funds due in respect of future or contingent debts are expressly excluded from release (subs.(4)).

Provided the period of 14 weeks has elapsed from the date of the final decree under s.73C(2) has elapsed, or from the date of the service of the schedule of the arrestment, the arrestee may release the sums calculated under s.73K to the creditor, provided those sums have not already been released as a result of the debtor signing a mandate authorising the release of that sum to the creditor (subs.(2)).

This section is subject to s.73L which, amongst other things, provides an opportunity for the debtor to object to the automatic release.

Section 73K

GENERAL NOTE
The sum released is as indicated in the section. The sum attached by the arrestment in subs.(a) is calculated under s.73E but limited by the protected minimum balance provisions in s.73F. The sum in (b) that the arrestee holds for the debtor will exclude any sums relating to future or contingent debts, since those debts will not yet have been paid. The sum in (c) is calculated in a similar manner to s.73E(2)(b) but takes no account of the estimated expenses of an action of furthcoming since no action of furthcoming is needed,

Section 73 L

GENERAL NOTE

This section gives the debtor, the arrestee and anyone else with an interest in the arrested funds the opportunity to object to the release and prevent it taking place. The process of objection is explained in the next section, but where the debtor alone is objecting to the release on the grounds of its undue harshness, this must be done under s.73Q(2).

The release of the funds will also be prevented if an action of multiplepoinding is raised in relation to the fund. An action of multiplepoinding takes place when several different creditors all claim an interest in a disputed fund, and the only remedy, if the creditors cannot agree their claim, is to have the matter resolved in court.

The release may be recalled or restricted or cease to have effect, perhaps because the creditor has been paid in full, or because there is a time to pay order in place in terms of the 1987 Act Pt I.

Section 73 M

DEFINITIONS
"Final decree": 1987 Act s.73C(2)
"Schedule of arrestment": 1987 Act s.73B

GENERAL NOTE

As indicated earlier, the debtor, the arrestee and a third party with an interest in the funds due to be released may by notice of objection apply to the sheriff for an order to recall or restrict the release (subs.(1)). The objector must do so on a form yet to be devised, give a copy of the notice within four weeks of the date of service of the final notice or of the date of service of the schedule of arrestment (as the case may be) to the creditor, the sheriff clerk, the debtor, the arrestee and any third party (subs.(3)). The grounds for the objection have to be specified, and those grounds may only be that the warrant for the arrestment was invalid, the execution of the arrestment was incompetent or irregular, or that the funds are due to the third party either solely or in common with the debtor (subs.(4)).

If one of the objectors has applied by notice as above, he may not simultaneously raise an action of multiplepoinding or any other action (save under the "unduly harsh" grounds of s.73Q) concerning the same funds (subs.(5)), except where he wishes to enter any action raised by someone else, or wishes to raise an action where the sheriff has sisted the proceedings to allow a multiplepoinding or any other proceedings on the disputed fund to take place.

Section 73 N

GENERAL NOTE

Where a notice of objection is made under s.73M(1), there will be a hearing for the sheriff to consider the objection. This must take place within eight weeks of the day the application for notice of objection is made to the sheriff (subs.(1)). At the hearing, the debtor, the creditor, the arrestee and any third party may be heard (subs.(2)).

The sheriff may uphold the objection and thereby recall or restrict the arrestment (subs.(3)). If the objection is not upheld, the funds will be released in accordance with s.73J(3) (i.e. within 14 weeks of the final decree or the service of the schedule under s.73B).

The sheriff may at any time decide that the matter is too complex for immediate consideration and may remit the matter for an action of multiplepoinding or other procedure, and if so, may sist the proceedings of the objection (subs.(5)).

The sheriff also has discretion to make any other order as he sees fit (subs.(6)), the order being intimated to all those involved. Any of them who feel aggrieved by his decision may appeal to the sheriff principal, on a point of law only, within 14 days (subs.(8)).

Section 73 P

GENERAL NOTE

Where the arrestee releases funds in good faith, unaware of any irregularity in the validity, competence or execution of the warrant or the arrestment, he will not be liable.

Section 73Q

DEFINITIONS
"Final decree": 1987 Act s.73C(2)

GENERAL NOTE
This applies where a creditor has obtained a final decree on the dependence of which he executed an arrestment or arrested in execution of a decree or document of debt and the arrestment has duly taken place (subs.(1)). The debtor may apply to the sheriff for an order requiring that the arrestment cease to have effect over any funds or property of the debtor's or any portion thereof, and requiring the release of the funds and property to the debtor (subs.(2)).

This must be applied for, at any time during the arrestment, in a form yet to be devised (subs.(3)).

Section 73R

GENERAL NOTE
If there is a hearing under s.73Q(2) the sheriff may not make an order without giving an opportunity for the creditor, the arrestee and anyone else with an interest the opportunity to be heard (subs.(1)). If the sheriff is satisfied that the arrestment is unduly harsh to the debtor or to those mentioned in para.(4) (subs.(2)), he will make an order that the arrestment cease to have effect over any funds or property of the debtor's or any portion thereof, and require the release of the funds and property to the debtor (subs.(3)). In particular, before making the order, and where the debtor is an individual, he will have to have regard to all the circumstances including the source of the funds and where the source of the funds is the debtor's earnings, whether any current arrestment order, current maintenance arrestment or conjoined arrestment order is in place.

Subsection (4) explains those whose interests the sheriff should consider before making an order. They are mostly close family, but do not include parents or siblings.

The sheriff may refuse to make an order restricting or recalling the arrestment, and require the arrestee to pay the required sum under s.73J(3) at the end of the 14 week period or as soon as possible thereafter (subs.(5)). This must be intimated to the creditor, the arrestee and anyone else with an interest. There is a right of appeal to the sheriff principal.

Section 73S

GENERAL NOTE
This section allows the Scottish Ministers to draw up a standard form of mandate which would be used by debtors to authorise the arrestee to make over funds or property to the creditor.

Where the arrestee makes over the funds or the property in good faith in accordance with the mandate, he will not liable in damages to the debtor or anyone else for handing over the property even if the mandate is invalid.

Section 73T

GENERAL NOTE
This explains that this part of the Act does not apply to ships or other maritime property. These are subject to other rules, namely Pt V of the Administration of Justice Act 1956 which is amended by Pt 14 of and Sch.4 to this Act.

PART 11

MAILLS AND DUTIES, SEQUESTRATION FOR RENT AND LANDLORD'S HYPOTHEC

GENERAL NOTE
This part deals with two forms of diligence that are not much used nowadays, mainly because there are other methods of achieving the same result or because their use is much circumscribed anyway.

Maills and duties were a type of diligence that allowed a creditor holding a debt secured over land (*debitum fundi*) (effectively a heritable security) over a property to collect the rents directly from the debtor's tenants. This is not available with a modern standard security, though it was available with the older forms of security, such as bonds and dispositions in security. The Abolition of Feudal Tenure etc. (Scotland) Act 2000 abolished the right of a creditor in a ground annual to enforce payment by this means. Indeed, there do not appear to have been any reported cases of actions for maills and duties for many years and their loss does not appear to be regretted. The word "maill" is an old Scots and Norse word for a stipulation or agreed payment, as in the word "blackmail".

Landlord's hypothec and sequestration for rent collectively form a diligence allowing certain landlords under limited circumstances to seize a tenant's assets and sell them. More accurately, it gives the landlord security over the tenant's property, known as *invecta et illata* (i.e. articles brought in or carried in) for one year's rent, but not arrears. The type of lease to which it applies is restricted to leases of commercial premises and agricultural holdings less than two acres in size, such as market gardens and nurseries. *Invecta et illata* do not cover property belonging to the tenant's family or on hire purchase, but can cover property sold to a third party and not uplifted, or property belonging to a sub-tenant. The security over the debtor's property gives a landlord a preferred right, relative to other creditors, for the rent in respect of the let premises.

If the rent is not paid, the property may be sold following an action for sequestration for rent. What has excited concern about this diligence is the fact that a third party, such a sub-tenant, may well find that his assets are taken by the landlord because the tenant has failed to pay the rent, and while no doubt a sub-tenant should always be aware of that possibility, and there are mechanisms to enable him to seek recall, he may, nevertheless, find that through no fault of his own, the landlord is entitled to sell his property and, given that the tenant is the one who has defaulted, any redress against the tenant is probably futile. There are several instances of unhappy subtenants in this situation: see *Ditchburn Organisation (Sales) Ltd v Dundee Corporation* 1971 SLT 218; *DH Industries Ltd v R E Spence and Co Ltd* 1973 SLT 26; *Scottish & Newcastle Breweries Ltd v Edinburgh District Council* 1979 SLT 11; *Cumbernauld Development v Mustone Ltd* 1983 SLT 55. Happily, it seems that an action for sequestration is uncommon nowadays and there are other fairer methods, such as attachment, for landlords to recover their rent.

The changes that the 2007 Act implements are to abolish sequestration for rent but to preserve the landlord's hypothec, effectively meaning that the security is only of use in the event of the debtor's insolvency.

Abolition of maills and duties

207. Abolition of maills and duties

(1) The diligence of maills and duties is abolished and any enactment or rule of law enabling an action of maills and duties to be raised ceases to have effect.

(2) Subsection (1) above does not affect an action of maills and duties brought before this section comes into force.

GENERAL NOTE

This section abolishes the diligence of maills and duties, although any such action brought before the courts before the section is brought into force may be continued to its conclusion.

Landlord's hypothec and sequestration for rent

208. Abolition of sequestration for rent and restriction of landlord's hypothec

(1) The diligence of sequestration for rent is abolished and any enactment or rule of law enabling an action of sequestration for rent to be raised ceases to have effect.

   (2) Notwithstanding that abolition, the landlord's hypothec-

      (a) continues, subject to subsections (3) to (9) below, as a right in security over corporeal moveable property kept in or on the subjects let; and-

      (b) ranks accordingly in any-

         (i) sequestration;

         (ii) insolvency proceedings; or

         (iii) other process in which there is ranking,

   in respect of that property.

   (3) The landlord's hypothec no longer arises in relation to property which is kept-

      (a) in a dwellinghouse;

      (b) on agricultural land; or

      (c) on a croft.

   (4) It no longer arises in relation to property which is owned by a person other than the tenant.

   (5) Property which is acquired by a person from the tenant-

      (a) in good faith; or

      (b) where the property is acquired after an interdict prohibiting the tenant from disposing of or removing items secured by the hypothec has been granted in favour the landlord, in good faith and for value,

ceases to be subject to the hypothec upon acquisition by the person.

   (6) Subsection (5)(b) above does not affect the tenant's liability for breach of the interdict.

   (7) Where property is owned in common by the tenant and a third party, any right of hypothec arises only to the extent of the tenant's interest in that property.

   (8) The landlord's hypothec-

      (a) is security for rent due and unpaid only; and

      (b) subsists for so long as that rent remains unpaid.

   (9) Any enactment or rule of law relating to the landlord's hypothec ceases to have effect in so far as it is inconsistent with subsections (2) to (8) above.

   (10) Subsections (1) to (3), (8) and (9) above do not affect an action of sequestration for rent brought before this section comes into force.

   (11) Subsection (3) above does not affect a landlord's right of hypothec which arose before and subsists on the coming into force of this section.

   (12) In subsection (2) above, "insolvency proceedings" means-

      (a) winding up;

      (b) receivership;

      (c) administration; and

      (d) proceedings in relation to a company voluntary arrangement,

within the meaning of the Insolvency Act 1986 (c.45).

   (13) In subsection (3) above-

      "agricultural land" has the same meaning as in section 1(2) of the Agricultural Holdings (Scotland) Act 1991 (c.55);

      "croft" has the same meaning as in section 3(1) of the Crofters (Scotland) Act 1993 (c.44); and

      "dwellinghouse" includes-

         (a) a mobile home or other place used as a dwelling; and

    (b) any other structure or building used in connection with
the dwellinghouse.

GENERAL NOTE

Sequestration for rent is abolished (subs.(1)), though any continuing action extant at the time this section comes into force may be continued to its conclusion (subs.(10)). Landlord's hypothec remains in force to give a security for rent due and unpaid over the debtor's moveable property (subs.(8)), and therefore ranking ahead of unsecured creditors in the event of the debtor's insolvency (subs.(2)). It also enables the creditor to obtain an interdict to prevent the debtor selling or removing his property, though the interdict's effect is limited where third parties are involved (see subs.(5)(b)).

Its use, already limited (see the general note to Pt 11) is now further restricted. It may not be used in respect of a dwellinghouse (which includes a mobile home or other place used as dwelling and any structure or building associated with the dwellinghouse (subs.(13)), nor agricultural land, as defined in the Agricultural Holdings (Scotland) Act 1991 s.1(2), nor a croft, as defined in the Crofters (Scotland) Act 1993 s.3(1). It may not be used where the property in question is owned by someone other than the tenant, thereby reversing the previous position whereby subtenants' property could be subject to the hypothec (subs.(4)). If someone has bought property from the tenant in good faith, or even if there is an interdict in place forbidding the debtor from disposing of his property, and the debtor has sold the property in defiance of the interdict, the purchaser in each case, providing he has acted in good faith and paid a proper price, is protected from the landlord's claim (subs.(5)). The tenant, of course, will still be liable for breach of his interdict (subs.(6)).

The existing common law relating to landlord's hypothec ceases to have effect so far as it is inconsistent with this section (subs.(9)).

This section came into force on April 1, 2008.

PART 12

SUMMARY WARRANTS, TIME TO PAY AND CHARGES TO PAY

GENERAL NOTE

Summary warrants permit local authorities (recovering council tax, commercial rates and community charge arrears) water authorities (recovering water and sewerage charges) and Her Majesty's Revenue and Customs (recovering arrears of tax and customs duty) to proceed directly to execute diligence without the need to serve a charge first. The rationale for this was that debtors would have ample warning beforehand, and to save money both for the debtors (who might otherwise have to pay the expenses of the charge, plus the interest on the outstanding sum) and for the creditors (who would bear the cost of the expenses if the debtor was unable to pay them).

A charge is when a judicial officer (in practice usually two judicial officers) attends at the debtor's home or business premises with an extract or certified copy of the decree or document of debt, and attempts to serve it upon the debtor. If the debtor is out, the copy is left at the home or premises and a recorded delivery copy posted as well. The debtor then has 14 days within the United Kingdom and 28 days outside the United Kingdom in which to pay the debt (see 1987 Act s.90).

This Part of the 2007 Act changes the rules so that a charge is now required for a summary warrant.

The rationale for this is that debtors apparently often ignore letters requiring them to pay their debts, but they do take the requirement to appear in court seriously. Because summary warrants did not involve any appearance in court, debtors often did not understand the significance of the fact that judicial officers could effect diligence without any further procedure. It is thought that the serving of a charge on a debtor gives the debtor one last chance either to pay the outstanding debt or to seek financial advice.

A time to pay direction is one granted under Pt I of the 1987 Act and effectively allows a debtor to pay off his debts by instalments after decree has been taken against him. During this time, the creditor may not enforce payment of the debt by diligence, nor sequestrate the debtor, unless the debtor defaults on paying the instalments. While the time to pay direction is in place, it is a "diligence stopper". Certain debts may not be subject to a time to pay direction, such as maintenance for a former spouse, capital sum payable on divorce, sums owed to HMRC, etc. (see 1987 Act s.1(5)). A time to pay order is similar, save that it proceeds after a charge followed by an arrestment or (at least until the passing of the 2007 Act), an adjudication for debt, though now it would be a land attachment.

The second section in this Pt 11 widens the grounds under which time to pay directions or orders may be granted.

This part came into force on April 1, 2008.

209.   Summary warrants, time to pay and charges to pay

(1) Section 10(4) of the 2002 Act (no charge required for attachment in pursuance of summary warrant) is repealed.

(2) In section 1 of the 1987 Act (time to pay direction)-

    (a) subsection (5)(e) (certain debts in relation to which a time to pay direction cannot be granted); and

    (b) subsection (9) (interpretation),

are repealed.

(3) In section 5 of the 1987 Act (time to pay order)-

    (a) subsection (4)(c) and (e) (certain debts in relation to which a time to pay order cannot be granted); and

    (b) subsection (9) (interpretation),

are repealed.

(4) In section 15(3) of the 1987 Act (interpretation)-

    (a) in the definition of "decree or document of debt", after paragraph (a) insert-

        "(aa) a summary warrant;" ; and

    (b) the words "or a summary warrant" are repealed.

(5) In section 90 of the 1987 Act (provisions relating to charges)-

    (a) in subsection (1), the words "Subject to subsection (2) below," and "an attachment or" are repealed;

    (b) after subsection (1) insert-

        "(1A) The following subsections of this section apply to any case where it is competent to execute diligence only if a charge for payment has been served on the debtor.";

    (c) subsection (2) (no charge required for attachment or earnings arrestment in pursuance of summary warrant) is repealed;

    (d) in subsection (5), for "an attachment or an earnings arrestment" substitute "diligence"; and

    (e) in subsection (6), for "an attachment or an earnings arrestment" substitute "diligence".

GENERAL NOTE

Subsection (1) narrates that summary warrants no longer may dispense with a charge. Henceforth the execution of diligence under a summary warrant must, like any other debt, be preceded by a charge.

Consequentially, subs.(5)(e) of s.1 of the 1987 Act is repealed, as is s.9. This means that it is now possible to have a time to pay direction for rates, council tax, community charge and water rates (subs.(2)).

Subsection (3) is of similar effect, amending paras (c) and (e) of s.5(4) of the 1987 Act so that time to pay orders may now be granted where a summary warrant is in place, or where there has been an action raised for rates, council tax, community charge and water rates. Time to pay orders will remain prohibited for the other items in subs.(4) of s.5.

Subsection (5) makes various amendments to s.90 of the 1987 Act consequential to the amendment in subs.(1) to remove the references in s.90 to an attachment being incompetent unless a charge is served. Subsection (5) also amends s.90 so that a charge to pay is needed before a creditor with a debt enforceable under a summary warrant may use an earnings arrestment. Paragraphs (b), (d) and (e) of subs.(5) also amend s.90 so that the provisions relating to charges to pay (i.e. that they must conform to the rules of court, that diligence must be executed within two years of the charge and that a further charge may be served to reconstitute the entitlement to execute diligence) apply to all diligences where a charge to pay must be served before diligence is competent.

210. Time to pay directions and time to pay orders

(1) The 1987 Act is further amended as follows.

(2) In section 1 (time to pay directions)-

    (a) in subsection (1)-

        (i) after "Act," insert "on an application by the debtor,"; and

        (ii) for the words "may, on an application by the debtor," substitute ", shall, if satisfied that it is reasonable in all the circumstances to do so, and having regard in particular to the matters mentioned in subsection (1A) below,"; and

    (b) after subsection (1) insert-

        "(1A) The matters referred to in subsection (1) above are-

            (a) the nature of and reasons for the debt in relation to which decree is granted;

            (b) any action taken by the creditor to assist the debtor in paying that debt;

            (c) the debtor's financial position;

            (d) the reasonableness of any proposal by the debtor to pay that debt; and

            (e) the reasonableness of any refusal by the creditor of, or any objection by the creditor to, any proposal by the debtor to pay that debt.".

(3) In section 5 (time to pay orders)-

    (a) in subsection (2), for the words "may, on an application by the debtor," substitute ", on an application by the debtor, shall, if satisfied that it is reasonable in all the circumstances to do so, and having regard in particular to the matters mentioned in subsection (2A) below,"; and

    (b) after subsection (2), insert-

        "(2A) The matters referred to in subsection (2) above are-

            (a) the nature of and reasons for the debt in relation to which the order is sought;

            (b) any action taken by the creditor to assist the debtor in paying that debt;

            (c) the debtor's financial position;

            (d) the reasonableness of any proposal by the debtor to pay that debt; and

            (e) the reasonableness of the objection by the creditor to the offer by the debtor to pay that debt.".

GENERAL NOTE

This extends the grounds on which the court may grant time to pay directions and time to pay orders, in ss.1 and 5 of the 1987 Act respectively, and, in essence, they permit the debtor to apply for such directions and orders and for the court to grant such directions and orders where it is satisfied in all the circumstances that it is reasonable to do so, taking into account, in particular, the matters in subss.1A and 2A. The matters include the nature of and reasons for the debt, any help the creditor has given the debtor, the debtor's financial position, the reasonableness of the debtor's proposals to pay off the debt and the reasonableness of any refusal by the creditor to accept the debtor's proposals for paying off the debt.

The effect of this is that creditors must be seen to taking more steps to help their debtors manage their debts and must not be unreasonable in rejecting the debtor's efforts to pay off his debts, although, equally, debtors must come up with sensible proposals for the management of their debts, proposals that are likely to be realistic from the creditor's point of view.

PART 13

AMENDMENTS OF THE DEBT ARRANGEMENT AND ATTACHMENT (SCOTLAND) ACT 2002

GENERAL NOTE

The Debt Arrangement and Attachment (Scotland) Act 2002 was the Act that introduces a new method of attachment to replace poinding and also introduced the Debt Arrangement Scheme. This is a method whereby a debtor may obtain advice and help from a "money adviser" who will set up a "debt payment programme" which is binding upon creditors and acts as a "diligence stopper". The money adviser, having set up the scheme, would arrange for a portion of the debtor's earnings to be set aside by and paid out by a payments distributor to the debtor's creditors. In some respects it replicated the effect if not the exact form of a trust deed for creditors, but because it does not involve insolvency practitioners and is relatively non-legalistic, it is perhaps a more approachable method for some debtors of dealing with their debts than a trust deed. In particular, money advisers are quite often connected with local citizens advice bureaux, or other sources of financial advice, which some debtors may find less intimidating than having to visit an accountant's office.

Unfortunately, despite the benevolent intentions of Debt Arrangement, it has not worked quite as well as might have been hoped. As at February 19, 2006 there were 90 approved advisers and 202 debt arrangement programmes. The major difficulty (which had been widely predicted) was that it was only very useful to those already receiving regular income but who realised that they needed help in ensuring that a portion of their earnings was siphoned off and paid to creditors before they could be tempted to spend the money themselves, or, as the cynics said, it was only useful for relatively sensible, but weak-willed, debtors already in employment. A second difficulty was that interest and expenses were not, initially, written off. That has since been changed (see The Debt Arrangement Scheme (Scotland) Amendment Regulations 2007 (SSI 2007/ 262) and interest and expenses are now written off. A third difficulty was that the training to be a debt adviser was laborious. This section allowed the Scottish Ministers to introduce new regulations to deal with these matters. These were produced and are known as The Debt Arrangement Scheme (Scotland) Regulations No. 2 2007 (SSI 2007/ 187) (in force June 30, 2007). They deal with certain previous difficulties to the following effect (the following is taken from the Scottish Justice Department circular dated August 28, 2007):

> Enforcement may be suspended on request by the debtor for 6 weeks, once in every 12 month period, when creditors are asked to agree a debt payment programme;
> Enforcement is suspended while an application for approval of a debt payment programme is being considered by the DAS administrator;
> A money adviser approval will last 3 years instead of 2;
> A money adviser will be required to review a debt payment programme once every 12 months instead of once every 6 months;
> A money adviser will no longer need to seek revocation of a 'failed' programme;
> The DAS administrator will be able to revoke failed debt payment programmes;
> A fee charging money adviser will not be required to tell the debtor about any 'free' alternative service, for example a local authority money advice service;
> Creditors will no longer be entitled to object to programmes on the grounds that a debtor has too much equity in land, or should be sequestrated;
> The DAS administrator will be able to take into account information

about land and buildings when deciding whether or not to approve an application for a debt payment programme;

The sheriff will no longer determine any application for approval of a debt payment programme; and

There will be a final right of appeal to the sheriff alone, and not to either the sheriff or the sheriff principal.

211. Debt payment programmes with debt relief

(1) The 2002 Act is amended as follows.

(2) In section 2 (debt payment programmes)-

    (a) after subsection (1) insert-

        "(1A) Subsection (1) above is subject to any provision in regulations made under section 7A(1) below." ; and

    (b) in subsection (4), after "section 7(1)" insert "or 7A(1)".

(3) After section 7 insert-

"7A Debt payment programmes: power to make provision about debt relief

(1) The Scottish Ministers may, by regulations, make such further provision as they think fit in connection with debt payment programmes for the purposes of-

    (a) enabling such programmes to provide for the payment of part only of money owed by debtors; and

    (b) on the completion of such programmes or otherwise, enabling any liability of debtors to pay any part of such money owed as is outstanding to be discharged.

(2) The regulations may, in particular, make provision about-

    (a) the minimum proportion or percentage of debts which shall be paid under such debt payment programmes;

    (b) without prejudice to section 7(2)(h) to (j) above, the consent of creditors for the purposes of section 2(4) above (including the circumstances in which consent by a majority by number or in value shall be sufficient);

    (c) the effect of such programmes on debtors' liabilities for interest, fees, penalties and other charges in relation to debts being paid under such programmes;

    (d) the effect of such programmes on the rights of creditors to charge interest, fees, penalties or other charges in relation to debts being paid under such programmes;

    (e) circumstances in which, on completion of such programmes or otherwise, any liability of debtors to pay-

        (i) part of any debts as are outstanding; or

        (ii) any interest, fees, penalties or other charges in relation to such debts,

    is to be discharged.

(3) Subsections (3) and (4) of section 7 above apply for the purposes of regulations under this section as they apply for the purposes of regulations under subsection (1) of that section.".

(4) In section 62 (regulations and orders)-

(a) in subsection (3), for "of this Act", where those words second occur, substitute "above or regulations made under section 7A above"; and

(b) in subsection (4), after "section 7 above" insert ", any regulations made under section 7A above".

GENERAL NOTE
This section permits the Scottish Ministers to make various regulations in connection with debt payment programmes and related matters, as indicated in the General Note above. This section came into force on March 8, 2007.

212. Further amendments of the Debt Arrangement and Attachment (Scotland) Act 2002

(1) The 2002 Act is further amended as follows.

(2) In section 2(3) (form and content of applications for debt payment programmes), the words "shall be signed by the debtor and" are repealed.

(3) In section 3 (application by debtor for approval of debt payment programme), after subsection (2) insert-

   (3) Subsections (1) and (2) above are subject to any contrary provision in regulations made under section 7(1) below.".

(4) In section 5(4) (form and content of applications for variation of debt payment programmes), paragraph (b) and the word "and" immediately preceding it are repealed.

(5) In section 7(2) (examples of provision that may be made by regulations under section 7(1))-

   (a) after paragraph (b) insert-

      "(ba) circumstances in which some or all of the functions of a money adviser under section 3 above may instead be carried out by an approved intermediary;

      (bb) circumstances in which a debtor is entitled to make an application for the approval, or the variation, of a debt payment programme where the debtor has not obtained advice under section 3(1) above;

      (bc) the manner in which-

         (i) the seeking of the consent of creditors to applications for approval of debt payment programmes; or

         (ii) the making of such applications,

      affects the rights and remedies of creditors or other third parties;";

   (b) after paragraph (s) insert-

      "(sa) the class of person who may act as an approved intermediary;" ; and

   (c) after paragraph (u) insert-

      "(ua) the functions of an approved intermediary;".

(6) In section 9(1) (interpretation), before the definition of "money adviser" insert-

   ""approved intermediary" means any person, not being a money adviser, who has been approved by the Scottish

Ministers as a person who may give advice to a debtor for the purposes of section 3(1) above;".

(7) In section 10(5) (attachment), in the definition of "debt advice and information package", for "Scottish Ministers" substitute "Scottish Civil Enforcement Commission".

(8) In section 19(1) (removal and auction of attached articles), for "The officer who attached articles" substitute "An officer".

(9) After section 19 insert-

"19A   Urgent removal of attached articles

(1) The officer may at any time remove an attached article without notice if-

    (a) the officer considers it necessary for-

        (i) the security; or

        (ii) the preservation of the value,

    of the article; and

    (b) there is insufficient time to obtain an order under section 20(1)(a) below.

(2) The officer shall remove an article under subsection (1) above-

    (a) to the nearest convenient premises of the debtor or the person in possession of the articles; or

    (b) if-

        (i) no such premises are available; or

        (ii) the officer considers such premises to be unsuitable,

    to the nearest suitable secure premises.

(3) Subsections (2) and (6) of section 19 above shall apply to this section as they apply to that section.".

(10) In section 20(2)(b) (applications for orders for security etc. of articles), after "officer" insert-

    (i) who attached articles; or

    (ii) who is authorised to arrange the auction".

(11) In section 21(7) (notice of theft of attached articles), after "officer" insert-

    (i) who attached articles; or

    (ii) who is authorised to arrange the auction,".

(12) In section 26(5)(b) (return of removed articles), for "the officer" substitute "an officer".

(13) In section 27(4) (notice of auction), the words "authorised to arrange the auction" are repealed.

(14) In section 31 (disposal of proceeds of auction)-

    (a) after subsection (1), insert-

        "(1A) Where an article is sold at the auction at a price below the value of the article, the difference between that price and that value shall, prior to the proceeds of the auction being disposed of under subsection (1) above, be credited against the sum recoverable.

        (1B) Where-

        (a) an article to which subsection (1A) above applies has been damaged and revalued under section 21(10)(b) above;

> (b) the damage was not caused by the fault of the
> debtor; and
> (c) no sum has been consigned into court by a third
> party under section 21(11) above,
>
> the revaluation shall be disregarded for the purposes of
> subsection (1A) above." ; and

(b) in subsection (4), after "subsections" insert "(1A),".

(15) After section 60 insert-

"60A Electronic signatures

(1) This section applies where-
  (a) a report or declaration under this Act requires to be
      signed; and
  (b) provision is made by virtue of this Act or any other
      enactment permitting the report or declaration to be an
      electronic communication.

(2) Where the report or declaration is an electronic communi-
    cation, the requirement is satisfied by a certified electronic
    signature.

(3) Subsection (2) above is to be read in accordance with
    section 7(2) and (3) of the Electronic Communications Act
    2000 (c.7) (electronic signatures and certification).".

(16) In schedule 1 (expenses)-
  (a) in paragraph 1, after sub-paragraph (o), insert-
      (oa) in serving notice on the debtor under section
           49(1)(b) above;" ; and
  (b) after that paragraph, insert-

> "1A The expenses referred to in sub-paragraphs (i), (j)
> and (k) of paragraph 1 above shall not be chargeable
> against the debtor if the articles are removed under
> section 19A(1) above.".

GENERAL NOTE

This section makes further amendments to the 2002 Act, in particular allowing someone who is not a money adviser to represent the debtor, and generally making the whole process of obtaining a debt arrangement programme less bureaucratic. Subsections (1) to (6) came into force on March 8, 2007. Subsection (7) is unlikely to be brought into force as the Commission referred to therein is not, at the time of writing, to be set up.

Subsection (2) repeals the requirement that a debtor needs to sign his application for a debt payment programme.

Subsection (3) provides that the requirements set out in s.3(1) and (2) of the 2002 Act for an application for the approval or the variation of a debt payment programme, including the requirement that the debtor obtain the advice of a money adviser, may be changed by regulations made under s.7(1).

Subsection (4) repeals the requirement that a debtor or creditor, as the case may be, should sign an application for a variation of a debt payment programme.

Subsection (5) amends s.7(2) to enable regulations to be made about the circumstances in which some or all of the duties of a money adviser may be carried out instead by an approved intermediary, about the circumstances that allow the debtor to apply for the approval or variation of a debt payment programme even without the benefit of the advice of a money adviser, and about the manner in which obtaining creditors' consent to the approval of debt payment programmes, and the application itself, may affects creditors' or anyone else's rights.

Subsection (6) explains that an approved intermediary is someone other than a money adviser who has been approved by the Scottish Ministers as a person who may give a debtor money advice in terms of s. 3(1) of the 2002 Act.

Subsection (7) amends the definition of "debt advice and information package" to allow the Scottish Civil Enforcement Commission, set up under s.50 of the 2007 Act, the power to decide what should be included within the package, and take away the power of the Scottish Ministers to do so.

Subsections (8) and (10)-(13) make various amendments to the 2002 Act to permit each step in the attachment process to be carried out by any judicial officer. Hitherto it was unclear whether it had to be the same judicial officer throughout.

Subsections (8)-(14) have been in force since March 31, 2007.

Subsection (9) inserts new s.19A into the 2002 Act. This permits a judicial officer power to remove articles swiftly if, under subs.(1), he considers it necessary to secure the article, for fear of damage or destruction, or to preserve its value and there is insufficient time to obtain an order from a sheriff under s.20(1)(a) of the 2002 Act permitting such removal). Should this happen, he will take the article in question to the nearest convenient premises of the debtor or the person in possession of the item, but if there are no such premises, or the judicial officer believes them unsuitable, he may take it to other secure premises (see subs.(2)). Subsection (3) (which applies s.19(4)) permits the judicial officer to open shut and lockfast places in order to take away the attached articles.

Subsection (14) inserts new subss.(1A) and (1B) into s.31 of the 2002 Act. Subsection (1A) states that where an article is sold at auction at less than the value assigned to it when it was attached, the difference between that price and the value will be credited against the sum owed. So the debtor benefits from having the debt reduced by the amount the item was valued at, even if it sells for less than that value at auction. No doubt this will lead to conservative valuation of articles. Subsection (1B) states that where an article has been damaged and revalued and the damage was not occasioned by the fault of the debtor and no sum has been consigned into the court by a third party to compensate for the damage, the revaluation is disregarded for the purposes of subs.(1A). The original value is thus the value that is credited against the debt after the sale even if the sale price of the item was less, and even if the creditor only receives the sale price.

Subsections (15) and (16) also came into force on March 31, 2007.

Subsection 15 inserts a new s.60A into the 2002 Act and permits electronic signatures to be used where any document that requires to be signed under the 2002 Act is submitted in electronic form. The signature has to be a certified electronic signature which complies with the requirements of the Electronic Communications Act 2000 (c.7).

Subsection (16)(a) inserts sub-para.(oa) into para.1 of Sch.1 to the 2002 Act. This explains that the expenses of serving a notice on the debtor indicating the date when an officer proposes to enter a dwellinghouse to execute an exceptional attachment order are chargeable against the debtor.

Subsection (16)(b) inserts new para.1A into Sch.1 to the 2002 Act. This explains that the expenses of removing attached articles, opening shut and lockfast places to remove the articles and store them cannot be charged against the debtor if the articles are removed under the "urgent removal" provisions of s.19A(1) above as inserted by s.212.

PART 14

ADMIRALTY ACTIONS AND ARRESTMENT OF SHIPS

213. Admiralty actions and the arrestment of ships: modification of enactments

Schedule 4 makes modifications of enactments relating to admiralty actions and the arrestment of ships.

GENERAL NOTE

Schedule 4 deals with this.

The Schedule makes certain amendments to the Administration of Justice Act 1956, broadly speaking to make Scots law conform to maritime law as it is generally understood elsewhere in the United Kingdom, as well as removing some areas of doubt. Part V of this Act applies to Scotland, and the Schedule introduces various new sections into the Act as well as supplying some new definitions.

Paragraph 1 changes s.48 of the Act in order to allow a new subs.(2) to be introduced. The new subsection defines the words "maritime lien" to mean a hypothec over a ship, cargo or other maritime property. "Maritime lien" is an international term for a creditor's right in security over a ship, its cargo or its property, even if the creditor does not actually have the ship, the cargo or her property in his possession. It is necessary to insert the definition because under Scots law a lien requires the creditor to have the debtor's possession in his possession, while a hypothec is a security over an asset not in the creditor's possession. So under Scots law, the term "maritime lien" is a contradiction in terms, but in order to be conform to international usage, this paragraph gives a special definition of the phrase. Paragraph 2 inserts the word "maritime" in front of the word "lien" on each occasion of its use throughout Pt V, and para.3 widens the scope of s.47(2)(r) by the insertion of the words "or existence of any other charge" lest the wording "mortgage or hypothecation" not cover the range of charges nowadays available in maritime matters.

Paragraph 4 defines what is meant by "admiralty action" and clarifies some other points. The words "or contract of respondentia" are added to the phrase "bottomry bond." A bottomry bond is a type of mortgage securing a loan to the shipowner over the ship and her freight, the loan generally being used to help fit out the ship. If the ship is lost, the lender loses his security, so the risk of the loan is partly borne by the lender, though he generally compensates for this by charging a higher, or "maritime" rate of interest.

A contract of respondentia is a bond secured on the cargo of a ship for a particular voyage.

An "admiralty action" is defined as any one of the 20 or so claims stated in subs.(2) of s.47.

Paragraph 6 clarifies the rules relating to a warrant to arrest *in rem* of a ship, cargo or other maritime property. To arrest a ship *in rem* means to arrest the ship herself (since a ship can hardly be said to be in the hands of a third party) and thus prevent her leaving harbour, perhaps by disabling her or otherwise preventing her leaving port. The warrant may be executed in the sheriffdom where the warrant was granted or provided the ship, cargo or maritime property was actually in the sheriffdom at the time of the grant of the warrant, anywhere in Scotland. Furthermore, an order for the sale of the ship, cargo or other maritime property may be made even though the ship, cargo or maritime property is no longer in the sheriffdom where the order for sale was granted.

Paragraph 7 introduces certain changes to s.47 of the Act. It clarifies that when there is an arrestment of a ship or maritime property which is not cargo (i.e. wreck, flotsam and jetsam), at the time the arrestment is executed the defender must either own at least one share in the ship, is the demise charterer of the ship, or own all the shares in the ship. A demise charterer is one who hires the entire ship and crew for the duration of a particular time, and while not the owner of the ship, in practice will take on many of the responsibilities of an owner. It remains permissible for the pursuer to arrest any other ships wholly belonging to the defender (subs.(1)(b)). It will be noted that cargo is specifically exempted.

Paragraph 7(3) inserts new subss.(1A) and (1B) into s.47 of the 1956 Act. If a ship has been arrested on the dependence of an action, no further warrant will be granted to arrest on the dependence of the same action the same ship or any other ship of which the defender owns at least a share, unless the pursuer can demonstrate good cause for the second arrestment. This is to conform with the wording in Art.3(1) of the Brussels Arrest Convention of 1952, the generally accepted international convention on the arrestment of ships.

Paragraph 7(4) allows for the arrestment of the defender's share in a ship rather than the whole ship.

Paragraph 8 inserts a new s.47B into the Act and deals with expenses. The pursuer is entitled to the expenses of obtaining any warrant for the arrestment on the dependence of an action of any ship, cargo and other maritime property and executing any warrant of arrestment unless the pursuer was acting unreasonably in applying for them under all the circumstances, in which case the defender will be entitled to the expenses of opposing the warrant. The court has discretion to modify or refuse expenses if the pursuer was acting unreasonably and has the power to make such findings as it sees fit in relation to the expenses payable by each side.

The rules relating to the recovery of the expenses of the warrant and execution of the arrestment on the dependence are not altered by the entitlements just mentioned.

The court may make such findings as it sees fit in relation to expenses incurred in obtaining a warrant for arrestment of a ship *in rem* (as opposed to on the dependence) and its subsequent execution, or, as the case may be, opposing the warrant.

Paragraph 9 inserts a new s.47C, forbidding the arrestment of cargo unless it is actually on a ship at the time of execution of the arrestment. Cargo not on board ship could normally only be attached, but if it is in the possession of the defender or his agent, as an exception to the normal rule it may be arrested (this being the point of para.10 which adds a new subs.(3) to s.11 of the 2002 Act, being a list of the articles exempt from attachment). Section 47D states that where cargo is arrested, the ship is treated as arrested until the ship is unloaded. The ship may therefore not leave the harbour.

Paragraph 11, by inserting new subss.(5A) and (5B) into s.47, clarifies where it is competent to arrest a ship, cargo or other maritime property. Even being on land (as in a repair yard or dry dock) does not prevent the ship, cargo or her maritime property being arrested. However, neither she nor her cargo may be arrested on the high seas.

Paragraph 12, by introducing a new s.47E, deals with the situation where a ship is arrested on the dependence of an admiralty action raised against the demise charterer of the ship and obtains decree (subs.(1)). Where either the owner or the demise charterer pays the sum under the decree to the pursuer or his agent, or tenders the sum and the tender is not accepted within a reasonable time, the arrestment ceases to have effect (subs.(2)). Should that not happen, however, the pursuer is entitled to sell the ship (subs.(3)). The ranking arrangements of the proceeds of sale are explained in subsequent sections (subs.(4)). The ship itself is sold under these circumstances free of any incumbrances (subs.(5)). What is distinctive about subs.(5) is that the purchaser gets a better title than the demise charterer may have had, and the owner may lose his ship, subject to s.47F and G below. On the other hand, many ships are registered in flag of convenience countries and many owners would be hard to find, so that if this provision were not in existence pursuers would be unable to have any form of redress. Furthermore, if the owner is rash enough to permit an unreliable demise charterer to charter his ship, that is surely a matter between the owner and the charterer and if the owner loses his ship, he has a claim against the charterer, for what it is worth.

As regards the ranking of arrestments, under new s.47F, a creditor, carrying out arrestment in an action against the owner of the ship ranks in preference to a creditor carrying out any arrestment on the dependence of an admiralty action against the demise charterer.

Where the owner of the ship is sequestrated or wound up (as the case may be) and the ship has previously been arrested on the dependence of an admiralty action against the demise charterer, the creditor in that admiralty action is entitled to rank on the proceeds of the sale of the ship following the owner's sequestration or winding up. The arresting creditor has no rights against the sequestrated estate or the assets in the winding up other than a right to his portion of the sale proceeds of the ship (subs.(2)).

Subsection (3) deals with equalisation of diligence, so that the normal rules which apply to diligence carried out 60 days prior to sequestration or winding up fail to give a preference to the arresting creditor except to the extent of the expenses of the arrestment.

New s.47H permits the pursuer to obtain a warrant to arrest the ship to found jurisdiction when the defender is both the demise charterer of the ship and the defender in an action raised against him by the pursuer.

Paragraph 13 amends the Sheriff Court (Scotland) Act 1907 to allow a sheriff to grant warrant to arrest to found jurisdiction against a demise charterer as well as an owner. This will bring the demise charterer into the jurisdiction of the sheriff which hitherto he was not.

PART 15

ACTIONS FOR REMOVING FROM HERITABLE PROPERTY

GENERAL NOTE

These sections are designed to tidy up the legislation and improve the position of tenants who may be required to leave their rented premises. It is also designed to bring some consistency into the manner in which tenants or other occupiers, authorised or not, may be required to leave premises. Over the years there have been many different pieces of legislation dealing with different types of tenant, or different types of occupier, such as squatters or owners who cannot maintain their mortgage payments, and the process of making the tenant or occupier quit the premises varies from Act to Act. This Part tries to rationalise and make consistent the rules on this matter.

It should be explained that "removing" is a wide term, covering the removal of someone from premises, whether he is there lawfully or lawfully. "Ejecting" is more forceful and applies particularly to occupiers who are not in the premises lawfully, or having been there lawfully originally, are no longer there lawfully. A "warrant of ejection" is required where judicial officers are to be used to evict the occupiers of premises.

214.   Expressions used in this Part

(1) In this Part-

"a decree for removing from heritable property" means-

(a) a decree or warrant such as is mentioned in subsection (2) below; or

(b) a document such as is mentioned in subsection (3) below; and

"an action for removing from heritable property" means, in the case of a decree or warrant, the proceedings in which such a decree or warrant is obtained.

(2) The decrees and warrants referred to in subsection (1) above are-

(a) a decree of removing and warrant of ejection obtained in an action of removing;

(b) a decree and warrant of ejection obtained in an action of ejection;

(c) a summary warrant of ejection obtained by virtue of section 36 of the Sheriff Courts (Scotland) Act 1907 (c.51) (in this section, the "1907 Act");

(d) a warrant for summary ejection obtained by virtue of section 37 of the 1907 Act;

(e) a decree obtained by virtue of a summary application for removing under section 38 of the 1907 Act;

(f) a decree for recovery of possession of heritable property obtained by virtue of a summary cause under section 35(1)(c) of the Sheriff Courts (Scotland) Act 1971 (c.58);

(g) an order for possession (within the meaning of section 115(1) of the Rent (Scotland) Act 1984 (c.58)) obtained by virtue of the Housing (Scotland) Act 1987 (c.26) or the Housing (Scotland) Act 1988 (c.43);

(h) a warrant for ejection of a crofter granted under section 22(3) of the Crofters (Scotland) Act 1993 (c.44);

(i) an order of removal or ejection made under section 84(1)(e) of the Agricultural Holdings (Scotland) Act 2003 (asp 11); and

(j) a warrant of ejection obtained by virtue of a summary application under section 38(1) of, or paragraph 3(1) of schedule 5 to, the Housing (Scotland) Act 2006 (asp 1),

being decrees or warrants which, or extracts of which, authorise the removing or ejection of persons from subjects or premises.

(3) The documents referred to in subsection (1) above are-

(a) a lease, or an extract of a lease, having, by virtue of section 34 of the 1907 Act, the same force and effect as an extract decree of removing; and

(b) a letter of removal having, by virtue of section 35 of the 1907 Act, the same force and effect as an extract decree of removing.

(4) The Scottish Ministers may by order modify subsections (2) and (3) above by-

(a) adding types of decree, warrant or document to;

(b) removing types of decree, warrant or document from; or

(c) varying the description of,

the types of decree, warrant or document referred to in those subsections.

215. Procedure for execution of removing

The procedure and practice to be followed in the execution of any decree for removing from heritable property may be regulated and prescribed by Act of Sederunt and, without prejudice to that generality, such Act may, in particular-

(a) prescribe the form of any notices or certificates to be used in or for the purposes of any such execution; and

(b) prescribe the procedure for removal from subjects or premises of any property in or on those subjects or premises.

GENERAL NOTE

This gives authority for an Act of Sederunt to prescribe the various forms, practice and procedure for the execution of any decree for removing both persons and their property from the heritable property.

216. Service of charge before removing

(1) A defender and any effects of the defender may, by virtue of a decree for removing from heritable property, be removed from subjects or premises but only if-

(a) the defender has been charged to remove from those subjects or premises within 14 days after the giving of the charge; and

(b) the period of charge has expired without the defender so removing.

(2) Where-

(a) the subjects or premises are occupied by an occupant deriving right or having permission from the defender;

(b) the defender has been charged, under subsection (1) above, to remove from those subjects or premises; and

(c) the period of charge has expired without the occupant so removing,

that occupant and any effects of that occupant may be removed from the subjects or premises.

(3) The judicial officer removing the defender, any other occupant and any effects of such a defender or occupant from the subjects or premises-

(a) may, if necessary for the purposes of such removing, open shut and lockfast places; and

(b) must make an inventory of any effects removed.

(4) Where the decree for removing from heritable property is granted by a court, the court may, on cause shown, dispense with or vary the period of charge.

(5) It is no longer necessary to obtain from the Court of Session letters of ejection before removing a person by virtue of subsection (1) or (2) above.

(6) The Scottish Ministers may, by regulations, prescribe the form of charge under subsection (1) above.

GENERAL NOTE

This section is designed to give more notice to occupiers that they will have to leave the premises they may be inhabiting. The defender (this meaning any tenant, occupier or other person against whom an action of removing is being raised) will have to be served a charge, on a form yet to be devised, giving him 14 days' notice in which to remove himself and his belongings. Only if the defender and his belongings are still there after the period of 14 days has elapsed may the defender and his belongings be removed (subs.(1)). On cause shown, it may be possible to dispense with or vary the period of the charge (subs.(4)). This might be necessary if the defender is carrying on some nefarious activity or wrecking the premises.

Subsection (2) deals with a subtenant or other person who is occupying the premises and deriving his right, or having obtained permission to do so, from the defender. If the defender is required to remove himself following a charge, as in subs.(1), so must the subtenant or other person remove himself and his belongings too.

Subsection (3) permits a judicial officer to open shut and lockfast places as part of the process of removing, but must make an inventory of any effects removed (presumably by the judicial officer). The legislation does not elaborate on the practicalities of how a judicial officer makes the inventory or what should be done with that inventory.

The former procedure of letters of ejection, obtained from the Court of Session, is no longer required (subs.(5)). The warrant for removing will suffice.

There is a consequential amendment in para.6(3) of Sch.5. The period of charge for removings under s.7 of the Sheriff Courts (Scotland) Extracts Act 1892 is amended in s.7(4) of that Act, changing it from 48 hours to 14 days.

217. When removing not competent

(1) It is not competent to execute a decree for removing from heritable property on-
    (a) a Sunday;
    (b) a day which is a public holiday in the area in which the decree is to be executed; or
    (c) such other day as may be prescribed by Act of Sederunt.

(2) The execution of such a decree must not-
    (a) begin before 8 a.m. or after 8 p.m.; or
    (b) be continued after 8 p.m.,

unless the judicial officer has obtained prior authority from the sheriff for the district in which the subjects or premises are situated for such commencement or continuation.

GENERAL NOTE

This section restricts the execution of a decree for removing from heritable property to certain days and to certain hours within those days, although it is possible to obtain an order from the court to vary those days or hours.

218. Preservation of property left in premises

(1) A court, when granting decree for removing from heritable property, may direct that the pursuer takes such steps as the court considers appropriate for the preservation of any effects removed from the subjects or premises.

(2) The court may, when making a direction under subsection (1) above, order that the defender is to be liable for any costs incurred in taking such steps as are specified by virtue of that subsection.

GENERAL NOTE

Although it is not perhaps absolutely clear, this section seems to refer to the preservation of the defender's property left behind in the premises, and states that the court may direct the pursuer to take such steps as the court thinks appropriate to preserve the defender's effects removed from the premises, albeit, if the court so directs, at the defender's cost.

This rule may well cause more difficulties than it hopes to solve. A pursuer, anxious to regain his premises, will be unlikely to want to look after any of the defender's belongings and if the defender is unable to pay his rent, he is even less likely to be able to pay the pursuer's costs in preserving the belongings. In practice many a pursuer will take a more ruthless approach and throw the defender's belongings away rather than be troubled with looking after them. There appears to be no legislative mechanism to permit the pursuer to do this if the pursuer has been positively ordered to look after the defender's belongings. A prudent pursuer should therefore try to resist any attempt to make the court order him to preserve the debtor's belongings, for if there is no such order, there will be no requirement to preserve the belongings. A prudent defender will take his belongings with him.

219. Caution for pecuniary claims

(1) In an action for removing from heritable property, the court may, on cause shown, order the defender to find caution for any payment claimed (other than by way of expenses) by the pursuer for loss arising from the occupation of the subjects or premises by the defender or any other occupant deriving right or having permission from the defender.

(2) Notwithstanding subsection (1) above, it is no longer competent to order a defender to find caution for violent profits.

(3) Where an order is made under subsection (1) above, the defender may provide caution-

    (a) by means of a bond of caution or other guarantee; or

    (b) by consigning an appropriate sum in court.

(4) For the avoidance of doubt, the loss referred to in subsection (1) above includes loss arising from the lawful occupation of the subjects or premises by the defender or such other occupant.

GENERAL NOTE

The defender may be required to find caution for any payment, other than expenses, claimed by the pursuer for loss arising out of the defender's occupation of the premises, or from anyone deriving the right to be in the premises from the defender. It is no longer permissible for the pursuer to seek caution for violent profits, which is effectively a penal form of rent for being in premises illegally or without authority. Formerly, where a defender was occupying premises illegally, the pursuer could demand that he provide caution for violent profits, and if this was not forthcoming, the pursuer could proceed directly to a warrant for ejection.

Violent profits themselves may still be claimed, but caution therefor may not be claimed, though caution may still be obtained for any loss arising out of the defender's use (or his authorisee's use) of the premises.

The Ejection Caution Act 1594 is also repealed (see Sch.6 Pt 1).

PART 16

DISCLOSURE OF INFORMATION

GENERAL NOTE

This Part is connected with a project being undertaken by the Department of Constitutional Affairs in England, and was inserted at its request so that should equivalent legislation take place in England the two jurisdictions would work from the same legislative principles. In 2001 the DCA introduced a Green Paper, "A Single Piece of Bailiff Law and a Regulatory Structure for Enforcement" (also loosely known as the Enforcement Review) which was issued by the Lord Chancellor's Department. Chapter 6 "Information Disclosure and Data Sharing" is probably most relevant to this Part of the 2007 Act, (see:*http://www.dca.gov.uk/enforcement/enfrev01/rep06.htm*). What it does is to discuss how creditors might be allowed access to financial information about debtors at an early stage in order to identify at an early stage debtors who are in a position to pay their debts and to avoid wasting time and money chasing debtors who cannot pay their debts. At the moment, in both England and Scotland, much effort is expended using debt collection agencies, bailiffs and judicial officers tracking down debtors, and while within certain areas, these officials have a good local knowledge and can advise creditors on the likelihood of recovery, it is still not a very efficient method of enforcing payment. The Green Paper hopes to find a better way by allowing creditors, subject to certain safeguards, the opportunity to access court records and thus to see, at any early stage, whether pursuing certain debtors is a worthwhile exercise. The DCA seems, however, to have lost interest in the Enforcement Review for the time being and not to have taken it any further. There seem to be no further references to it on the DCA website and it is quite possible that in the wider discussion of the problems arising out of Data Protection and Freedom of Information, the Enforcement Review has been sidelined. So it is also possible that this Part may not in fact ever be used.

A perhaps more suspicious approach would be that there is little political mileage for politicians in bringing in legislation that makes it easier for creditors to extract payment out of debtors: while better payment might gladden the heart of some creditors and the tax-payer, creditors overall have fewer votes that debtors. Furthermore, the whole concept throws up some very difficult issues to do with privacy and the intrusion of the State, never mind creditors, into citizens' personal behaviour.

220. Information disclosure

(1) The Scottish Ministers may, by regulations, make provision for-
    (a) the obtaining, on the application to the sheriff by creditors, by the sheriff of information about debtors; and
    (b) the disclosure of that information to creditors to facilitate diligence to enforce payment of debts due by virtue of decrees and documents of debt.

(2) Regulations under subsection (1) above may, in particular-
    (a) provide about applications by the creditor;
    (b) prescribe persons who may make an application on the creditor's behalf;
    (c) provide about the functions of the sheriff on such applications;
    (d) prescribe the information about the debtor which may be obtained;
    (e) prescribe the persons from whom such information may be required;
    (f) provide about the consequences (if any) of such a prescribed person failing to disclose information when required to do so;
    (g) provide about the disclosure of information obtained by the sheriff to-
        (i) the creditor; and
        (ii) such other persons as the regulations may prescribe;
    (h) provide for unauthorised use or disclosure of such information to be an offence; and
    (i) make such other provision as the Scottish Ministers think fit.

(3) Regulations under subsection (1) above may not prescribe the debtor as a person from whom information may be required.

(4) A person who commits an offence under regulations made under subsection (1) above is liable to such penalties, not exceeding the penalties mentioned in subsection (5) below, as are provided for in the regulations.

(5) Those penalties are-
    (a) on summary conviction, imprisonment for a term not exceeding 12 months or a fine not exceeding the statutory maximum or both;
    (b) on conviction on indictment, imprisonment for a term not exceeding 2 years or a fine or both.

(6) Any provision made under regulations under subsection (1) above does not prejudice any power to disclose or use information (or to order such disclosure or use) that exists under any other enactment or rule of law.

(7) The disclosure or use of information by virtue of regulations under subsection (1) above is not to be taken to breach any restriction on the disclosure or use of such information (however imposed).

(8) The Scottish Ministers may by order modify, for the purposes of this section, the definitions of "decree" and "document of debt" in section 221 of this Act by-

    (a) adding types of decree or document to;

    (b) removing types of decree or document from; or

    (c) varying the description of,

the types of decree or document to which those definitions apply.

GENERAL NOTE

Subsection (1) allows the Scottish Ministers to draw up regulations allowing creditors to apply to the sheriff for certain information about debtors and for the disclosure of that information for the better enforcement of the payment of debts.

Subsection (2) provides for the various types of regulation that might be drawn up, as well as indicating that criminal penalties would apply for the unauthorised use or disclosure of the information obtained.

The remaining subsections detail further penalties for misuse, prevent the debtor from having to supply information about himself, provide that the information may be used under any other power to use such information, and allow the Scottish Ministers to modify the terms "decree" and "document of debt".

PART 17

GENERAL AND MISCELLANEOUS

221. Interpretation

In this Act-

    the "1985 Act" means the Bankruptcy (Scotland) Act 1985 (c.66);

    the "1987 Act" means the Debtors (Scotland) Act 1987 (c.18);

    the "2002 Act" means the Debt Arrangement and Attachment (Scotland) Act 2002 (asp 17);

    "certified electronic signature" is to be read in accordance with section 7(2) and (3) of the Electronic Communications Act 2000 (c.7);

    the "Commission" means the Scottish Civil Enforcement Commission;

    "debt advice and information package" has the meaning given by section 81(8) of this Act;

    "decree" means-

        (a) a decree of the Court of Session, of the High Court of Justiciary or of the sheriff;

        (b) a decree of the Court of Teinds;

        (c) a summary warrant;

        (d) a civil judgement granted outside Scotland by a court, tribunal or arbiter which, by virtue of any enactment or rule of law, is enforceable in Scotland;

        (e) an order or determination which, by virtue of any enactment, is enforceable as if it were an extract registered decree arbitral bearing a warrant for execution granted by the sheriff;

(f) a warrant granted in criminal proceedings for enforcement by civil diligence;

(g) an order under section 114 of the Companies Clauses Consolidation (Scotland) Act 1845 (c.17);

(h) a determination under section 46 of the Harbours, Docks and Piers Clauses Act 1847 (c.27); or

(i) a liability order within the meaning of section 33(2) of the Child Support Act 1991 (c.48);

"document of debt" means-

(a) a document registered for execution in the Books of Council and Session or in the sheriff court books;

(b) a bill protested for non-payment by a notary public; or

(c) a document or settlement which, by virtue of an Order in Council made under section 13 of the Civil Jurisdiction and Judgments Act 1982 (c.27), is enforceable in Scotland;

"electronic communication" has the meaning given by section 15(1) of the Electronic Communications Act 2000 (c.7);

"judicial officer" shall be construed in accordance with section 57(1) of this Act; and

"professional association" shall be construed in accordance with section 63(1)(a) of this Act.

GENERAL NOTE

This section provides a number of definitions referred to throughout the Act.

Execution of diligence: electronic standard securities

222. Registration and execution of electronic standard securities

(1) The Requirements of Writing (Scotland) Act 1995 (c. 7) is amended as follows.

(2) In section 6(1) of that Act (recording and registration of documents), after "subsection (3) below" insert "and section 6A of this Act".

(3) After section 6 of that Act insert-

"6A Registration for preservation and execution of electronic standard securities

(1) This section applies where an electronic document, which creates a standard security over a real right in land, is presumed under section 3A of this Act to have been authenticated by the granter.

(2) An office copy of the electronic document may be registered for preservation and execution in the Books of Council and Session or in the sheriff court books.

(3) An office copy so registered is to be treated for the purposes of executing any diligence (including, for the

271

avoidance of doubt, for the purposes of sections 1 and 2 of the Writs Execution (Scotland) Act 1877 (c. 40)) as if-

(a) the standard security were created by a document to which section 6(2) of this Act applies; and

(b) the office copy were that document.".

GENERAL NOTE

This section, which came into force on January 16, 2007, allows for the registration and execution of electronic standard securities. Given that electronic standard securities have no tangible existence, a mechanism needed to be drawn up to allow paper copies to be made if necessary, not least for the purpose of preservation and execution should they ever get lost or the computer networks fail. This section introduces a new s.6A into the Requirements of Writing (Scotland) Act 1995 (the "1995 Act"). New s.6A permits an office copy of an electronic standard security, already registered in the Land Register of Scotland, to be registered for preservation and execution in the Books of Council and Session or in the sheriff court books (the "court books"). This means that diligence may proceed on it as if it were the original. An office copy is a paper copy issued by the Keeper of the Registers of Scotland under s.6(5) of the Land Registration (Scotland) Act 1979 (the "1979 Act"). Electronic standard securities may be registered in the Land Register using Automated Registration of Title to Land ("ARTL"). The law relating to this system may be seen in ss.1(2A), (2B) and 2(A)-(C) of the 1995 Act, together with s.4(2A)-(C) of the 1979 Act (inserted by the Automated Registration of Title to Land (Electronic Communications) (Scotland) Order 2006 (SSI 2006/491)).

General

223. Crown application

(1) Subject to subsection (2) below, this Act binds the Crown acting in its capacity as a creditor.

(2) An amendment or other modification by this Act of an enactment binds the Crown to the same extent as the enactment being amended or modified.

GENERAL NOTE

Section 223(1) provides that this Act binds the Crown but only when the Crown is a creditor, not as a debtor. Subsection (2) clarifies that amendments made by this Act of other Acts (such as the 2002 Act) bind the Crown to the same extent which those existing Acts provide.

224. Orders and regulations

(1) Any power conferred by this Act on the Scottish Ministers to make orders or regulations is exercisable by statutory instrument.

(2) Any power conferred by this Act on the Scottish Ministers to make orders or regulations-

(a) may be exercised so as to make different provision for different cases or descriptions of case or for different purposes; and

(b) includes power to make such incidental, supplementary, consequential, transitory, transitional or saving provision as the Scottish Ministers think fit.

(3) A statutory instrument containing an order or regulations made under this Act (other than an order under section 227(3) of this Act) is, subject to subsections (4) and (5) below, subject to

annulment in pursuance of a resolution of the Scottish Parliament.

(4) No statutory instrument-

    (a) containing an order which makes provision such as is mentioned in section 225(2) of this Act; or

    (b) containing-

        (i) regulations made under section 50(4), 83(3), 92(2) or (3), 97(7)(b) or 98(6) of this Act; or

        (ii) the first regulations made under section 220(1) of this Act,

may be made unless a draft of it has been laid before, and approved by a resolution of, the Scottish Parliament.

(5) Subsection (3) above does not apply to a statutory instrument containing further regulations made under section 220(1) of this Act where a draft of it has been laid before, and approved by a resolution of, the Scottish Parliament.

GENERAL NOTE

This section gives power to the Scottish Ministers to make orders or regulations by means of statutory instruments. Most of these statutory instruments, and in particular the less contentious ones, will be subject to annulment ("the negative resolution procedure") by the Scottish Parliament (subs.(3)) but the more contentious ones, as outlined in subs.(4), require the positive approval ("the affirmative resolution procedure") of the Scottish Parliament, generally because they raise significant issues of political import.

Subsections (3) and (5) provide that further regulations made under s.220(1) (court-based information disclosure orders) do not need the affirmative resolution procedure where a draft has already been laid before and approved by the Scottish Parliament.

225. Ancillary provision

(1) The Scottish Ministers may, by order made by statutory instrument, make such incidental, supplemental, consequential, transitory, transitional or saving provision which they consider necessary or expedient for the purposes of this Act or in consequence of any provision made by or under this Act.

(2) An order under subsection (1) above may modify any enactment (including this Act) or instrument.

GENERAL NOTE

This allows the Scottish Ministers to make such provisions by statutory instrument as they see fit for the purposes of this Act.

226. Minor and consequential amendments and repeals

(1) Schedule 5 to this Act, which contains minor amendments and amendments consequential on the provisions of this Act, has effect.

(2) The enactments mentioned in the first column of Part 1 of schedule 6 to this Act are repealed to the extent specified in the second column of that schedule.

(3) The enactment mentioned in the first column of Part 2 of schedule 6 to this Act is revoked to the extent specified in the second column of that schedule.

GENERAL NOTE

This states that Schs 5 and 6 have effect.

This section came into effect April 1, 2008 to the extent of those specific parts of those two Schedules which were commenced by the Bankruptcy and Diligence etc (Scotland) Act 2007 (Commencement No.3, Savings and Transitionals) Order 2008 (SSI 2008/115).

227. Short title and commencement

(1) This Act may be cited as the Bankruptcy and Diligence etc. (Scotland) Act 2007.

(2) Section 222 of this Act comes into force on the day after Royal Assent.

(3) The remaining provisions of this Act, except this section and sections 224 and 225, come into force on such day as the Scottish Ministers may, by order, appoint.

(4) Different days may, under subsection (3) above, be appointed for different purposes.

GENERAL NOTE

This gives the short title and allows the Scottish Ministers to appoint days for the various provisions to come into force.

SCHEDULES

SCHEDULE 1

Minor and Consequential Amendments of the 1985 Act

(introduced by section 36)

1. The 1985 Act is amended as follows.

2. In section 1A (supervisory functions of the Accountant in Bankruptcy)-
    (a) in subsection (1)(a)(ii), for "permanent trustees" substitute "trustees (not being the Accountant in Bankruptcy)"; and
    (b) in subsection (2), for "court which" substitute "sheriff who".

3.
    (1) Section 2 (appointment and functions of interim trustee) is amended as follows.
    (2) For the word "court", in each place where it occurs, substitute "sheriff".
    (3) In subsection (1), for the word "interim", where it first and third occurs, substitute "the".
    (4) In subsection (2)-
        (a) for "it" substitute "he"; and
        (b) for the word "interim", where it first and third occurs, substitute "the".
    (5) In subsection (3)(c), for sub-paragraphs (i) and (ii) substitute "as the trustee".
    (6) In subsection (7), for the words from "the", where it first occurs, to "trustee", where it second occurs, substitute-
            (a) a trustee is appointed in a sequestration where the petition was presented by a creditor or the trustee acting under a trust deed; or
            (b) an interim trustee is appointed in pursuance of subsection (5) above,
    he".

4.
    (1) Section 5 (sequestration of the estate of living or deceased debtor) is amended as follows.
    (2) In subsection (2A), for "petition" substitute "application".
    (3) In subsection (2B)-
        (a) in both paragraphs (a) and (b), for "of presentation of the petition" substitute "the debtor application is made"; and

(b) in sub-paragraph (ii) of paragraph (c), for the words from "and" to the end of the sub-paragraph substitute "which is not a protected trust deed by reason of the creditors objecting, or not agreeing, in accordance with regulations under paragraph 5 of Schedule 5 to this Act, to the trust deed,".

(4) In subsection (2C), for "(2)(c)" substitute "(2)(b)(iv)".

(5) In subsection (4), after "petition" insert "or, as the case may be, the date the debtor application is made".

(6) In subsection (5), after "petition" insert "or, as the case may be, the date the debtor application is made".

(7) For subsection (6A) substitute-

(6A) In the case of a debtor application, the debtor shall send a statement of assets and liabilities to the Accountant in Bankruptcy along with the application.".

(8) After subsection (7), insert-

(7A) Where, after a debtor application is made but before the sequestration is awarded, the debtor dies, then the application shall fall.".

(9) After subsection (8), insert-

(8A) Where, after a debtor application is made but before the sequestration is awarded, a creditor who concurs in the application withdraws or dies, any other creditor who was a qualified creditor at the date the debtor application was made and who remains so qualified may notify the Accountant in Bankruptcy that he concurs in the application in place of the creditor who has withdrawn or died.".

(10) In subsection (9)(a), for "(6A)(b)" substitute "(6A)".

(11) In subsection (10)(a), for "(6A)(b)" substitute "(6A)".

5. In section 6(5) (combination of certain petitions for sequestration), for "subsection (4)(aa) to (b)" substitute "subsection (4)(b)".

6. In section 7(2)(c) (end of apparent insolvency), for "when" substitute "until".

7. In section 9(5) (jurisdiction), after "petition" insert ", the date the debtor application is made".

8. For section 10 (concurrent proceedings for sequestration or analogous remedy) substitute-

"10. Duty to notify existence of concurrent proceedings for sequestration or analogous remedy

(1) If, in the course of sequestration proceedings (referred to in this section and in section 10A of this Act as the "instant proceedings")-

(a) a petitioner for sequestration;

(b) the debtor; or

(c) a creditor concurring in a debtor application,

is, or becomes, aware of any of the circumstances mentioned in subsection (2) below, he shall as soon as possible take the action mentioned in subsection (3) below.

(2) Those circumstances are that, notwithstanding the instant proceedings-

(a) a petition for sequestration of the debtor's estate is before a sheriff or such sequestration has been awarded;

(b) a debtor application has been made in relation to the debtor's estate or sequestration has been awarded by virtue of such an application;

(c) a petition for the appointment of a judicial factor on the debtor's estate is before a court or such a judicial factor has been appointed;

(d) a petition is before a court for the winding up of the debtor under Part IV or V of the Insolvency Act 1986 (c.45) or section 372 of the Financial Services and Markets Act 2000 (c.8); or

(e) an application for an analogous remedy in respect of the debtor's estate is proceeding or such an analogous remedy is in force.

(3) The action referred to in subsection (1) above is-

(a) in a case where the instant proceedings are by petition for sequestration, to notify the sheriff to whom that petition was presented; and

(b) in a case where the instant proceedings are by debtor application, to notify the Accountant in Bankruptcy,

of the circumstance referred to in subsection (2) above.

(4) If a petitioner fails to comply with subsection (1) above, he may be made liable for the expenses of presenting the petition for sequestration.

(5) If a creditor concurring in a debtor application fails to comply with subsection (1) above, he may be made liable for the expenses of making the debtor application.

(6) If a debtor fails to comply with subsection (1) above, he shall be guilty of an offence and liable, on summary conviction, to a fine not exceeding level 5 on the standard scale.

(7) In this section and in section 10A of this Act "analogous remedy" means a bankruptcy order under the Bankruptcy Act 1914 (c.59) or an individual voluntary arrangement or bankruptcy order under the Insolvency Act 1986 (c.45) or an administration order under section 112 of the County Courts Act 1984 (c.28) in England and Wales or under any enactment having the like effect in Northern Ireland or a remedy analogous to any of the aforesaid remedies, or to sequestration, in any other country (including England, Wales and Northern Ireland).

10A Powers in relation to concurrent proceedings for sequestration or analogous remedy

(1) Where, in the course of instant proceedings which are by petition, any of the circumstances mentioned in paragraphs (a) to (d) of section 10(2) of this Act exists, the sheriff to whom the petition in the instant proceedings was presented may, on his own motion or at the instance of the debtor or any creditor or other person having an interest, allow that petition to proceed or may sist or dismiss it.

(2) Without prejudice to subsection (1) above, where, in the course of instant proceedings which are by petition, any of the circumstances mentioned in paragraphs (a), (c) or (d) of section 10(2) of this Act exists, the Court of Session may, on its own motion or on the application of the debtor or any creditor or other person having an interest, direct the sheriff before whom the petition in the instant proceedings is pending, or the sheriff before whom the other petition is pending, to sist or dismiss the petition in the instant proceedings or, as the case may be, the other petition, or may order the petitions to be heard together.

(3) Without prejudice to subsection (1) above, where, in the course of instant proceedings which are by petition, the circumstance mentioned in paragraph (b) of section 10(2) of this Act exists, the sheriff to whom the petition in the instant proceedings was presented may, on his own motion or at the instance of the debtor or any creditor or other person having an interest, direct the Accountant in Bankruptcy to dismiss the debtor application.

(4) Where, in the course of instant proceedings which are by debtor application, any of the circumstances mentioned in paragraphs (a) to (d) of section 10(2) of this Act exists, the Accountant in Bankruptcy may dismiss the debtor application in the instant proceedings.

(5) Where, in respect of the same estate-
    (a) a petition for sequestration is pending before a sheriff; and
    (b) an application for an analogous remedy is proceeding or an analogous remedy is in force,
the sheriff, on his own motion or at the instance of the debtor or any creditor or other person having an interest, may allow the petition for sequestration to proceed or may sist or dismiss it.

(6) Where, in respect of the same estate-
    (a) a debtor application has been made and has not been determined; and
    (b) an application for an analogous remedy is proceeding or an analogous remedy is in force,
the Accountant in Bankruptcy may proceed to determine the application or may dismiss it.".

9. In section 11 (creditor's oath)-
    (a) in subsection (1), for "petition by a debtor" substitute "debtor application"; and
    (b) in subsection (4)-
        (i) for "court to which" substitute "sheriff to whom"; and
        (ii) after "presented" insert "or, in the case of a creditor concurring in a debtor application, the Accountant in Bankruptcy".

10. In section 12 (when sequestration is awarded)-
    (a) in subsection (1)(c), for "subsections (6) and" substitute "subsection";

(b) in subsection (2)-
    (i) for "court to which" substitute "sheriff to whom"; and
    (ii) for "it" substitute "him";
(c) in subsection (3)-
    (i) for "court" substitute "sheriff"; and
    (ii) for "it" substitute "he"; and
(d) in subsection (4)-
    (i) in paragraph (a), for "the petition for sequestration is presented by the debtor" substitute "a debtor application is made"; and
    (ii) in paragraph (b)(i), for "court" substitute "sheriff".

11.
(1) Section 13 (resignation, removal etc. of interim trustee) is amended as follows.
(2) Before subsection (1), insert-
    (A1) This section applies where an interim trustee is appointed under section 2(5) of this Act and the petition for sequestration has not been determined.".
(3) For the word "court", in each place where it occurs, substitute "sheriff".
(4) In subsection (3), for "it" substitute "the sheriff".
(5) In subsection (6), for "disqualified from acting as permanent" substitute "ineligible to be elected as replacement".

12.
(1) Section 14 (registration of court order) is amended as follows.
(2) In subsection (1)-
    (a) for "clerk of the court" substitute "sheriff clerk"; and
    (b) in paragraph (a), for "relevant court order" substitute "order of the sheriff granting warrant under section 12(2) of this Act".
(3) After subsection (1), insert-
    (1A) Where the Accountant in Bankruptcy awards sequestration on a debtor application he shall forthwith after the date of sequestration send a certified copy of his determination of the application to the keeper of the register of inhibitions for recording in that register.".
(4) In subsection (2), after "subsection (1)(a)" insert "or (1A)".
(5) In subsection (3)-
    (a) after paragraph (a), insert-
        (aa) on the recording under paragraph 11(4)(a) of Schedule 4 to this Act of a certified copy of a certificate;" ; and
    (b) in paragraph (b), for "paragraph (a)" substitute "paragraphs (a) and (aa)".
(6) The heading to that section becomes "Registration of warrant or determination of debtor application".

13. In section 15 (further provision relating to award of sequestration), after subsection (3), insert-
    "(3A) Where the Accountant in Bankruptcy, on determining a debtor application, refuses to award sequestration, the debtor or a creditor concurring in the application may appeal against such a determination within 14 days of it being made to the sheriff.".

14. In section 16 (petition for recall of sequestration)-
    (a) in subsection (1)(a), for "petition" substitute "debtor application"; and
    (b) in subsection (2), for "petition", where it first occurs, substitute "debtor application".

15. In section 17 (recall of sequestration)-
    (a) in subsection (1)(c), for "section 10(5)" substitute "section 10(7)";
    (b) in subsection (3)(a)-
        (i) after "sequestration" insert "or, as the case may be, the debtor application"; and
        (ii) for "permanent" substitute "the";
    (c) in subsection (3)(b), for "petition" substitute "debtor application"; and
    (d) in subsection (5)-
        (i) in paragraph (a), after "sequestration" insert ", the making of the debtor application";
        (ii) in paragraph (b), for "permanent" substitute "the"; and
        (iii) after paragraph (b) insert-

"(c) affect a bankruptcy restrictions order which has not been annulled under section 56J(1)(a) of this Act.".

16.

(1) Section 18 (interim preservation of estate) is amended as follows.

(2) In subsection (1), after "may" insert ", in pursuance of the function conferred on him by section 2(6A) of this Act,".

(3) In subsection (2)-
(a) for "functions" substitute "function"; and
(b) for "2(4)(a)" substitute "2(6A)".

(4) After subsection (2) insert-
(2A) Section 43 of this Act applies to an interim trustee as it applies to a trustee.".

(5) In subsection (3)-
(a) for "court" substitute "sheriff"; and
(b) in paragraph (c), for "it" substitute "he".

(6) In subsection (4)-
(a) for "court", in both places where it occurs, substitute "sheriff"; and
(b) for "it", in both places where it occurs, substitute "he".

(7) The italic cross-heading preceding that section becomes "Initial stages of sequestration".

17.

(1) Section 19 (statement of assets and liabilities) is amended as follows.

(2) In subsection (1)-
(a) for "petitioner for sequestration is the debtor" substitute "debtor has made a debtor application";
(b) for "interim trustee", where it first occurs, substitute "trustee under section 2 of this Act"; and
(c) for "lodged in court in pursuance of section 5(6A)(a)" substitute "sent to the Accountant in Bankruptcy in pursuance of section 5(6A)".

(3) In subsection (2), for "2(7)" substitute "2(7)(a)".

18. In section 20 (trustee's duty to send information to Accountant in Bankruptcy before statutory meeting)-
(a) in subsection (2)-
(i) after "meeting" insert "or, where the trustee does not intend to hold such a meeting, not later than 60 days after the date on which sequestration is awarded,";
(ii) in paragraph (a), after "liabilities" insert "(unless the statement has already been received by the Accountant in Bankruptcy by virtue of section 5(6A) of this Act)"; and
(iii) in paragraph (b), at the beginning insert "subject to subsection (2A) below," and
(b) after that subsection insert-
(2A) The trustee need not send a statement of the debtor's affairs to the Accountant in Bankruptcy in accordance with subsection (2)(b) above if the trustee has sent a copy of the inventory and valuation to the Accountant in Bankruptcy in accordance with section 38(1)(c) of this Act.".

19. The italic cross-heading preceding section 21 becomes "Statutory meeting of creditors and trustee vote".

20. In section 21A(2) (time limit for giving notice of intention to call statutory meeting), for "of the sequestration" substitute "on which sequestration is awarded".

21. In section 21B (report where no statutory meeting called)-
(a) in subsection (1)(a), for "sheriff" substitute "Accountant in Bankruptcy"; and
(b) after subsection (1), insert-
"(1A) This section does not apply in any case where the Accountant in Bankruptcy is the trustee.".

22. In section 22(3)(a) (trustee's duty to inform creditors outside Scotland), for "21(2)" substitute "21A(2)".

23.

(1) Section 24 (election of permanent trustee) is amended as follows.

(2) In subsection (2), for the word "permanent", where it first and second occurs, substitute "replacement".

(3) In subsection (3), for the words "election of the permanent trustee" substitute "trustee vote".

(4) In subsection (3A)-

    (a) for the word "interim" substitute "original";

    (b) in paragraph (a), for the words "election of the permanent trustee" substitute "trustee vote";

    (c) in paragraph (b), for the word "permanent" substitute "replacement"; and

    (d) for the words "section 25A of this Act shall apply" substitute "shall continue to act as the trustee".

(5) In subsection (4)-

    (a) for the word "interim", where it first and second occurs, substitute "original";

    (b) for the words "election of the permanent trustee" substitute "trustee vote";

    (c) for the word "permanent", where it second occurs, substitute "replacement"; and

    (d) after paragraph (b), insert-

        "and he shall continue to act as the trustee.".

24.

(1) Section 25 (confirmation of permanent trustee) is amended as follows.

(2) In subsection (1)-

    (a) for the word "permanent", in both places where it occurs, substitute "replacement"; and

    (b) for the word "interim", in both places where it occurs, substitute "original".

(3) In subsection (2)-

    (a) for "permanent trustee" substitute "trustee in the sequestration"; and

    (b) for the words from "confirm" to "Bankruptcy" substitute "make an order appointing him as such".

(4) In subsection (4), in paragraph (b)-

    (a) for "interim" substitute "original"; and

    (b) for "for the election of a permanent trustee" substitute "at which a new trustee vote shall be held".

(5) In subsection (5), for "confirmation" substitute "appointment".

(6) In subsection (6)-

    (a) for the word "permanent", where it first occurs, substitute "replacement"; and

    (b) in paragraph (b), for "confirmed in office" substitute "appointed".

25.

(1) Section 26 (provisions relating to termination of interim trustee's functions) is amended as follows.

(2) Before subsection (1), insert-

    "(A1) This section applies where a replacement trustee is appointed under section 25 of this Act.".

(3) In subsection (1), for the words from "Where" to "office" substitute "The original trustee, shall, on the appointment of the replacement trustee".

(4) In subsection (2)-

    (a) for the words from "confirmation" to "interim", where it first occurs, substitute "appointment of the replacement trustee, the original"; and

    (b) in paragraph (b), for "permanent", where it first occurs, substitute "replacement".

(5) After subsection (2), insert-

    "(2A) Where the original trustee was appointed under section 2(5) of this Act as the interim trustee in the sequestration, his accounts and the claim referred to in subsection (2)(a) above shall include accounts and a claim for the period of his appointment as interim trustee.".

(6) In subsection (3)-

    (a) in paragraph (a)(ii), for "interim" substitute "original";

    (b) in paragraph (b)(i), for "interim", where it first occurs, substitute "original"; and

    (c) in paragraph (b)(ii)-

        (i) for "interim" substitute "original"; and

        (ii) for "permanent" substitute "replacement".

(7) In subsection (4)-

    (a) for "interim" substitute "original"; and

    (b) for "permanent" substitute "replacement".

(8) In subsection (5)-

    (a) for "permanent" substitute "replacement";
    (b) for "confirmed in office" substitute "appointed";
    (c) for "confirmation" substitute "appointment"; and
    (d) for "interim" substitute "original".
(9) In subsection (5A), for "interim" substitute "original".
(10) The heading to that section becomes "Provisions relating to termination of original trustee's functions".

26.

(1) Section 26A (Accountant in Bankruptcy to account for intromissions) is amended as follows.
(2) In subsection (1)-
    (a) for "interim" substitute "original"; and
    (b) for "becomes the permanent trustee" substitute "is appointed as replacement trustee under section 25 of this Act".
(3) In subsection (2)-
    (a) for "confirmation of the permanent trustee in office" substitute "the appointment of the replacement trustee";
    (b) for the word "permanent", where it second occurs, substitute "replacement"; and
    (c) for the word "interim", where it first occurs, substitute "original".
(4) In subsection (3)-
    (a) for "confirmation in office of the permanent" substitute "appointment of the replacement";
    (b) for the word "permanent", where it second occurs, substitute "replacement"; and
    (c) in paragraph (a), for "interim" substitute "original".
(5) In subsection (5), for "permanent" substitute "replacement".
(6) In subsection (8)-
    (a) for "permanent" substitute "replacement";
    (b) for "confirmed in office" substitute "appointed"; and
    (c) for "confirmation" substitute "appointment".

27.

(1) In section 27 (discharge of interim trustee)-
    (a) in subsection (2), after "debtor", where it first occurs, insert ", to all creditors known to the original trustee";
    (b) for the word "interim", in each place where it occurs, substitute "original"; and
    (c) for the word "permanent", in each place where it occurs, substitute "replacement".
(2) The heading to that section becomes "Discharge of original trustee".

28.

(1) Section 28 (resignation and death of permanent trustee) is amended as follows.
(2) In subsections (1), (1A) and (2), for "sheriff", in each place where it occurs, substitute "Accountant in Bankruptcy".
(3) In subsection (4)-
    (a) for "and confirmation in office of the", substitute "of a replacement trustee and the appointment of that"; and
    (b) for "confirmation in office", where it second occurs, substitute "appointment".
(4) In subsection (5), for ", the provisions of section 25A of this Act shall apply" substitute-
        (a) the Accountant in Bankruptcy; or
        (b) such person as may be nominated by the Accountant in Bankruptcy (being a person who is not ineligible for election as replacement trustee under section 24(2) of this Act) if that person consents to the nomination,
may apply to the sheriff for appointment as trustee in the sequestration; and, on such application, the sheriff shall make an order so appointing the Accountant in Bankruptcy or, as the case may be, the person nominated by him.".
(5) The heading to that section becomes "Resignation and death of trustee".
(6) The italic cross-heading preceding that section becomes "Replacement of trustee".

29.

(1) Section 29 (removal of permanent trustee and trustee not acting) is amended as follows.

(2) In subsection (7)-
  (a) for "and confirmation in office of the", substitute "of a replacement trustee and the appointment of that"; and
  (b) for "confirmation in office", where it second occurs, substitute "appointment".

(3) After subsection (9), insert-
  "(10) This section does not apply in any case where the Accountant in Bankruptcy is the trustee.".

(4) The heading to that section becomes "Removal of trustee and trustee not acting".

30.

(1) Section 31 (vesting of estate at date of sequestration) is amended as follows.

(2) In subsection (2), for "the act and warrant" substitute "his appointment".

(3) In subsection (4), for "the act and warrant" substitute "his appointment".

(4) In subsection (6)-
  (a) for "court", in both places where it occurs, substitute "sheriff"; and
  (b) for "it" substitute "he".

(5) In subsection (7), for "court" substitute "sheriff".

(6) The italic cross-heading preceding that section becomes "Vesting of estate in trustee".

31. Section 31A (proceedings under EC regulation: modified definition of "estate") as inserted by regulation 12 of the Insolvency (Scotland) Regulations 2003 (S.I. 2003 No. 2109) is renumbered as section 31ZA.

32. In section 32 (vesting of estate and dealings of debtor after sequestration), in subsection (6)-
  (a) for "act and warrant" substitute "order"; and
  (b) for "confirming the permanent trustee's appointment" substitute "or, as the case may be, by the Accountant in Bankruptcy appointing the trustee".

33. In section 37(1) (effect of sequestration on diligence), for "court" substitute "sheriff or, as the case may be, the determination of the debtor application by the Accountant in Bankruptcy".

34.

(1) In section 38(1)(a) (taking possession of estate by permanent trustee), for "confirmation in office" substitute "appointment".

(2) The heading to that section becomes "Taking possession of estate by trustee"

(3) The italic cross-heading preceding that section becomes "Administration of estate by trustee".

35.

(1) Section 39 (management and realisation of estate) is amended as follows.

(2) In subsection (1)-
  (a) for "confirmation in office" substitute "appointment";
  (b) for "subsection (6)" substitute "subsections (1A), (6) and (9)"; and
  (c) in paragraph (b), for "court" substitute "sheriff".

(3) After subsection (1), insert-
  "(1A) Subsection (1) above does not apply in any case where the Accountant in Bankruptcy is the trustee.".

(4) In subsection (2)-
  (a) in paragraph (a), after "on" insert "or close down"; and
  (b) after paragraph (d), insert-
      "(e) borrow money in so far as it is necessary for the trustee to do so to safeguard the debtor's estate;
      (f) effect or maintain insurance policies in respect of the business or property of the debtor.".

(5) In subsection (4)(c), for "court" substitute "sheriff".

36. In section 40 (power in relation to family home)-
  (a) in subsection (1), for "court" substitute "sheriff";
  (b) in subsection (2)-
      (i) for "court", in both places where it occurs, substitute "sheriff"; and

      (ii) for "it", in both places where it occurs, substitute "he"; and

  (c) the heading to that section becomes "Power of trustee in relation to the debtor's family home".

37. In section 41(1) (protection of occupancy rights of non-entitled spouse)-

  (a) for "of issue of the act and warrant of" substitute "the order is made appointing";

  (b) for "such act and warrant is issued" substitute "trustee is appointed";

  (c) for "such issue" substitute "order making such an appointment"; and

  (d) in paragraph (b)-

      (i) for "Court of Session" substitute "sheriff";

      (ii) after "date", where it second occurs, insert "of the award";

      (iii) for "it", in both places where it occurs, substitute "he"; and

      (iv) after "sequestration", where it third occurs, insert "or, as the case may be, the debtor application".

38. In section 41A(1) (protection of occupancy rights of civil partner)-

  (a) for "of issue of the act and warrant of" substitute "the order is made appointing";

  (b) for "such act and warrant is issued" substitute "trustee is appointed";

  (c) for "such issue" substitute "order making such an appointment"; and

  (d) in paragraph (b)-

      (i) for "Court of Session" substitute "sheriff";

      (ii) after "date", where it second occurs, insert "of the award";

      (iii) for "it", in both places where it occurs, substitute "he"; and

      (iv) after "sequestration", where it third occurs, insert "or, as the case may be, the debtor application".

39. In section 42 (contractual powers of permanent trustee)-

  (a) in subsection (2), for "court" substitute "sheriff"; and

  (b) the heading to that section becomes "Contractual powers of trustee".

40. The heading to section 43 becomes "Money received by trustee".

41. In section 46(1) (warrant to apprehend)-

  (a) in paragraph (a), for "messenger-at-arms or sheriff officer" substitute "judicial officer"; and

  (b) in the proviso, for "court" substitute "sheriff".

42. In section 48 (submission of claims to permanent trustee)-

  (a) in subsection (2), in paragraph (b), for the words from "and" to the end of that paragraph, substitute "which has not been rejected in whole";

  (b) in subsection (3), for the words from "for", where it second occurs, to "trustee", where it second occurs, substitute "after the word "trustee" there were inserted the words""; and

  (c) the heading to that section becomes "Submission of claims to trustee".

43. In section 51(1)(d) (order of priority in distribution), for "the petition" substitute "a debtor application".

44.

(1) Section 52 (estate to be distributed in respect of accounting periods) is amended as follows.

(2) In subsection (2)-

  (a) for "6", in both places where it occurs, substitute "12"; and

  (b) in paragraph (a)-

      (i) at the beginning insert "subject to subsection (2ZA) below,"; and

      (ii) for "of sequestration" substitute "on which sequestration is awarded".

(3) After subsection (2), insert-

    "(2ZA) Where the trustee was appointed under section 2(5) of this Act as interim trustee in the sequestration, the first accounting period shall be the period beginning with the date of his appointment as interim trustee and ending on the date 12 months after the date on which sequestration is awarded.".

45. In section 53 (procedure after end of accounting period)-

  (a) in subsection (2A)(c), for "have not determined that the account should" substitute "or, if there are no commissioners, the Accountant in Bankruptcy, have determined that the account need not"; and

    (b) after subsection (6A) (as inserted by section 30(2)(b) of this Act) insert-
        (6B) Before-
           (a) a debtor; or
           (b) a creditor,
        appeals under subsection (6) above, he must give notice to the trustee of
        his intention to appeal.".

46. After section 53, insert-

"53A Modification of procedure under section 53 where Accountant in Bankruptcy is trustee

    (1) In any case where the Accountant in Bankruptcy is the trustee, section 53 of this Act shall have effect subject to the following modifications.

    (2) For subsections (1) to (7) of that section, there shall be substituted-

       "(1) At the end of each accounting period, the Accountant in Bankruptcy shall prepare accounts of his intromissions with the debtor's estate and he shall make a determination of his fees and outlays calculated in accordance with regulations made under section 69A of this Act.

       (2) Such accounts and determination shall be available for inspection by the debtor and the creditors not later than 6 weeks after the end of the accounting period to which they relate.

       (3) In making a determination as mentioned in subsection (1) above, the Accountant in Bankruptcy may take into account any adjustment which he may wish to make in the amount of his remuneration fixed in respect of any earlier accounting period.

       (4) Not later than 8 weeks after the end of an accounting period, the debtor (subject to subsection (5) below) or any creditor may appeal to the sheriff against the determination of the Accountant in Bankruptcy; and the decision of the sheriff on such an appeal shall be final.

       (5) A debtor may appeal under subsection (4) above if, and only if, he satisfies the sheriff that he has, or is likely to have, a pecuniary interest in the outcome of the appeal.

       (6) Before-
          (a) a debtor; or
          (b) any creditor,
        appeals under subsection (4) above, he must give notice to the Accountant in Bankruptcy of his intention to appeal.

       (7) On the expiry of the period within which an appeal may be made under subsection (4) above, the Accountant in Bankruptcy shall pay to the creditors their dividends in accordance with the scheme of division.".

    (3) In subsection (10) for the words "the audited" there shall be substituted the word "his".".

47. In section 55, subsection (3) (references to a fine or penalty to include a confiscation order), as inserted by paragraph 15(5) of Schedule 11 to the Proceeds of Crime Act 2002 (c.29), is renumbered as subsection (2A).

48. The italic cross-heading preceding section 57 becomes "Discharge of trustee".

49. The heading to section 57 becomes "Discharge of trustee".

50. In section 58A(7) (discharge of Accountant in Bankruptcy), after "sequestration" insert "including, where the Accountant in Bankruptcy was the interim trustee, the functions of the interim trustee".

51. In section 59A(1) (petition for conversion into sequestration), for "court", where it first occurs, substitute "sheriff".

52. In section 59B(1)(c) (contents of affidavit), for "court", in both places where it occurs, substitute "sheriff".

53. In section 59C (power of court)-
    (a) for "court", in each place where it occurs, substitute "sheriff";
    (b) in subsection (1), for "it" substitute "he"; and
    (c) the heading to that section becomes "Power of sheriff".

54. In section 60B(2) (trustee to give notice or provide copies of documents to member State liquidator)-
(a) for "or a permanent" substitute "trustee or a"; and
(b) for "court", where it second occurs, substitute "sheriff".

55. In section 61 (extortionate credit transactions), for "court", in both places where it occurs, substitute "sheriff".

56. The heading to section 64 becomes "Debtor to co-operate with trustee".

57. In section 65(1) (arbitration and compromise), for "court" substitute "sheriff".

58. The heading to section 69 becomes "Outlays of insolvency practitioner in actings as interim trustee or trustee".

59. In section 70(1)(a) (supplies by utilities), for "the petition was presented by the debtor" substitute "a debtor application was made".

60.
(1) Section 73 (interpretation) is amended as follows.
(2) In subsection (1)-
(a) after the definition of "associate", insert-
""bankruptcy restrictions order" has the meaning given by section 56A(1) of this Act;
""bankruptcy restrictions undertaking" has the meaning given by section 56G(1) of this Act;";
(b) after the definition of "debtor", insert-
""debtor application" means an application for sequestration made to the Accountant in Bankruptcy under sections 5(2)(a) or 6(3)(a), (4)(a) or (6)(a) of this Act;";
(c) after the definition of "the EC regulation", insert-
""enactment" includes an Act of the Scottish Parliament and any enactment comprised in subordinate legislation under such an Act;";
(d) in the definition of "interim trustee", for "2" substitute "2(5)";
(e) after the definition of "ordinary debt", insert-
""original trustee" shall be construed in accordance with section 24(1)(a) of this Act;";
(f) after the definition of "relevant person", insert-
""replacement trustee" shall be construed in accordance with section 24(1)(b) of this Act;";
(g) after the definition of "sederunt book", insert-
""sequestration proceedings" includes a debtor application and analogous expressions shall be construed accordingly;"; and
(h) after the definition of "trust deed", insert-
""trustee" means trustee in the sequestration;
"trustee vote" shall be construed in accordance with section 24(1) of this Act;".
(3) In subsection (5)(b), for "such a petition" substitute "a debtor application".
(4) In subsection (6), for "clerk of the court" substitute "sheriff clerk".
(5) After subsection (6), insert-
"(6A) Any reference in this Act, howsoever expressed, to the time when a debtor application is made shall be construed as a reference to the time when the application is received by the Accountant in Bankruptcy.".

61. In Schedule 6 (meetings of creditors and commissioners)-
(a) for "court", in each place where it occurs, substitute "sheriff"; and
(b) in paragraph 15(1), for "shall", in both places where it occurs, substitute "may".

62. In Part II of Schedule 7 (re-enactment of certain provisions of the Bankruptcy (Scotland) Act 1913), in paragraph 24(5), for "(5)" substitute "(4)".

GENERAL NOTE
    This Schedule deals with changes to the 1985 Act, and many of the provisions are there to take account of the fact that sequestration henceforth will take place either in the sheriff court or under the auspices of the Accountant in Bankruptcy by means of debtor applications. This has consequential effects on procedural terms (the use of application in the sheriff court as opposed to

petition in the Court of Session, for example). Paragraph 8 outlines the requirement to notify the court or the Accountant in Bankruptcy of concurrent procedures either having taken place or taking place, thus allowing the later proceedings to be sisted or as the case may be dismissed.

SCHEDULE 2

THE SCOTTISH CIVIL ENFORCEMENT COMMISSION

(introduced by section 50(7))

Status

1.
(1) The Commission-
    (a) is not a servant or agent of the Crown; and
    (b) does not enjoy any status, immunity or privilege of the Crown.
(2) The Commission's property is not property of, or property held on behalf of, the Crown.

Membership

2. The Commission is to consist of-
    (a) the following persons appointed by the Scottish Ministers-
        (i) a Senator of the College of Justice nominated by the Lord President of the Court of Session;
        (ii) a sheriff principal or a sheriff, so nominated;
        (iii) a person who is an advocate or solicitor;
        (iv) a judicial officer nominated by the professional association; and
        (v) 3 other persons, not being persons holding an office or, as the case may be, possessing a qualification referred to in paragraphs (i) to (iv) above;
    (b) the Lord Lyon King of Arms; and
    (c) the Keeper of the Registers of Scotland.

3. No person may be appointed as a member of the Commission if that person is, or has at any time during the previous year been, a member of-
    (a) the House of Commons;
    (b) the Scottish Parliament; or
    (c) the European Parliament.

Tenure of office

4. Subject to paragraphs 5 to 14 below, a member appointed by the Scottish Ministers holds and vacates office on terms and conditions determined by the Scottish Ministers.

5. Subject to paragraphs 6 to 10 below, members are appointed for a period of not more than 5 years and are eligible for reappointment.

6. A member who is-
    (a) a Senator of the College of Justice; or
    (b) a sheriff principal or a sheriff,
holds office only so long as that member retains the office of Senator of the College of Justice or, as the case may be, sheriff principal or sheriff.

7. A member who is-
    (a) a solicitor or advocate; or
    (b) a judicial officer,
holds office only so long as that member retains the qualification of solicitor or advocate or, as the case may be, officer.

8. A member who becomes a member of-
    (a) the House of Commons;
    (b) the Scottish Parliament; or
    (c) the European Parliament,
ceases to be a member of the Commission.

9. A member may at any time resign by notice in writing to the Scottish Ministers.

10. The Scottish Ministers may remove a member from office if they consider-
    (a) that the member is unable or unfit to discharge the functions of a member; or
    (b) that the member has not complied with the terms and conditions of the office as determined under paragraph 4 above.

11. Where-
    (a) a person makes a complaint to the Commission about the conduct of a member; or
    (b) a member is charged with an offence,
the Commission may suspend the member from office.

12. The Commission may revoke or extend a suspension made under paragraph 11 above.

Filling vacancies

13.
(1) This paragraph applies where a person ceases to be a member (whether by resignation or otherwise) prior to the expiry of that member's period of appointment.
(2) The Scottish Ministers must appoint a person to fill the vacancy.
(3) A person so appointed-
    (a) must hold the same office or, as the case may be, possess the same qualification as the member that person succeeds; and
    (b) holds and vacates office as a member on terms and conditions determined by the Scottish Ministers.

14. Paragraphs 5 to 13 above apply in relation to a member appointed under paragraph 13(2) above as they apply to a member appointed under paragraph 4 above.

Chairperson

15. The Commission must select one member as chairperson of the Commission for a period determined by the Commission.

Disciplinary Committee

16. The Commission must appoint a disciplinary committee (which may include persons who are not members of the Commission) for the purposes of carrying out disciplinary proceedings under section 71 and making decisions under sections 68(2) and 72 of this Act.

Remuneration

17. The Commission must pay to its members (and to members of its committees and subcommittees who are not members of the Commission) any-
    (a) remuneration; and
    (b) allowances in respect of expenses properly incurred in the performance of their functions,
as the Scottish Ministers may determine.

General powers

18. The Commission may do anything which it considers is necessary or expedient for the purpose of exercising or in connection with its functions.

19. The power in paragraph 18 above includes, in particular, power to-
    (a) appoint committees and sub-committees (including committees and subcommittees which include persons who are not members of the Commission);
    (b) delegate any of its functions to-
        (i) its committees or sub-committees; or
        (ii) its chief executive officer appointed under paragraph 24 below;

    (c) with the approval of the Scottish Ministers, borrow and lend money;
    (d) acquire and dispose of land and other property;
    (e) enter into contracts;
    (f) specify its own procedures, so far as not provided for by this Act or by regulations or rules made under this Act; and
    (g) levy a charge for services it may provide in accordance with its functions.

20. Where the Commission levies charges under paragraph 19(g) above, it must-
    (a) publish a list of; and
    (b) annually review,
those charges.

Quorum

21. Subject to any regulations as may be made under paragraph 22 below, the quorum of the Commission, the disciplinary committee and any committee or sub-committee appointed under paragraph 19(a) above is such as the Commission may determine.

Structure and procedures

22. The Scottish Ministers may, by regulations, make further provision about the structure and procedures of the Commission as they consider appropriate.

Chief executive officer and other staff

23. Subject to paragraph 24 below, the Commission may appoint as employees any persons (other than its members) it considers necessary for the performance of its functions.

24. The Commission must appoint, as a member of staff, a chief executive officer who is responsible to the Commission for the general exercise of its functions.

25. The Commission may determine the remuneration and conditions of service of a chief executive officer appointed under paragraph 24 above.

26. The Commission may-
    (a) pay, or make arrangements for the payment of;
    (b) make payments towards the provision of; and
    (c) provide and maintain schemes (whether contributory or not) for the payment of,
pensions, allowances and gratuities to or in respect of such of its employees, or former employees, as it considers appropriate.

27. The reference in paragraph 26 above to pensions, allowances and gratuities includes a reference to pensions, allowances and gratuities by way of compensation for loss of employment or reduction in remuneration.

28. Anything done by virtue of paragraphs 24 to 27 above must be approved by the Scottish Ministers.

Location of office

29. The Commission-
    (a) must not determine where its office premises are to be located without that location being approved by the Scottish Ministers; and
    (b) must comply with any direction as to the location of those premises given by the Scottish Ministers.

Financing by the Scottish Ministers

30. The Scottish Ministers may-
    (a) pay grants;
    (b) make loans,
to the Commission of amounts that they determine.

31. Any-
    (a) grant paid in pursuance of paragraph 30(a) above;

(b) loan made in pursuance of paragraph 30(b) above,

may be paid or, as the case may be, made on such terms and subject to such conditions (including, in the case of a loan, conditions as to repayment) as the Scottish Ministers consider appropriate.

32. The Scottish Ministers may, from time to time after any grant is paid or loan made, vary the terms and conditions on which it was paid or, as the case may be, made.

Account and audit

33. The Commission must-
(a) keep proper accounts and accounting records;
(b) prepare for each financial year a statement of accounts giving a true and fair view of the state of its financial affairs; and
(c) send the statement of accounts, by the time directed by the Scottish Ministers, to the Auditor General for Scotland for auditing.

34. Every statement of accounts prepared by the Commission in accordance with paragraph 33 above must comply with any direction given by the Scottish Ministers relating to-
(a) the information to be contained in the statement of accounts;
(b) the manner in which that information is to be presented; or
(c) the methods and principles according to which the statement of accounts is to be prepared.

35. The financial year of the Commission is-
(a) the period beginning with the date on which the Commission is established and ending with 31 March next following that date; and
(b) each successive period of 12 months ending with 31 March.

GENERAL NOTE
At the time of writing, the Commission appears unlikely to be set up, not least because there is a certain political hostility to Quangos, of which this would be one more. The terms and members of the Quango are not in themselves exceptionable: there is lay representation, as may be expected, and to continue the sense of tradition, the Lord Lyon King of Arms is a member.

For further information on the Commission, see s.50 of the 2007 Act.

SCHEDULE 3

EXPENSES OF MONEY ATTACHMENT

(introduced by section 196 (1))

Expenses chargeable against the debtor

1. There is to be chargeable against the debtor any expenses incurred-
(a) subject to section 90(7) of the 1987 Act, in serving a charge;
(b) in executing a money attachment;
(c) in relation to a valuation arranged under section 180(1) of this Act (including the fees and outlays of the person who carried out the valuation);
(d) in making a report under section 182(1) of this Act but not in applying for an extension of time for the making of such a report;
(e) in applying for a payment order under section 183(2) of this Act;
(f) in granting a receipt and making a report to the sheriff under section 188(4) of this Act;
(g) in giving a statement under section 189(1) of this Act;
(h) in removing money from the place at which is was found;
(i) in opening shut and lockfast places for that purpose;
(j) by a solicitor in instructing a judicial officer to take any of the steps specified in this paragraph.

2. Expenses chargeable against the debtor by virtue of paragraph 1(e) above must be calculated, whether or not the application is opposed by the debtor, as if it were unopposed.

Circumstances where no expenses are due to or by either party

3. Subject to paragraph 4 below, the debtor shall not be liable to the creditor nor the creditor to the debtor for any expenses incurred by the other party in connection with-
  (a) an application under section 181(1), 185(1) or 186 of this Act;
  (b) any objections to such an application;
  (c) an opposition, under section 183(6) of this Act, to an application for a payment order;
  (d) a hearing held by virtue of section 183(8), 186(6) or 190(7) of this Act.

4. If-
  (a) an application mentioned in paragraph 3(a) above is frivolous;
  (b) such an application is opposed on frivolous grounds;
  (c) an application for a payment order is opposed on frivolous grounds; or
  (d) a party requires, on frivolous grounds, a hearing mentioned in paragraph 3(d) above to be held,
the sheriff may award a sum of expenses, not exceeding such amount as may be prescribed by the Scottish Ministers by regulations, against the party acting frivolously in favour of the other party.

5. Paragraphs 3 and 4 above do not apply to expenses incurred in connection with an appeal under section 194(1).

GENERAL NOTE
  This is introduced by s.196(1).

SCHEDULE 4

MODIFICATIONS OF ENACTMENTS RELATING TO ADMIRALTY ACTIONS AND THE ARRESTMENT OF SHIPS

(introduced by section 213)

Definition of "maritime lien"

1. In section 48 of the Administration of Justice Act 1956 (c.46) (in this Act, the "1956 Act")-
  (a) the existing words become subsection (1);
  (b) paragraph (d) is repealed; and
  (c) at the end insert-
        "(2) In this Act and in any other enactment (including an Act of the Scottish Parliament and any enactment comprised in subordinate legislation under such an Act), "maritime lien" means a hypothec over a ship, cargo or other maritime property.".

2. In sections 45(5) and 47(3)(b), (4)(b) and (5) of the 1956 Act, before the word "lien" in each place where it occurs, insert the word "maritime".

3. In section 47(2)(r) of the 1956 Act, for "or hypothecation of" substitute ", hypothecation of or existence of any other charge on".

The term "admiralty action"

4. In section 47 of the 1956 Act-
  (a) in subsection (2)(h), after "bond" insert "or contract of respondentia";
  (b) after subsection (2), insert-

"(2A) An action having a conclusion appropriate for the enforcement of a claim to which subsection (2) above applies shall be known as an "admiralty action".";

(c) in subsection (3), for "the last preceding subsection" substitute "subsection (2) above".

5.

(1) In paragraph 7 of schedule 5 to the Civil Jurisdiction and Judgements Act 1982 (c.27), for "Admiralty cause" substitute "admiralty action".

(2) In paragraph 6 of schedule 9 to that Act, for "causes" substitute "actions".

Arrestment in rem granted by the sheriff

6. After section 47 of the 1956 Act, insert-

"47A   Execution of warrant to arrest in rem and of order for sale

(1) A warrant for the arrestment in rem of a ship, cargo or other maritime property granted by the sheriff may be executed-
(a) within the sheriffdom in which the warrant was granted; or
(b) where the ship, cargo or other maritime property was situated within that sheriffdom when the warrant was granted, anywhere in Scotland.
(2) For the avoidance of doubt, where a warrant for arrestment in rem granted by the sheriff has been executed, an order for the sale of the arrested ship, cargo or other maritime property may be made notwithstanding that it is not situated within the sheriffdom when the order is made.".

Arrestment on the dependence

7.

(1) Section 47 of the 1956 Act is amended as follows.
(2) In subsection (1)-
(a) after "arrest", where it second occurs, insert "a ship or other maritime property which is not cargo";
(b) after "unless", where it second occurs, insert "at the time when the arrestment is executed";
(c) in paragraph (a), after "concerned" insert "and the defender against whom that conclusion is directed owns at least one share in it or is the demise charterer of it"; and
(d) in paragraph (b), the words "against whom that conclusion is directed" are repealed.
(3) After subsection (1), insert-
"(1A) Where a warrant to arrest on the dependence referred to in subsection (1) above (an "initial arrestment") has been executed, then, subject to subsection (1B) below, no further warrant may be granted to arrest on the dependence-
(a) the subjects of the initial arrestment; or
(b) while the initial arrestment continues to have effect, any other ship in which the defender owns at least one share,
in respect of the claim to which the initial arrestment relates.
(1B) A further warrant to arrest on the dependence may be granted if-
(a) the further arrestment complies with the requirements of subsection (1) above; and
(b) cause is shown for granting the further warrant.".
(4) In subsection (3)-
(a) in paragraph (a), after "ship" insert "or of any share in it"; and
(b) after "ship", where it last occurs, insert "or, as the case may be, any share in a ship other than in the ship,".

Liability for losses and expenses

8. After section 47A of the 1956 Act (as inserted by paragraph 6 above), insert-

"47B   Expenses

(1) Subject to subsection (3) below, a pursuer shall be entitled to such expenses as are incurred-

(a) in obtaining warrant for the arrest of a ship, cargo or other maritime property on the dependence of an action; and

(b) in executing the arrestment.

(2) Subject to subsection (4) below, a defender shall be entitled, where-

(a) warrant for the arrest of a ship, cargo or other maritime property on the dependence of an action is granted; and

(b) the court is satisfied that the pursuer was acting unreasonably in applying for it,

to such expenses as are incurred in opposing that warrant.

(3) The court may modify or refuse such expenses as are mentioned in subsection (1) above if it is satisfied that-

(a) the pursuer was acting unreasonably in applying for the warrant; or

(b) such modification or refusal is reasonable in all the circumstances and having regard to the outcome of the action.

(4) The court may modify or refuse such expenses as are mentioned in subsection (2) above if it is satisfied as to the matter mentioned in subsection (3)(b) above.

(5) Subject to subsections (1) to (4) above, the court may make such findings as it thinks fit in relation to such expenses as are mentioned in subsections (1) and (2) above.

(6) Expenses incurred as mentioned in subsections (1)(a) and (2) above shall be expenses of process.

(7) Subsections (1) to (4) above are without prejudice to any enactment or rule of law as to the recovery of expenses chargeable against a debtor as are incurred in executing an arrestment on the dependence of an action.

(8) Where warrant is granted for the arrest of a ship in rem in proceedings to which section 47(3)(b) of this Act applies, the court may make such findings as it thinks fit in relation to expenses incurred-

(a) in obtaining the warrant and, as the case may be, executing the arrestment;

(b) in opposing the application for the warrant.

(9) For the avoidance of doubt, expenses incurred in applying for and executing the arrest of a ship, cargo or other maritime property in rem in respect of a conclusion appropriate for the making good of a maritime lien shall be expenses of process.".

Factors affecting arrestments

9. After section 47B of the 1956 Act (as inserted by paragraph 8 above), insert-

"47C   Competence of arresting cargo

(1) It is not competent to execute an arrestment of cargo unless the cargo is on board a ship when the arrestment is executed.

(2) For the avoidance of doubt, it is competent to execute an arrestment of cargo where it is in the possession of the defender or of a person acting on behalf of the defender.

47D   Arrestment of cargo: restriction on movement of ship

Where cargo is arrested, the ship is treated as if arrested until the cargo is unloaded.".

Cargo on board a ship exempt from attachment

10. In section 11 of the 2002 Act (articles exempt from attachment), at the end insert-

"(3) It is not competent to attach cargo which it is competent to arrest by virtue of section 47C of the Administration of Justice Act 1956 (c.46) (competence of arresting cargo).".

Location of a ship when arrestment executed

11. In section 47 of the 1956 Act-

(a) after subsection (5), insert-

(5A) Subject to subsection (6) below, it is competent to execute an arrestment of a ship, cargo or other maritime property regardless of whether the ship or other maritime property is in non-tidal or tidal waters or on land.

(5B) In subsection (5A) above, "tidal waters" means any part of the sea and any part of a river within the ebb and flow of the tide at ordinary spring tides."; and

(b) in subsection (6), for the words from "Nothing" to "of", where it second occurs, substitute, "It is not competent to execute an arrestment of a ship or cargo on board".

Demise charters

12. After section 47D of the 1956 Act (as inserted by paragraph 9 above) insert-

Special provision in relation to charters by demise

47E Sale of ship arrested on the dependence of action against demise charterer

(1) This section applies where-
  (a) a ship is arrested on the dependence of an admiralty action against the demise charterer of it; and
  (b) the pursuer obtains decree for payment for all or part of a principal sum concluded for in the action.

(2) Where the owner or demise charterer of the ship-
  (a) pays the sum due under the decree to-
    (i) the pursuer; or
    (ii) any person who has authority to receive payment on behalf of the pursuer; or
  (b) tenders that sum to any of those persons and the tender is not accepted within a reasonable time,
  the arrestment ceases to have effect.

(3) The court may, on the application of the pursuer, make an order for the sale of the ship.

(4) Subject to sections 47F and 47G below, the court shall rank any claims made on the proceeds.

(5) A ship sold under subsection (3) above vests in the purchaser free of any security or other encumbrance.

(6) The Court of Session may, by Act of Sederunt, make provision relating to proceedings under this section.

47F Ranking of arrestments on sale of ship chartered by demise

In any ranking process relating to the proceeds of sale of a ship (or any share in a ship), an arrestment of the ship (or share) executed before the sale by a creditor of the owner of the ship (or share) shall rank in preference over any arrestment of the ship executed on the dependence of an admiralty action against the demise charterer of the ship.

47G Ranking of arresting creditor of demise charterer in sequestration or winding up of owner

(1) This section applies where-
  (a) a ship is arrested on the dependence of an admiralty action against the demise charterer of it; and
  (b) at any time after the arrestment is executed-
    (i) the owner of the ship's estate is sequestrated; or
    (ii) where the owner is a company, it is wound up.

(2) The creditor who executed the arrestment is entitled to rank on the proceeds of any sale of the ship resulting from the sequestration or, as the case may be, winding up.

(3) Section 37(4) and (5) of the Bankruptcy (Scotland) Act 1985 (c.66) (effect of sequestration on arrestment or attachment) and section 185(1)(a) and (2) (in so far as applying and modifying section 37(4) and (5)) of the Insolvency Act 1986 (c.45) (application of sequestration provisions relating to diligence

on winding up) shall apply to such an arrestment as they apply to any other arrestment.

47H   Arrestment to found jurisdiction in action against demise charterer

Where the defender in an admiralty action is the demise charterer of the ship with which the action is concerned, the court may, on the application of the pursuer, grant warrant to arrest the ship to found jurisdiction.".

13. In section 6(c) of the Sheriff Courts (Scotland) Act 1907 (c.51) (competence of arresting a ship to found jurisdiction in sheriff court), after "owner", where it second occurs, insert "or demise charterer".

GENERAL NOTE
See the notes above to s.213.

SCHEDULE 5

Minor and Consequential Amendments

(introduced by section 226)

1.   The Companies Clauses Consolidation (Scotland) Act 1845 (c.17)

In section 114 of the Companies Clauses Consolidation (Scotland) Act 1845 (summary remedy against parties failing to account), after "attachment" insert "or money attachment".

2.   The Harbours, Docks and Piers Clauses Act 1847 (c.27)

In section 46 of the Harbours, Docks and Piers Clauses Act 1847 (power of justice or sheriff to settle disputes over costs of diligence), after "attachment" insert "or money attachment".

3.   The Titles to Land Consolidation (Scotland) Act 1868 (c.101)

In section 3 of the Titles to Land Consolidation (Scotland) Act 1868 (definitions), in the definition of the "deed" and "conveyance"-
    (a) after "adjudged" insert "in implement"; and
    (b) after "adjudication", where it third occurs, insert "in implement".

4.   The Writs Execution (Scotland) Act 1877 (c.40)

In section 3(a) of the Writs Execution (Scotland) Act 1877 (warrant in extract writ to authorise diligence)-
    (a) after "arrestment" insert ", a land attachment, a residual attachment, a money attachment"; and
    (b) after "executing the" insert "land attachment, residual attachment, money attachment or".

5.   The Judicial Factors (Scotland) Act 1889 (c.39)

In section 11A of the Judicial Factors (Scotland) Act (application for judicial factor on estate of deceased person)-
    (a) in subsection (1)-
        (i) for "petition to the Court of Session or" substitute "application"; and
        (ii) for "petition", where it second occurs, substitute "application"; and
    (b) in subsection (2), for "petition" substitute "application".

6.   The Sheriff Courts (Scotland) Extracts Act 1892 (c.17)

(1) The Sheriff Courts (Scotland) Extracts Act 1892 is amended as follows.
(2) In section 7(1)(a) (warrant in extract decree to authorise diligence)-
    (a) after "arrestment" insert ", a land attachment, a residual attachment, a money attachment"; and

(b) after "executing the" insert "land attachment, residual attachment, money attachment or".

(3) In section 7(4) (warrant in extract decree of removing), for the words "forty-eight hours" in both places where they occur substitute "14 days".

(4) In section 8 (persons who may execute on extracts), for the words "messengers-at-arms, officers of court," substitute "judicial officers".

7. The Execution of Diligence (Scotland) Act 1926 (c.16)

(1) The Execution of Diligence (Scotland) Act 1926 is amended as follows.

(2) In section 2 (execution by registered letter)-

    (a) in subsection (1)(b), for "sheriff officer" substitute "judicial officer";

    (b) in subsection (2)(b)-

        (i) for the words from "sheriff officer", where they first occur, to "situated" substitute "judicial officer";

        (ii) for "sheriff officer, or messenger-at-arms" substitute "judicial officer"; and

        (iii) for "law agent enrolled in such sheriffdom" substitute "solicitor";

    (c) in subsection (2)(c), for "law agent, messenger-at-arms or sheriff officer" substitute "solicitor or judicial officer"; and

    (d) in subsection (2)(g), for "rule 111" substitute "rule 6.1".

(3) In section 3 (authorisation by sheriff to do diligence)-

    (a) for "messenger-at-arms or sheriff officer", in both places where it occurs, substitute "judicial officer"; and

    (b) for "law agent" substitute "solicitor".

(4) In section 6 (regulations, forms and fees), for "messengers-at-arms, sheriff officers" substitute "judicial officers".

8. The Local Government (Scotland) Act 1947 (c.43)

(1) The Local Government (Scotland) Act 1947 is amended as follows.

(2) In section 247(3) (diligences which can be used to recover rates), after paragraph (a) insert-

    "(aa) a money attachment;".

(3) In section 247A(1) (sheriff officer's fees and outlays), after "attachment)" insert "and section 196(1) of the Bankruptcy and Diligence etc. (Scotland) Act 2007 (asp 3) (expenses of money attachment)".

9. The Taxes Management Act 1970 (c.9)

(1) The Taxes Management Act 1970 is amended as follows.

(2) In section 63(2) (diligences which can be used to recover tax), after paragraph (a) insert-

    "(aa) a money attachment;".

(3) In section 63A(1) (sheriff officer's fees and outlays), after "attachment)" insert "and section 196(1) of the Bankruptcy and Diligence etc. (Scotland) Act 2007 (asp 3) (expenses of money attachment)".

10. The Sheriff Courts (Scotland) Act 1971 (c.58)

In section 32(1) of the Sheriff Courts (Scotland) Act 1971 (power of Court of Session to regulate sheriff court civil procedure), in paragraph (l), for the words "an attachment" substitute "an interim attachment, an attachment, a money attachment, a land attachment or a residual attachment".

11. The Animal Health Act 1981 (c.22)

In section 92(3) of the Animal Health Act 1981 (power of local authority to apply to sheriff for warrant), for the words "the officers of the court" substitute "a judicial officer".

12. The Civil Jurisdiction and Judgments Act 1982 (c.27)

In section 27 of the Civil Jurisdiction and Judgments Act 1982 (power of Court of Session to grant provisional and protective measures in respect of proceedings outwith Scotland)-

    (a) in subsection (1), after paragraph (b), insert-

        "(ba) subject to subsection (2)(c) below, grant a warrant for the interim attachment of corporeal moveable property situated in Scotland;" ; and

(b) in subsection (2)(c), for the words "and (b)" substitute ", (b) and (ba)".

13. The Bankruptcy (Scotland) Act 1985 (c.66)

(1) The 1985 Act is amended as follows.

(2) In section 31 (vesting of estate in trustee), in subsection (1)-

    (a) after "shall", where it first occurs, insert ", by virtue of the trustee's appointment,"; and

    (b) after "vest", where it first occurs, insert "in the trustee".

(3) In section 37 (effect of sequestration on diligence)-

    (a) in subsection (1)(b), for "a completed poinding" substitute "an attachment";

    (b) in subsection (2), for "No" substitute "Where an";

    (c) in subsection (4)-

        (i) after "arrestment" insert ", money attachment, interim attachment"; and

        (ii) after "attached" insert ", or any funds released under section 73J(2) of the Debtors (Scotland) Act 1987 (c.18) (automatic release of funds)";

    (d) in subsection (5)-

        (i) after "arrestment", where it first occurs, insert ", money attachment, interim attachment";

        (ii) in paragraph (a), after "obtaining" insert-

            (i) warrant for interim attachment; or

            (ii) ";

        (iii) after "arrestment", where it second occurs, insert ", money attachment"; and

        (iv) in paragraph (b), after "arrestment" insert ", money attachment, interim attachment";

    (e) after subsection (5A) insert-

        (5B) No land attachment of heritable property of the debtor created within the period of six months before the date of sequestration and whether or not subsisting at that date shall be effectual to create a preference for the creditor.

        (5C) A creditor who creates a land attachment within the period of six months mentioned in subsection (5B) above shall be entitled to payment, out of the attached land or out of the proceeds of the sale of it, of the expenses incurred

            (a) in obtaining the extract of the decree, or other document, containing the warrant for land attachment; and

            (b) in-

                (i) serving the charge for payment;

                (ii) registering the notice of land attachment;

                (iii) serving a copy of that notice; and

                (iv) registering certificate of service of that copy.";

    (f) after subsection (8) insert-

        "(8A) A notice of land attachment registered-

            (a) on or after the date of sequestration against land forming part of the heritable estate of the debtor (including any estate vesting in the trustee by virtue of section 32(6) of this Act); or

            (b) before that date in relation to which, by that date, no land attachment is created,

        shall be of no effect.

        (8B) Subject to subsections (8C) to (8F) below, it shall not be competent for a creditor to insist in a land attachment-

            (a) created over heritable estate of the debtor before the beginning of the period of six months mentioned in subsection (5B) above; and

            (b) which subsists on the date of sequestration.

        (8C) Where, in execution of a warrant for sale, a contract to sell the land has been concluded-

            (a) the trustee shall concur in and ratify the deed implementing that contract; and

            (b) the appointed person shall account for and pay to the trustee any balance of the proceeds of sale which would, but for the sequestration, be due to the debtor after disbursing those proceeds in accordance with section 116 of the Bankruptcy and Diligence etc. (Scotland) Act 2007 (asp 3) (disbursement of proceeds of sale of attached land).

(8D) Subsection (8C) above shall not apply where the deed implementing the contract is not registered before the expiry of the period of 28 days beginning with the day on which-
  (a) the certified copy of the order of the sheriff granting warrant is recorded under subsection (1)(a) of section 14 of this Act; or
  (b) the certified copy of the determination of the Accountant in Bankruptcy awarding sequestration is recorded under subsection (1A) of that section,
  in the register of inhibitions.

(8E) Where a decree of foreclosure has been granted but an extract of it has not registered, the creditor may proceed to complete title to the land by so registering that extract provided that the extract is registered before the expiry of the period mentioned in subsection (8D) above.

(8F) The Scottish Ministers may-
  (a) prescribe such other period for the period mentioned in subsection (8D) above; and
  (b) prescribe different periods for the purposes of that subsection and subsection (8E) above,
  as they think fit." ; and

-(g) at the end insert-

"(10) Expressions used in subsections (5B), (5C) and (8A) to (8F) above which are also used in Chapter 2 of Part 4 of the Bankruptcy and Diligence etc. (Scotland) Act 2007 (asp 3) have the same meanings in those subsections as they have in that Chapter.".

14. The Insolvency Act 1986 (c.45)

(1) The Insolvency Act 1986 is amended as follows.

(2) After section 61(1) (which sets out the process by which a receiver may dispose of property subject to both the floating charge and to another security, other encumbrance or diligence) insert-

"(1B) For the purposes of subsection (1) above, an arrestment is an effectual diligence only where it is executed before the floating charge, by virtue of which the receiver was appointed, attaches to the property comprised in the company's property and undertaking.".

(3) In section 185(1)(a) (effect of diligence in the winding up of a company registered in Scotland), after "subsection (6)" insert ", (8A) to (8F) and (10)".

15. The Legal Aid (Scotland) Act 1986 (c.47)

In Part 2 of Schedule 2 to the Legal Aid (Scotland) Act 1986 (proceedings in which civil legal aid is not available)-
  (a) in paragraph 4, after "(asp 17)" insert "or Part 8 of the Bankruptcy and Diligence etc. (Scotland) Act 2007 (asp 3)"; and
  (b) in paragraph 5, after "(asp 17)" insert "or Part 8 of the Bankruptcy and Diligence etc. (Scotland) Act 2007 (asp 3)".

16. The Debtors (Scotland) Act 1987 (c.18)

(1) The 1987 Act is amended as follows.

(2) In section 2 (effect of time to pay direction on diligence)-
  (a) in subsection (1)(b), after sub-paragraph (iv) insert-
    '(v) a money attachment;
    (vi) a land attachment;
    (vii) a residual attachment,";
  (b) in subsection (2), at beginning insert "Subject to subsection (2A) below,";
  (c) after that subsection insert-
    "(2A) Where the arrestment which remains in effect as mentioned in subsection (2) above is an arrestment such as is mentioned in subsection (1) of section 73J of this Act, while the time to pay direction is in effect-
      (a) it shall not be competent to release funds under subsection (2) of that section; and
      (b) the period during which the direction is in effect shall be disregarded for the purposes of determining whether the period mentioned in subsection (3) of that section has expired.

      (2B) While a time to pay direction is in effect an interim attachment shall remain in effect
        (a) if it has not been recalled; or
        (b) to the extent that it has not been restricted under subsection (3) below.";
  (d) in subsection (3), after "restrict" insert "an interim attachment or";
  (e) in subsection (4)-
    (i) after "If" insert "an interim attachment or"; and
    (ii) after "restriction of the" insert "interim attachment or"; and
  (f) after subsection (5) insert-
    "(5A) Where-
      (a) a time to pay direction is recalled or ceases to have effect as mentioned in subsection (5) above; and
      (b) an arrestment such as is mentioned in section 73J(1) of this Act is in effect,
   the clerk of court or sheriff clerk shall intimate the fact of that recall or cessation to the arrestee.".
(3) In section 3 (variation and recall of time to pay direction and arrestment)-
  (a) in subsection (1)(a), after "reasonable" insert "in all the circumstances";
  (b) in subsection (1)(b)-
    (i) after "if" insert "an interim attachment or";
    (ii) after "restrict the" insert "interim attachment or"; and
  (c) in subsection (2), after "If" insert "an interim attachment or".
(4) In section 5 (time to pay orders)-
  (a) in subsection (5), for paragraph (a) substitute-
    "(a) articles belonging to the debtor have been attached and notice of an auction given under section 27(4) of the Debt Arrangement and Attachment (Scotland) Act 2002 (asp 17) but no auction has yet taken place;
    (aa) money owned by the debtor has been attached and removed;";
  (b) for paragraph (c) and the word "or" immediately preceding it substitute-
    "(c) land owned by the debtor has been attached and an order under section 97(2) of the Bankruptcy and Diligence etc. (Scotland) Act 2007 (asp 3) (in this Part, the "2007 Act") granting warrant for sale of the land has been made but that warrant has not yet been executed; or
    (d) property owned by the debtor has been attached by residual attachment and a satisfaction order under section 136(2) of the 2007 Act has been made but not yet executed," ; and
  (c) after subsection (5) insert-
    "(5A) Where, in respect of a debt to which this section applies, an arrestment such as is mentioned in subsection (1) of section 73J of this Act has been executed, the sheriff may make a time to pay order in respect of that debt only if less than 8 weeks of the period mentioned in subsection (3) of that section have expired.".
(5) In section 6 (application for time to pay order), in subsection (6), leave out paragraph (b) and the word "and" immediately preceding it and insert-
    "(b) serve on-
      (i) the creditor; and
      (ii) where an arrestment such as is mentioned in section 73J(1) of this Act is in effect, the arrestee,
   a copy of the interim order; and
    (c) serve on the creditor a copy of any order under subsection (4) above.".
(6) In section 7 (disposal of application for time to pay order), in subsection (4)(a), for "and the creditor" substitute ", the creditor and, where an arrestment such as is mentioned in section 73J(1) of this Act is in effect, the arrestee".
(7) In section 8 (effect of interim order on diligence)-
  (a) in subsection (1)-
    (i) before paragraph (a) insert-
      "(za) to attach in execution of the decree any articles which have been attached by interim attachment;";
    (ii) in paragraph (a), for "auction any articles which have been attached" substitute "give, in relation to any articles which have been attached, notice of an auction under section 27(4) of the Debt Arrangement and Attachment (Scotland) Act 2002 (asp 17)";

      (iii) after paragraph (a) insert-

          "(aa) to execute a money attachment;";

      (iv) in paragraph (c), at the beginning insert "subject to subsection (1A) below,"; and

      (v) for paragraph (d) substitute-

          "(d) subject to subsection (1B) below, to register, under section 83(1)(c) of the 2007 Act, a notice of land attachment;

          (e) subject to subsection (1C) below, to apply, under section 130(1) of the 2007 Act, for a residual attachment order."; and

  (b) after subsection (1) insert-

      "(1A) Where the arrestment mentioned in subsection (1)(c) above is an arrestment such as is mentioned in subsection (1) of section 73J of this Act, while the interim order is in effect-

      (a) it shall not be competent to release funds under subsection (2) of that section; and

      (b) the period during which the order is in effect shall be disregarded for the purposes of determining whether the period mentioned in subsection (3) of that section has expired.

      (1B) Where, before the interim order is made-

      (a) a notice of land attachment is registered, it shall not be competent to take any steps other than-

          (i) serving, under subsection (5) of section 83 of the 2007 Act, a copy of that notice; and

          (ii) registering, under subsection (6) of that section, a certificate of service; or

      (b) a land attachment is created, it shall not be competent to make, under section 97(2) of the 2007 Act, an order granting a warrant for sale of the attached land.

      (1C) Where, before the interim order is made, a residual attachment order has been made, it shall not be competent-

      (a) to take any steps other than serving, under section 133(1) of the 2007 Act, a schedule of residual attachment; or

      (b) to make, under section 136(2) of the 2007 Act, a satisfaction order.".

  (8) In section 9 (effect of time to pay order on diligence)-

    (a) in subsection (1)(b), after sub-paragraph (iv) insert-

      '(v) a money attachment;

      (vi) a land attachment;

      (vii) a residual attachment,";

    (b) in subsection (2), for paragraph (c) substitute-

      "(c) where a notice of land attachment has been registered under section 83(1)(c) of the 2007 Act, shall make an order prohibiting the taking of any steps other than-

          (i) the serving, under subsection (5) of that section, of a copy of the notice; and

          (ii) the registration, under subsection (6) of that section, of a certificate of service;

      (ca) where a residual attachment order has been made under section 132(2) of the 2007 Act, shall make an order prohibiting the taking of any steps other than the serving, under section 133(1) of the 2007 Act, of a schedule of residual attachment;

      (cb) may make an order recalling an interim attachment;";

    (c) after subsection (2) insert-

      "(2A) While a time to pay order is in effect, it shall not be competent in respect of the debt-

      (a) to make, under section 97(2) of the 2007 Act, an order granting warrant for sale of attached land; or

      (b) to make, under section 136(2) of the 2007 Act, a satisfaction order.";

    (d) in subsection (3)-

      (i) after "If" insert "an interim attachment," and

      (ii) for "or the recall of" substitute ", the recall of the interim attachment or";

    (e) in subsection (4)-

      (i) at the beginning insert "Subject to subsection (4A) below,"; and

(ii) for "(2)(d) or (e)" substitute "(2)(cb), (d) or (e)";

(f) after subsection (4) insert-

"(4A) Where, in relation to an arrestment such as is mentioned in subsection (1) of section 73J of this Act, the sheriff does not exercise the power conferred on him by subsection (2)(e) above to recall that arrestment, he shall make an order-

(a) prohibiting, while the time to pay order is in effect, the release of funds under subsection (2) of section 73J of this Act; and

(b) providing that the period during which the time to pay order is in effect shall be disregarded for the purposes of determining whether the period mentioned in subsection (3) of that section has expired.";

(g) in subsection (6), for "(2)(d) or (e)" substitute "(2)(cb), (d) or (e)";

(h) in subsection (7), after paragraph (b) insert

"; and

(c) where any order under subsection (4A) above is made in relation to an arrestment such as is mentioned in section 73J(1) of this Act is in effect, intimate that order to the arrestee." ; and

(i) in subsection (8)-

(i) for paragraph (a) substitute-

"(a) to sell articles which have been attached (other than by virtue of section 20(1) or 22(3) of the Debt Arrangement and Attachment (Scotland) Act (asp 17);" ; and

(ii) in paragraph (b), at the beginning insert "to grant".

(9) In section 10 (variation and recall of time to pay order and arrestment)-

(a) in subsection (1)(a), after "reasonable" insert "in all the circumstances";

(b) in subsection (1)(b), after "if" insert "an interim attachment,"; and

(c) in subsection (2), after "If" insert "an interim attachment,".

(10) In section 13 (saving of creditor's rights and remedies), in the full-out words to subsection (2), for "poinding", in any place where it occurs, substitute "attachment".

(11) In section 87(2)(a) (warrant in extract decree to authorise diligence)-

(a) after "arrestment" insert ", a land attachment, a residual attachment, a money attachment"; and

(b) after "executing the" insert "land attachment, residual attachment, money attachment or".

(12) In section 104 (regulations), after "Regulations" insert "and orders".

(13) In section 105 (application to Crown)-

(a) the existing words become subsection (1);

(b) after "1947" insert "and subject to subsection (2) below"; and

(c) at the end insert-

"(2) Section 70B of this Act does not affect Her Majesty in Her private capacity as an employer."

(14) In section 106 (interpretation)-

(a) after the definition of "current maintenance", insert-

""debt advice and information package" has the meaning given to it in section 47(4) of this Act;";

(b) after the definition of "employer", insert-

""enactment" includes an Act of the Scottish Parliament and any enactment comprised in subordinate legislation under such an Act;" ; and

(c) in the definition of "officer of court", for the words from "a" where it first occurs to the end substitute "a judicial officer".

17. The Abolition of Domestic Rates etc. (Scotland) Act 1987 (c.47)

(1) Schedule 2 to the Abolition of Domestic Rates etc. (Scotland) Act 1987 is amended as follows.

(2) In paragraph 7(3) (diligences which can be used to recover community charge), after paragraph (a) insert-

"(aa) a money attachment;".

(3) In paragraph 8(1) (sheriff officer's fees and outlays), after "attachment)" insert "and section 196(1) of the Bankruptcy and Diligence etc. (Scotland) Act 2007 (asp 3) (expenses of money attachment)".

18. The Child Support Act 1991 (c.48)

In section 38 of the Child Support Act 1991 (enforcement of liability orders by diligence)-
   (a) in subsection (1)-
      (i) after paragraph (a) insert-
         "(aa) for the Secretary of State-
            (i) to charge the person to pay the appropriate amount; and
            (ii) to execute, in respect of the person's land, a land attachment;" ; and
      (ii) for the words from "and", where it fifth occurs, to the end, substitute-
         (c) for an inhibition." ; and
   (b) for subsection (2) substitute-
      "(2) In subsection (1)-
         (a) the "appropriate amount" means the amount in respect of which the order was made, to the extent that it remains unpaid; and
         (b) in paragraph (aa), "land" has the same meaning as in section 82 of the Bankruptcy and Diligence etc. (Scotland) Act 2007 (asp 3).".

19. The Social Security Administration Act 1992 (c.5)

In section 121B of the Social Security Administration Act 1992-
   (a) in subsection (1) (diligences which can be used to recover unpaid contributions), after paragraph (a) insert-
      "(aa) a money attachment;" ; and
   (b) in subsection (4) (sheriff officer's fees and outlays), after "attachment)" insert "and section 196(1) of the Bankruptcy and Diligence etc. (Scotland) Act 2007 (asp 3) (expenses of money attachment)".

20. The Local Government Finance Act 1992 (c.14)

   (1) Schedule 8 to the Local Government Finance Act 1992 is amended as follows.
   (2) In paragraph 2(3) (diligences which can be used to recover council tax etc.), after paragraph (a) insert-
      "(aa) a money attachment;".
   (3) In paragraph 4(1) (sheriff officer's fees and outlays), after "attachment)" insert "and section 196(1) of the Bankruptcy and Diligence etc. (Scotland) Act 2007 (asp 3) (expenses of money attachment)".

21. The Tribunals and Inquiries Act 1992 (c.53)

In Part II of Schedule 1 to the Tribunals and Inquiries Act 1992 (tribunals under the supervision of the Scottish Committee of the Council on Tribunals), after paragraph 54A insert-

   "Judicial Officers 54B. The disciplinary committee of the Scottish Civil Enforcement Commission constituted under paragraph 16 of Schedule 2 to the Bankruptcy and Diligence etc. (Scotland) Act 2007 (asp 3).".

22. The Proceeds of Crime (Scotland) Act 1995 (c.43)

In section 32 of the Proceeds of Crime (Scotland) Act (inhibition of property affected by restraint order or by interdict)-
   (a) in subsection (1)-
      (i) for the words "Lord Advocate, the Court of Session" substitute "prosecutor, the court";
      (ii) in paragraph (a), for the words "Lord Advocate" substitute "prosecutor"; and
      (iii) in paragraph (b), for the words from "have" to the end substitute "forthwith be registered by the prosecutor in the Register of Inhibitions.";
      and
   (b) in subsection (5), for the words "Lord Advocate" substitute "prosecutor".

23. The Criminal Procedure (Scotland) Act 1995 (c. 46)

In section 221 of the Criminal Procedure (Scotland) Act 1995 (fines: recovery by civil diligence), in subsection (1)(a)-

 (a) for "the execution of an arrestment and the attachment of articles belonging to him" insert-

   "(i) the execution of an arrestment;

   (ii) the attachment of articles belonging to him; and

   (iii) the execution of a money attachment," ; and

 (b) after "attachment", where it second occurs, insert "or the money attachment".

24. The Finance Act 1997 (c.16)

In section 52 of the Finance Act 1997-

 (a) in subsection (2) (diligences which can be used to recover certain taxes), after paragraph (a) insert-

   "(aa) a money attachment;" ; and

 (b) in subsection (3) (sheriff officer's fees and outlays), after "attachment)" insert "and section 196(1) of the Bankruptcy and Diligence etc. (Scotland) Act 2007 (asp 3) (expenses of money attachment)".

25. The Ethical Standards in Public Life etc. (Scotland) Act 2000 (asp 7)

In schedule 3 to the Ethical Standards in Public Life etc. (Scotland) Act (devolved public bodies), after the entry "Scottish Children's Reporter Administration", insert-

 The Scottish Civil Enforcement Commission".

26. The Water Industry (Scotland) Act 2002 (asp 3)

(1) Schedule 4 to the Water Industry (Scotland) Act 2002 is amended as follows

 (2) In paragraph 2(3) (diligences which can be used to recover unpaid charges), after sub-paragraph (za) insert-

   "(zb) a money attachment;".

 (3) In paragraph 4(1), at the beginning insert "Without prejudice to section 39(1) of the Debt Arrangement and Attachment (Scotland) Act 2002 (asp 17) (expenses of attachment) and section 196(1) of the Bankruptcy and Diligence etc. (Scotland) Act 2007 (asp 3) (expenses of money attachment),".

27. The Scottish Public Services Ombudsman Act 2002 (asp 11)

In Part 2 of schedule 2 to the Scottish Public Services Ombudsman Act 2002 (Scottish public authorities), after paragraph 37 insert-

 37A The Scottish Civil Enforcement Commission".

28. The Freedom of Information (Scotland) Act 2002 (asp 13)

In schedule 1 to the Freedom of Information (Scotland) Act (public authorities within the meaning of section 3), after paragraph 80 insert-

 "80A The Scottish Civil Enforcement Commission.".

29. The Proceeds of Crime Act 2002 (c.29)

In section 123 of the Proceeds of Crime Act (inhibition of property affected by a restraint order)-

 (a) in subsection (1), for the words "Lord Advocate, the Court of Session" substitute "prosecutor, the court";

 (b) in subsection (3)-

   (i) in paragraph (a), for the words "Lord Advocate" substitute "prosecutor"; and

   (ii) for paragraph (b) substitute-

    "(b) must forthwith be registered by the prosecutor in the Register of Inhibitions"; and

 (c) in subsection (7) , for the words "Lord Advocate" substitute "prosecutor".

30. The Debt Arrangement and Attachment (Scotland) Act 2002 (asp 17)

(1) The 2002 Act is amended as follows.

(2) In section 10(3) (competence of attachment), for paragraphs (a) and (b) substitute-

> (a) the debtor has been charged to pay the debt;
> (b) the period for payment specified in the charge has expired without payment being made; and
> (c) where the debtor is an individual, the creditor has, no earlier than 12 weeks before taking any steps to execute the attachment, provided the debtor with a debt advice and information package.".

(3) In section 11 (articles exempt from attachment)-

> (a) in subsection (1), after paragraph (d) insert-
>> "(e) any money."; and
> (b) after subsection (2) insert-
>> "(3) In subsection (1)(e) above, "money" has the same meaning as in section 175 of the Bankruptcy and Diligence etc. (Scotland) Act 2007 (asp 3).".

(4) After section 13 insert-

"13A   Schedule of attachment

(1) The officer must, immediately after executing an attachment, complete a schedule such as is mentioned in subsection (2) below (in this section, the "attachment schedule").

(2) An attachment schedule-

> (a) must be in (or as nearly as may be in) the form prescribed by Act of Sederunt; and
> (b) must specify-
>> (i) the articles attached; and
>> (ii) their value, so far as ascertainable.

(3) The officer must-

> (a) give a copy of the attachment schedule to the debtor; or
> (b) where it is not practicable to do so-
>> (i) give a copy of the schedule to a person present at the place where the attachment was executed; or
>> (ii) where there is no such person, leave a copy of it at that place.

(4) An attachment is executed on the day on which the officer complies with subsection (3) above.".

(5) In section 14 (procedure for attachment of articles kept outwith dwellinghouses), for "19" substitute "19A".

(6) In section 15, the title to that section becomes "Valuation".

(7) In section 28(1)(b) (restriction on alteration of arrangements for auctions), for "19" substitute "19A".

(8) In section 32 (report of auction)-

> (a) in subsection (2)(a), after sub-paragraph (iii) insert-
>> (iiia) any sums paid by the debtor to account of the sum recoverable;"
>> ; and
> (b) in subsection (4), for the words from "Court" to the end substitute "Scottish Civil Enforcement Commission under section 67(1)(b) of the Bankruptcy and Diligence etc. (Scotland) Act 2007 (asp 3).".

(9) In section 33 (audit of report of auction)-

> (a) in subsection (7), for the words from "providing" to the end substitute-
>> (a) giving-
>>> (i) the debtor;
>>> (ii) the creditor; and
>>> (iii) any third party who claims ownership (whether alone or in common with the debtor) of any attached article,
>> an opportunity to make representations; or
>>> (b) holding a hearing." ; and
> (b) in subsection (8), for "debtor" substitute "persons mentioned in subsection (7)(a) above.".

(10) In section 34 (articles belonging to third parties), in subsection (1)(b)(ii), for "so satisfied" substitute "satisfied that the claim is valid".

(11) In section 40 (recovery from debtor of expenses of attachment)-

> (a) in subsection (3)-
>> (i) in paragraph (a), for "9(2)(a), (d) or (e)" substitute "9(2)(d) or (10)(b)"; and

(ii) in paragraph (c), for "presentation of a petition for an administration order" substitute "appointment of an administrator"; and

(b) in subsection (4)(b), for "administration order" substitute "appointment".

(12) In section 41(2)(a) (ascription of sums recovered by attachment), after sub-paragraph (i) insert-

"(ia) any previous interim attachment the expenses of which are chargeable against and recoverable from the debtor under section 9Q(1)(a) of this Act;"

(13) In section 45 (interpretation of Parts 2, 3 and 4 of that Act), in the definition of "officer", for the words from "the" where it first occurs to the end substitute "a judicial officer appointed by a creditor".

(14) In section 60(2) (application of the Act to sequestration for rent and arrestment) for the words "such a" substitute "the landlord's".

(15) In schedule 1, in paragraph 1, before "2" insert "1A,".

31. The Public Appointments and Public Bodies etc. (Scotland) Act 2003 (asp 4)

In schedule 2 to the Public Appointments and Public Bodies etc. (Scotland) Act (the specified authorities to which the Commissioner for Public Appointments in Scotland's code of practice applies), after the entry "Scottish Children's Reporter Administration", insert-

"Scottish Civil Enforcement Commission".

32. The Finance Act 2003 (c.14)

In paragraph 3(2) of Schedule 12 to the Finance Act 2003 (diligences which can be used to recover stamp duty land tax), after sub-paragraph (a) insert-

"(aa) a money attachment;".

33. The Civil Partnership Act 2004 (c.33)

In section 103(6) of the Civil Partnership Act 2004 (warrant to enter premises), for "messenger-at-arms or sheriff officer" substitute "judicial officer".

GENERAL NOTE

These are mostly amendments that update existing legislation to take account of the new diligences set up by this Act or the use of the word "judicial officer" to replace "sheriff officer" and "messenger at arms".

Paragraph 10 allows lay representation at sheriff court hearings in proceedings relating to interim attachment, attachment, money attachment, land attachment and residual attachment.

Paragraph 13 introduces certain sections into the 1985 Act explaining the interaction between land attachment and sequestration. These are dealt with in the introduction to land attachment at the beginning of Pt 4.

Paragraph 14 attempts to clarify the point that where a creditor has executed arrestment of a company's property before the attachment of a floating charge, it will be an effectual diligence. This is a somewhat vexed area. In *Iona Hotels Ltd*, 1991 SLT 11, a creditor arrested an item of a company's property and the company subsequently granted a floating charge. A receiver later appointed by the floating charge holder was unable to seize that item since it was litigious; on the other hand, where a company had granted a floating charge, and a creditor later arrested in the hands of a third party an asset of that company's, but failed to carry out an action of furthcoming before the appointment of a receiver under the floating charge, the receiver successfully took possession of the asset on the grounds that an arrestment not followed up by an action of furthcoming was not effectually executed diligence (see the Insolvency Act 1986, s.55, Schd.2; *Gordon Anderson (Plant) v Campsie Construction*, 1977 S.L.T. 7; *Lord Advocate v Royal Bank of Scotland*, 1977 S.C. 155). There is considerable debate about the meaning of the words "effectually executed diligence", but their continuing use in s.45(3)(a) of the 2007 Act suggests that the much questioned interpretation of the Inner House in *Lord Advocate v Royal Bank of Scotland* remains in place. To further confuse the issue, the Insolvency Act 1986 ss.61 and 61A, and indeed, this new s.61B, refer to "effectual diligence". For a critique of this case, see *Squaring the circle: revisiting the receiver and "effectually executed diligence"*, Scott Wortley, Jur. Rev. 2000, 5, 325-346.

It would appear, though it is not beyond doubt, that what is meant by s.61B here is that an executed arrestment takes priority over a floating charge that has not yet attached (or crystallised, as it sometimes known) and that "execution" merely requires the service of the schedule of arrestment on the arrestee holding the debtor company's assets, but does not mean that an action of furthcoming, the signing of a mandate, an application for a warrant for sale or an automatic forthcoming is required.

Paragraph 16 makes certain changes to the 1987 Act to allow the debtor more opportunities to apply for time to pay directions and time to pay orders.

Paragraph 30 extends the effect of time to pay orders to the new diligences in the 2007 Act, so that a time to pay order will prevent the relevant diligence taking place while the order is operational. While the court considers whether or not to grant a time to pay order, an interim "stop" may be obtained pending the final decision and this will "freeze" any existing diligence for the time being. If the relevant diligence has started, it is still not too late to obtain a time to pay order provided that as regards an auction under the s.27 of the 2002 Act it has not yet taken place; as regards money attachment, the debtor's money has not actually been attached and removed; as regards land attachment, the warrant for the sale of land has not actually been executed; as regards property subject to residual attachment, the property has been attached but a satisfaction order has not been obtained; and as regards arrestment, the time to pay order must be made within eight weeks of the 14 week period before automatic release have elapsed.

Paragraph 30 introduces a new s.13A into the 2002 Act and outlines the procedure for giving a schedule to the debtor indicating what has been attached by an attachment. The day that the schedule is given to the debtor, or someone present at the time of the attachment, will be deemed to be the day the attachment is executed, even if a valuation of the attached articles takes place at a later date.

SCHEDULE 6

REPEALS AND REVOCATION

(introduced by section 226)

PART I

REPEALS

Enactment	Extent of repeal
Decrees in Absence Act 1584 (c.10) (Act of the Parliaments of Scotland)	The whole Act.
Ejection Caution Act 1594 (c.27) (Act of the Parliaments of Scotland)	The whole Act.
Arrestments Act 1617 (c.17) (Act of the Parliaments of Scotland)	The whole Act.
Diligence Act 1621 (c.6) (Act of the Parliaments of Scotland)	The whole Act.
Adjudication Act 1621 (c.7) (Act of the Parliaments of Scotland)	The whole Act.
Diligence Act 1661 (c.344) (Act of the Parliaments of Scotland)	The whole Act.
Minority Act 1663 (c.4) (Act of the Parliaments of Scotland)	The whole Act.

Enactment	Extent of repeal
Adjudications Act 1672 (c.45) (Act of the Parliaments of Scotland)	The whole Act.
Debtors (Scotland) Act 1838 (c.114)	Section 17. Section 22.
Hypothec Amendment (Scotland) Act 1867 (c.42)	The whole Act.
Titles to Land Consolidation (Scotland) Act 1868 (c.101)	In section 3, in the definition of the "deed" and "conveyance", the words "of adjudication for debt, and" and the words "whether for debt or implement,". In section 62, the words ", whether for debt or", in both places where they occur. In section 129, the words ", whether for debt or", in both places where they occur. In section 159, the words "for debt or in security or". Schedules PP and RR.
Hypothec Abolition (Scotland) Act 1880 (c.12)	The whole Act.
Judicial Factors (Scotland) Act 1889 (c.39)	In section 11A(2), the words "Court or"; and in paragraph (a), the word "permanent".
Heritable Securities (Scotland) Act 1894 (c.44)	Sections 3, 6 and 7. Schedules A to C
Sheriff Courts (Scotland) Act 1907 (c.51)	In section 5(4), the words "actions of adjudication save in so far as now competent and". In section 29, the words "of a warrant of sequestration for rent, or". In section 40, the word "officers,".
Conveyancing (Scotland) Act 1924 (c.27)	In section 44, subsection (1); and in subsection (2), in paragraph (a)(i), the words "and Adjudications", and paragraph (b).
Execution of Diligence (Scotland) Act 1926 (c.16)	Section 1. Section 4. In section 5, the words from "a law agent" to the end.
Public Registers and Records (Scotland) Act 1948 (c.57)	In section 1(2), the words "and Adjudications".
Reserve and Auxiliary Forces (Protection of Civil Interests) Act 1951 (c.65)	Section 8(2)(e).
Taxes Management Act 1970 (c.9)	In section 64(1), the words "poinding, sequestration for rent, or".
Sheriff Courts (Scotland) Act 1971 (c.58)	In section 35(1)(b), the words "and actions of sequestration for rent" and the words "or the rent in respect of which sequestration is asked,".
Prescription and Limitation (Scotland) Act 1973 (c.52)	Section 1(4).
Land Registration (Scotland) Act 1979 (c.33)	In section 6(1)(c), the words "and Adjudications". In section 12(3)(k), the words "and Adjudications".

Enactment	Extent of repeal
Sale of Goods Act 1979 (c.54)	In section 62(5), the words "or sequestration for rent".
Rent (Scotland) Act 1984 (c.58)	Section 110.
Family Law (Scotland) Act 1985 (c.37)	Section 19.
Bankruptcy (Scotland) Act 1985 (c.66)	In section 1A, in subsection (1)(b)(ii), the words "under paragraph 5(1)(e) of Schedule 5 to this Act"; and in subsection (3)(c), the word "permanent".

In section 2(4).

In section 3, the word "permanent" in each place where it occurs.

In section 4, the words "(other than one to which Schedule 2 to this Act applies)"; and the word "permanent".

In section 5, in subsection (4A), the word "permanent"; in subsection (7), paragraph (a); and in subsection (8)(a), the words "or concurs in a petition by the debtor".

In section 7(1), in paragraph (c), sub-paragraphs (iii), (iv), (v) and (vi); and the words ""confiscation order"", where they second occur.

In section 8, in subsection (1)(a), sub-paragraph (i); in subsection (5), the words ", or the concurring in,"; and in subsection (6), the words "or concurring" and "or concur".

Section 12(1A).

In section 13(2)(b), the words "in the sequestration".

In section 14, in subsection (1)(a), the words "and adjudications"; in subsection (2) the words "and of a citation in an adjudication"; in subsection (3)(a), the words ", or by virtue of paragraph 11 of Schedule 4 to,"; in subsection (4), the word "permanent" and the words "and adjudications"; and subsection (5).

In section 15, in subsection (3), the words "or a creditor concurring in the petition for sequestration"; in subsection (5)(a), the words "and adjudications"; in subsection (6), the word "interim"; and in subsection (8)(a), the words from "permanent", where it first occurs, to "interim".

In section 16, in subsection (1)(b), the words "interim trustee, the permanent"; and in subsection (2), the words "interim trustee or permanent".

In section 17(8), in paragraph (a), the words "and adjudications"; and in paragraph (b)(ii), the word "permanent".

Section 18(2)(g).

In section 19, in subsection (1), the word "interim", where it second occurs; and in subsections (2) to (4), the word "interim", in each place where it occurs.

In section 20, the word "interim", in each place where it occurs; and subsections (4) and (5).

Enactment	*Extent of repeal*
	In section 20A, the words "interim" and "21 or".
	In section 21A, in subsection (1), the word "interim", where it second occurs; in subsections (2) to (7), the word "interim", in each place where it occurs; and subsection (9).
	In section 21B, in subsection (1), the word "interim", where it first occurs and paragraph (b) and the word "and" immediately preceding that paragraph; and subsection (2).
	In section 22, the word "interim", in each place where it occurs; and in subsection (5)(b)(ii), the words "or permanent trustee".
	In section 23, the word "interim", in each place where it occurs.
	In section 24, in subsection (2), the word "permanent", where it third and fourth occurs; and in subsection (4)(b), the words from "who" to the end.
	In section 25, in subsection (6), paragraph (a) and the word "and" immediately following that paragraph; and in paragraph (b), the words "where he is not the same person as the interim trustee," and the word "permanent".
	Section 25A.
	In section 26, in subsection (2)(b), the words "(unless the interim trustee has himself become the permanent trustee)"; and in subsection (3)(b)(i), the words "(except where the interim trustee has himself become the permanent trustee)".
	In section 26A, in subsection (2), the word "interim", where it second occurs; and in subsections (4), (5) and (7), the word "interim", in each place where it occurs.
	Section 27(7).
	In sections 28 to 30, the word "permanent", in each place where it occurs.
	In section 31, in subsection (1), the words "in the permanent trustee" and paragraphs (a) and (b) and the word "; and" immediately preceding them; in subsection (2), the words "(reserving any effect of such inhibition on ranking)"; and in subsections (2) to (7) and (10) the word "permanent", in each place where it occurs.
	In section 31A(2) (as inserted by paragraph 15 of Schedule 11 to the Proceeds of Crime Act 2002 (c.29)), the word "permanent".
	In section 31B, in subsection (1), the word "and" following paragraph (a); and in subsection (2), the word "permanent"
	In sections 31C to 36C, 36E and 36F, the word "permanent", in each place where it occurs.
	In section 37, subsection (1)(a); in subsection (2), the word "which", the words "shall be effectual to create a preference for the inhibitor and" and the word "permanent"; in subsection (4), the word "permanent" in

Enactment	Extent of repeal
	both places where it occurs; in subsection (6), the word "permanent" in both places where it occurs; and in subsection (8), the words from "to", where it first occurs, to "or", where it second occurs; and in subsection (9), the word "permanent".
	In section 38, the word "permanent" in each place where it occurs.
	In section 39, in subsection (1), the word "permanent", in both places where it occurs, and the words "with the commissioners or, if there are no commissioners,"; and in paragraph (c), the words "if there are no commissioners,"; and in subsection (2), the word "permanent", the words from "but" to "court" and the words from "if", where it second occurs, to "estate", where it first occurs; and in subsections (3) to (6) and (8), the word "permanent" in each place where it occurs.
	In sections 40 to 45, the word "permanent" in each place where it occurs.
	In section 46, in subsection (1), in paragraph (a), the word "permanent" and in paragraph (b) the words "the Court of Session or" and the word "permanent"; and in subsection (4), the word "permanent".
	In section 47, the word "permanent" in both places where it occurs.
	In section 48, in subsection (1), the word "permanent"; in subsection (2), in paragraph (a), the word "interim" and in paragraph (b), the word "permanent"; in subsection (3), the words from ", and", where it second occurs, to the end of the subsection; in subsections (4) and (5), the word "permanent", in each place where it occurs; in subsection (7), paragraph (a) and in paragraph (b) the words ""interim" and", "respectively" and ""permanent" and"; and in subsection (8), the word "permanent".
	In sections 49 to 53, the word "permanent", in each place where it occurs.
	In section 54, the word "permanent", in each place where it occurs; in subsection (4)(b)(ii), the words "interim or"; and in subsection (7)(a), the words "and adjudications".
	In sections 56 and 57, the word "permanent", in each place where it occurs.
	In section 58A, in subsections (1), (4), (5) and (7), the word "permanent", in each place where it occurs; and subsection (9).
	In section 60(2), the word "permanent".
	In sections 61 to 65, the word "permanent", in each place where it occurs.
	In section 67, in subsection (4), the word "permanent"; and in subsection (5), in paragraph (b), the words "interim or permanent".
	In sections 69 and 70, the word "permanent", in each place where it occurs.

Enactment	Extent of repeal
	In section 73(1), the definition of "permanent trustee".
	In section 75, in subsection (4), the words "by the permanent trustee"; in subsection (5), paragraph (b); in subsection (7), the word "permanent"; and in subsection (11), the words from "permanent", where it first occurs, to "interim".
	In Schedule 1, the word "permanent", in each place where it occurs.
	In Schedule 4, in paragraph 1(1), the word "permanent", where it second occurs; in paragraph 2, the word "permanent"; in paragraph 4, the word "permanent", where it first occurs; in paragraph 9, in sub-paragraphs (1) and (1A), the word "permanent", in each place where it occurs; in paragraph 12, the word "permanent", in both places where it occurs; in paragraph 17, in subparagraphs (1), (3) and (4), the word "permanent", in each place where it occurs; and in paragraph 18, in sub-paragraphs (3) and (4), the word "permanent", in each place where it occurs.
	In Schedule 5, in paragraph 2(1), the words "and adjudications"; and in paragraph 4, sub-paragraphs (b)(ii) and (d).
	In Schedule 6, the word "permanent", in each place where it occurs (including the occurrence in the italic cross-heading preceding paragraph 7); and in paragraph 11(2), the words "the interim trustee or, as the case may be,".
	In Schedule 7, in paragraph 25(a), the words "interim or permanent".
Law Reform (Miscellaneous Provisions) (Scotland) Act 1985 (c.73)	In section 8(7), the words "and Adjudications".
Insolvency Act 1986 (c.45)	In section 185(2)(d), the word "permanent".
Debtors (Scotland) Act 1987 (c.18)	Section 2(1)(b)(iv). In section 5, subsection (1)(c). Section 8(3). In section 9, subsection (1)(b)(iv); and, in subsection (8), the words "to grant". Section 15(1). Part V. Section 101. In Schedule 6, paragraph 3.
Proceeds of Crime (Scotland) Act 1995 (c.43)	In section 32, in subsection (2), the words from "as" to the end; subsection (3); and in subsection (5)(b), the words "and Adjudications". In Schedule 1, in paragraph 7(c), the words from "raise" to "property" where it first occurs
Terrorism Act 2000 (c.11)	In Schedule 4, in paragraph 21, in sub-paragraph (2)(b) the words from "shall", where it first occurs, to "and", where it first occurs, and the words "and adjudications"; in sub-paragraph (3), the words from "as"

Enactment	Extent of repeal
	to the end; and in subparagraph (5)(b), the words "and adjudications".
Mortgage Rights (Scotland) Act 2001 (asp 11)	In section 3(1) , the words "and Adjudications".
International Criminal Court (Scotland) Act 2001 (asp 13)	In Schedule 6, in paragraph 6, in sub-paragraph (2)(b) the words from "shall", where it first occurs, to "and", where it first occurs, and the words "and Adjudications"; in sub-paragraph (3), the words from "as" to the end; and in subparagraph (6)(b), the words "and Adjudications".
	In Schedule 6, in paragraph 10(6) , the words "and Adjudications".
Proceeds of Crime Act 2002 (c.29)	In section 123, in subsection (4), the words from "as" to the end; and in subsection (7)(b), the words "and Adjudications".
	Section 285(7).
	In Schedule 3, paragraph 7(5), the words from "raise" to "property" where it first occurs.
Debt Arrangement and Attachment (Scotland) Act 2002 (asp 17)	Section 4(2A)(d).
	Section 15(1).
	Section 60(1), (2)(b), (4) and (5).
	Schedule 1, paragraph 4(a), the words "of court".

PART 2

REVOCATION

Enactment	Extent of revocation
The Bankruptcy (Scotland) Regulations 1985 (S.I. 1985 No. 1925)	Regulation 13.

INDEX

References are to sections and Schedules